Encountering extremism

Manchester University Press

Encountering extremism

Theoretical issues and local challenges

Edited by

Alice Martini, Kieran Ford and
Richard Jackson

Manchester University Press

Published by Manchester University Press
Oxford Road, Manchester M13 9PL

www.manchesteruniversitypress.co.uk

British Library Cataloguing-in-Publication Data
A catalogue record for this book is available from the British Library

ISBN 978 1 5261 3660 2 hardback
ISBN 978 1 5261 9565 4 paperback

First published 2020
Paperback published 2026

EU authorised representative for GPSR:
Easy Access System Europe – Mustamäe tee 50, 10621 Tallinn, Estonia
gpsr.requests@easproject.com

Typeset by
Sunrise Setting Ltd, Brixham

Contents

Contributors

Alice Martini is Associate Professor of International Security Studies at the Comillas Pontifical University, Spain, and is currently teaching International Relations (IR) for the Queen Mary, University of London Online Programme, UK. She is also an Associate Researcher in International Relations at the Autonomous University of Madrid, Spain, and at the Sant'Anna School of Advanced Studies, Italy. She is co-convenor of the British International Studies Association's Critical Studies on Terrorism Working Group, and she sits on the board of EISA's Early Career Development Group. She is a member of several working groups, such as GERI (International Relations Study Group) and ERIS Emerging Research on International Security (Sant'Anna)), and an editor for *Relaciones Internacionales* and *Security Praxis*. Her research focuses on the deconstruction of global discourses of (counter)terrorism, and, more recently, countering (violent) extremism.

Kieran Ford graduated with a PhD in Peace and Conflict Studies from the University of Otago, New Zealand, in 2019. His research focuses on critical approaches to countering extremism, with a particular interest in exploring educational approaches to countering extremism and P/CVE (Prevention/Countering of Violent Extremism) more broadly. His published research includes work on the securitisation of education development, and the normalisation of violence in school textbooks. His current research projects focus on developing agonistic alternatives to CVE strategies.

Richard Jackson is Professor of Peace Studies and Director of the National Centre for Peace and Conflict Studies (NCPACS), University of Otago, New Zealand. He is the founding editor and current editor-in-chief of the journal *Critical Studies on Terrorism*, and the author and editor of eleven books and more than seventy journal articles and book chapters. His recent books include *Critical Terrorism Studies at Ten: Contributions, Cases and Future Challenges* (Routledge, 2019, co-edited with Harmonie Toros, Lee Jarvis and Charlotte Heath-Kelly), *Contemporary Debates on Terrorism* (Routledge, 2018, 2nd edition, co-edited with Daniela Pisiou), *The Routledge Handbook of Critical Terrorism Studies* (Routledge, 2016), *Confessions of a Terrorist* (Zed Books, 2014) and *Terrorism: A Critical Introduction* (Palgrave-Macmillan, 2011, co-authored with Marie Breen-Smyth, Jeroen Gunning and Lee Jarvis). His most recent research focuses on pacifism and non-violence in international relations.

Jessica Auchter is Assistant Professor at University of Tennessee at Chattanooga, US. Her research focuses primarily on visual politics and culture. Her book *The Politics of Haunting and Memory in International Relations* (Routledge 2014), examines the politics and ethics of being haunted by lives, deaths and dead bodies. She has recently published articles in the *Journal of Global Security Studies, Review of International Studies, Journal for Cultural Research, International Feminist Journal of Politics* and *Critical Studies on Security,* among others. She is currently working on a book manuscript on the politics of the global dead in security studies.

Marie Breen-Smyth has held academic posts at universities in the US and the UK. She is a founding editor of the Taylor and Francis journal *Critical Studies on Terrorism* and an initiator of the field of Critical Terrorism Studies. She founded the Institute for Conflict Research in Belfast. She was 2002–2003 Jennings Randolph Senior Fellow at the United States Institute of Peace and has worked with the Special Representative of the Secretary General of United Nations for Children and Armed Conflict. She publishes on political violence and its impact, ethics and methods in violent contexts, the Northern Ireland conflict, truth recovery and managing violent pasts, victim politics and counting casualties of political violence. She has also made two documentary films.

Mariela Cuadro holds a PhD in International Relations from the National University of La Plata, Argentina. She is a sociologist at the University of Buenos Aires, Argentina; a researcher at the National Council of Research (CONICET), Argentina; Professor of Theory of International Relations at the National University of General San Martín (UNSAM), Argentina; and Coordinator of the Latin American Council of Social Sciences (CLACSO) working group Latin America and the Middle East. Her latest publications include 'International Relations and peripheral orientalism: sectarian readings from Latin America' (*CIDOB Revista d'Afers Internacionals*) and 'Multipolarity under construction: new paths and difficult balances in Argentina–Middle East relations during the Kirchner governments' (in Tawil Kuri, M. (ed.), *Latin American Foreign Policies towards the Middle East: Actors, Contexts, and Trends* (Palgrave Macmillan, 2016)).

Priya Dixit is Associate Professor at the Department of Political Science, Virginia Tech, US. Her research interests are qualitative methods and Critical Security Studies. She is the author of various articles and books on global security, including *The State and 'Terrorists' in Nepal and Northern Ireland* (Manchester University Press, 2015). She is currently researching ideologies and narratives of far-right and militia violent actors in the US.

Tanja Dramac Jiries holds a PhD from the School of Advanced Studies Sant'Anna in Pisa, Italy. Her research focuses on the recruitment and radicalisation process of foreign fighters from the Balkans. She holds a BA in Journalism from the University of Banja Luka, Bosnia and Herzegovina, and MA in Political Science from the Central European University in Budapest, Hungary. For her Master's thesis she conducted fieldwork in Srebrenica in order to understand the role of women-led NGOs in peacebuilding. She has worked for the Office of the European Union Special Representative to Bosnia and Herzegovina (EUSR), for the Permanent Mission of Bosnia and Herzegovina to the United Nations in New York City and for a number of grass-roots civil society organisations in the Balkans.

Laura Fernández de Mosteyrín is Lecturer in Sociology at Universidad a Distancia de Madrid, Spain. She is a member of the Group for the Studies in Society and Politics (UCM-UNED). Her research focuses on how security shapes state–citizens relations, and she teaches in the field of sociology of conflict, deviance and security policy. Her most recent publication is 'Imagining the future in a difficult present: storylines from Spanish youth', co-authored with M.L. Moran (*Contemporary Social Science*, 2017).

Sondre Lindahl is Associate Professor at Østfold University College, Norway. He holds a PhD from the National Centre for Peace and Conflict Studies, University of Otago, New Zealand. His research interests are international relations, terrorism, counterterrorism, security and philosophy. He is a regular commentator in Norway on terrorism and counterterrorism, and he is the author of *A Critical Theory of Counterterrorism: Ontology, Epistemology, Normativity* (Routledge, 2018).

Aislinn O'Donnell is Professor of Education in the Department of Education in Maynooth University, Ireland. She has developed a number of creative pedagogical projects, including the Erasmus+-funded The Enquiring Classroom (www.enquiring-classroom.eu). Her current research develops approaches to engage educationally with complex and difficult political questions, such as polarisation, intolerant extremism and hate speech. She is Principal Investigator on EDURAD: Addressing Violent Radicalisation: A Multi-Actor Response through Education, funded by the EU's Internal Security Fund-Police (ISF-P).

Akinyemi Oyawale holds a PhD from the University of East Anglia, Norwich, UK, where he is also Associate Tutor in Politics. His research looks at the impact of counterterrorism on the (in)security of the public in Nigeria. His research interests are terrorism, counterterrorism, extremism, radicalisation and de-radicalisation, and security more broadly.

Afiya Shehrbano Zia is a feminist scholar with a doctoral degree in Women and Gender Studies from the University of Toronto, Canada. She is the author of *Sex Crime in the Islamic Context* (ASR, 1994) and has contributed essays to several edited volumes, including *Contesting Feminisms: Gender and Islam in Asia* (SUNY Press, 2015) and *Voicing Demands* (Zed Books, 2014). Her peer-reviewed essays have been carried in *Feminist Review* and the *International Feminist Journal of Politics*. She has taught at Habib University, Karachi, Pakistan and the University of Toronto, Canada, and she is an active member of the Women's Action Forum, Pakistan. Her most recent book is *Faith and Feminism in Pakistan: Religious Agency or Secular Autonomy?* (Sussex Academic Press, 2018).

Guendalina Simoncini is a doctoral researcher in Political Sciences at the University of Pisa, Italy. She holds a Bachelor's degree in Arabic and Islamic Studies from the University of Granada, Spain, and a Joint Master's degree in Mediterranean Studies from the Autonomous University of Barcelona, Spain, Université UPVM Montpellier, France, and Ca'Foscari of Venice, Italy. She is conducting research into counter-terrorism in post-revolutionary Tunisia from a discursive perspective.

Chin-Kuei Tsui is an Assistant Professor at the Graduate Institute of International Politics, National Chung Hsing University, Taiwan, ROC. He was awarded his PhD from the National Centre for Peace and Conflict Studies, University of Otago, New Zealand. His research interests are US foreign and security policies, the American-led war on terror, Critical Terrorism Studies and peace and conflict studies. His book *Clinton, New Terrorism and the Origins of the War on Terror* was published by Routledge in 2016.

Acknowledgements

This book is a collective enterprise and it would not have been possible without the efforts and collaboration from all its contributors. Therefore, as editors, Alice, Kieran and Richard would like to thank the authors of the following chapters for believing in the project from the first moment, and for making it possible. They also would like to thank all the team at Manchester University Press, and, above all, Tony Mason, Jonathan de Peyer and Robert Byron, for making this volume a reality.

Introduction

Encountering extremism: a critical examination of theoretical issues and local challenges

Alice Martini, Kieran Ford and Richard Jackson

From countering terrorism to countering extremism: wider discourse, same problems?

The term extremism has thoroughly permeated counter-terrorism discourses and policies. The word is currently widely employed across the security sector and it has become the 'explanatory core' of understandings of terrorism and radicalisation (Fernández de Mosteyrín and Limón López, 2016, p. 806). In contemporary discourse, extremism has almost become synonymous with terrorism, to the point that, at times, the words are used interchangeably (Kundnani and Hayes, 2018, p. 2; Martini, this volume; Tsui, this volume). The term terrorism, both in its inconsistency in usage, and its inherent subjectivity, has drawn substantial criticism from critical scholars as an explanatory term for political violence (e.g., Breen-Smyth et al., 2008). The recent emergence of extremism as the explanatory term *du jour* does not present a lesser degree of inconsistency when used. On the contrary, through various discursive processes, 'extremism' has come to encompass wider dynamics than terrorism and thus lost even further any specificity (Richards, 2011, 2015).

Since its emergence within wider discourses of radicalisation over ten years ago, extremism has established itself in the literature as a term that is supposed to capture ideological processes behind the use of violence by individuals, or, roughly speaking, the relationship between ideology and terrorism (Ford, 2017; Heath-Kelly, 2013). Peter R. Neumann (2013), for instance, delineates two different types of radicalisation: 'cognitive radicalisation' and 'behavioural radicalisation'. While the latter relates to someone becoming convinced to utilise political violence, the former relates to someone becoming more 'extreme' in their political beliefs. While debate ensues as to the apparent relationship between these two forms of radicalisation, the implication of this distinction is that radicalised, extreme beliefs threaten, or *could* threaten, political violence.

On both sides of the Atlantic, concurrent political processes catalysed extremism's ascendency. In the UK, the attacks on the London transport network in 2005 by so-called 'homegrown terrorists' (Crone and Harrow, 2011; Schuurman and Horgan, 2016) prompted searching questions regarding how and why individuals would attack their own country and fellow citizens. Theories of 'radicalisation' offered answers, and the role of ideology became increasingly important (Ford, 2019; Payne, 2009).

In the US, new ideas were needed in the failing Global War on Terror. As Kundnani and Hayes explain, 'the "shock and awe" that had failed in Iraq would be complemented by new programmes aimed at winning "hearts and minds" [. . .] the "battle of ideas" would be engaged alongside the battle for territory' (2018, p. 4). Radicalisation processes offered, however, further confusion rather than clarity. In particular, there remains no conclusive evidence of there being a causative relationship between 'extreme' ideologies and the use of political violence. Not only are there much larger populations of individuals who hold onto 'extreme' views, but who never engage in political violence, than the population size of those who do, but also political violence appears a popular strategy of those who hold onto more 'moderate' ideologies as well.

The term extremism remains murkily defined. Across the globe there is diversity in whether countries might seek to counter, or to prevent, extremism, or *violent* extremism more specifically. Beyond this uncertainty, it is evident also that certain forms of extremism are more worthy of attention than others. The US and the UK have both been critiqued for focusing almost entirely on Islamist extremism, while ignoring the threat of white nationalist organisations in particular (Dixit, this volume; Kundnani, 2015).

This diversity in terminology ensures that there is no comprehensive global answer as to what is being countered, or indeed what it is that threatens. As this volume demonstrates, many approaches around the world focus on countering violent extremism (CVE). However, 'non-violent extremism' is also, according to some counter-extremism strategies such as Prevent in the UK, something to eradicate. This term is deployed to loosely describe the ideologies of those who hold onto 'extreme' beliefs, but who do not pose a direct violent threat. According to the UK's Prevent strategy, non-violent extremists are a threat in that, it is argued, violent extremists often rely on such 'non-violent extremist' ideologies to legitimise their violence. Britain's definition of extremism as 'opposition to fundamental British values' (Her Majesty's Government, 2011, p. 107) defines anything which strays too far from moderate, mainstream British values as 'extreme' and potentially threatening, considering that in the future someone might take up those ideas and employ violence to see their fruition.

Another key question within the radicalisation literature concerns where and when within the radicalisation journey, from moderate through extremism to terrorism, the act of countering should take place. In particular, four terms appear to be widely deployed, with overlapping meanings. CVE appears to concern itself with responding to more immediate threats of violent extremism, though it is increasingly hard to say how CVE might distinguish itself from counter-terrorism. After all, both appear to be concerned with halting threats of political violence. Preventing violent extremism (PVE) is a widely used term referring to the more holistic approach to ensure that society holds a level of cohesion and stability such that violent extremism is less likely to occur (Nash and Nesterova, 2017, p. 45). PVE approaches include educational strategies, and often employ medical metaphors such as 'early indication' and 'resilience'. Counter-extremism then appears to be a more overarching, umbrella term to incorporate everything from the promotion of democratic values in a kindergarten through to the armed intervention in a planned act of political violence. The UK's definition of extremism is illustrative here. The UK defines both the opposition to a set of fundamental values such as democracy, alongside threats to the lives of members of the armed forces, as examples of extremism needing to be countered (Her Majesty's Government, 2011, p. 107).

In other words, 'extremism' is nowadays used to refer to phenomena that lie on a broad spectrum from specific ideas and ideologies, the display of certain behaviours and ideological sympathy, to the actual use of violence (Kundnani and Hayes, 2018, p. 4). Furthermore, the word is currently used also to refer to everyone from terrorist organisations, such as ISIL and Boko Haram (Martini, 2019), to activist groups. At the same time, it is often *not* used to describe other violent actors – and white nationalist violent attackers in particular (Dixit, this volume).

Underlying this level of uncertainty remains the core question of which values or ideologies should be considered 'extreme'. In short, extremism indicates a subjective term to identify those values and ideas that appear at a great distance from those of the articulator (see, for example, Cuadro, this volume; Ford, 2019). What might be 'extreme' to one person may appear the most sensible idea to another. The curious nature of deploying such a subjective term within government policy is that governments now find themselves attempting to grasp an objective centre-ground from which to identify the extremes. Such a position ensures that moderation is associated with the status quo, and extremism with change (Kundnani, 2015). It is of little surprise therefore that the desire for political or social change, under a counter-extremism logic, is transformed from being an indicator of active engagement in political life, into an indicator of vulnerability to radicalisation and a threat. As such, countering extremism poses questions and concerns not only for those examining how best to reduce levels of political violence, but also for those examining the status of democracy more broadly.

Despite these inconsistencies and the wide range of phenomena it identifies, the mainstream literature has enthusiastically and unquestioningly supported this shift in focus towards extremism. Specifically, from 2010 onwards, it has widely adopted the 'extremism' language (Kundnani and Hayes, 2018, p. 5), even though concrete definitions of (violent) extremism or countering (violent) extremism remain elusive (Nasser-Eddine et al., 2011, p. 16). As this volume notes, the 'terrorism industry' (Herman and O'Sullivan, 1989) surrounding CVE and PVE is truly globalised. Kundnani and Hayes (2018, p. 2) note that such strategies exist 'from Finland to the Philippines'. At an international level, the UN Secretary-General published a Plan of Action on PVE in 2016 (Martini, this volume), and funding prevention initiatives remains a high priority for civil society groups and non-governmental organisations.

Driven by this shift, politics and policies have also been centred on this matter, resulting in highly problematic behaviour. Reproducing this language, without fixing a clear delimitation of the concept, implied that policies have been implemented without a clear goal, rendering it difficult to assess whether they worked or not, but also to specify what their main aim was. As Harris-Hogan et al. put it, 'many CVE approaches cannot define the specifics of what they are preventing, let alone how or whether they have prevented it' (Harris-Hogan et al., 2016, p. 6), a reflection that underlines the problems behind the use of this term.

Overall, the new language of extremism serves to recreate the legitimacy of the 'war on terror' in a phase where previous discourses and categories are losing legitimacy, popularity and political support (Jackson and Tsui, 2016). As a consequence, and to paraphrase Kundnani's critique of 'radicalisation', the language of countering (violent) extremism has 'inherited at birth a number of in-built, limiting assumptions (from the language of counter-terrorism)' (Kundnani, 2012, p. 5). Although eluding specific definitions of what extremism means or what the processes of countering and preventing it involve, the term has been shaped and influenced by the same constructed characteristics of (countering-) terrorism. The construction of extremism presents thus the same problematic aspects of the discourse on terrorism, it depicts the threat in a similar way and it subjugates similar knowledge, above all, about its political nature (Jackson, 2012). Furthermore, based on the same epistemological and ontological problems (Jackson, 2015), counter-extremism measures have, for example, several harmful consequences on societies in terms of human rights and civil rights abuses or restrictions (Kundnani and Hayes, 2018).

Here, the wider meaning of extremism and its focus on violence or physical behaviours, and also on certain ideas and beliefs, has broadened the discourse – and the legitimacy of specific counter-measures – to other aspects. The understanding that extremism encompasses also ideologies and ideas has led to the securitisation of more abstract, private and personal realms, and created a 'pre-criminal space' (Heath-Kelly, 2017) where preventive measures could be implemented in the name of countering extremism before a crime takes place. In other words, preventing and countering extremism have managed to direct and govern behaviours and thoughts. They have allowed the implementation of a wider governmentality of subjects in societies through various 'technologies of the Self' (Elshimi, 2015), based on the promotion of hegemonic moderate beliefs and subjectivities – and, thus, the neglecting or silencing of different or dissident ideas (Martin, 2018; O'Donnell, 2016). From this perspective, the task of countering extremism goes far beyond that of countering terrorism. While the latter can be understood to encompass the task of reducing the level of political violence in a society, the former entails the promotion of a set of 'moderate' values, a task only complete once an entire society's beliefs and values sit within a pre-ordained realm of moderation (Ford, 2017).

Depicting certain (non-Western) subjectivities as 'at risk of being risky' (Heath-Kelly, 2013, p. 12), the discourse has not only securitised Muslims and Muslim identities but also, in more general terms, multiculturalism and diversity in societies (Ragazzi, 2016). As a consequence, it has created, othered and securitised (Muslim) 'suspect communities' (see, among others, Awan, 2012; Breen-Smyth, 2014; Pantazis and Pemberton, 2009).

It has also entered different spheres of the welfare state such as education (Brown and Saeed, 2015; O'Donnell, 2016) or healthcare (Heath-Kelly and Strausz, 2018), securitised these spheres and allowed the implementation of exceptional measures. Moreover, as Jessica Auchter (this volume) and Alice Martini (this volume; 2019) argue, the discourse has allowed the penetration of security measures into the personal and domestic sphere, securitising all spheres of society. This securitisation allowed the implementation of exceptional (abusive) measures and surveillance, a problematic dynamic for democratic principles and human and civil rights (Kundnani and Hayes, 2018).

As said, despite its problematic nature, the mainstream literature had adopted the extremism language almost uncritically, with only a few exceptions (see, for example, Richards, 2015). In a similar dynamic, the discourse has fully entered the political realm and, as noted, it has profoundly shaped the counter- and preventive measures implemented. These processes are nowadays quite standardised and have reached an international level, to the point that Kundnani and Hayes talk about 'the globalisation of countering violent extremism policies' (Kundnani and Hayes, 2018). We have noted, however, the series of problematic dynamics within this surge of popularity of the term. From the term's definition through to its deployment, countering extremism is riddled with problematic processes. It is these processes that this volume aims at critiquing and deconstructing.

Aims of the volume: encountering extremism

Critical voices have produced extensive critique of the discourses (see, among others, Baker-Beall, 2016; Holland, 2012; Jackson, 2005; Jarvis, 2009), and practices of countering terrorism and radicalisation (Blakeley, 2009; Heath-Kelly et al., 2016; Jackson, 2016; Jarvis and Lister, 2015a, 2015b). Yet, unlike terrorism and radicalisation, fewer opportunities have been given to examine extremism in depth and from multiple perspectives. It is this lacuna that this book wants to address. Born out of the concern that the discourse is rapidly evolving around this new language of extremism, and thus legitimising new practices, this volume seeks to provide a space to critique and deconstruct these aspects.

In other words, the aim of this volume is to interrogate and reflect critically on this shift in the discourse, from a wide variety of points of view. The volume aims at deconstructing the category of extremism and the discourses constructing it. Moreover, it attempts to reveal the practices legitimised by this shift in the understanding of the 'threat of terrorism' and reflect upon its consequences for politics and society.

It should, however, be acknowledged that, by doing this, the volume will also inevitably function to reify the status of the discourse and this shift. This work will follow the mainstream literature and will support this change in the construction by producing further knowledge on the matter. It will thus produce a turn also in critical and poststructuralist literature on the subject which will somehow inevitably reify the status of 'extremism' in the world. Nevertheless, given the status the language of extremism has reached (Kundnani and Hayes, 2018), it has been considered that the literature greatly needs the critique this work provides.

Based on these premises, this volume offers a space of reflection on a wide variety of theoretical and empirical points of view. It provides an original space of resistance to the discourse and of critique from a wide variety of theoretical and empirical perspectives in an original combination of voices in, mainly, International Relations. Responding to the call put forward by Critical Terrorism Studies scholars, the volume is aimed at widening the voices and perspectives that have not received enough attention within the mainstream literature (Jackson et al., 2009, p. 4). With the intention of enriching the discussion but also the critique of this concept, this volume not only brings together critical and poststructuralist scholars, but also feminist, postcolonial and peace studies academics. Furthermore, the book seeks to transcend the institutional blinkers that focus the bulk of the academy towards the issue of Islamist extremism, examining in detail other violent actors and ideologies, such as white nationalism. The volume thus provides a multidimensional deconstruction of the language of extremism.

Moreover, in contrast to many existing works, and in line with a more culture-sensitive turn, this volume brings together local experts that examine local realities, in the majority of the cases through ethnographic work and using interviews carried out in the field with a wide variety of actors – from policymakers to activists and the local population. Thus, this volume opens up a space for many non-Western voices, something that is often missing in the existing literature and which renders the volume unique in its kind.

This is thus a work that is aimed at 'encountering extremism' – at interrogating this concept through a plethora of theoretical perspectives and backgrounds and exploring counter-extremism as it has materialised in plural local contexts. Seeking to encounter, rather than counter, extremism entails not only a research approach, but a normative commitment. *Encountering extremism* recognises the socially embedded nature of knowledge construction surrounding the discourses of extremism. It seeks to understand the dangers in constructing the problem of extremism as a problem to be eliminated, and a problem of the Other. Instead, an encounter with extremism seeks to examine, and learn from, this phenomenon, as well as the social and political dynamics that have contributed to its (re) production.

Therefore, the volume offers an inquiry into the concepts, discourses and practices of (countering) extremism articulated on two levels: the theoretical and the local analysis. This is motivated by the need to discuss the theoretical implications of the move to extremism, while also giving equitable attention to analyses sensitive to local dynamics, specifically from a critical perspective.

Overview of the chapters

The rationale of this volume is to deconstruct and unpack extremism on various levels and from different points of view. This was motivated by the will to provide the widest perspective on the issues related to this concept. Moreover, the intention was to show how the adoption of this new language has specific consequences in many ways and in many social spheres. To this end, the volume is organised in two parts. The first, 'What's in a name? Theoretically deconstructing extremism', draws together theoretical reflections on extremism, from a critical point of view in the social sciences. Each chapter in this section adopts contrasting approaches or perspectives. Collectively, the section analyses extremism and counter-extremism from multiple angles, offering a holistic examination of the issue. Here, authors from Critical Terrorism Studies examine the construction of extremism and the implications of counter-extremism strategies from a critical perspective. Moreover, this section also explores extremism from complementary schools of thought such as feminism, poststructuralism and peace studies and from an educational perspective.

The second part of the book, 'Extremism, countering extremism and preventing extremism: from theory to international and local challenges', examines various global and local contexts where counter-extremism strategies have been implemented. Often presented in isolation, this compilation of case perspectives will allow for comparison and cross-examination. Furthermore, acknowledging that the little existing literature on the subject overwhelmingly focuses empirically on the strategic and operational policies of major Western states such as the US or the UK, this volume – although not discarding these examples entirely – emphasises lesser-known examples of countries implementing counter-extremism strategies, shedding light on cases of counter-extremism rarely discussed outside of their local context, such as Bosnia and Herzegovina, Tunisia and Spain. Moreover, chapters in this section also contribute to the theoretical discussion by highlighting their relevance in specific cases.

The volume starts with a genealogical study of the concept of extremism in International Relations. In 'Interrogating the concept of (violent) extremism: a genealogical study of terrorism and counter-terrorism discourses', Chin-Kuei Tsui traces the genealogical evolution of the concept of (violent) extremism from its original inception in the US and other Western states to recreate legitimacy for their actions. Moreover, the author reflects on the discursive shift the introduction of the extremism language has implied in contemporary terrorism and counter-terrorism. Specifically, it analyses the resulting policy practices prompted and implemented by states, and the political consequences these had on societies in terms of racism, discrimination and exclusion of (Muslim) minorities.

Chapter two, 'Conceptualising violent extremism: ontological, epistemological and normative issues', by Sondre Lindahl, puts forward a critical theory of (counter-)extremism. The chapter is based on Weber's conceptualisation of ideal types, a scientific construct that allows studying a specific phenomenon through the focus on some of its main characteristics (Weber, 1949, 1978). The discussion presented here is a follow-up to the author's previous construction of an ideal type for 'terrorism' (Lindahl, 2018). In this chapter, Lindahl explores how the construction of the ideal types of terrorism and extremism can be used to maintain the ontological, epistemological and normative commitments of Critical Terrorism Studies when researching violent extremism. In this respect, the author puts forward a methodological reflection that could improve scholars' coherency and consistency when working with these issues.

The third chapter, 'Knowledge, power, subject: constituting the extremist/moderate subject', by Mariela Cuadro, studies extremism from a poststructuralist point of view. Departing from Foucault's insights, the chapter analyses the inter-relation between knowledge, power and the subject. Specifically, the author interrogates the discourse on extremism from the perspective of the formation of identity and political subjectivities. She traces the formation of knowledge about extremism and the construction of the extremist subject, but also of the discursive formation of their opposite categories, moderation and the moderate subjects. Through the study of these categories, the author reflects on how the discourse on extremism, from a poststructuralist point of view, can be seen as a way of exercising power through knowledge and as a way of enforcing and establishing desirable (moderate) subjectivities. As the author argues, in this light, the discourse of extremism can thus be seen as the bearer of global governmentality which regulates acceptable and unacceptable behaviours.

In chapter four, 'The lone (white) wolf, "terrorism" and the suspect community', Marie Breen-Smyth explores how countering extremism is rooted in the politics of colonialism and, as a consequence, it reproduces similar dynamics. She argues that the concept serves to subordinate particular 'Others' in a colonial world order reproduced both at a domestic and at an international level. Departing from her previous studies on the 'suspect communities' (Breen-Smyth, 2014), she reflects on the racialised nature of the discourse on extremism and on the reason why the violent nature of white right-wing nationalists has failed to produce a suspect community of white right-wing individuals, despite the fact that these people may also, at times, be labelled 'extremists'.

Jessica Auchter puts forward a feminist reading of countering extremism in chapter five, 'The personal is political: feminist critiques of countering violent extremism'. Drawing from the famous feminist claim that 'the personal is political', this chapter proposes two main critiques of the policies of countering extremism. The first regards the fact that these programmes are based on the premise that security threats such as extremism should be countered in the private realm. Therefore, they invade the domestic sphere, rendering the private realm a security theatre. The second problem is linked to the fact that these counter- and preventive measures are constructed on gendered understandings. They identify women as responsible actors in these security measures based on their supposed feminine peaceful nature, rendering women the gate-keepers of their communities and their families. These approaches thus also reproduce specific (desirable) subjectivities reinforcing gender biases in society and at an international level.

Chapter six formulates a peace studies approach to countering extremism. In 'A peace studies approach to countering extremism: do counter-extremism strategies produce peace?', Kieran Ford assesses the strategies implemented to counter extremism from a peace studies perspective. In this chapter, the author develops a matrix of peace and violence to evaluate whether approaches to countering extremism engender peace or violence. The author argues that current counter-extremism measures produce various kinds of violence: epistemic and cultural violence through the promotion of homogeneity and the securitisation of diversity, and direct violence in the way these measures are enacted. Underlining the counter-productive and damaging nature of contemporary counter-extremism, Ford formulates a peaceful counter-extremism model, built on the framework of agonism and agonistic peace (Mouffe, 2013; Shinko, 2008).

Closing the theoretical section is Aislinn O'Donnell's chapter, 'What is an educational response to extreme and radical ideas and why does it matter?' From a pedagogical and educational point of view, O'Donnell reflects on the impact countering-extremism approaches have on the realm of education. She analyses how these approaches frame education in security terms and encompass it within countering-extremism strategies. The author provides an assessment of the changed role of education, educational relationships and the educational engagement with ideas, but also of the promotion of certain values over others as part of these approaches.

The second part of the book, 'Extremism, countering extremism and preventing extremism: from theory to international and local challenges', takes many of the themes discussed in the theoretical part and analyses them empirically in relation to local dynamics. This part starts with a reflection on the role of the United Nations within the standardisation and legitimisation of countering extremism at an international level. In chapter eight, 'Legitimising countering extremism at an international level: the role of United Nations Security Council', Alice Martini provides an analysis of the discourses and policies produced by the Security Council in relation to extremism. Martini follows the genealogical shift of the international discourse from terrorism to extremism and underlines its loss of focus and specificity. Moreover, she analyses how the concept of extremism has been discursively assigned a wide range of meanings – from ideas to physical violence. This issue not only contributes to the incongruous use of the word, but it has also permitted the implementation of all-encompassing governmentality which has merged the domestic and the international sphere, and the private and public social realms. In this sense, Martini highlights how the institution has contributed to the formation of a Foucauldian *dispositif* of extremism at a global level and how the UN has played a central role in the enforcement of international standardised governmentality.

Chapter nine bridges the international level with local dynamics. In 'International PVE and Tunisia: a local critique of international donors' discourses', Guendalina Simoncini offers an analysis of the PVE discourses produced by international donors in Tunisia. The author reflects on the main categories of individuals that have been the main beneficiaries of these initiatives, specifically women and youth. Simoncini looks at the securitisation of these groups within the intersection of the discourse on extremism, the security–development nexus, but also, more in general, Orientalist and Western understandings of this Arab country. Lastly, the author provides a critique of the donors' conceptualisations of peace and social cohesion, aimed at boosting the status quo and maintaining specific relations of power.

In chapter ten, Laura Fernández de Mosteyrín focuses on how the global CVE paradigm is being transposed in the case of Spain. In 'Communication as legitimation in Spanish CVE: bringing lessons from the past', the author examines the communication of the CVE strategy, mainly in public events of dissemination. Tracing the origin of this practice from past counter-terrorism campaigns in the country, Fernández de Mosteyrín reflects on how past discourses create the basis for, but also shape, the reception of global discourses on CVE in local contexts. In Spain, the author argues, legitimisation has been central to past counter-terrorism practices and it has thus been transposed into contemporary dynamics too. Within this understanding, the author analyses how communication of CVE in contemporary Spain has become a central practice in the legitimisation of current measures, but she also discusses how this communication takes place through specific dynamics.

Priya Dixit discusses in chapter eleven the racialisation of the discourse on extremism in the US. In 'Extremists or patriots? Racialisation of countering violent extremism programming in the United States', Dixit analyses the racial biases of CVE discourses and programmes in the US. Although US far-right extremists have killed people and armed militias have occupied government lands, Dixit argues that these individuals are rarely described as extremists by the media and government. Differently, CVE discourses in the US mainly focus on Muslim and Arab people. Therefore, Dixit formulates a race-based analysis of violent extremism in the US, taking into consideration the concepts of Islamophobia and 'suspect communities' to illustrate how linking extremism mainly to 'brown bodies' erases and neglects violence by white men in public debates and from the public's understanding of extremism.

In chapter twelve, 'The CVE paradox: inapplicability and necessity in Bosnia and Herzegovina', Tanja Dramac Jiries discusses the case of Bosnia and Herzegovina. Dramac discusses and problematises the implementation of CVE practices in the country. A post-war political scenario, Bosnia and Herzegovina had to confront the challenge of an important number of foreign fighters joining the wars in Syria and Iraq, which the government tried to counter through the implementation of a specific formulation of CVE. Nevertheless, these policies presented various problematic aspects. Dramac discusses the inapplicability of the mainstream CVE logic and its orthodox approach to Islamic fundamentalism in a country that is both highly multi-ethnic and has significant socio-economic problems. Therefore, the author calls instead for a more cultural and context-sensitive implementation of CVE grounded in peacebuilding practices.

Chapter thirteen, 'Drivers or decoys? Women and the narrative of extremist violence in Pakistan', is by Afiya Shehrbano Zia. Here, the author analyses the case of CVE in Pakistan, specifically in relation to the disciples of the *Lal Masjid* (the Red Mosque) in the capital city of Islamabad. She underlines how CVE in the country is driven by military logic and how it fails to understand religious extremism and the place of religion in the country. Consequently, discussions about CVE are shaped by masculine narratives and imbricated in religious nationalism and exclude the voices of women, minorities, civilians or secular sensibilities. Focusing on the uprising of the women of the seminary of the Jamia Hafsa, the author challenges previous understandings of women pivoting around their piety. She thus argues for a CVE that may be able to grasp the connectivity between piety and radical religious narratives and that includes women's voices in policymaking spheres for CVE.

Lastly, chapter fourteen deals with the Nigerian case. In 'The Mayor of Abuja and the "Pied Piper" of Maiduguri: extremism and the "politics of mutual envy" in Nigeria?', Akinyemi Oyawale discusses the politics of extremism and radicalisation in the country from a postcolonial and poststructuralist perspective. The author problematises existing literature and current understandings about extremism in Nigeria. These, Oyawale argues, foreclose the possibilities of a rich, nuanced and critical understanding of political violence. He then puts forward a critique of extremism as an ideological tool adopted by the state with the aim of practising a 'politics of mutual envy' – a manifestation of the uncritical perpetuation of (post)colonial mimicry. Oyawale underlines in this chapter how the binary of the 'Islam vs. the West' narrative – at the basis of the understanding of this kind of political violence – flounders when analysed in relation to the historical, political and cultural background of Nigeria, a country where, with all its different varieties, Islam has constituted the fulcrum for both hegemonic and counterhegemonic struggles for almost a millennium.

Conclusion

As this short overview shows, this book brings together various points of view on the issue of extremism and preventing and countering it. Despite the very wide theoretical and empirical perspectives on the issue, all the authors agree that measures implemented in CVE and PVE and the same concept of extremism are highly problematic. Before proceeding to the rest of the volume, it is worth highlighting the common themes shared by the following chapters – and thus, by the discourse on (violent) extremism.

The first issue that emerges from these analyses is the unjustified shift in the discourse from terrorism to extremism. As the following chapters illustrate, there is no real empirical or scientific evidence that extremism plays a central role in inducing individuals to embrace violence. Although models and scientific studies have tried to demonstrate the link between thoughts, ideas and violence (Borum, 2011; Canna, 2011; King and Taylor, 2011), they have so far failed to prove this relation. Moreover, as mentioned, the word still lacks an agreed definition and its use so far appears even more inconsistent than that of terrorism (Richards, 2015). In other words, analysed from within, the shift in the discourse does not seem to be justified outside of the political logic of renewing the legitimacy of existing discourses (Jackson and Tsui, 2016).

Second, the term does not seem to add to existing understandings of political violence, but appears instead to further neglect the political element of this violence and to further its decontextualisation and its ahistoricisation. Its use shifts the analysis towards these elements by further denying a focus on the political and social root causes of terrorist violence (Lindekilde, 2016). In this sense, the use of this word reflects an established dynamic within the discourse and understandings of terrorism, namely, that of neglecting the political causes, the inequalities of societies and the socio-economic causes that may bring individuals to embrace violence. As for terrorism (Jackson, 2012; Jackson and Dexter, 2014), the focus on extremism further depoliticises this violence, neglecting its political message and shifting the focus towards other elements.

A third aspect to be highlighted as a general critique to CVE and PVE that can be learned from this volume is the growing standardisation of these practices and the internationalisation of the discourse in an unproblematic way. This has already been denounced by Kundnani and Hayes (Kundnani and Hayes, 2018) and it is further illustrated by the combination of theory and practice present in this volume's chapters. In other words, it is interesting to note that the categories highlighted by the two chapters analysing international institutions (chapters eight and nine) are present in the analyses of more specific, local contexts. Here, as the following chapters will describe, the internationalisation of CVE and PVE (Kundnani and Hayes, 2018) has led to the implementation of these measures in a decontextualised way, blind to cultural aspects and sensitivities. In most cases, this has brought about counter-productive results that have not managed to enter the various levels of society; they have thus not adapted to their specific context of intervention, instead reproducing sterile, external understandings of local conflicts.

Linked to the counter-productivity of these measures is the question of peace. Overall, the chapters of this volume all criticise CVE and PVE because they fail to produce peace, and they fail to engage with and solve social conflicts. Moreover, they are counter-productive in the sense that, in some instances, they produce more violence than peace. On the one hand, this violence is the result of these same approaches and it is visible in the establishment of suspect communities, of human and civil rights abuses and in the more violent ways these measures are put into practice. On the other side, by neglecting the political element of terrorism, and thus the peaceful expression of political claims, they further produce frustration and marginalisation that may result in bursts of violence (Mouffe, 2005, pp. 76–83; Shinko, 2008).

Lastly, as most of the chapters show, the discourse on extremism is once again placed at the intersection between Orientalist (Croft, 2012; Grosfoguel and Mielants, 2006; Hurd, 2003) and gendered understandings of violence (Enloe, 2014; Martini, 2018; Sjoberg and Gentry, 2011, 2007; Sylvester and Parashar, 2011). Inheriting from the gendered and racial conceptualisation of terrorism, the discourse on extremism reproduces the same subject-positions. On this, most of the chapters show how Muslim identities are highly securitised by the discourse, even in Muslim countries. Here, the extremist subject is again the brown man, whereas brown women are depicted as peaceful and non-violent, and thus rendered the ideal gate-keepers of their own communities. This theme is widely examined throughout most of the chapters, where authors reflect from specific perspectives on the consequences of this gendered and racialised understanding of extremism and, above all, of counter-extremism.

In conclusion, despite a wide and generalised critique of its problematic nature, the discourse on extremism and its relative practices reproduce many of the assumptions of the discourse on terrorism, while at the same time broadening its governmentality at all spheres of society. It is because of this reason that critical literature needs to make its voice heard. And it is with this aim that this volume brings together so many perspectives on the matter. Its goal is not that of presenting ways or strategies of preventing or countering extremism. Before that, this volume wants to provide a space of resistance to these dominant understandings, a space where non-mainstream and critical voices can be heard and a space where a deep reflection can take place while, through the following chapters, the reader is 'encountering extremism'.

References

Awan, I., 2012. '"I am a Muslim not an extremist": How the Prevent strategy has constructed a "suspect" community: Extremism and terrorism', *Politics & Policy*, 40, 1158–1185.

Baker-Beall, C., 2016. *European Union's Fight Against Terrorism: Discourse, Policies, Identity*. Manchester University Press, Manchester.

Blakeley, R., 2009. *State Terrorism and Neoliberalism. The North in the South*. Routledge, London and New York.

Borum, R., 2011. 'Radicalization into violent extremism II: A review of conceptual models and empirical research', *Journal of Strategic Security*, 4, 37–62.

Breen-Smyth, M., 2014. 'Theorising the "suspect community": Counterterrorism, security practices and the public imagination', *Critical Studies on Terrorism*, 7(2), 223–240.

Breen-Smyth, M., Gunning, J., Jackson, R., Kassimeris, G. and Robinson, P., 2008. 'Critical Terrorism Studies – an introduction', *Critical Studies on Terrorism*, 1(1), 1–4.

Brown, K.E., Saeed, T., 2015. 'Radicalization and counter-radicalization at British universities: Muslim encounters and alternatives', *Ethnic and Racial Studies*, 38, 1952–1968.

Canna, S. (ed.), 2011. *Countering Violent Extremism: Scientific Methods & Strategies*. NSI, Washington DC.

Croft, S., 2012. *Securitizing Islam: Identity and the Search for Security*. Cambridge University Press, Cambridge.

Crone, M., Harrow, M., 2011. 'Homegrown terrorism in the West', *Terrorism and Political Violence*, 23, 521–536.

Elshimi, M.S., 2015. 'De-radicalisation interventions as technologies of the self: A Foucauldian analysis', *Critical Studies on Terrorism*, 8(1), 110–129.

Enloe, C., 2014. *Bananas, Beaches and Bases. Making Feminist Sense of International Politics*. University of California Press, Berkeley, Los Angeles and London.

Fernández de Mosteyrín, L., Limón López, P., 2016. 'Paradigmas y Políticas de Seguridad: una aproximación al Plan Estratégico Nacional de Lucha contra la Radicalización Violenta PEN-LCRV 2015', *Política y Sociedad*, 54(3), 801–823.

Ford, K., 2017. 'Developing a peace perspective on counter-extremist education', *Peace Review*, 29(2), 144–152.

Ford, K., 2019. 'Defending a castle under siege: A critical examination of the British counter-extremism in schools strategy' (Thesis, Doctor of Philosophy). University of Otago. Available at http://hdl.handle.net/10523/9420 (accessed 10 July 2019).

Grosfoguel, R., Mielants, E., 2006. 'The long-durée entanglement between Islamophobia and racism in the modern/colonial capitalist/patriarchal world-system: An introduction', *Human Architecture: Journal of the Sociology of Self-Knowledge*, 5, 1–13.

Harris-Hogan, S., Barrelle, K. and Zammit, A., 2016. 'What is countering violent extremism? Exploring CVE policy and practice in Australia', *Behavioral Sciences of Terrorism and Political Aggression*, 8, 6–24.

Heath-Kelly, C., 2013. 'Counter-terrorism and the counterfactual: Producing the "radicalisation" discourse and the UK PREVENT Strategy', *The British Journal of Politics and International Relations*, 15, 394–415.

Heath-Kelly, C., 2017. 'The geography of pre-criminal space: Epidemiological imaginations of radicalisation risk in the UK Prevent Strategy, 2007–2017', *Critical Studies on Terrorism*, 10, 297–319.

Heath-Kelly, C., Strausz, E., 2018. 'The banality of counterterrorism "after, after 9/11"? Perspectives on the Prevent duty from the UK health care sector', *Critical Studies on Terrorism*, 12(1), 1–21.

Heath-Kelly, C., Baker-Beall, C. and Jarvis, L. (eds), 2016. *Neoliberalism and Terror: Critical Engagements*. Routledge, London and New York.

Herman, E.S., O'Sullivan, G., 1989. *The Terrorism Industry. The Experts and Institutions that Shape Our View of Terror*. Pantheon Books, New York.

Her Majesty's Government, 2011. *Prevent Strategy*. Crown Copyright, London.

Holland, J., 2012. *Selling the War on Terror: Foreign Policy Discourses after 9/11*. Routledge, New York.

Hurd, E., 2003. 'Appropriating Islam: The Islamic other in the consolidation of Western modernity', *Critique: Critical Middle Eastern Studies*, 12, 25–41.

Jackson, R., 2005. *Writing the War on Terrorism. Language, Politics and Counter-terrorism*. Manchester University Press, Manchester.

Jackson, R., 2012. 'Unknown knowns: The subjugated knowledge of terrorism studies', *Critical Studies on Terrorism*, 5(1), 11–29.

Jackson, R., 2015. 'The epistemological crisis of counterterrorism', *Critical Studies on Terrorism*, 8(1), 33–54.

Jackson, R. (ed.), 2016. *Routledge Handbook of Critical Terrorism Studies*. Routledge, London and New York.

Jackson, R., Dexter, H., 2014. 'The social construction of organised political violence: An analytical framework', *Civil Wars*, 16, 1–23.

Jackson, R., Tsui, C.-K., 2016. 'War on terror II: Obama and the adaptive evolution of US counterterrorism', in Bentley, M. and Holland, J. (eds), *The Obama Doctrine: A Legacy of Continuity in US Foreign Policy?* Routledge, Abingdon, pp. 70–83.

Jackson, R., Breen-Smyth, M. and Gunning, J. (eds), 2009. *Critical Terrorism Studies: A New Research Agenda*. Routledge, London.

Jarvis, L., 2009. *Times of Terror. Discourse, Temporality and the War on Terror*. Palgrave Macmillan, New York.

Jarvis, L., Lister, M. (eds), 2015a. *Critical Perspectives on Counter-terrorism*. Routledge, London and New York.

Jarvis, L., Lister, M., 2015b. *Anti-terrorism, Citizenship and Security*. Oxford University Press, Oxford.

King, M., Taylor, D.M., 2011. 'The radicalization of homegrown jihadists: A review of theoretical models and social psychological evidence', *Terrorism and Political Violence*, 23, 602–622.

Kundnani, A., 2012. 'Radicalisation: The journey of a concept', *Race & Class*, 54, 3–25.

Kundnani, A., 2015. *The Muslims Are Coming! Islamophobia, Extremism and the Domestic War on Terror*. Verso Books, London.

Kundnani, A., Hayes, B., 2018. *The Globalisation of Countering Violent Extremism Policies. Undermining Human Rights, Instrumentalising Civil Society*. Transnational Institute, Amsterdam.

Lindahl, S., 2018. *A Critical Theory of Counterterrorism: Ontology, Epistemology and Normativity*. Routledge, London.

Lindekilde, L., 2016. 'Radicalization, de-radicalization and counter-radicalization', in Jackson, R. (ed.), *Routledge Handbook of Critical Terrorism Studies*. Routledge, London and New York, pp. 248–259.

Martin, T., 2018. 'Identifying potential terrorists: Visuality, security and the Channel project', *Security Dialogue*, 49, 254–271.

Martini, A., 2018. 'Making women terrorists into "Jihadi brides": An analysis of media narratives on women joining ISIS', *Critical Studies on Terrorism*, 11(3), 458–477.

Martini, A., 2019. 'On international barbarians and global civilisations. A Critical Discourse Analysis of the evolution of the Security Council's fight against terrorism'. (Thesis, Doctor of Philosophy). Sant'Anna School of Advanced Studies. Unpublished work.

Mouffe, C., 2005. *On the Political. Thinking in Action*. Routledge, New York.

Mouffe, C., 2013. *Agonistics. Thinking the World Politically*. Verso, London.

Nash, C., Nesterova, Y., 2017. *Youth Waging Peace: Youth Led Guide on Prevention of Violent Extremism through Education*. UNESCO Mahatma Gandhi Institute of Education for Peace and Sustainable Development, New Delhi.

Nasser-Eddine, M., Garnham, B., Agostino, K. and Caluya, G., 2011. *Countering Violent Extremism (CVE) Literature Review, Counter Terrorism and Security Technology Centre*. Department of Defense, the Australian Government, Edinburgh, South Australia.

Neumann, P.R., 2013. 'The trouble with radicalisation', *International Affairs*, 89(4), 873–893.

O'Donnell, A., 2016. 'Securitisation, counterterrorism and the silencing of dissent: The educational implications of Prevent', *British Journal of Educational Studies*, 64, 53–76.

Pantazis, C., Pemberton, S., 2009. 'From the "old" to the "new" suspect community: Examining the impacts of recent UK counter-terrorist legislation', *British Journal of Criminology*, 49, 646–666.

Payne, K., 2009. 'Winning the battle of ideas: Propaganda, ideology, and terror', *Studies in Conflict and Terrorism*, 32(2), 109–128.

Ragazzi, F., 2016. 'Suspect community or suspect category? The impact of counter-terrorism as policed multiculturalism', *Journal of Ethnic and Migration Studies*, 4, 724–741.

Richards, A., 2011. 'The problem with "radicalization": The remit of "Prevent" and the need to refocus on terrorism in the UK', *International Affairs*, 87, 143–152.

Richards, A., 2015. 'From terrorism to "radicalization" to "extremism": Counterterrorism imperative or loss of focus?', *International Affairs*, 91, 371–380.

Schuurman, B., Horgan, J.G., 2016. 'Rationales for terrorist violence in homegrown jihadist groups: A case study from the Netherlands', *Aggression and Violent Behavior*, 27, 55–63.

Shinko, R.E., 2008. 'Agonistic peace: A postmodern reading', *Millennium: Journal of International Studies*, 36, 473–491.

Sjoberg, L., Gentry, C.E. (eds), 2011. *Women, Gender, and Terrorism*. University of Georgia Press, Athens, GA.

Sjoberg, L., Gentry, C.E., 2007. *Mothers, Monsters, Whores: Women's Violence in Global Politic*. Zed Books, New York.

Sylvester, C., Parashar, S., 2011. 'The contemporary "Mahabharata" and the many "Draupadis": Bringing gender to critical terrorism studies', in Jackson, R., Breen-Smyth, M., Gunning, J. and Jarvis, L. (eds), *Terrorism: A Critical Introduction*. Palgrave Macmillan, New York, pp. 194–215.

Weber, M., 1949. *The Methodology of the Social Sciences*. The Free Press, Glencoe, IL.

Weber, M., 1978. *Economy and Society: An Outline of Interpretive Sociology. Volume 1*. University of California Press, London.

Part I

What's in a name? Theoretically deconstructing extremism

1

Interrogating the concept of (violent) extremism: a genealogical study of terrorism and counter-terrorism discourses

Chin-Kuei Tsui

Tracing the discursive origins of '(violent) extremism': terrorism, radicalisation and extremism

Recently, the terms *terrorism*, *radicalisation* and *extremism* have been utilised interchangeably by scholars, decision makers and policy practitioners to interpret the so-called 'terrorist threat'. The tendency is to increasingly merge these terms into a sole discursive framework that is perceived to affect the modern epistemological understanding of terrorism and the subsequent practices of countering (violent) extremism in many Western countries (Richards, 2015, 2017). However, through the lens of Critical Discourse Analysis (CDA), which aims to try and understand the relationship between discursive phenomena and social processes and practices (Jackson, 2018; Jorgensen and Phillip, 2002), this chapter contributes to a genealogical study of terrorism-related discourse and illustrates an intrinsic link among the concepts of terrorism, radicalisation and extremism. The present research suggests that the discursive foundation of violent extremism is actually the more widely accepted US war on terror discourse and the recent radicalisation discourse, particularly constructed by counter-terrorism elites and intellectuals in the UK around the mid-2000s. In addition, as much of the existing literature has demonstrated, besides the US-led war on terror, the discursive construction of radicalisation and extremism can be attributed to the notions about a series of significant incidents in the 2000s plotted by perpetrators with Middle East and North African backgrounds, such as the 2004 Madrid train bombings and the 7/7 London bombings.

(Countering) violent extremism in the US's 'war on terror' discourse

Although recent research (Nasser-Eddine et al., 2011) has argued that so-called 'violent extremism' is an evolving concept and, thus, there is no real distinction between violent extremism and other forms of political violence, the concept of violent extremism has its specific meaning in counter-terrorism initiatives conducted mainly by Western countries. The construction of '(countering) violent extremism' discourse should be better understood in the wider context of the US-led war on terror.

Subsequent to the terrorist attacks of 9/11 in 2001, the Bush administration acted vigorously to instigate the global war on terror. In the name of counter-terrorism, the Bush administration conducted two major military operations in the greater Middle East – namely, Operation Enduring Freedom and Operation Iraqi Freedom – overthrowing the Taliban and Saddam Hussein regimes in Afghanistan and Iraq. However, after major military combat in both countries, the US turned to a bloody war of counter-insurgency in Iraq, trying reluctantly to win the war of 'hearts and minds'; it also fought various campaigns against jihadist groups in Yemen, Libya, Somalia, Mali, the Philippines and elsewhere under the Bush presidency. Accordingly, many (Jackson, 2012; Leffler, 2003; Miller, 2010; Winkler, 2007) have argued that the military-oriented counter-terrorism approach was the focus of the Bush administration's global war on terror, though other approaches like the anti-terrorism legislation and enforcement marked by the PATRIOT Act of 2001 were simultaneously implemented by the Bush administration.

Despite the material practices mentioned above, during the Bush presidency, the war on terror discourse – the particular way of talking about and understanding terrorism and counter-terrorism – was successfully framed, constructed, circulated and institutionalised in the wider American society (Croft, 2006; Jackson, 2012). Terrorism was consequently comprehended as a severe threat to the US, its citizens and the American way of life. During these years, the political rhetoric of 'terrorism' and 'terrorists' mainly referenced Islamic extremism characterised by bin Laden, al Qaida and their affiliates. Despite the notion of Islamic extremism in the mid-2000s, terms such as 'extremism', 'extremists' and 'radicalisation' rarely appeared in America's public discourse; when these terms were used, they usually referred to the far right and neo-Nazism (Kundnani and Hayes, 2018, pp. 6–7).

Unlike the Bush administration's global war on terror and its counter-insurgency missions in Iraq, which were the major policy focus of President Bush's second term, the Obama administration continued the 'war' but relocated it to Afghanistan and Pakistan, with the implicit argument that these countries, not Iraq, were the true 'epicenter of violent extremism practised by Al Qaida' and that 'it is from here that new attacks are being plotted' (Obama, 2009c). Most of the coercive approaches to counter-terrorism – such as the drone-killing programme and the reliance on US special military forces – were adopted and even broadly utilised by the Obama administration; indeed, Obama and his political aides contributed to a discursive shift in US counter-terrorism; that is, the language changed from 'the war on terror' to 'the war against al Qaida and violent extremism' (Jackson and Tsui, 2016). More specifically, during the Obama presidency, terms such as *extremist*, *extremism* and *violent extremism* were adopted to replace phrases related to the war on terror and were particularly utilised by officials to interpret the threats posed by al Qaida and ISIS because these groups were the focus of President Obama's counter-extremism initiatives. The discursive shift of US counter-terrorism, in part, illustrates Obama's determination to change his predecessor's controversial foreign and security policies, which had been argued against and criticised by many American citizens and US foreign allies. It partially demonstrates the Obama administration's political goal to ease the tension between the Muslim world and the US that was caused by the tragedy of 9/11 and the so-called global war on terror.

In 2009, in his address to the joint session of Congress, Obama (2009a) said, 'With our friends and allies, we will forge a new and comprehensive strategy for Afghanistan and Pakistan to defeat Al Qaida and combat extremism'. In the same speech, he emphasised that, 'To overcome extremism, we must also be vigilant in upholding the values our troops defend, because there is no force in the world more powerful than the example of America'. On 4 June 2009, when he delivered his remarkable speech at Cairo University and tried to release the tension between the US and the Islamic world, Obama (2009b) stressed that, among many significant issues (such as Palestinian–Israeli relations and the proliferation of nuclear weapons), violent extremism was undoubtedly the top issue that the US had to confront in the Muslim world in the foreseeable future. As he mentioned unequivocally, 'The US and the Muslim world will, however, relentlessly confront violent extremists who pose a grave threat to our security, because we reject the same thing that people of all faiths reject: the killing of innocent men, women, and children'.

In short, in the first term of Obama's presidency, there was still no firm consensus about the meaning and definition of *extremism* in the US political arena. In official language, *extremism* usually referred to a specific form of brutal violence targeting innocent civilians and committed mainly by al Qaida. To deal with the threats posed by extremism, a specific Countering Violent Extremism Working Group was built by the US Department of Homeland Security. The Obama administration introduced and published the first preventing violent extremism (PVE) strategy in August 2011 (Kundnani and Hayes, 2018, p. 11). Besides, during Obama's first term as president, international cooperation on issues related to terrorism and extremism was prompted and supported by US government authorities, such as the US–EU security dialogue on countering violent extremism (CVE) and the establishment of the EU's Radicalisation Awareness Network (RAN), built based on the shared interests of the US and EU in CVE (Kundnani and Hayes, 2018, p. 11, pp. 23–25).

However, the notion of domestic (violent) extremism and relevant policy practices notably can be dated to 2009 and 2010 due to the lessons learnt from several incidents in the US, namely, the Little Rock recruiting office shooting in Arkansas, the Fort Hood shooting in Texas and two attempted bombings in New York plotted by Najibullah Zazi and Faisal Shahzad (Kundnani and Hayes, 2018, p. 11). Prior to these events, officials thought radicalisation and the extremist threat in the US homeland occurred relatively rarely, compared with many European countries; thus, issues related to radicalisation and extremism were initially discussed internally by Federal Bureau of Investigation (FBI) and New York Police Department (NYPD) officials, and were not explicitly perceived as policy programmes (Kundnani and Hayes, 2018, pp. 10–11). Yet, after these incidents, European and particularly UK-style CVE programmes, which emphasise the significance of risk analysis and management, were imported and stressed by US policymaking elites and counter-terrorism practitioners (Kundnani and Hayes, 2018).

In Obama's second term, the term (*violent*) *extremism* was particularly utilised by US political elites to interpret the threats posed by ISIS and so-called 'foreign fighters' residing in many European countries. In 2014, when he gave his UN General Assembly speech on the so-called 'violent extremism' that the world faced, Obama quoted President Kennedy's words:

> 'Terror is not a new weapon', he said. 'Throughout history, it has been used by those who could not prevail, either by persuasion or example'. In the 20th century, terror was used by all manner of groups who failed to come to power through public support. But, in this century, we have faced a more lethal and ideological brand of terrorist who have perverted one of the world's great religions. . . . They have embraced a nightmarish vision that would divide the world into adherents and infidels – killing as many innocent civilians as possible, and employing the most brutal methods to intimidate people within their communities. (Obama, 2014)

Additionally, although the post-war situation in Afghanistan was controlled by the US in 2014, Obama (2014) continued to urge the international community to beware of the danger posed by some 'religiously motivated fanatics' (i.e., members of ISIS) who were thought to be the cause of violent extremism. As he pointed out, 'Extremist ideology has shifted to other places – particularly in the Middle East and North Africa, where a quarter of young people have no job; food and water could grow scarce; corruption is rampant; and sectarian conflicts have become increasingly hard to contain' (Obama, 2014). Clearly, for the Obama administration, the roots of violent extremism are associated with twisted religious ideologies, economic and political grievances and sectarian conflicts. Obama's political discourse argues and illustrates that, besides al Qaida and the Taliban, the threat of (violent) extremism originated from the greater Middle East and was noted and discussed by US officials in Obama's second term.

In 2015, the Obama administration further explained the concept of violent extremism and introduced the outlines for the US-led counter-extremism coalition. As Obama indicated at the summit on CVE hosted by the US in Washington, DC:

> By violent extremism, we don't just mean the terrorists who are killing innocent people. We also mean the ideologies, the infrastructure of extremists – the propagandists, the recruiters, the funders who radicalise and recruit or incite people to violence. (Obama, 2015a)

Regarding the feasible counter-extremism policies targeting al Qaida and ISIS, Obama (2015a) emphasised the necessity of a *prevention* policy – that is, preventing these groups from radicalising, recruiting or inspiring individuals to violence in the first place. Based on the idea of prevention, relevant policies were argued to be indispensable at discrediting extremist ideologies, addressing issues related to political and economic grievances, and enlarging the counter-extremism community composed of both Muslim and non-Muslim members (Obama, 2015b). Moreover, a pilot programme on CVE prompted by the US Justice Department was beginning to be implemented in Los Angeles, Greater Boston and Minneapolis (Kundnani and Hayes, 2018; Smith et al., 2018).

Additionally, Obama claimed that leaders of al Qaida and ISIS were, in fact, terrorists who portrayed themselves as religious leaders and therefore justified violence in the name of Islam. To discredit extremist thought and improve the relationship between the US and the Islamic world, Obama (2015a) emphasised that the US was not at war with Islam, as extremist groups like al Qaida and ISIS constantly claimed; instead, the US was at war with those who perverted Islam.

In summary, an analysis of US terrorism-related discourse illustrates that the prevalence of the words *extremism* or *violent extremism* in the US political arena can largely be traced to the Obama presidency, although, in the mid-2000s, officials from the Bush administration had debated the utilisation of the *war on terror* and suggested a new phrase – *struggle against violent extremism* (SAVE) – to rebrand the US-led counter-terrorism efforts after the terrorist attacks of 9/11 in 2001 (Burkeman, 2009; Nasser-Eddine et al., 2011). The internal debate among

US officials illustrates that US policymaking elites had indeed considered and discussed the request for counter-terrorism policy to change from its specific focus on a terrorist organisation – namely, al Qaida – to a broader perceived problem with radical Islam. However, President Bush still opted to use the 'war on terror' rhetoric (Schmitt and Shanker, 2005).

During the years of Obama's presidency, terms like *extremist, extremism* and *violent extremism* were widely employed by officials to structure the terrorism-related discourse and interpret the threats posed by al Qaida and its affiliates. Nonetheless, with the emergence of ISIS and the pressing threats from 'foreign fighters', Obama, especially in his second term, clearly defined terrorists, ideologies and the infrastructure of extremists as so-called 'violent extremism'. To fight violent extremism, the president urgently insisted that the UN cooperate internationally to solve issues associated with sectarian conflicts, fanatical beliefs and economic and political grievances.

CVE in the UK and Europe's radicalisation discourse

The notion of CVE in the UK and European countries can be understood in the broader context of the 'radicalisation' discourse, which was initially produced for the purpose of counter-terrorism among government authorities, rather than in scholarly discussion (Kundnani, 2012). As many argue, the epistemological understanding of 'radicalisation' and '(countering) violent extremism', in particular the notion of 'home-grown terrorism', can be attributed to several terrorist attacks in European countries – such as the 2004 Madrid train bombings in which 192 people died, the 7 July 2005 London bombings in which 52 lives were lost, the murder of Dutch filmmaker Theo Van Gogh in 2004 and the killing of British soldier Lee Rigby in 2013. However, the US government had been alerted to scenarios of domestic terrorist attacks carried out by national citizens since the 1990s due to the impact of the 1995 Tokyo sarin gas attacks and the 1996 Oklahoma City bombings (Tsui, 2015, 2016).

It has been argued that the emphasis on countering extremism or preventing violent extremism in the UK and many European countries is closely associated with the discursive construction of radicalisation in the mid-2000s (Kundnani, 2012; Thomas, 2016). After the 2001 terrorist attacks in New York and Washington, DC, the Dutch government noted the potential threat of radicalisation and implemented relevant anti-radicalisation measures. Yet the most noticeable and influential anti-radicalisation effort in Europe is the UK's Prevent programme. It is one of the core elements of the UK's Counter-terrorism Strategy (CONTEST) drafted by the Home Office in 2003 and updated in 2006, 2009 and 2011 (Briggs, 2010; Richards, 2017; Kundnani and Hayes, 2018).[1] Alerted by the London bombings on 7 July 2005 plotted by four home-grown perpetrators, the Tony Blair-led British government reformulated its counter-terrorism policy and emphasised the threat of radicalisation, featuring the notion of home-grown (or British-born) terrorism and the al Qaida-related terrorist network in the UK. The new counter-terrorism policy, to some extent, illustrates an evolution of terrorist threats in the UK. That is, although threats from al Qaida and its affiliates remain persistent, the risk of terrorist attacks conducted by national citizens with apocalyptic thinking is quite high. In addition, recent attacks have shown that perpetrators who adopted extremist ideologies do not differentiate their targets. It is believed that the weapons they use might include weapons of mass destruction (Croft and Moore, 2010). As the former director of the British Security Service noted:

> The terrorist threat from AQ and related group[s] is, quite simply, unprecedented in scale, ambition and ruthlessness: They have a global reach, and they are willing to carry out mass casualty attacks, including suicide attacks, without warning. It remains a very real possibility that they may, sometime, somewhere, attempt a chemical, biological, radiological or even nuclear attack. (quoted in Croft and Moore, 2010, p. 830)

Official concerns regarding the post-9/11 and post-7/7 terrorist attacks were articulated in CONTEST, in which a major assumption of the so-called 'radicalisation process' was made by counter-terrorism elites and experts (Heath-Kelly, 2012). With the particular concept of radicalisation, officials believed that it should be understood as a *process* in which individuals – usually Muslim youths – are radicalised by extremist ideologies and, therefore, are likely incited by terrorists to commit violence. As UK's CONTEST indicates, 'Radicalisation is being driven by ideology, by a number of people who set out to disseminate these ideologies and by vulnerabilities in people which make them susceptible to a message of violence' (Home Office, 2011, p. 60). Thus, the aim of Prevent, or CONTEST as a whole, is to stop people from becoming terrorists or supporting terrorism (Home Office, 2011, p. 60).

As recent research (Kundnani, 2012; Schmid, 2014) has demonstrated, the discursive construction of radicalisation indeed contributed to the epistemological understanding of radicalisation and violent extremism and further affected the UK and its allies' counter-terrorism practices. That is, the 'problem' of radicalisation (and violent extremism) could be investigated, analysed and effectively prevented with the implementation of extraordinary measures, such as the establishment of early-warning and community-based policing networks (Kundnani and Hayes, 2018). Consequently, the shift of the UK's counter-terrorism policy led to new funds and posts for anti-radicalisation and the Prevent programme. For example, a local authority activity targeting groups of British

Muslim youths was financed by the Department for Communities and Local Government, and over 300 Prevent-dedicated police posts were established during 2008–2011 (Thomas, 2016, p. 171). Apart from that, in 2005, over 400,000 public sector agents received the so-called 'Prevent' training, and approximately 4,000 individuals were reported as probable extremists – including many youths under the age of 18 (Kundnani and Hayes, 2018, p. 9).

With the emergence of the radicalisation discourse, the significance of CVE was emphasised by the UK government. In 2006, subsequent to the London bombings on 7 July 2005, the PVE Pathfinder Fund was introduced to support local authorities with tackling the threat of violent extremism (Briggs, 2010, p. 975). In 2008, along with National Indicator 35, the UK's Prevent programme expanded the scope of anti-radicalisation and directly engaged several Muslim communities in the country. Consequently, the role of schools and educators in PVE was increased; the authorities also sought to provide necessary support for individuals vulnerable to violent extremism (Briggs, 2010). Additionally, Channel, a police-led multi-agency partnership that evaluates referrals of individuals at risk of being drawn into terrorism, was considered indispensable. In the 2011 revised version of Prevent, the British government stated that, in addition to the notion of violent extremism and terrorism, it was necessary to respond to the 'ideological challenge of terrorism', especially focusing on individuals who held certain extremist but non-violent views and preventing them from being drawn towards the trajectory of terrorism-related activities (Home Office, 2011, p. 62; see also Richards, 2017, pp. 117–118). According to the UK government, *extremism* refers to 'vocal or active opposition to fundamental British values, including democracy, the rule of law, individual liberty and mutual respect and tolerance of different faiths and beliefs' (Home Office, 2011, p. 63).

The UK's counter-terrorism initiatives prompted in the mid-2000s, especially CONTEST, profoundly affected the formulation of the EU's 2005 Counterterrorist Strategy, which is characterised by a framework consisting of four crucial elements, namely *prevent* (individuals from turning to terrorism), *protect* (citizens and infrastructure by reducing their vulnerability to attack), *pursue* (investigate terrorists and disrupt support networks) and *respond* (manage and minimise the consequences of attack). Similarly, the UK's CONTEST also outlined its four Ps: *pursue, prevent, protect* and *prepare*. The pressing threat of radicalisation and violent extremism was explicitly articulated in the EU's counter-terrorism-related document. EU officials argued that 'radicalisation and recruitment to terrorism are not confined to one belief system or political persuasion. . . . But the terrorism perpetrated by Al-Qaida and extremists inspired by Al-Qaida has become the main terrorist threat to the Union' (White and McEvoy, 2012, p. 12).

Besides the EU's warning, its members also acted vigorously to address the threats posed by radicalisation. For example, following the murder of Theo van

Gogh in 2004, the Dutch government developed and implemented a policy to counter violent extremism in Amsterdam, concentrating its counter-terrorism policy on localism and multi-agency cooperation (Kundnani and Hayes, 2018, pp. 7–8). Unlike the wider understanding that terrorist attacks are often religiously motivated, the Dutch government attributed radicalisation to socio-political exclusion and the difficulties of integration shared by many Dutch Muslims. Accordingly, feasible solutions, such as the importance of prevention and early intervention, were emphasised and articulated in the *Dutch Polarisation and Radicalisation Action Plan of 2007–2011* (White and McEvoy, 2012, pp. 17–18). To fight radicalisation, the Dutch Security Services (Algemene Inlichtingen- en Veiligheidsdient, AIVD) defined *radicalisation* as the 'growing readiness to pursue and/or support – if necessary by undemocratic means – far-reaching changes in society that conflict with, or pose a threat to, the democratic order' (Borum, 2011, p. 12), while the Danish Intelligence Service (Politlets Efterretningstjeneste, PET) argued that *violent radicalisation* is 'a process by which a person to an increasing extent accepts the use of undemocratic or violent means, including terrorism, in an attempt to reach a specific political/ ideological objective' (Borum, 2011, p. 12).

Similarly, after the 2004 Madrid bombings, the Spanish government introduced a series of initiatives targeted at terrorism, radicalisation and violent extremism. The Madrid train bombings plotted by al Qaida-linked perpetrators killed over 190 civilians and injured approximately 1,800. Given that Muslims constituted Spain's second-largest religious group and the difficulties of integration challenged many Muslim immigrants, the Spanish government modified its counter-terrorism policies and began focusing on immigrant issues (White and McEvoy, 2012, p. 20). For example, the Spanish government urged the Ministry of Labour and Social Affairs to take over immigration affairs that were originally handled by the Ministry of the Interior. The policy *per se* marked a discursive shift in Spain's counter-terrorism policy; that is, terrorism or radicalisation is not merely a policing issue. Instead, it could be better understood as a broader socio-cultural issue (White and McEvoy, 2012, p. 20.). With the formulation of a new counter-terrorism policy, the Spanish government, following the 2004 Madrid attacks, reallocated significant funding to programmes related to immigration, facilitating Muslim integration and working closely with domestic Muslim communities, such as the Islamic Commission of Spain (Comisión Islámica de España, CIE) and the Spanish Islamic Council, as they were the crucial partner agencies for CVE (White and McEvoy, 2012, pp. 20–21).

In addition to the threat of home-grown terrorism associated with al Qaida and its global network, concerns about ISIS and foreign fighters have recently been articulated in the Western-centred radicalisation discourse. Since 2014, ISIS has plotted and been the mastermind of various terrorist attacks in

European countries, such as the terrorist attacks in Paris, Nice, Brussels, Berlin, London and Manchester. In 2014, David Cameron, the then UK prime minister, stressed the threat from foreign fighters at a UN Security Council meeting. The UK's domestic intelligence agency, the Security Service (MI5), also expressed specific concerns regarding UK nationals who travelled to undergo radicalisation in Pakistan, Yemen and Somalia, and established connections with local extremist groups like Pakistan's Tehrik-e-Taliban, Yemen's al Qaida in the Arabian Peninsula (AQAP) and Somalia's al-Shabab (Counter Extremism Project, 2017). To address threats posed by Islamic extremism and foreign fighters, Jonathan Evans, the former head of MI5, warned: 'It is only a matter of time before we see terrorism on our streets inspired by those who are today fighting alongside al-Shabab' (quoted in Norton-Taylor, 2010). Alex Younger, the head of the UK's intelligence agency, has also argued that ISIS is 'plotting ways to project violence against the UK and our allies without ever having to leave Syria' (quoted in MacAskill, 2016). Considering the significant recent attacks, both the UK and French governments instituted travel bans to prevent their citizens from radicalisation and joining extremist groups abroad.

In short, an examination of the recent counter-terrorism efforts made by Western countries illustrates a significant discursive change in contemporary terrorism and counter-terrorism. Moreover, as the present research has analysed and discussed, it demonstrates the interplay between the US and European terrorism-related discourses. Prior to the London bombings on 7 July 2005, European counter-terrorism practices could be understood in the context of the US-led war on terror. To respond to President George W. Bush's global war on terror and his assertion 'Either you are with us, or you are with the terrorists', most European countries joined the US-led war on terror, fighting the war against al Qaida and its affiliates.

However, in the mid-2000s, following the specific attacks in London and other deadly attacks in European countries, home-grown terrorism and radicalisation alerted government authorities and counter-terrorism practitioners. The experiences and lessons learnt by European countries in the mid-2000s later enriched US counter-terrorism practices both discursively and materially. Until the emergence of ISIS in 2014, al Qaida and its related groups were the major focuses of European and American counter-terrorism, as they were explicitly articulated in the UK's CONTEST and US terrorism discourse. In the official lexicon, *terrorism* and *radicalisation* often referred to the threats posed by Islamic terrorism and al Qaida, in particular. Yet, in contrast to *terrorism, radicalisation* is framed and comprehended as a process in which individuals are radicalised to become members of terrorist groups and commit violence.

Importantly, as the discourse on radicalisation illustrates, the problem of radicalisation is not inevitable; instead, it can be managed, monitored and controlled through a prevention strategy. Concerning (violent) extremism, the specific concept has been frequently discussed in the context of radicalisation and anti-radicalisation and has been recently utilised to interpret ISIS, particularly its extremist thoughts and behaviours, which severely challenge Western democracies and values. Overall, the practices of Western counter-terrorism and intensive cooperation among nations on antiracialisation and countering extremism demonstrate that the CVE (or PVE) discourse has become globalised.[2]

Rethinking the discursive construction of radicalisation and violent extremism

As discussed previously, the concept of (violent) extremism can be studied and understood in the broader context of the US-led war on terror and the emergence of a radicalisation discourse in European countries. As with the concept of terrorism, to date, there is no firm consensus or universal definition of *radicalisation* and (violent) *extremism*, and these terms are, in fact, utilised interchangeably by decision makers and counter-terrorism experts in Western countries – although they might have different meanings in different political contexts at different times. However, with the discursive convergence of terrorism, radicalisation and extremism, and the discursive practices of so-called (violent) extremism (i.e., the way that extremism discourse is framed, understood, circulated and accepted by the public), extremism was eventually perceived as an existential threat to Western cultures, values and civilisation. According to a survey administered by the Pew Research Center in 2017, majorities in Europe and North America had pervasive concerns about the threat of extremism (Poushter, 2017), with 72% of American citizens concerned about Islamic extremism, while the percentages of nationals who worried about extremism in the name of Islam in the UK, France, the Netherlands and Spain were 79%, 79%, 76% and 82%, respectively (Poushter, 2017).

In addition to the construction of an extremist threat, the discursive formation of radicalisation and (violent) extremism caused many socio-political consequences in Western societies – in particular, racism and discrimination. Initially, the radicalisation and (violent) extremism discourse was created by certain political demands, helping counter-terrorism practitioners prevent violent attacks conducted mainly by nationals and suspect communities with particular Muslim identities. The understanding of radicalisation (as a process) and violent extremism also affected real-world policy practices in many ways. Since the 2000s, government authorities in the UK, the Netherlands and Spain have executed specific programmes targeting internal Muslim minorities to prevent Muslims from radicalising and being recruited by terrorist groups, especially al

Qaida and ISIS. Besides, considering the severe threats posed by ISIS and foreign terrorist fighters, international organisations, such as the United Nations and the European Union, have also urged the leaders of member states to be concerned with the threats posed by (violent) extremism. Consequently, a series of political summits and policies related to CVE or PVE issues were organised, prompted and practised. Though the relevant initiatives aim to reduce further terrorist attacks and seek to integrate Muslim minorities into mainstream societies, critics argue that, in the long term, Muslim minorities – the groups most vulnerable to radicalisation, according to Western government authorities – might be isolated and marginalised due to the distinction between Muslims and non-Muslims.

Recently, issues related to Islamophobia, anti-immigration, populism and the emergence of right-wing political parties have been widely discussed and debated by the public, and are attributed to several deadly attacks in European countries and the worst refugee crisis since the Second World War. Reports of Islamophobia and xenophobia have also illustrated that prejudice and anger towards Muslims has been dramatically increasing in many European countries (Al Jazeera, 2018). For example, in 2017, around 950 attacks focused on Muslims and mosques occurred in Germany; at least 500 Islamophobic incidents took place in Spain (Al Jazeera, 2018). Data from the Competence Centre for Right-Wing Extremism and Democracy Research also shows that more than 44% of Germans believe Muslims should be prohibited from immigrating. A great proportion of the German population argues that the number of Muslims has made them feel like strangers in Germany (Osborne, 2018). Besides, in 2017, a survey conducted in the US illustrates that 75% of Muslim-Americans think that discrimination is frequent in US society, and 48% of American Muslims express that they have experienced at least one incident of discrimination in the past year (Pew Research Center, 2017). Many US Muslims argue that their fellow Americans do not think Islam can be a part of mainstream American society (Pew Research Center, 2017).

In fact, besides Islamic extremism, right-wing extremism has recently challenged the values broadly shared by Western democracies, for example, the rule of law, individual liberty and mutual respect and tolerance of different faiths and beliefs. These values were clearly articulated in the official lexicon and counter-terrorism-related documents. Additionally, attacks conducted by right-wing extremists aimed at Muslim minorities have occurred occasionally in many Western countries.

However, very recently, the US government began noting the pressing threat posed by far-right terrorism, and the British government began defining certain groups – such as National Action, Britain First and the English Defence League – as right-wing extremists (Counter Extremism Project, 2017). In December 2016, due to the murder of the Labour MP Jo Cox, UK Home Secretary Amber Rudd officially banned National Action, an anti-semitic white supremacist group, out-lawing membership and support of this group and classifying it as a terrorist organisation (Elgot, 2016). The legal legislation *per se* has special meaning in UK counter-terrorism, marking the first time that membership of a far-right group has been prohibited in the UK (Elgot, 2016). In addition to extremism in the UK, a 2017 study on US domestic terrorism indicated that, in the few years prior to the study, the large majority of attacks that occurred in the US were mainly committed by right-wing extremists rather than Islam-inspired terrorists and left-wing extremists (Neiwert, 2017). Besides, unlike the mainstream under-standing of terrorist threats, right-wing extremist terrorism was deadly more often than Islamist extremism (Neiwert, 2017). On one hand, the notion of right-wing extremism in Western countries illustrates that the radicalisation and (violent) extremism discourse indeed has fallacies and, therefore, cannot pro-vide full comprehension regarding the existing threat of extremism. On the other hand, the specific notion shows the discourse *per se* is actually quite West-ern-centred and seldom mentions threats posed by non-Muslim actors.

Accordingly, the radicalisation and (violent) extremism discourse also failed to provide a clear definition of the threat of extremism. The British government indicated that any 'vocal or active opposition to fundamental British values could be perceived as extremism' (Home Office, 2011, p. 63). The US adminis-tration also mentioned in its 2011 CVE strategy that *extremists* are 'individuals who support or commit ideologically motivated violence to further political goals' (quoted in Kundnani and Hayes, 2018, p. 12). Other Western nations have made similar statements that the readiness to pursue or support far-reaching change in Western societies fits the definition of *extremism*.

In fact, to some extent, the vague definitions given by government authorities have led to misperceptions of extremism. For example, according to the US 2011 CVE strategy, American citizens can be categorised and understood as extrem-ists if they embrace the idea of American exceptionalism and support military violence for official US political goals, such as regime change and foreign human-itarian intervention (Kundnani and Hayes, 2018, p. 12). However, no US CVE programme exists to prevent American teens from being indoctrinated into American exceptionalism (Kundnani and Hayes, 2018, p. 12). Moreover, as the UK's CONTEST has explicitly articulated, a *non-violent* extremist ideology is arguably conducive to terrorism. The 2011 revised CONTEST illustrates that the idea of countering extremist ideologies has been broadly shared by government authorities in Western countries and has been practised by counter-terrorism experts in their anti-radicalisation initiatives.

Yet, to date, there is no clear distinction between *extremism of thought* and *extremism of method* (Richards, 2015, 2017). Critics argue that individuals who have extremist thoughts might not necessarily adopt extremist methods to achieve their goal, and people who participate in extremist activities might not all have extremist thoughts. The term *extremism*, indeed, includes both violent and non-violent forms (Malik, 2008). As with the concept of terrorism, the meaning of *extremism* is not neutral and is, in fact, very subjective. It depends on who supplies the definition and why, and who has the authority to distinguish between violent and non-violent forms (Vermeulen, 2014). For some Western countries, individuals who propagate and act to support ideas, such as the caliphate, *ummah* (Muslim community) and the practice of Islamic law (Sharia), might constitute so-called 'extremism' and 'extremists' because they seek to challenge and destabilise dominant values and norms like sovereignty, the nation-state and the separation of church and state.

However, notably, individuals, groups and communities who advocate those ideas might not all employ violent methods to realise their ideals and goal. For instance, according to Vidino (2009), several orthodox political Islamic organisations like the Muslim Brotherhood adopt flexible policies to engage their Western counterparts, avoiding an immediate radical change in the West. Given this, it is very unlikely to demonstrate a causal link between violent extremism and non-violent extremism and to clarify a distinct causal relationship between an extremist ideology and extremist activities (or physical violence). Hence, the extremism of method (i.e., the use of violence or the threat of violence), rather than the extremism of thought, should be the primary concern of counter-terrorism practitioners.

Notably, the current radicalisation and (countering) extremism discourse lacks an insightful discussion of the causes of terrorism and critical reflections on the current counter-terrorism practices conducted by Western countries, particularly their military presences and foreign international interventions, the use of drones and targeted killing programmes, and torture and extrajudicial rendition programmes (Calhoun, 2015; Jackson and Tsui, 2016; Mearsheimer and Walt, 2016). As with the mainstream terrorism-related discourse, which tends to attribute terrorism to other-worldly ideologies and perspectives, the present radicalisation and extremism discourse concentrates on Islam-related terrorism, with very few interpretations regarding right-wing or other types of terrorism. The essence of the radicalisation and extremism discourse is literally policy-oriented, arguing the significance of interventions at the early stage of the radicalisation process. Due to the special demands of officials and counter-terrorism experts, extraordinary measures for risk management were manifestly articulated in the particular security discourse.

Hence, the causes of radicalisation or extremism were omitted by policymakers and perceived as policy-irrelevant. However, notably, the present research does not aim to judge government authorities' current efforts to counter violent extremism. Instead, it suggests that, to fully understand (violent) extremism, reflections on current and previous counter-terrorism initiatives are indispensable. These include military-oriented counter-terrorism initiatives in the Middle East and North Africa region, the wider utilisation of unmanned aerial vehicles (UAVs), public surveillance targeting certain minority groups (such as Muslim youths) and policies based on the UK's CONTEST with the possibility of eroding human rights, individual liberty and freedom of speech and expression.

Conclusion

This chapter provides a genealogical and discursive analysis of the current radicalisation and (violent) extremism discourse. It argues that the discursive foundation of radicalisation and recent (violent) extremism can be traced to the American-led war on terror since 2001. During the years of Bush's presidency, the specific term *violent extremism* rarely appeared in the official lexicon and public discourse. However, with the pressing threats posed by radical Islam in the Middle East and many European countries, violent extremism was widely utilised by the Obama administration to interpret the terrorist threats that the US has faced, such as al Qaida and its affiliates in Obama's first term and ISIS and foreign fighters in his second term. The Obama administration also contributed to the current US CVE programmes funded by the US Department of Homeland Security. Many of Obama's counter-terrorism initiatives, including the controversial CVE programmes targeting Muslim and other minority groups, were adopted and followed by his successor. According to the Brennan Center for Justice at the New York University School of Law, the Trump administration has almost tripled CVE funding, from about $764,000 to $2,340,000 to monitor Muslim communities in the US (Patel et al., 2018).

Concerning the meaning of *extremism*, in the US, violent extremism in general refers to terrorist threats originating outside the American homeland, usually with specific Middle Eastern origins. However, unlike the US understanding of violent extremism, the British and European comprehension of the concept has particularly emphasised the notion of home-grown terrorism and radicalisation, such as the initial al Qaida-related groups and recent ISIS networks. The divergence of understanding also led to different counter-terrorism practices conducted by Western government authorities. Despite the recent CVE measures and programmes, US counter-terrorism policy mainly relies on a coercive approach marked by a series of foreign military interventions and the use of lethal force. The UK and European approaches stress the importance of risk management, as characterised by the UK's CONTEST and its Prevent programme.

Since the mid-2000s, violent extremism has been perceived as an existential threat by civilians living in Europe and North America and understood as a severe threat to Western cultures and civilisation. However, as the present research has argued, the dominant discourse on radicalisation and (violent) extremism is, in fact, not unassailable; instead, it reveals certain fallacies and represents European-centred terrorism and counter-terrorism. Thus, to fully understand the problem of extremism, further research and more critical reflections are necessary regarding present and previous counter-terrorism practices.

Acknowledgement

I acknowledge the support of the Ministry of Science and Technology (MOST), Taiwan, the Republic of China, in the preparation of this chapter. The research was conducted under the project funded by the MOST, 104-2410-H-005-062-MY3, 'President Obama's Counterterrorism Approach: War on Extremism Discourse and Policy Practices'.

Notes

1   In December 2002, the Dutch General Intelligence and Security Service (Algemence Inlichtingen- en Veiligheidsdienst, AIVD) released a public report, introducing the first attempt to develop a model of the radicalisation process. The 2002 report, according to Kundnani and Hayes (2018), contains many significant key themes of modern radicalisation which dominate and direct the analysis of radicalisation and policymaking aimed at countering violent extremism.
2   To date, there is no universal consensus regarding the concepts and forms of CVE and PVE. However, in contrast to the orthodox counter-terrorism and CVE approaches aimed at detecting, prohibiting and tackling violent extremism and terrorist plots, PVE-related programmes seek to particularly address the factors and drivers that make vulnerable individuals join violent groups (Macdonald and Waggoner, 2016).

References

Al Jazeera, 2018. 'Anti-Muslim "incidents" surge in Germany, Spain', *Al Jazeera*, 4 March. Available at www.aljazeera.com/news/2018/03/anti-muslim-hate-crimes-surge-germany-spain-180303142227333.html (accessed 23 December 2018).
Borum, R., 2011. 'Radicalization into violent extremism I: A review of social science theories', *Journal of Strategic Security*, 4(4), 7–36.
Briggs, R., 2010. 'Community engagement for counterterrorism: Lessons from the United Kingdom', *International Affairs*, 86(4), 971–981.

Burkeman, O., 2009. 'Obama administration says goodbye to "war on terror"', *Guardian*, 25 March. Available at www.theguardian.com/world/2009/mar/25/obama-war-terror-overseas-contingency-operations (accessed 10 March 2018).

Calhoun, L., 2015. *We Kill Because We Can: From Soldiering to Assassination in the Drone Age*. Zed Books, London.

Counter Extremism Project, 2017. *United Kingdom: Extremism & counter-extremism*. Available at www.counterextremism.com/countries/united-kingdom (accessed 20 March 2018).

Croft, S., 2006. *Culture, Crisis and America's War on Terror*. Cambridge University Press, Cambridge.

Croft, S., Moore, C., 2010. 'The evolution of threat narratives in the age of terror: Understanding terrorist threats in Britain', *International Affairs*, 86(4), 821–835.

Elgot, J., 2016. 'Neo-Nazi group national action banned by UK home secretary', *Guardian*, 12 December. Available at www.theguardian.com/world/2016/dec/12/neo-nazi-group-national-action-banned-by-uk-home-secretary (accessed 20 March 2018).

Heath-Kelly, C., 2012. 'Counter-terrorism and the counterfactual: Producing the "radicalisation" discourse and the UK Prevent strategy', *The British Journal of Politics and International Relations*, 15(3), 394–415.

Heath-Kelly, C., 2017. 'Forgetting ISIS: Enmity, drive and repetition in security discourse', *Critical Studies on Security*, November 2017, 85–99. Available at www.tandfonline.com/doi/full/10.1080/21624887.2017.1407595

Home Office, 2011. *CONTEST: The United Kingdom's Strategy for Countering Terrorism*, July 2011. Available at www.gov.uk/government/uploads/system/uploads/attachment_data/file/97995/strategy-contest.pdf (accessed 5 March 2018).

Jackson, R., 2012. *Writing the War on Terrorism: Language, Politics and Counter-Terrorism*. Manchester University Press, Manchester.

Jackson, R., 2018. 'Pacifism: The anatomy of a subjugated knowledge', *Critical Studies on Security*, 6(2), 160–175.

Jackson, R., Tsui, C.-K., 2016. 'War on terror II: Obama and the adaptive evolution of US counterterrorism', in Bentley, M. and Jack Holland (eds), *The Obama Doctrine: A Legacy of Continuity in US Foreign Policy?* Routledge, Abingdon, pp. 70–83.

Jorgensen, M., Phillip, L., 2002. *Discourse Analysis as Theory and Method*. SAGE, London.

Kundnani, A., 2012. 'Radicalisation: The journey of a concept', *Race & Class*, 54(2), 3–25.

Kundnani, A., Hayes, B., 2018. 'The globalisation of countering violent extremism policies: Understanding human right instrumentalising civil society', Transnational Institute, Amsterdam, February 2018. Available at www.tni.org/files/publication-downloads/the_globalisation_of_countering_violent_extremism_policies_executive_summary.pdf (accessed 10 April 2018).

Leffler, M., 2003. '9/11 and the past and future of American foreign policy', *International Affairs*, 79(5), 1045–1063.

MacAskill, E., 2016. 'Hostile states pose "fundamental threat" to Europe, says MI6 chief', *Guardian*, 8 December. Available at www.theguardian.com/uk-news/2016/dec/08/hostile-states-pose-fundamental-threat-to-europe-says-mi6-chief (accessed 25 March 2018).

Macdonald, G., Waggoner, L., 2016. 'From countering to preventing violent extremism', *openDemocracy*, 22 November. Available at www.opendemocracy.net/geoffrey-macdonald-luke-waggoner/from-countering-to-preventing-violent-extremism (accessed 15 March 2018).

Malik, M., 2008. 'Engaging with extremists', *International Relations*, 22(1), 85–104.

Mearsheimer, J., Walt, S., 2016. 'The case for offshore balancing: A superior US grand strategy', *Foreign Affairs*, 95(4), 70–83.

Miller, B., 2010. 'Explaining changes in US grand strategy: 9/11, the rise of offensive liberalism, and the war in Iraq', *Security Studies*, 19(1), 26–65.

Nasser-Eddine, M., Garnham, B., Agostino, K. and Caluya, G., 2011. 'Countering violent extremism (CVE) literature review', Department of Defense, Australian Government. Available at www.dtic.mil/dtic/tr/fulltext/u2/a543686.pdf (accessed 5 March 2018).

Neiwert, D., 2017. 'Alt-America: The time for talking about white terrorism is now', *Guardian*, 26 November. Available at www.theguardian.com/world/2017/nov/26/alt-america-terrorism-rightwing-hate-crimes (accessed 25 March 2018).

Norton-Taylor, R., 2010. 'MI5 chief warns of terror threat from Britons trained in Somalia', *Guardian*, 17 September. Available at www.theguardian.com/politics/2010/sep/17/mi5-chief-somalia-terro-threat (accessed 25 March 2018).

Obama, B., 2009a. 'Address before a joint session of the Congress', 24 February. Available at www.presidency.ucsb.edu/documents/address-before-joint-session-the-congress-1 (accessed 17 February 2018).

Obama, B., 2009b. 'Remarks in Cairo', 4 June. Available at www.presidency.ucsb.edu/documents/remarks-cairo (accessed 17 February 2018).

Obama, B., 2009c. 'Remarks at the United States Military Academy at West Point, New York', 1 December. Available at www.presidency.ucsb.edu/documents/remarks-the-united-states-military-academy-west-point-new-york-1 (accessed 17 February 2018).

Obama, B., 2014. 'Remarks as prepared for delivery by President Barack Obama, address to the United Nations General Assembly', 24 September. Available at https://obamawhitehouse.archives.gov/the-press-office/2014/09/24/remarks-prepared-delivery-president-barack-obama-address-united-nations- (accessed 17 February 2018).

Obama, B., 2015a. 'Remarks by the President in closing of the summit on countering violent extremism', 18 February. Available at https://obamawhitehouse.archives.gov/the-press-office/2015/02/18/remarks-president-closing-summit-countering-violent-extremism (accessed 17 February 2018).

Obama, B., 2015b. 'Remarks by the President at the summit on countering violent extremism', 19 February. Available at www.presidency.ucsb.edu/documents/remarks-the-white-house-summit-countering-violent-extremism-0 (accessed 17 February 2018).

Osborne, S., 2018. 'Islamophobia and xenophobia on the rise in Germany, new study claims', *Independent*, 7 November. Available at www.independent.co.uk/news/world/europe/germany-islamophobia-xenophobia-racism-study-survey-extremism-a8622391.html (accessed 22 December 2018).

Patel, F., Lindsay, A. and DenUyl, S., 2018. 'Countering violent extremism programs in the Trump era', Brennan Center, 15 June. Available at www.brennancenter.org/countering-violent-extremism-programs-trump-era (accessed 24 December 2018).

Pew Research Center, 2017. 'US Muslims concerned about their place in society, but continue to believe in the American dream: Findings from Pew Research Center's 2017 survey of US Muslims', 26 July. Available at www.pewforum.org/2017/07/26/findings-from-pew-research-centers-2017-survey-of-us-muslims/ (accessed 23 December 2018).

Poushter, J., 2017. 'Majorities in Europe, North America worries about Islamic Extremism', Pew Research Center, 24 May. Available at www.pewresearch.org/fact-tank/2017/05/24/majorities-in-europe-north-america-worried-about-islamic-extremism/ (accessed 20 March 2018).

Richards, A., 2015. 'From terrorism to "radicalization" to "extremism": Counterterrorism imperative or loss of focus?', *International Affairs*, 91(2), 371–380.

Richards, A., 2017. 'Some thoughts on constructions of terrorism and the framing of the terrorist threat in the United Kingdom', in Stohl, M., Burchill, R. and Englund, S. (eds), *Constructions of Terrorism: An Interdisciplinary Approach to Research and Policy*. University of California Press, Oakland, CA, pp. 108–124.

Schmid, A., 2014. 'Violent and non-violent extremism: Two sides of the same coin?', *ICCT Research Paper*, May 2014. Available at www.icct.nl/download/file/ICCT-Schmid-Violent-Non-Violent-Extremism-May-2014.pdf (accessed 10 March 2018).

Schmitt, E., Shanker, T., 2005. 'US officials retool slogan for terror war', *The New York Times*, 26 July. Available at www.nytimes.com/2005/07/26/politics/us-officials-retool-slogan-for-terror-war.html (accessed 10 March 2018).

Smith, B., Stohl, M. and al Gharbi, M., 2018. 'Discourses on countering violent extremism: The strategic interplay between fear and security after 9/11', *Critical Studies on Terrorism*, 12(1), 151–168. Available at www.tandfonline.com/doi/full/10.1080/17539153.2018.1494793 (accessed 21 December 2018).

Thomas, P., 2016. 'Britain's Prevent programme: An end in sight?', in Jarvis, L. and Lister, M. (eds), *Critical Perspectives on Counter-Terrorism*. Routledge, Abingdon, pp. 169–187.

Tsui, C-K., 2015. 'Framing the threat of catastrophic terrorism: Genealogy, discourse and President Clinton's counterterrorism initiatives', *International Politics*, 52(2), 66–88.

Tsui, C-K., 2016. *Clinton, New Terrorism and the Origins of the War on Terror*. Routledge, Abingdon.

Vermeulen, F., 2014. 'Suspect communities – targeting violent extremism at the local level: Policies of engagement in Amsterdam, Berlin, and London', *Terrorism and Political Violence*, 26(2), 286–306.

Vidino, L., 2009. 'Islamism and the West: Europe as a battlefield', *Totalitarian Movements and Political Religions*, 10(2), 165–176.

White, S., McEvoy, K., 2012. *Countering Violent Extremism: Community Engagement Programmes in Europe*, Volume 1, Phase 2. Qatar International Academy for Security Studies. Available at http://qiass.org/wp-content/uploads/2016/05/QIASS-CVE_Community-Engagement-Programmes-in-Europe-final-101514.pdf (accessed 15 March 2018).

Winkler, C., 2007. 'Parallels in preemptive war rhetoric: Reagan on Libya; Bush 43 on Iraq', *Rhetoric & Public Affairs*, 10(2), 303–334.

2

Conceptualising violent extremism: ontological, epistemological and normative issues

Sondre Lindahl

Introduction

As the two preceding chapters have documented, it would not be an overstatement to suggest that Western countries embraced a kind of terrorism/counterterrorism hyperbole after the 9/11 attacks. The almost singular focus and frenzied attention on waging war on terror was at the same time, as a recent article shows, supported by a similar singular focus and attention in academia on jihadism (Schuurman, 2019). As a result, other terrorisms or forms of violent extremism were subjugated or simply ignored. However, with several attacks perpetrated by so-called foreign fighters or home-grown terrorists, violent extremism was conceptualised and understood by many as a severe threat to both national and international security. More recently, with attacks in New Zealand, the US and Norway by people who share a brand of right-wing extremist views, the threat of violent extremism has received much greater attention. Not surprisingly, perhaps, there is a debate with considerable disagreement as to what violent extremism is: is it an ideology or disease? Maybe it is about perceived grievances, groupthink, propaganda, a specific online culture or perhaps the work of psychologically unstable madmen? To make matters even more complicated, the rhetoric of political leaders like Donald Trump and Viktor Orbán resonates among right-wing extremists. If terrorism can be said to be an 'essentially contested concept', then the description seems apposite for violent extremism as well.

This volume seeks, in part, to offer a critical examination of theoretical issues in relation to research on extremism. To contribute to this effort, this chapter will revolve around two crucial points that are at the centre of the critical research agenda, be it on terrorism or violent extremism. First is a concern with *content* of reason, or the need for reflexivity of emancipatory, ontological and epistemological content. Second is a concern with how, or from where, a critical research agenda on violent extremism obtains the necessary justificatory force to assert its normative *function*. In other words, how can a critical approach to violent extremism produce methodologically rigorous knowledge, and how does it justify and legitimate its normative function as preferable to other approaches to violent extremism? Both points are essential to a research agenda which aims at normative action and social change.

As such, this chapter begins with an overview of the core commitments of the Critical Terrorism Studies (CTS) research agenda before discussing in detail Weber's theory of the ideal type. One reason for this focus is the increased attention given to Weber by leading scholars in the field (Bjørgo and Ravndal, 2019). The main reason, however, for this discussion is that Weber's theory is a potentially fruitful avenue for pursuing a critical research agenda. The primary aim of the chapter is therefore to illustrate how this theory encompasses the core commitments of the CTS research agenda, and how scholars can utilise it in order to produce methodologically rigorous knowledge that can inform and sustain emancipatory policies and actions.

Ontological and epistemological commitments

CTS can be said to be based upon a specific set of ontological and epistemological commitments which informs its critical research agenda and pertains thus to the *content* of knowledge. At the core is the 'acceptance of the basic insecurity of all knowledge and the impossibility of neutral or objective knowledge about terrorism' (Jackson, 2007, p. 246). Indeed, according to Jackson, CTS is 'acutely sensitive to the need for historical, political and cultural context in understanding the use of terrorism as a strategy' (Jackson, 2007, p. 248). This ontological position forms a central critique of an orthodoxy of traditional terrorism studies, namely that terrorism is presumed to be a thing-in-itself and mirrors more or less accurately how the world really is. Although terrorism might seem to be a complex phenomenon, it would be possible to articulate general laws about terrorism. More specifically, in setting out the CTS research agenda Jackson et al. argued for an ontological position which holds that terrorism should be recognised as a social fact with no objective essence, contending that 'while acts of violence are a brute physical fact for the victims and onlookers, the meaning or labelling of the acts [. . .] is a social process that depends upon different actors making judgements about its nature' (Jackson et al., 2011, p. 35).

Epistemologically, then, creating knowledge about terrorism is understood as ultimately a social process in which scholars must remain sensitive to, and be aware of, the various ways in which context and process impact knowledge about terrorism (Jackson et al., 2011, p. 37). This approach includes a recognition that it is impossible for any individual to engage in value-free and presuppositionless research and academic activity. Indeed, research is dominated by the *perspectival* character of the knowledge that is produced and conditioned by the direction of each researcher's knowledge interest. These commitments resonate with arguments made by Max Weber that human beings are cultural beings with the capacity and the will to take a deliberate attitude towards the world and to lend it *significance*. Whatever this significance may be, it will lead us to judge certain phenomena of human existence in its light and to respond to them as being (positively or negatively) meaningful (Weber, 1949, p. 81). Thus, social sciences, and studies on terrorism and violent extremism, are productive of the world, beholden to a set of cultural values that orient the investigation from the beginning. The ontological and epistemological commitments have traditionally been held together by an ethical-normative commitment to emancipation. Inspired by the dictum that philosophers should not only interpret the world but work to change it, the commitment to emancipation is integral to the CTS approach to terrorism. Although emancipation is a contested concept within CTS, it can broadly be summarised by Booth's four points: (1) emancipation is inextricably bound with security, and security is conceived of broadly and as a positive value; (2) there is a conceptual harmony between emancipation and security, so that the means must be commensurate with the ends; (3) the struggle against terrorism should be part of the struggle seeking to emancipate humans everywhere from the oppressions of political violence; and (4) the struggle for emancipation must be universal if it is to be successful (Booth, 2007, p. 112). The reconstructive potential of CTS scholarship rests in large part on its ability to produce methodologically rigorous knowledge, and to use this knowledge to inform normative action and social change. Wyn-Jones once argued that it is only this possibility of emancipatory change that gives critical theory coherence, and indeed, purpose (Wyn-Jones, 1999, p. 56). This description seems apt for CTS as well, and by extension, critical approaches to violent extremism.

As such, CTS has taken seriously Cox's crucial understanding that knowledge production is a social process wherein knowledge is produced for someone and for some purpose (Cox, 1981, p. 128). The ontological and epistemological commitments, anchored as they are in critical theory, are therefore meant to rescue the *content* of reason from the flaws of positivist, or traditional, approaches to terrorism studies. These commitments, it seems fair to argue, provide a logically consistent perspective through which matters of political violence are constituted, inquired into, understood, explained and critiqued. However, as Heath-Kelly argued in her 2010 article (Heath-Kelly, 2010), CTS fails to account from where it obtains the necessary justificatory force to assert its normative *function* as preferable to the function of traditional reason. For CTS this last point is crucial because it goes to the heart of the reconstructive potential and ability of its knowledge production. The point is not to merely interpret the world in various ways, but to change it. This, it seems to me, is the core of a critical approach to both terrorism and violent extremism: all theory is understood to be political, and the task is therefore to produce methodologically rigorous knowledge (content of reason) coupled with a clear normative commitment (function of reason).

I will return to a discussion on normativity later in the chapter, but at this juncture I would like to introduce Weber's theory of the ideal type. Weber's scholarship has attracted more attention recently, with scholars at the Center for Research on Extremism (C-REX) at the University of Oslo using it to conceptualise various forms of violent extremism (Bjørgo and Ravndal, 2019). The increased attention given to Weber's scholarship by leading scholars in the field is an important reason for the focus on Weber in this chapter. Furthermore, I hope with this discussion to show how Weber's scholarship can be utilised to bring together the ontological, epistemological and normative commitments of CTS and thereby harness a critical research agenda on violent extremism.

The ideal type

Weber, in his scholarship, assumed a role for social scientists where the purpose of social scientific analysis and inquiries was not only to examine the uniqueness of particular social phenomena, or generate universal laws, but to 'synthesize meaningful, characteristic aspects of individual phenomena in order to explain the occurrence of social events' (Hekman, 1983, p. 121). As such, one might say that it is event driven, or at the very least it takes as a point of departure that 'real' phenomena take place in a shared reality that we can know something about. Weber was therefore interested in a type of social science which dealt with concrete reality, and which aimed at understanding the relationships and the cultural significance of individual events in their contemporary manifestations, on the one hand, and the causes of their being historically so and not otherwise, on the other (Weber, 1949, p. 72). Ontologically, Weber argued that the 'data' for social scientists is constituted by the social actors' bestowal of meaning, which in modern academic terms is akin to a social constructivist position. Weber's philosophically monist position argues that the category of facts, from which an ideal type eventually is constructed, is the meaning social actors bestow on their actions. Human action, and the associated bestowal of meaning, form the horizon within which the facts for social analysis take place. Moreover, Weber argues that human action takes place in a great many different contexts, and the ways in which life confronts us in immediate concrete situations represent 'an infinite multiplicity of successively and coexistently emerging and disappearing events'

(Weber, 1949, p. 72). This multiplicity remains undiminished even when we turn and fix our attention on a single object of study. Consequently, any aspect of our shared reality cannot be apprehended without presuppositions, that is, without assuming a certain point of view.

Weber therefore argued that all knowledge is abstraction from the concreteness of reality, which means that knowing anything or any aspect of this infinite multiplicity of successively and coexistently emerging and disappearing events necessarily involves abstracting particular elements. Thus, knowledge production is impossible without conceptualisations, because 'concepts are the means by which abstraction from the concreteness of reality is effected' (Hekman, 1983, p. 20). The question then becomes how an investigator chooses a particular segment of facts as topic for investigation. To answer that question, Weber highlighted the importance of personal value-judgements, arguing that 'without the investigator's evaluative ideas, there would be no principle of selection of subject-matter and no meaningful knowledge of concrete reality' (Weber, 1949, p. 82). Furthermore: 'all the analysis of infinite reality which the finite human mind can conduct rests on the tacit assumption that only a finite portion of the reality constitutes the object of scientific investigation, and that only it is "important" in the sense of being "worthy of being known"' (Weber, 1949, p. 72). This volume demonstrates a great variety of different views, definitions and conceptualisations of violent extremism, but there can be no doubt that there is an infinitude of complex causes and relationships involved – not least because acts of violent extremism take place in a wide range of different contexts and with very different individuals. Thus, as scholars and researchers we select a finite portion of this complex and infinite reality as the object of study based on specific value-judgements. That naturally implies that, as researchers, we prioritise certain aspects of this reality and base our inquiry on specific value-judgements, whether or not we are explicit and rigorous about spelling them out (Jackson, 2008, p. 147). This element is at the heart of the CTS critique of orthodox terrorism studies, where the latter has been critiqued for constituting terrorism as an external object of study without making clear the value-judgements which guide the research or who the research is for. Weber, on his part, argued that all knowledge is ideal-typical, meaning that it is a 'deliberately partial way of configuring the world, arising from a subtle combination of empirical observation and the value-commitments made by the researcher' (Jackson, 2008, p. 147). In the most famous passage on the ideal type, and building on the theory described in the previous paragraphs, Weber explains that they are

> formed through a one-sided *accentuation* of *one* or *more* points of view, and through bringing together a great many diffuse and discrete, more or less present and occasionally absent *concrete individual* events, which are arranged

according to these emphatically one-sided points of view in order to construct a unified *analytical construct* (Gedankenbild). In its conceptual purity, this analytical construct (Gedankenbild) is found nowhere in empirical reality; it is a utopia. (Weber, 1949, p. 90, italics in original)

As such, the knowledge that we produce about violent extremism is necessarily ideal-typical, and it forms the horizon within which the facts about extremism arise. In Weber's conception there is no apprehendable 'world', externally existing objects, that could be used to limit the application of an ideal type or to falsify and improve it. Instead, Weber argues that 'the fate of an epoch which has eaten of the tree of knowledge is that it must know that we cannot learn the *meaning* of the world from its analysis, be it ever so perfect; it must rather be in a position to create this meaning itself' (Weber, 1949, p. 57).

The main implication of this reasoning is that the knowledge produced about violent extremism is ideal-typical, and it can make no claim to correspond to an external 'truth' of violent extremism. In relation to studies on violent extremism, this view entails an approach that would not aim to describe the world in a definitely incorrect or correct way. Instead, it would serve as a systematic demonstration of what it would be like to construct the world in that way. It seems to me that CTS as a research agenda has not aimed to produce accurate knowledge of an object somehow exogenous to our societies, or identified such a pursuit as the element that gives the agenda worth. Rather, the aim has been to systematically show how terrorism could be of use (and abuse perhaps) as a term to describe an act of violence as we give meaning to concrete physical events. P.T. Jackson summarises Weber's argument thus:

social scientific investigation should be regarded not merely as an analytical wager concerning what the world is like – although it is certainly that – but also as a thought-experiment about what such a world *would* be like. The creation of meaning and value remains central to the enterprise, even though (and perhaps even *because*) there is no definitive way to adjudicate between value-orientations and the worlds that they produce. (Jackson, 2008, p. 149)

In sum, Weber shows how two sets of presuppositions enter into the selection of facts for research on social events, namely: the meanings of the social actors, and the investigator's individual values which guide, and are reflected in, the theoretic interest. As Weber points out: 'science can make him [the scientist] realize that all action and naturally, according to the circumstances, inaction imply in their consequences the espousal of certain values – and herewith – what is often overlooked – the rejection of certain others. The act of choice itself is his own responsibility' (Weber, 1949, p. 53). As such, Weber's theory of the ideal type encompasses many of the commitments CTS has identified at the core of its critical research agenda. Indeed, a case can be made that Weber's ideal type also rescues the *content* of reason from the flaws of traditional theory. The focus then turns to the *function* of reason, and this is the point where I would like to argue that the ideal type can help advance and guide normative action in a way that critical theory and minimal foundationalism perhaps is incapable of. Before turning our attention to specific constructions of ideal types, it is worth spending some time on the issue of normativity because this is where a coherent critical research agenda ideally comes together.

Normativity

CTS has traditionally looked to the Boothian version of emancipation (Booth, 2007) as the normative basis for research and praxis. While highly attractive as a normative concept, making emancipation the cornerstone of the normative agenda has not been without problems. Heath-Kelly argued, as mentioned earlier, that CTS had failed to provide sufficient normative force to sustain an emancipatory agenda based on a flawed engagement with the wider philosophical implications of critical theory. One potential source of confusion could be found in the doctrine of minimal foundationalism, which is an attempt to maintain a minimum of material existence.[1] Minimal foundationalism seeks to establish the possibility of objective regularities within a socio-historical context as a middle way between foundationalism and anti-foundationalism. It still has to retain a faith in reality so as to not succumb to relativism, but from this minimal foundation it is possible to produce knowledge and launch normative projects. This move allows for the investigator to operate with context-dependent objective regularities. The challenge is that they are treated as if they were objective realities, and it is from this position that normative arguments are conjured.

Indeed, when minimal foundationalism posits that objective regularities within socio-historical epochs exist, the latter can be seen as a cognitive tool we use to designate a certain era and not a quality it possesses *in itself*. The existence of objective regularities then rests on a subjective notion of what constitutes a socio-historic event or era. Without due consideration, this move might just resemble a more refined dualistic and positivist stance. As such, scholars might find themselves facing the paradox that, on the one hand, they critique positivist attempts to approximate the objective truth, or nature of violent extremism. On the other hand, they themselves also attempt to approximate the truth of violent extremism but now within a subjectively defined specific context. Heath-Kelly's objection, that CTS fails to account from where it obtains the necessary justificatory force to assert its normative function, largely remains unresolved. This discussion is therefore not merely an academic pursuit. It goes to the very core of any research agenda which takes seriously Cox's argument that all theory comes from somewhere, and it is for someone and a purpose.

Both CTS and Weber broadly share the same ontological and epistemological commitments, although articulated with different vocabularies and with many years apart. However, on the issue of normativity the difference is greater. This obviously has something to do with the fact that social change and normative action were not the main priorities for Weber, while CTS has drawn heavily on the Frankfurt School of critical theory for whom social change was the main priority. To understand how issues of normativity come into Weberian scholarship, we must begin with his argument that humans are cultural beings with the will and capacity to take a deliberate attitude towards the world and lend it significance. This will lead us to judge certain social phenomena in its light as either positively or negatively meaningful. Thus, the theoretic interest and values combine to make up the investigator's specific attitude towards the world, and what elements of reality are worthy of being known. For Weber all knowledge represents abstractions from reality; they are ideal types. They may or may not be meaningful concepts and interpretations of concrete social events, and the investigator's values will be reflected in the research. Indeed, these values should be clearly stated and properly discussed.

Weber argues that such a discussion has three functions: first, an elaboration and explication of the ultimate and internally consistent value axioms; second, a deduction of implications which follow from the irreducible value axioms, when the practical evaluation of factual situations is based on these axioms; and third, the determination of the factual consequences which the realisation of a certain practical evaluation must have (a) in consequence of being bound to certain indispensable means; and (b) in consequence of the inevitability of certain, not directly desired repercussions (Weber, 1949, pp. 20–21). For our purposes, this process can be useful as a way of reflexively engaging with 'emancipation' as the ultimate, internally consistent value axiom in research because it addresses a point made by several scholars that the idea of self-reflexivity ironically has been missing from CTS scholarship (Joseph, 2011; Michel and Richards, 2009).

The major implication when the practical evaluation of factual situations is based on emancipation as the ultimate value axiom is that all theory of social and cultural life is understood to be political. This approach does not try to legitimise normative arguments through ought-is argumentation by establishing emancipation as a 'good' or the 'truth'. Like an ideal type it can describe and make the case for what *could* happen, but also what *should* happen. The point therefore is not to dispense with values or succumb to relativism, because we simply cannot do without our own value axioms and value evaluations in research.

While this is a deeper philosophical and methodological debate, it is now possible to argue that a consequence of this discussion is that knowledge about violent extremism will be based on the selection of facts which depends on the theoretic interest and values of the investigator. As such, this knowledge will to some degree vary from investigator to investigator, and they bring forth various elements from the 'infinite flux' of reality that they deem worthy of being known. Weber did not state a specific normative project as basis for his own research, but I would like to go further than Weber and argue that values do more than play a part in selecting facts for analysis. Indeed, values give research meaning and purpose, and they can help realise concrete emancipatory utopias. Indeed, given the unresolved tensions within minimal foundationalism, and the philosophical roots of emancipation in which it is tied to the goal of rationally creating a better society, the Weberian approach offers several benefits which should be of interest to readers of this volume: first, it provides an approach that rescues the *content* of reason from the flaws of traditional theory by setting out a coherent set of ontological and epistemological commitments. Second, it accounts from where it obtains the justificatory force to assert its normative *function*. In sum, it can provide a detailed and coherent account of the process of how knowledge is produced, for what purpose and who it is for.

Constructing an ideal type

In Weberian terms we may state that because violent extremism can never correspond to a fact 'out there', it can only be one or more competing conceptualisations trying to explain the occurrence of a social phenomenon which is defined by social actors' bestowal of meaning. Consequently, these concepts must be ideal-typical. The starting point, however, must be the occurrence of concretely real events, institutions or practices, which means that we begin from the position that we take part in, and understand, a shared common reality. This argument may seem tautological, but it is an important one. While ideal types, like all forms of knowledge, necessarily are 'abstract' in the sense that they are syntheses selected from the concrete totality of reality, they are perspectival, and hence it is still presupposed that there must be a reality on which to have those different perspectives. That does not mean that violent extremism exists as a thing-in-itself, but there must be an existence of concrete acts that we subsequently may, or may not, label violent extremism in a meaningful way.

Weber argued that the construction of ideal types is based on a distinctive process of selection and synthesis. These two features make up the epistemological basis for the ideal type, and it provides a shared foundation for the different varieties of ideal types that a researcher might use in empirical research. It should be noted that Weber's methodological discussion was a result of the debates of his day. This means that although the general formula of ideal type construction is useful, it is not a blueprint or dogma. The ideal type of terrorism that will be presented later in the chapter is an example of what Weber labelled the sociological ideal type. It is meant to answer questions concerning a social institution or practice found across societies in various time periods, and so it aims to transcend the specific historical and societal aspects of the institution or practice under investigation. They are therefore, to some extent, ahistorical. The primary interest in this chapter is thus whether it is possible to construct a sociological ideal type of violent extremism as a meaningful concept to describe and explain its occurrence.

The first step in the construction is to determine the category of facts from which the ideal type is constructed. Something becomes a 'fact' for analysis because the social actors bestow it with meaning. Second, emphasis is placed on the selection of facts out of a broad range, such as historic and economic factors. Third, the researcher chooses particular elements of a selected group of facts to construct a concept which is determined by the nature of the question that is posed in the inquiry. As a way of illustrating how the ideal type can be constructed, the next paragraphs will present the ideal type of terrorism that I have made use of in my attempt to construct a theory and model of counter-terrorism (Lindahl, 2018). The ideal type is drawn from CTS scholarship where meaningfully relevant, logically compatible aspects have been selected and synthesised according to the theoretic interest of the investigator. Thus, terrorism refers to a phenomenon which involves the use, and in some cases the threat, of physical force to communicate a political message. It is a phenomenon with a history which is not reducible to an act in the here and now, and which might or might not be justifiable in accordance with some or other conception of justice. Finally, it can be seen to force into the open issues that are already present, but beneath the surface, ignored or subjugated.

This ideal type can be broken into several components. First, terrorism is the use of brute, physical force in a symbolically communicative action (Jackson, 2011, pp. 124–127). In recent years terms like cyber-terrorism, economic terrorism and eco-terrorism have been employed by states, security services and the media although the use of physical force is not essential to, or a big component of, these forms of 'terrorism'. They can thus be excluded from the ideal type. Second, the threat of violence, as physical force, can be included when the threat is specific and credible. In other words, if a threat is made within a specific context marked by violence, such that it is part of a history, then it may be included. A threat from ISIS of an imminent attack in Paris could be included because the group has perpetrated attacks there before. This would remove a great many nonsense threats that have been logged as terrorism threats, which is important to maintain terrorism as a meaningful category of violence.

Third, an act of terrorism must be deliberate and premeditated, and is not reducible to an act in the here and now. This means, on the one hand, that it requires a methodological logic and seriality, and that 'every discrete instance of terrorism is only part of an organized campaign with a purpose and depth in time' (Aran, 2017, p. 7). Terrorism therefore is not meaningless, random violence, but perpetrated by self-aware actors who comprehend the potential consequences of employing terrorism as a strategic choice. On the other hand, it will exclude acts of so-called lone-actor terrorism. This is a key conceptual move and it is necessary to sharpen and refine terrorism in this ideal-typical construction. The Breivik attacks in 2011 are commonly understood as terrorism, although it is not obvious what one would gain from labelling the Breivik attacks as terrorism compared with other possible categories, such as mass shootings. The ideal type proposed here is concerned with understanding acts of violence which are part of a history of violence and counterviolence. Lone-actor attacks, such as the case with Breivik, can be meaningfully excluded from this ideal type.

Fourth, and as a consequence of the third point, terrorism is distinct from other types of direct intentional violence such as criminal activities perpetrated for material or egoistic interests, hooliganism or domestic violence. Keeping with the previous discussion, violent acts perpetrated for the purpose of control or status in themselves, or a desire for publicity, will also be excluded from the ideal type. Breivik was not interpolated in a violence/counter-violence cycle due to the actions of the Norwegian state, nor did his actions interpolate Norwegians in a similar cycle against right-wing extremists. One could therefore view the attacks as a way for Breivik to gain publicity for his cause, but they do not satisfy the requirement for it to be terrorism. Fifth, terrorism is not exclusive to non-state actors. States can use physical force to communicate a political message in a way that goes beyond the coercive power that states possess. There is a crucial difference between the use of force and coercion, and a state that can use coercion to make sure inhabitants pay taxes, obey traffic laws and make sure criminals serve their sentences. Most people accept these various roles that the state performs, but states can also engage in violent acts that interpolate people in this repetition effect of violence and counter-violence from which they cannot free themselves.

Sixth, terrorism is primarily directed at civilians, when it can be said that: 'the victims of terrorism are not part of the defense forces – soldiers, policemen, intelligence agents – but rather non-combatants; nor are the victims part of the government or its agents, but rather its subjects' (Aran, 2017, p. 8). Defining civilian status this way makes sense because it acknowledges that actors who represent a state in some capacity potentially take part in processes that eventually are forced into the open through acts of terrorism. A soldier on leave therefore is not a civilian, and at any rate, if such an attack were to occur, it still would not be random. It would only highlight the conflict between the state and the opposing group(s).

In conclusion, these paragraphs detail an ideal type of terrorism which says something about what terrorist violence is (symbolically communicative act which is part of a history), the intentions of the terrorist act (to communicate a message, intimidate an audience and produce a psychological effect of fear within a specific context) and the broader aims of terrorist violence (the achievement of narrow or broad political goals).

Violent extremism

An ideal-typical construction of violent extremism could take a great many different shapes and forms depending on the theoretic interest of the investigator. For example, researchers from the Center for Research on Extremism (C-REX) at the University of Oslo have conceptualised various forms of violent extremism as ideal types. More specifically, they have presented a family tree of the far right, making a division between radical-right and extreme-right groups. These two groups are further subdivided into cultural, ethnic and racial nationalism (Bjørgo and Ravndal, 2019, p. 3). Although not fleshed out by the authors in that particular publication, one assumes that these various categories are selected and synthesised according to the epistemological pattern described above. Nonetheless, this study indicates an increasing general interest in Weber's theory of the ideal type and its potential utility. In the remainder of the chapter I will not propose an ideal type of violent extremism. Instead, I would like to expound on the basics of the ideal type further by including one element from the discussion of the ideal type of terrorism. Namely, the exclusion of the Breivik attacks even though they are often described as terrorism. Based on the belief that Muslims were taking over Europe, and that the Norwegian Labour Party had helped facilitate this take-over, Breivik wanted to send a message to the population to wake up. The targets for the attack were deliberately chosen, although the direct victims were random. Killing kids at a political youth camp to send a political message to a wider audience does correspond with most definitions of terrorism.

However, one of the points the ideal type accentuated was that every discrete instance of terrorism is part of a history of violence and counterviolence. In the case of Breivik, it was only him. He did talk to other people online, but he was not part of an organisation which perpetrated attacks over a longer period of time. Nor did the attacks interpolate more people into a repetition effect of violence and counterviolence. If he had been part of an organisation or movement in Norway that held beliefs and opinions deemed to be extremist, and the government had cracked down on the group through the use of violence in the past, one could then make the case that the attacks were part of a violent history. Say, for example, that the Norwegian government in the aftermath of the attacks had abducted, rendered and tortured members of that group to send a clear message, then the two parties would be interpolated into a violent repetition effect. It would then be possible to explain the occurrence of these concrete events by pointing out how they are part of a violent history. There would be a method-ological logic and seriality to the attacks by either party, which would mean that they are not random acts of violence in the here and now. Importantly, the group would not perpetrate attacks because they have been mysteriously radicalised, but because there is a history of real, concrete acts of violence. This realisation would not absolve the group of any responsibility, but it would help to explain the occurrence of terrorist attacks in Norway.

Thus, to explain the occurrence of the Breivik attacks and violent extremism, an ideal type of violent extremism could meaningfully include several of the characteristics of terrorism, including the use of brute, physical force in a sym-bolically communicative action. However, while terrorism is constructed to explain the occurrence of violent acts that are part of a specific history of vio-lence and counterviolence, violent extremism could be seen to be different. Indeed, there are good reasons for why they should be different, not least because of how the focus on extremism now can be said to form the explana-tory core of international terrorism. As Martini (this volume) points out, the term extremism now identifies two main elements: (1) the ideology or beliefs that may bring an individual to perpetrate violent attacks; and (2) through a process of strict causation and, at the same time, semantic confusion, extrem-ism has become a synonym of terrorism. In this regard, a logic prevails that perceives a two-stage linear process of radicalisation which eventually leads to terrorism. First, through cognitive radicalisation a person can develop extrem-ist ideas – they become cognitive extremists – and, second, through behavioural radicalisation a person becomes a terrorist. This process and trajectory is reflected in the British government's definition of radicalisation (Home Office, 2009, p. 11), and Neumann notes that the US Department of Homeland Secu-rity's definition also implies that 'terrorists become cognitive extremists first, and then – for whatever reason – decide to pursue their extremist aims by vio-lent means' (Neumann, 2013, p. 876). As such, a connection is made between extremism and terrorism which I will suggest is unhelpful and confusing because it adds even more actors, potential causes and socio-political factors onto the already loaded concept of terrorism. In my own attempt at creating a model of counter-terrorism I found it useful to sharpen the concept of terror-ism and exclude the Breivik attacks. It seems reasonable to argue that such events could be more meaningfully explained by using other concepts, perhaps violent extremism.

Conclusion

The discussions in this chapter have revolved around two important elements that are at the centre of the critical research agenda on violent extremism. The first element pertains to the *content* of reason, or the need for reflexivity of emancipatory, ontological and epistemological content. The second element pertains to how, or from where, a critical research agenda on violent extremism obtains the necessary justificatory force to assert its normative *function*. In short, these elements are essential to a research agenda that takes seriously two important strands of critical reasoning: (1) that theory is from somewhere, for someone and for a purpose; and (2) that scholars should not only merely interpret the world, but work to change it in various ways. As such, research on violent extremism must address these two points, and hopefully this chapter has been able to show why such discussions are important, and perhaps how Weber's ideal type can be of great use in a critical research agenda.

Note

1   Minimal foundationalism holds that: 'through mutually constitutive relationships, both subject and object can be said to exist. Their constitution does not collapse into intersubjective meanings and objective regularities, so objective regularities can be said to exist within socio-historical epochs' (Heath-Kelly, 2010, p. 246).

References

Aran, G., 2017. 'Striking home: Ideal-type of terrorism', *Terrorism and Political Violence*, 31(5), 987–1005.

Bjørgo, A.T., Ravndal, J.A., 2019. 'Extreme-right violence and terrorism: Concepts, patterns, and responses', *ICCT policy brief*, September. International Centre for Counter-Terrorism, The Hague, pp. 1–22. Available at https://icct.nl/publication/extreme-right-violence-and-terrorism-concepts-patterns-and-responses/ (accessed 2 October 2019).

Booth, K., 2007. *Theory of World Security*. Cambridge University Press, Cambridge.

Cox, R., 1981. 'Social forces, states and world orders: Beyond international relations theory', *Millennium – Journal of International Studies*, 10(2), 126–155.

Heath-Kelly, C., 2010. 'Critical Terrorism Studies, critical theory and the "naturalistic fallacy"', *Security Dialogue*, 41(3), 235–254.

Hekman, S.J., 1983. 'Weber's ideal type: A contemporary reassessment', *Polity*, 16(1), 119–137.

Home Office, 2009. *Pursue Prevent Protect Prepare: The United Kingdom's Strategy for Countering International Terrorism*. Home Office, London. Available at

https://assets.publishing.service.gov.uk/government/uploads/system/uploads/
attachment_data/file/228907/7833.pdf (accessed 1 October 2019).

Jackson, P.T., 2008. 'Foregrounding ontology: Dualism, monism, and IR theory', *Review
of International Studies*, 34(1), 129–153.

Jackson, R., 2007. 'The core commitments of Critical Terrorism Studies', *European
Political Science*, 6, 244–251.

Jackson, R., 2011. 'In defence of "terrorism": Finding a way through a forest of
misconceptions', *Behavioral Sciences of Terrorism and Political Aggression*, 3(2),
116–130.

Jackson, R., Jarvis, L., Gunning, J. and Breen-Smyth, M., 2011. *Terrorism: A Critical
Introduction*. Palgrave Macmillan, New York.

Joseph, J., 2011. 'Terrorism as a social relation within capitalism: Theoretical and
emancipatory implications', *Critical Studies on Terrorism*, 4(1), 23–37.

Lindahl, S., 2018. *A Critical Theory of Counterterrorism: Ontology, Epistemology,
Normativity*. Routledge, Abingdon.

Michel, T., Richards, A., 2009. 'False dawns or new horizons? Further issues and
challenges for Critical Terrorism Studies', *Critical Studies on Terrorism*, 2(3),
399–413.

Neumann, P.R., 2013. 'The trouble with radicalization', *International Affairs*, 89(4),
873–893.

Schuurman, B., 2019. 'Topics in terrorism research: Reviewing trends and gaps,
2007–2016', *Critical Studies on Terrorism*, 12(3), 463–480.

Weber, M., 1949. *The Methodology of the Social Sciences*. Edited by E.A. Shils and H.A.
Finch. The Free Press, Glencoe, IL.

Wyn-Jones, R., 1999. *Security, Strategy, and Critical Theory*. Lynne Rienner Publishers,
London.

3

Knowledge, power, subject: constituting the extremist/moderate subject

Mariela Cuadro

A critique is not a matter of saying that things are not right as they are. It is a matter of pointing out on what kinds of assumptions, what kinds of familiar, unchallenged, unconsidered modes of thought the practices that we accept rest. . . . Criticism is a matter of flushing out that thought and trying to change it: to show that things are not as self-evident as one believed, to see what is accepted as self-evident will no longer be accepted as such. Practicing criticism is a matter of making facile gestures difficult. (Foucault, 1990, p. 155)

Introduction

This is a theoretical chapter that aims at reflecting on the subject of extremism from a poststructuralist perspective. Therefore, the reader should not expect to find in it a detailed analysis of a particular aspect of specific debates concerning extremism today. Instead, it departs from Foucault's (1982) 'The subject and power' in order to address the question from a triple dimension: knowledge, power and subject. Indeed, addressing extremism from a poststructuralist perspective implies considering it as a discourse that produces political subjectivities. This way, in this chapter, I reflect upon how extremism as an object of knowledge and the extremist as its subject are constituted through their opposite: moderation and the moderate subject. Thus, the text analyses extremism as a way of exercising power through knowledge, constituting both the extremist other and the moderate self, asserting that discourses on extremism constitute not only otherness but, at the same time, a desirable self.

Inasmuch as the constitution of subjects takes place within historical modes of exercising power, the chapter contextualises the production of both the extremist and the moderate subjects within what is defined as global liberal government and its particular way of intervention on the conditions of freedom. This way, it concludes that discourses on extremism function to constitute a moderate liberal subject that actualises and reinforces this particular form of global governmentality.

Mostly, discourses on extremism make reference to two manifestations of contemporary politics: far-right ideology and political Islam. Both trends share links with religion and are constituted as threatening others. Nonetheless, they differ in important points, the most important of which is the specific bond established between political Islam and terrorism (a discursive feature not necessarily shared by the far-right other). This difference makes it difficult to address them together. Further, as this chapter focuses on the global effects of discourses on extremism, asserting that they constitute a moderate liberal subject through international interventionist policies in non-liberal spaces, it will mostly reflect on political Islam.

Besides this introduction, the chapter is divided into four sections and a conclusion. The first section focuses on poststructuralism's epistemological stance, its conception of the subject, and its particular way of addressing security issues, stressing its readings on extremism. The second section enquires into the definition of extremism, asking what extremism means and relating it to moderation theory. The third analyses the context of power relations where this conception develops, addressing the notion of global liberal government from analytics of governmentality. The fourth section provides some examples in order to illustrate the previous assertions. The conclusion delivers a summary of the main propositions of the text.

Poststructuralism and the subject of extremism

Poststructuralism is an ensemble of intellectual practices using a wide array of conceptual and methodological tools and multiple perspectives as genealogy, deconstruction, semiotics, psychoanalysis, intertextuality, etc. (Der Derian, 1989). Michel Foucault, Jacques Derrida, Jacques Lacan, Gilles Deleuze and Félix Guattari, among other thinkers, are considered the main referents of this perspective whose primary interest is to reflect upon knowledge, power and subject and their mutual relations. Foucault's 'The subject and power' (1982) is key to understanding the inherent relation between these three elements. From the very beginning of the text, the French philosopher shows that power is inextricably linked to subject; power, knowledge and subject working at the same time as conditions of possibility and effects of each other.

Poststructuralist approaches on extremism have taken place within Critical Security Studies. According to Charlotte Heath-Kelly, the main feature of poststructuralism's critical stance related to security studies resides in its injection of politics in a mainly normative field, constituted by normative categories (Heath-Kelly, 2016). Since its eruption in International Relations, poststructuralism has participated in these debates and moved them into Critical Terrorism Studies.

Poststructuralism emerged along with the epistemological debate in International Relations that opened the discipline's door to postpositivism (Lapid, 1989). The understanding of this paradigm is central to the comprehension of poststructuralism's stance on Critical Terrorism Studies in general, and to its approach to extremism in particular. For this reason, and in order to justify the importance of analysing the construction of extremism as an object of knowledge, this section starts with a quick review of it.

Postpositivism is an epistemological paradigm that emerged in opposition to positivism and its assumption that knowledge of the social world is value-free. This positivist assertion derives from the premise that subject and object of knowledge are separated. Indeed, positivism assumes that the object of knowledge has an existence and a logic of its own and that the function of the scientist (subject) is to discover it. Based on this discovering, the scientist can and must establish causal universally valid laws. This way, the subject of knowledge arrives at an objective universal truth.

As said before, postpositivism emerged in opposition to these assumptions. Thus, it does not conceive of the subject and the object of knowledge as separated. Instead, it assumes that they constitute each other. This way, the object is not deemed to have an existence of its own but to be constructed in its relation with the subject, making objectivity impossible and, therefore, dismissing the idea of a universally valid knowledge. Hence, not denying the existence of truth, postpositivism considers it the result of a construction, a product of intersubjective relations constituted by power relations. As a corollary, postpositivism emphasises the links between knowledge and power, asserting that knowledge cannot be separated from values nor from politics.

Based on these assumptions, poststructuralism does not conceive of security as a thing to achieve (or that can be achieved) but as a practice that constitutes subjects. Likewise, terrorism is not considered as an objective category, but as a functional discourse (Heath-Kelly, 2016). In fact, this conception allows poststructuralism to engage with terrorism not as an object existing independently from practices of knowledge and power, but as a discursive practice that constitutes subjects. Hence R.B.J. Walker's assertion: 'The crucial subject of security, in short, is the subject of security' (Walker, 1997, p. 68), because modern accounts of security 'tell us who we must be' (Walker, 1997, p. 72). Indeed, contrary to mainstream International Relations perspectives which depart from the subject (mainly the state) for their analysis, poststructuralism conceives of the subject as an arrival point. In other words, poststructuralism's focus on power is aimed at reflecting upon the question of the subject (Foucault, 1982). This way, the main concern of poststructuralists' analysis of security is with the subject of security: how are both the threatening other and the self constituted and for which political purposes, and which functions do these constructions perform within historical modes of exercising power?

Thus, poststructuralist readings of extremism have focused on the dimension of subjectivity, stressing the shift in the approach of terrorism that the emergence of a discourse on extremism has entailed. Indeed, whereas the former refers to actions and behaviours, the latter focuses on ideologies and beliefs appearing as a pre-terrorist stage delinked from the 'criminal justice model' (Elshimi, 2015; Heath-Kelly, 2012). This way, the discourse on extremism centres on subjectivities, constituting vulnerable, 'at-risk' subjects whose transformation and subsequent inclusion by refashioning its beliefs are intended (Martin, 2018). The focus on this dimension has allowed poststructuralist thinkers to frame counter-extremist policies within a governmental strategy (Elshimi, 2015; Heath-Kelly, 2012), different from the legal disciplinary one. Indeed, considered as a result of certain ideas, extremism opens up the possibility for a counter-terrorist preventive strategy that attacks the subjective causes of terrorism and encourages the adoption of liberal values as part of the 'cure' (Elshimi, 2015). Just as these authors have done, this chapter deals with extremism by conceiving of it as a discursive practice that allows the deployment of a series of technologies of anticipation. Nonetheless, different from them, it does not reflect on counter-violent extremism policies or counter-radicalisation policies within domestic contexts (Baker-Beall et al., 2015), but upon the discursive constitution of extremism itself. By putting the latter in relation to its opposite (as will be argued: moderation), it asserts that the discourse on extremism also works within global liberal interventionist strategies aiming at the transformation of non-liberal spaces.

Inasmuch as the subject is considered the result of discursive practices within specific contexts of power relations, discourse acquires a prominent position. Indeed, postpositivism is linked to a particular approach regarding the relationship between language and world that conceives of the former as constitutive of the latter. In this respect, the work of Ferdinand De Saussure has been fundamental for poststructuralist's theoretical developments. The French linguist affirmed that words' meanings are not natural, but arbitrary, derived from their differentiation from other words. Jacques Derrida (2017) picked up this premise and centred his deconstructive reading in the identification of dichotomies that function securing meanings. According to him, if words' meanings are not natural, if they depend on their relations of difference with other words, they must be secured. This is done through the establishment of dichotomies constituted by two opposite words hierarchically ordered. Thus, dichotomies such as West/ East, North/South, Man/Woman that organise Western thought allow the first signifier to acquire and secure its meaning.

However, the words in these dichotomies are not equal, the former being normatively superior to the latter. Nonetheless, the second, less valued word, is necessary in order to secure the former's meaning. Indeed, the aim of deconstruction is to detect these hierarchies and point out that the excluded element of these dichotomies is crucial to the existence of the more valued one. This way, identities, otherness and subjectivities are politically constituted through discursive dichotomies. The next section deals with the dichotomy within which extremism acquires its meaning.

Knowledge: what does extremism mean?

Defining extremism

In this section, I explore how extremism has been constructed as an object of knowledge and within which dichotomy its meaning has been secured. After a revision of mainstream literature, I conclude that extremism only makes sense when it is put in relation with its opposite: moderation. Indeed, the dichotomy of moderation/extremism functions to secure the meaning of the first signifier, turning it into a desirable political subjectivity. This way, I problematise the idea that extremism is a descriptive category that can be objectively identified.

Instead, I argue that extremism is a normative category functioning as a discursive practice of differentiation that entails a specific programme of action. According to Foucault, differentiations are at the same time conditions of possibility and effects of certain relations of power. This means that power operates through them; signalling what must be excluded, it points out the features of what can be included. And in the same vein as Derrida, he affirms that because 'deviances' from the norm help to define it, the latter's actualisation requires the existence of the former. Thus, my main hypothesis in this section is that extremism is brought into existence as a deviance from moderation in order to construct the latter as a norm of political subjectivity. This way, extremism allows defining moderation, securing its meaning.

Indeed, although many pages have been written about extremism, scholars and politicians coincide in the difficult task of defining it. Extremism appears as a 'contested term' (Halverson et al., 2011, p. 6), a 'diverse phenomenon, without clear definition' (United Nations General Assembly, 2015, p. 1). One of the reasons to explain the notion's slippery character is the allegedly extremist movements' heterogeneity. Indeed, the literature not only postulates the existence of two different categories of extremists (those holding on to far-right ideology and Islamists), but it also notes there are differences among the movements conforming to each of these categories.[1]

These difficulties lead some authors to appeal to instinct, stating that if extremism is almost impossible to define, instead it is easy to recognise (see, as examples, Michael, 2003; Mudde, 2002; Sotlar, 2004). Thus, 'we seem to know *who* they are even though we do not exactly know *what* they are' (Mudde, 2002, p. 7). The 'what' question is picked up by Irm Haleem in her book *The Essence of Islamic Extremism*. However, despite the announcement, her text does not deliver a definition of extremism but develops the 'dialectic reason' leading to its existence (Haleem, 2012). Unable to define extremism, and in order to demarcate the contours of their object of study, most authors restrict themselves to making a list of its alleged characteristics. Among them, violence, rigidity and a certain relation of opposition to (liberal) democracy are highlighted.

In fact, most authors and politicians agree in stating that violence is the main feature of extremism because it seeks to impose its will through violent means, disregarding consensus. From this perspective, violence is considered necessary to impose a rigid, non-negotiable belief, associating extremism with a lack of flexibility. Both characteristics lead them to assert that, in the end, it is a threat to democracy. At the same time, they affirm that extremism flourishes where democracy is absent or wavering. This way, extremism and democracy are interrelated.

According to the reviewed literature, the aforementioned characteristics are shared by far-right and Islamist extremism. Nonetheless, although it remains under suspicion, far-right extremism's stance towards democracy seems more 'difficult to discern given the obvious reasons in the contemporary West to hide anti-democratic sentiments' (Eatwell, 2004, p. 8). In other words, whereas Islamist extremism's rejection of democracy seems clear, the far right's appears blurred by the general democratic consensus reigning in the West. As a result, far-right extremism's threat is somehow tempered by its jelly-like, ill-defined stance towards democracy.

Similarly, while far-right extremism's violence is underlined, that of Islamist extremism is put in relation with terrorism, raising its level of danger. Indeed, extremism's lack of definition allows scholars and politicians (alike) to equate this signifier with others such as fascism, populism (in the case of far-right extremism) and terrorism (in the case of Islamist extremism). In this regard, the introduction to the 2015 United Nations Secretary General's Plan of Action to Prevent Violent Extremism is telling. It states: 'Violent extremism is a diverse phenomenon, without a clear definition. It is neither new nor exclusive to any region, nationality or system of belief. Nevertheless, in recent years, terrorist groups such as Islamic State in Iraq and the Levant (ISIL), Al-Qaida and Boko

Haram have shaped our image of violent extremism' (United Nations' General Assembly, 2015, p. 1). Besides equating violent extremism with terrorism, the Plan only uses Islamist groups to exemplify it. This way, it limits the links to terrorism to that category of extremism, contributing to the attachment of Islam with terrorism. With the latter being the 'single most important [global] security issue' (Jackson, 2007, p. 394), the terrorism–extremism association helps to emphasise the latent danger of relying on this kind of political subjectivity. This way, the series extremism – political Islam – terrorism implies a hierarchically ordered scale of danger at the top of which racialised Islamist extremism is placed. Further, it makes 'new terrorism' even more threatening than the old one due to its irrationality, fanaticism and extremism, thus constructing the threat of an unconstrained, unmanaged violence.

Some authors add another reason for the difficulties in defining extremism: the negative connotations of the term (Sotlar, 2004). Indeed, as with terrorism, the term extremism is never a self-referent one. This is why, according to Roger Eatwell, it 'is essentially an academic and antifascist construct designed to delegitimize groups' (Eatwell, 2004, p. 10). With this proposition, Eatwell highlights the political character of the term. Effectively, this is a symbolic, clearly performative label that in the instant that it is put to work carries with it an implicit programme of action. Thus, extremism is a 'term of damnation' (Eatwell and Goodwin, 2010, p. 7). This means that it has not a merely descriptive effect, but also a normative one, aimed at changing not only the subjects' behaviour but also their beliefs. Indeed, the labelling of a person or a group as extremist carries with it the instruction of excluding and transforming them. At the same time, it reveals the existence of other subjects and groups which can and must be included: moderates.

Moderation and the desirable political subject

Despite its importance in political thought, authors tackling the issue coincide in the difficulties of its definition, just as with extremism. In Murat Somer's words, moderation is a 'poorly defined and slippery concept' (Somer, 2014, p. 245) whose content is 'a variable by definition' (Somer, 2014, p. 246). In the same vein, Suveyda Karakaya and Kadir Yildrim argue that 'moderation has become an all-catch term' (2013, p. 1322) that 'takes on different meanings' (2013, p. 1326). In this sense, Vali Nasr's definition – moderation is moving away from extremism – acquires relevance (Nasr, 2009).

Most authors coincide in defining moderation as some kind of domestication, or adaptation. However, as cleverly pointed out by Somer, 'they do not specify "to what" the moderating actors adapt' (Somer, 2014, p. 246). This lack of specification leads Somer to look at it in more detail. Nonetheless, despite the rigorous work of the Turkish scholar in contextualising and historicising moderation, he ends up not answering the question and affirms that it has three universal characteristics: 'Preference for peaceful political strategies'; 'Ability to relax ideological priorities for appealing to greater segments of voters'; and 'Potential openness to other worldviews and to peaceful competition, cooperation and compromise with other actors' (Somer, 2014, p. 248). As can be noted, these characteristics oppose those of extremism (peaceful strategies vs. violence; flexibility vs. rigidity; friendship with democracy vs. enmity with democracy) and refer to subjective characteristics, pointing out preferences, abilities and worldviews. These features are of special interest to this chapter because they reveal the deep relationship between moderation (as opposed to extremism), (liberal) democracy and the subject of liberalism.

According to moderation theory's revision made by Somer, there are two main ways of defining moderation: a restricted way and an enlarged one. While the former equates moderation with 'upholding the norms and practices observed in Western, liberal and secular democracies' (Somer, 2014, p. 247), the latter assumes different characteristics as: 'acceptance of competitive politics', a movement 'from state-centered to society-centered, civil and reformist movements; (. . .) from monopoly of religious truth to the acknowledgment of ambiguity and multiplicity; from closed to more open worldviews tolerant of alternative truth-claims' (Somer, 2014, p. 247).

To fully grasp the sense of the latter way of defining moderation, the alleged characteristics must be put in relation with moderation theory and its assertion that moderation leads to or helps to consolidate democracy (Browers, 2009; El-Ghobashy, 2005; Michels, 1982; Robinson, 1997; Wickham, 2004). Thus, moderation is defined as a political subjectivity upholding democracy, diversity, secularism and tolerance, and praising civil society. This way, although not as explicit as the restricted definition as regards to the relation of moderation with liberalism and democracy, the link is evident. Nonetheless, this relation is not between moderation and democracy in the abstract, but with a certain form of democracy: liberal democracy. Indeed, most authors agree that moderation leads not only to democracy but to a political and economic liberalisation, as well (Nasr, 2009; Robinson, 1997). In this sense, Aurelian Craiutu conceives of moderation as part of the 'principles of liberal democracy', as a political virtue that 'can immunize the body politic against the seductions of perfectionism and the tyranny of abstraction in politics' (Craiutu, 2003, p. 293).

Thus read, this definition appears in clear opposition with the alleged aforementioned attributes of extremism. This way, moderation and extremism are interrelated, each being defined as mutually opposed. Whereas moderate political subjectivity is centred on democracy, civil society, diversity, secularism and tolerance, extremism is deemed undemocratic, state-centred, religiously driven and intolerant.

Although moderation theory has traditionally focused on behaviours and not on subjectivities, from a constructivist perspective Jillian Schwedler places moderation in the subjectivity field, turning moderation into an identity (Schwedler, 2006). Indeed, she asserts that moderation is a political identity whose construction is related to ideology because, in order to be a moderate, it is not enough to act like a moderate, but it is also necessary to think as one, to believe in moderation. In her words, this implies a 'change in ideology from a rigid and closed worldview to one relatively more open and tolerant of alternative perspectives' (Schwedler, 2006, p. 22). This apparently broad definition is tightened when the author specifies that openness and liberalisation can be equated. Certainly, according to her, political liberalisations are 'sometimes called political openings' (Schwedler, 2006, p. 36). This way, becoming moderate entails becoming a liberal subject.

Whereas moderation and liberalism are intertwined, extremism and liberalism are as well, although in an oppositional way. Thus, Manuela Caiani can assert: 'Extremists divide the world between friends (those who support their cause) and enemies (those who oppose it), without seeking a common ground among contending parties, nor does extremism seek common perspectives, as liberalism does' (Caiani, 2013, p. 2). This way, a series can be established through which moderation/extremism, that is, moderation as an objectified practice that gets its meaning through its opposition to extremism (and vice-versa), liberal democracy and liberalism enter into an inextricable relationship where moving away from extremism appears as a condition of possibility and effect of liberalism. Indeed, moderation/extremism produces a political subjectivity that is constituted within the liberal rationality of government, thus being an effect and condition of liberalism.

Power: liberal government and moderation/extremism

Objectified practices such as extremism do not appear in a vacuum but within specific contexts of power–knowledge–subject relations. The authors referred to in the previous section link moderation/extremism with liberalism conceived of as a political doctrine or ideology without contextualising the emergence of what is constituted as extremism. Contrary to this latter reading, hereinafter, my aim is to frame the dichotomy within liberalism conceived of from the perspective of governmentality, that is, as a mode of government.

Foucault identified different modes of analysing and exercising power, among them governmentality. As Mitchell Dean maintains, Foucault gave it 'several meanings and uses' (Dean, 2017), appearing in a clear but not fully defined relation with liberalism. Hence, some authors dealing with the issue establish a sort of homogenisation between both terms (for example, Joseph, 2011), whereas, on the contrary, others tend to pick up the concept of governmentality while setting aside that of liberalism (as is the case with Sending and Neumann, 2006). Governmentality and liberalism are indeed intertwined. As a conclusive example, Foucault asserts that it is with the emergence of liberalism that governmental technologies reach their maximum deployment. This way, they work as conditions of possibility and the effects of one another. In stating that moderation/extremism are possible in the context of a liberal government and, at the same time, function to reinforce it, in this section I especially focus on this latter form of governmental rationality (Gordon, 1991).

Global liberal government

Liberal rationality of government stems from a particular form of knowledge: political economy. According to Foucault, political economy's originary problem was linked to the limitation of public power, thus making 'possible the self-limitation of governmental reason' (Foucault, 2008, p. 12), based on the principle that government 'always risks governing too much' (Foucault, 2008, p. 16). Hence, the invisible hand theory's assertion that economic processes cannot be the field of government due to the sovereign power's impossibility of knowing the totality of the economic process. This incapacity to know a field reigned by natural individual interests has led to the *laissez-faire* mandate and to the sovereign's impossibility of intervening in the market.

If this is the case, 'what will government be concerned with if the economic process, and the whole of the economic process, is not in principle its object?' (Foucault, 2008, p. 286), Foucault asks. And he answers: civil society. This new domain appears as a 'new plane of reference' (Foucault, 2008, p. 295) which includes both juridical and economic subjects, law and market. This way, from a governmentality perspective, civil society is not the opposite of government, but its correlate.

How does government work in this new domain? Governmentality entails conceiving of power as 'a total structure of actions brought to bear upon possible actions; it incites, it induces, it seduces, it makes easier or more difficult; in the extreme it constrains or forbids absolutely; it is nevertheless always a way of acting upon an acting subject or acting subjects by virtue of their acting or being capable of action' (Foucault, 1982, p. 789). Two conclusions can be drawn from this statement. First, the object of government is not only conceived of as such, that is, as a passive thing on which power is exerted, but as an active subject. This way, power is not exerted on civil society, but through it. Second, a field of possible actions must be opened. Hence, central to this conception of power as government is freedom and its production, for power thus conceived of can only be exerted if the subject is free to act, that is, 'capable of action'. In Graham Burchell's words, it is a technology of government that 'requires the proper use of liberty' (Burchell, 1996, p. 24), actively responsible free selves.

Nonetheless, self-government based on freedom must not be confused with the absence of government. Liberalism governs through intervention on the conditions of freedom. This means that, as long as it is a power, it conducts conduct. However, it does not do so by directly intervening on the object's behaviour, but on the framework where the latter develops, thus not nullifying subjects' freedom, but conducting it. This way, the mode of intervention changes: 'action is brought to bear on the rules of the game rather than on the players' (Foucault, 2008, p. 260), 'an environmental type of intervention instead of the internal subjugation of individuals' (Foucault, 2008, p. 260). This intervention is done through law. According to Foucault, the use of this means has nothing to do with a 'supposedly natural legalism of liberalism' (Foucault, 2008, p. 321). Instead, law is the way liberal interventionism adopts because it 'defines forms of general intervention excluding particular, individual, and exceptional measures, and because participation of the governed in drawing up the law in a parliamentary system is the most effective system of governmental economy' (Foucault, 2008, p. 321).

Therefore, encouraging the participation of the governed in the drawing up of laws generating the framework within which their life develops, representative institutions allow the object of government to function as a subject of self-government as well. This way, the participation of the governed in their government is not due to their allegedly natural individual rights or freedoms, but 'because government already depends on the liberties and capacities of the governed exercised within an economy' (Dean, 1999, p. 174). Hence, notwithstanding there is not a natural relationship between liberalism, rule of law and democracy, Foucault's conception of liberal government enables putting them within this rationality of government.

Despite Foucault's conception of liberal government being restricted to the nation-state, he allows its globalisation when demarcating government from territory, asserting that the object of government is no longer the latter, but 'a sort of complex composed of men and things' (Foucault, 1991, p. 93). Hence, the emergence of the notion of global governmentality.[2] Herein, I will use the term global liberal governmentality with the intention of focusing on the liberal form of this particular mode of exercising power. Globalising governmentality is core to this text because, as mentioned, it aims to interrogate how extremism works within global interventionist strategies and not in domestic contexts.

Besides, the underlining of the global character of the liberal government is important so as to address an issue that is not defined by its territoriality. Indeed, as previously developed, extremism is understood as a normative, and thus political, non-territorial subjectivity. From now on, I will consider the linkages between global liberal government and the way moderation/extremism are discursively constructed, arguing that this construction functions as a condition of possibility and effect of liberal governmental practices. Indeed, each of the aforementioned elements that constitute liberal government (self-limitation, civil society as object and subject of government, self-government, freedom and intervention through law) are put into operation in the construction of moderation/extremism as referred to in the previous section.

In decentring the study of power from the state and, instead, conceiving of an active subject of government, governmentality puts subjectivity as a fundamental dimension of the study of power. In separating state from government, governmentality allows conceiving of the possibility of a government exercised from 'non-political' spaces. According to Castro-Gómez, as power is exerted through civil society, a particular feature of liberal practices is that they are agreed by those upon whom the technologies of government are applied. This consent is possible, since 'government is not only exerted through ideas or ideological agendas but mainly on (and through) people's desires, aspirations and beliefs' (Castro-Gómez, 2010, p. 41). This way, subjectification becomes a cornerstone of liberal power. Even more when liberalism needs freedom to work: 'to govern does not mean to force others to behave in a certain way (and against their will), but to reach that the governed themselves view that behaviour as good, honourable, worthy and, above all, as own, as resulting from their freedom' (Castro-Gómez, 2010, p. 43).[3] Hence, the idea of a self-governed, responsibly free subject.

Extremism and the shaping of the liberal subject

Law answers the question of how to produce the conditions of freedom enabling civil society to exercise self-government, because, as said, it works as a general frame and, through parliamentary devices, it encourages the participation of the governed in its drawing up. This way, Foucault's conception of the rule of law in liberal government has allowed me to insert democracy within this particular mode of exercising power. This is of interest because, as previously pointed out, liberal democracy is at the heart of the construction of the dichotomy moderation/extremism. Whereas the former is said to emerge from and consolidate democracy, the latter is supposed to weaken or destroy it. As long as moderation/extremism work as normative categories aiming at the establishment of a desirable political subjectivity, this dichotomy feeds the characterisation of liberal democracy as the only legitimate way of government.

This way, it works as a liberalising discursive force. Indeed, setting up a liberal democratic framework is not only conceived of as dissuading from extremism, but also as encouraging the development of civil society, which, as previously depicted, is deemed as a core agent of moderation. This way, moderation, civil society and liberal democracy reinforce each other. Thus, connecting rule of law, conditions of freedom, civil society, self-government and democracy, the dichotomy moderation/extremism functions as a global liberal governmental device, allowing for and stemming from an environmental juridical global interventionism.

The aforementioned principle of self-limitation leads liberal government to depend upon a self-governable subject that, in turn, must be produced. This text's main proposition is that extremism is one of many ways of producing it in the form of a moderate liberal political subject. Hence, the continuous insistence on the involvement of civil society (schools, communities, individuals, etc.) in counter-extremism policies, giving it a function in reporting suspicious behaviours or beliefs, making disaster readiness plans, requesting Muslim communities to respond to and manifest themselves against terrorist attacks, dissuading youth, women, family and friends from taking part in alleged extremist movements, mediating between communities and governments, etc.[4] This way, civil society is empowered as a key actor to counter extremism and, at the same time, is moulded and reinforced in specific normative ways of behaving and being.

Extremism is conceived of as having a cause (the subject's worldviews) and a (possible) consequence (terrorism). Thus, in order to avoid the latter, it is necessary to deal with the former. This way, the constitution of both the extremist and the moderate liberal subject is part of 'technologies of anticipation' (Heath-Kelly, 2016) that are supported by racialising practices identifying particular subjects' beliefs as 'vulnerable' to extremism. That is, democratising interventions in non-liberal states are deemed as enabling the constitution of a civil society inhabited by moderate subjects and distancing them from extremist subjectivities.

The 2015 United Nations Secretary General's Plan of Action to Prevent Violent Extremism can serve as an exemplifier of what has been affirmed up to now. The importance of this document must be highlighted not only in itself but also because it is the basis for regional and national policies of countering violent extremism. It emerged as a consequence of the speech by former United States President Barack Obama at the 2014 United Nations General Assembly. In that opportunity, he highlighted the necessity to 'reject the cancer of violent extremism'[5] and then sent Resolution 2178 to the United Nations Security Council, thus calling for the organ to 'counter violent extremism' (Ucko, 2018) for the first time. This way, extremism was introduced as a different way of approaching counter-terrorism, not dealing with its symptoms but with its causes. Therefore, a different strategy against terrorism arose, confronting extremism and the subjective conditions enabling it.

The Plan addresses global extremism by making particular reference to Islamist movements. Nonetheless, it departs from the assumption that extremism is a nation-state product, reinforcing the International Relations' foundational cleavage (inside/outside) and, at the same time, opening up the way to international interventions within nation-states' organisational frameworks. Indeed, the Plan points out certain socio-economic and political conditions leading to violent extremism. Among them, it highlights: 'poor governance, violations of human rights and the rule of law' (United Nations General Assembly, 2015, p. 7); 'democracy deficits, corruption and a culture of impunity' (United Nations General Assembly, 2015, p. 7); and 'absence or curtailment of democratic space' (United Nations General Assembly, 2015, p. 8), underlining non-democratic conditions of extremism's emergence.

Stemming from these diagnoses, the analysed document postulates a plan for action: 'the creation of open, equitable, inclusive and pluralist societies, based on the full respect of human rights and with economic opportunities for all' (United Nations General Assembly, 2015, p. 3). This way, once more extremism and democracy appear intertwined: 'National plans should fortify the social compact against violent extremism by promoting respect for the principle of equality before the law and equal protection under the law in all government-citizen relations, and developing effective, accountable and transparent institutions at all levels, as well as ensuring responsive, inclusive, participatory and representative decision-making' (United Nations General Assembly, 2015, p. 12). That is, the solution to extremism is the establishment of a democratic framework encouraging moderation.

The participatory element pointed out in relation to the democratic framework allegedly working to dissuade extremism leads to the aforementioned active character of the object/subject of government. Indeed, according to the Plan, with regard to civil society, development is encouraged through the creation of this democratic environment, and the opening of the government to its participation dissuades from extremist behaviours and beliefs, thus leading to moderation: 'When Governments embrace international human rights norms and standards, promote good governance, uphold the rule of law and eliminate corruption, they create an enabling environment for civil society and reduce the appeal of violent extremism. (. . .) create an environment where entrepreneurship can flourish' (United Nations General Assembly, 2015, p. 15).

This central role of civil society in the Plan has as a corollary the active participation of civil society in its own security, thus changing the sovereign idea that security must be provided by an externality. This way, according to the analysed document, the most effective response to and the better way to prevent extremism is the encouragement of civil society self-government enabled by a democratic framework established through the rule of law. At the same time, this latter is reinforced by a moderate responsibly free civil society. Thereby, the United Nations' plan for dealing with extremism puts into operation each of the aforementioned elements constituting the global liberal government, the dichotomy moderation/extremism working both as a condition of possibility and effect of this mode of exercising power.

Final words

Inasmuch as poststructuralism's main question with regards to security is the subject, and the latter is conceived of as a condition of possibility and an effect of knowledge and power, in this chapter I have addressed the issue of extremism from that triple dimension. This way, the main problem conducting these pages has been: which subject does the discourse on extremism constitute?

In order to answer this question, I started by asking: what is extremism? The impossibility of its definition highlighted in the literature addressing the issue led me to conclude that extremism is not a descriptive category, but a normative one. Indeed, during the research, the notion of moderation appeared with insistence as the desirable other of extremism. Nonetheless, as with the latter, the existent literature does not find a suitable definition for the former either, with most scholars replacing definitions with lists of alleged characteristics. Thus, while moderation is described as a peaceful, flexible and democratic way of acting and being, extremism is portrayed as being violent, rigid and undemocratic, these two notions working together securing the meaning of one another. So, I concluded that extremism is brought into existence as opposed to moderation in order to construct the latter as a norm of political subjectivity. Furthermore, the link between extremism and subjectivity opens up the door to preventive practices aiming at transforming the latter. Therefore, for this chapter the meaning of extremism was not relevant in order to discover some allegedly essential feature of it, but because the way it is constituted has power and subject effects. Thus, I have focused on two main effects of this discourse: as constitutive of a desirable political subjectivity, and as supporting democratising interventions in non-liberal spaces.

I have conceived of the dichotomy moderation/extremism as a practice and, as such, inserted within particular relations of power. Specifically, within liberalism understood from a governmentality perspective, that is, as a mode of analysing/exercising power. Global liberal government was characterised as centred on freedom and based on self-government of civil society. This conception of government through civil society entails a particular interventionism exerted through law in order to manipulate the conditions of freedom. The role given by Foucault to the law within this mode of power allowed me to link liberalism to democracy and, thus, to moderation/extremism, functioning as a condition of possibility as much as an effect of global liberal government. Indeed, I asserted that the dichotomy moderation/extremism works as a global governmental device enabling a legal global interventionism that transforms the social, political and economic structures of nation-states, establishing a democratic framework that shapes subjectivity.

The question about the subject implies conceiving of the subject both as a condition of possibility and as effect. This way, 'The subject produces the world of which it is a part at the same time as it is itself produced' (Edkins, 2007, p. 90). Hence, the question that has organised this text: which is the subject produced by the discourse on extremism? Of course, it produces an extremist subject, a violent, fanatical, rigid, authoritarian threatening other, incapable of self-government. However, more importantly yet, it also produces a moderate subject, a self-governed, tolerant, democratic self. This way, the discourse on extremism shows that discourse does not have a merely reflex function. Instead, it constructs reality through the constitution of subjects. Indeed, it encourages the desire for moderation, liberal democracy and liberalism.

During the research, lots of questions arose which I intentionally put aside in order to concentrate on the subjective effects of the dichotomy moderation/extremism. For example: How are Western far-right extremism and Islamic extremism differently constituted? What part does race play in that differentiation? What are the effects of pointing out extremist violence with respect to 'moderate' violence? Which types of violence are hidden in this underlining? These are certainly challenging questions that would deserve a major development. Nonetheless, this chapter's theoretical character demanded that I avoid focusing on specific issues and, instead, concentrate on the guiding question articulating extremism with liberal government from analytics of governmentality.

Notes

1   It is relevant to underline that heterogeneity is mainly highlighted in the case of far-right extremism, whereas so-called Islamist extremists movements are generally presented as homogenous.
2   See, for example, Larner and Walters, 2004; Sending and Neumann, 2006; Vrasti, 2013, among others.
3   Own translation.
4   See, for example, Department of State and USAID (2016); Organization for Security and Co-operation in Europe (2018).
5   Available at www.washingtonpost.com/politics/full-text-of-president-obamas-2014-address-to-the-united-nations-general-assembly/2014/09/24/88889e46-43f4-11e4-b437-1a7368204804_story.html (accessed 7 August 2018).

References

Baker-Beall, C., Heath-Kelly, C. and Jarvis, L. (eds), 2015. *Counter-Radicalisation: Critical Perspectives*. Routledge, Abingdon.

Browers, M., 2009. *Political Ideology in the Arab World: Accommodation and Transformation*. Cambridge University Press, Cambridge.

Burchell, G., 1996. 'Liberal government and techniques of the self', in Barry, A., Osborne, T. and Rose, N. (eds), *Foucault, and Political Reason. Liberalism, Neo-liberalism, and Rationalities of Government*. The University of Chicago Press, Chicago, pp. 19–36.

Caiani, M., 2013. 'Extremism', in Snow, D., Della Porta, D., Klandermans, B. and McAdam, D. (eds), *The Wiley-Blackwell Encyclopedia of Social and Political Movements*. Wiley-Blackwell, Chichester.

Castro-Gómez, S., 2010. *Historia de la gubernamentalidad. Razón de Estado, liberalismo y neoliberalismo en Michel Foucault*. Siglo del Hombre, Pontificia Universidad Javeriana, Universidad Santo Tomás de Aquino, Bogotá.

Craiutu, A., 2003. *Liberalism under Siege: The Political Thought of the French Doctrinaires*. Lexington Books, New York.

Dean, M., 1999. 'Normalising democracy: Foucault and Habermas on democracy, liberalism, and law', in Ashenden, S. and Owen, D. (eds), *Foucault contra Habermas: Recasting the Dialogue between Genealogy and Critical Theory*. SAGE, London, pp. 166–194.

Dean, M., 2017. 'Governmentality', in Turner, B., Kyung-Sup, C., Epstein, C., Kivisto, P., Outhwaite, W. and Ryan, M. (eds), *The Wiley Blackwell Encyclopedia of Social Theory*. Wiley-Blackwell, Chichester, pp. 1–2.

Department of State and USAID, 2016. *Joint Strategy on Countering Violent Extremism*. State Department/USAID.

Der Derian, J., 1989. 'The boundaries of knowledge and power in International Relations', in Der Derian, J. and Shapiro, M. (eds), *International/Intertextual Relations: Postmodern Readings of World Politics*. Lexington Books, New York.

Derrida, J., 2017. *De la gramatología*. Siglo XXI, México City.

Eatwell, R., 2004. 'Introduction: The new extreme right challenge', in Eatwell, R. and Mudde, C. (eds), *Western Democracies and the New Extreme Right Challenge*. Routledge, London, pp. 1–16.

Eatwell, R., Goodwin, M., 2010. 'Introduction: The new extremism in 21st century Britain', in Eatwell, R. and Goodwin, M. (eds), *The New Extremism in 21st Century Britain*. Routledge, Abingdon, pp. 1–20.

Edkins, J., 2007. 'Poststructuralism', in Griffiths, M. (ed.), *International Relations Theory for the Twenty-First Century. An Introduction*. Routledge, Oxford, pp. 88–98.

El-Ghobashy, M., 2005. 'The metamorphosis of the Egyptian Muslim Brothers', *International Journal of Middle East Studies*, 37(3), 373–395.

Elshimi, M., 2015. 'De-radicalisation interventions as technologies of the self: A Foucauldian analysis', *Critical Studies on Terrorism*, 8(1), 110–129.

Foucault, M., 1982. 'The subject and power', *Critical Inquiry*, 8(4), 777–795.

Foucault, M., 1990. 'Practicing criticism', in Kritzman, L. (ed.), *Michel Foucault. Politics, Philosophy, Culture. Interviews and Other Writings 1977–1984*. Routledge, New York, pp. 152–156.

Foucault, M., 1991. 'Governmentality', in Burchell, G., Gordon, C. and Miller, P. (eds), *The Foucault Effect. Studies in Governmentality*. The University of Chicago Press, Chicago, pp. 87–104.

Foucault, M., 2008. *The Birth of Biopolitics. Lectures at the Collège de France 1978–1979*. Palgrave Macmillan, Basingstoke.

Gordon, C., 1991. 'Governmental rationality: An introduction', in Burchell, G., Gordon, C. and Miller, P. (eds), *The Foucault Effect. Studies in Governmentality*. The University of Chicago Press, Chicago, pp. 1–51.

Haleem, I., 2012. *The Essence of Islamist Extremism: Recognition through Violence, Freedom through Death*. Routledge, New York.

Halverson, J., Goodall, H.L. and Corman, S.R., 2011. *Master Narratives of Islamist Extremism*. Palgrave Macmillan, New York.

Heath-Kelly, C., 2012. 'Counter-terrorism and the counterfactual: Producing the "radicalisation" discourse and the UK PREVENT strategy', *The British Journal of Politics and International Relations*, 15(3), 394–415.

Heath-Kelly, C., 2016. 'Post-structuralism and constructivism', in Jackson, R. (ed.), *Routledge Handbook of Critical Terrorism Studies*. Routledge, New York, pp. 137–159.

Jackson, R., 2007. 'Constructing enemies: "Islamic terrorism" in political and academic discourse', *Government and Opposition*, 42(3), 394–426.

Joseph, J., 2011. 'Governmentality of what? Populations, states, and international organisations', in Kiersey, N. and Stokes, D. (eds), *Foucault and International Relations. New Critical Engagements*. Routledge, New York, pp. 51–65.

Karakaya, S., Yildrim, K., 2013. 'Islamist moderation in perspective: A comparative analysis of the moderation of Islamist and Western communist parties', *Democratization*, 20(7), 1322–1349.

Larner, W., Walters, W. (eds), 2004. *Global Governmentality: Governing International Spaces*. Routledge, London.

Lapid, Y., 1989. 'The third debate: On the prospects of International Relations theory in a post-positivist era', *International Studies Quarterly*, 33(3), 235–254.

Martin, T., 2018. 'Identifying potential terrorists: Visuality, security and the Channel project', *Security Dialogue*, 49(4), 254–271.

Michael, G., 2003. *Confronting Right-Wing Extremism and Terrorism in the USA*. Routledge, New York.

Michels, R., 1982. *Sociologia dos partidos politicos*. Editora Universidade de Brasilia, Brasilia.

Mudde, C., 2002. *The Ideology of the Extreme Right*. Manchester University Press, Manchester.

Nasr, V., 2009. *The Rise of Islamic Capitalism: Why the Middle Class is the Key to Defeating Extremism*. Free Press, New York.

Organization for Security and Co-operation in Europe, 2018. *The Role of Civil Society in Preventing and Countering Violent Extremism and Radicalization that Lead to Terrorism: A Focus on South-Eastern Europe*, OSCE.

Robinson, G., 1997. 'Can Islamists be democrats? The case of Jordan', *Middle East Journal*, 51(3), 373–387.

Schwedler, J., 2006. *Faith in Moderation: Islamist Parties in Jordan and Yemen*. Cambridge University Press, New York.

Sending, O., Neumann, I., 2006. 'Governance to governmentality: Analyzing NGOs, states, and power', *International Studies Quarterly*, 50, 651–672.

Somer, M., 2014. 'Moderation of religion and secular politics, a country's "center" and democratization', *Democratization*, 21(2), 244–267.

Sotlar, A., 2004. 'Some problems with a definition and perception of extremism within a society', in Mesko, G., Pagon, M. and Dobovsek, B. (eds), *Policing in Central and Eastern Europe: Dilemmas of Contemporary Criminal Justice*. University of Maribor, Maribor, pp. 703–707.

Ucko, D., 2018. 'Preventing violent extremism through the United Nations: The rise and fall of a good idea', *International Affairs*, 94(2), 251–270.

United Nations General Assembly, 2015. *Plan of Action to Prevent Violent Extremism* (Report of the Secretary General), United Nations' General Assembly.

Vrasti, W., 2013. 'Universal but not truly "global": Governmentality, economic liberalism, and the international', *Review of International Studies*, 39(1), 49–69.

Walker, R.B.J., 1997. 'The subject of security', in Krause, K. and Williams, M. (eds), *Critical Security Studies: Concepts and Cases*. University College London Press, London, pp. 61–81.

Wickham, C., 2004. 'The path to moderation: Strategy and learning in the formation of Egypt's Wasat party', *Comparative Politics*, 9(1), 205–228.

The lone (white) wolf, 'terrorism' and the suspect community

Marie Breen-Smyth

Contemporary insecurities

Mamdani (2002) argues that the ability to see 'terrorism' as a 'new' problem that began in September 2001 is dependent on an ahistoricism that denies more recent histories. Organisations such as al Qaida are not purely products of 'radical Islam' but co-productions of interrelationships with the West. Al Qaida was born of local political conditions and rivalries between Muslims and co-opted and deployed by the US in the past to serve its anti-Soviet political projects.

During the Cold War, the 'other' was largely separated from the West by oceans. The 'far-war' of the past has morphed into a war nearer to home. The 'other' is no longer distant but lives among those whose security is the priority of the state. Western invasion and colonisation have equipped these 'others' with Western passports; 'they' speak the language and know the culture well. 'They' live in the heart of the coloniser's territory and such intimacy offers multiple and diverse possibilities for attack. Sara Ahmed points out:

> The nation becomes imagined and embodied as a space, not simply by being defined against other spaces, but by being defined as close to some others (friends), and further away from other others (strangers). . . The proximity of strangers within the nation space. . . is a mechanism for the demarcation of the national body, a way of defining borders within it. (Ahmed, 2000, p. 100)

Many of these 'others' have fled wars in which the West had a hand, raising anxieties about their loyalty and trustworthiness independent of any racial antipathy that they might arouse. Thus, a 'suspect community' comes into being. Hillyard's original study of the 'suspect community' (Hillyard, 1993) was of the Irish living in England – the British mainland – rather than of the Irish living in a militarised Northern Ireland, where the bulk of political violence occurred.

Hillyard's suspect community was rendered suspect under the Prevention of Terrorism Act (1989) whereby police no longer required 'reasonable suspicion' to justify stopping a person who only had to be in 'a category of person', namely Irish. Under random stop and search powers, in theory at least, everyone has an equal chance of being stopped, whereas the Prevention of Terrorism Act permitted specific categories of people – Irish people – to be picked out (Hillyard, 1993, p. 19). Hillyard's study can be seen in the context of a history of targeting Irish people in Britain and the US for racialised abuse and exclusion (see, for example, Fried, 2015; Hickman, 1998) in the context of the colonial relationship between Britain and Ireland.

Following the IRA ceasefires and the 1998 peace settlement in Northern Ireland and the 2001 global war on terror, Muslims in Britain and the US became the 'new suspect community'. A range of studies examined Muslim experiences of being suspect (Hickman et al., 2010a, 2010b, 2013). Pantazis and Pemberton (2009) described this Muslim suspect community as: 'a sub-group of the population that is singled out for state attention as being "problematic" . . . individuals may be targeted, not necessarily as a result of suspected wrong doing, but simply because of their presumed membership of that sub-group. Race, ethnicity, religion, class, gender, language, accent, dress, political ideology or any combination of these factors may serve to delineate the sub-group' (Pantazis and Pemberton, 2009, p. 649). However, there was nothing 'new' about this suspicion of Muslims, rather it was too 'natural' in the context of historical and contemporary Orientalist and colonial relations.

The 'othering' that constructs the 'suspect community' is enacted through surveillance, profiling, stopping, searching, arrest and detention of that suspect community. Government discourses of threat such as red/amber/green warning systems signalling the likelihood of terrorist attack marshal public fear and direct it at this 'suspect community'. Suspicion of Muslims, or the Irish before them, is encouraged by calls for vigilance; the public are urged 'if you see something, say something' (Cushing, 2013).

It is not only Muslims (or previously Irish) who are treated as members of the 'suspect community' (Breen-Smyth, 2014). Misidentification and ignorance of cultural, racial or ethnic markers mean that some non-Irish or non-Muslims have also experienced being suspect, sometimes with fatal effect. Jean Charles de Menezes, a Brazilian, was shot dead in 2005 by counter-terrorist police in London when they took him for an al Qaida member. Harry Stanley, a Scot, was shot dead in 1999 by police who mistook his Scottish accent for Irish.

The suspect community exists in the public's suspicious mind, which is informed by public discourses on security, terrorism and threat produced by government, media, security practitioners and political actors (Nickels et al., 2012). This 'suspect community' is imagined as malevolent and in possession of

violent agency. Once identified, a member of a 'suspect community' can be legitimately subjected to legal exceptionalism and extraordinary security practices.
The setting aside of their security is justified by threat conjured in the securitised
imagination of a fearful public, an imagination informed by historically embedded racialised stereotypes.

Hillyard's 'suspect community' is an embodied community with fixed characteristics, such as a location or a homogenous set of beliefs, identifications and so
on. However, as the cases of misidentification illustrate, the 'suspect community'
is not a fixed population, but rather is constructed in the *imagined fears of its
non-members* – in the securitised imagination of a fearful public (Breen-Smyth,
2014). This inverts Anderson's (1991) conceptualisation of an 'imagined community' as a grouping constructed in the imagination of their members. To be
considered one of a 'suspect community' it is not necessary to be a Muslim or
(previously) Irish. Rather, you only have to appear so to the security services
or a suspicious member of the public.

So, as distinct from Anderson's imagined community of nationalist identity,
where the individual imagines themselves into the community *ab initio*, members of this re-conceptualised suspect community 'discover' their membership
when suspicion is directed at them by the police, the media or a member of the
public. Unlike Anderson's national imagined community which 'regardless of
the actual inequality and exploitation that may prevail [. . .] is always conceived
as a deep, horizontal comradeship' (Anderson, 1991, p. 224), there is no auto-
matic solidarity between members of the suspect community. The racialised
public imagination is not limited to white people.

These processes of suspicion, consolidated by programmes such as Countering Violent Extremism (CVE), have the effect of instating and reinforcing
vertical lines of trust between government and a (non-suspect) population
while undermining horizontal lines of trust and solidarity between neigh-
bours in diverse communities. Government initiatives such as CVE that
encourage vigilance and the reporting of suspicious behaviour operate in a
wider context of a state-promoted 'hostile environment' that supports or
even lauds the often-violent and oppressive treatment of Black and ethnic
minorities and the stripping of racialised 'others' such as refugees and asylum seekers of rights to humanitarian treatment. Solidarity is based ultimately on trust of and loyalty to the state, not trust and care for our fellow
citizens.

De-radicalisation projects targeted particularly at young Muslims in the past
depended on 'culture talk' (Mamdani, 2002), whereby Islam was totalised and
demonised by thinking encapsulated in Huntingdon's (1996) *The Clash of Civilizations* (Mamdani, 2002, p. 766). More recently, the focus has been more

specifically on fundamentalisms associated with Salafi Islam (Alvi, 2014; Barton, 2018; Shavit and Andersen, 2016). Thereafter, the security forces aligned themselves with certain Muslim organisations and communities to isolate 'other' Muslims who supported 'terrorism' and to engage in a particular reading of Islam which justifies attacks on the Western infidel. Muslims were thus differentiated into 'good' and 'bad' Muslims.

To remain a 'good' Muslim, even mild commentary on foreign policy is too risky (see Mythen et al., 2009 on managing 'risky' identities) and makes for a form of Muslim quietism (Breen-Smyth, 2014). A 'good Muslim' must engage in specific forms of political performance, such as condemnation of violence by other Muslims or being 'responsibilised' into the role of ambassador for Islam (Mythen and Khan, n.d., p. 13).

According to David Anderson, the independent reviewer of terrorism laws, the UK's 2011 counter-terrorism 'Prevent' strategy and the 2015 Prevent duty which requires public authorities to have 'due regard to the need to prevent people from being drawn into terrorism' has disproportionately targeted Muslims. Prevent has thus become 'a significant source of grievance' among British Muslims, encouraging 'mistrust to spread and to fester' (Anderson, 2016). The targeting of Muslims has the effect of augmenting structural and cultural Islamophobia, according to Abbas (2018), which in turn amplifies both Islamist and far-right radicalisation. Goldberg (2006) asserts that the radicalised Muslim extremist 'other' functions as an unacknowledged racial reference whereby a form of racial ordering, endemic within policing and security operations, is imposed through a range of counter-terrorism measures that are laden with latent racism (Goldberg, 2009; Kapoor, 2013).

Security and citizenship

Counter-terrorism policies impact differentially the security and citizenship of the population. First, 'security' is implicitly presumed to be that of the dominant (white) population, so insecurities experienced by suspect communities are only a concern insofar as they might drive 'radicalisation'. Jarvis and Lister (2013) found that white participants in the UK viewed anti-terrorism measures as distanced from their everyday lives, whereas participants from ethnic minority backgrounds believed that anti-terrorism measures had reduced their rights, made them feel uneasy, made them vulnerable to arrest and detention, and that the measures contributed to increased racism. They found 'a widespread sense among ethnic minorities that it was *their* rights that were subject to curtailment'

(Jarvis and Lister, 2013, p. 667). Second, the perception that communities become 'suspect' – albeit often as 'invisible' citizens – is undermined. Rather, as Jamal and Naber (2008) argue, instead of citizens, they become 'visible subjects'. Thus, in a number of cases, the UK government has revoked the legal citizenship of British citizens under section 40 of the British Nationality Act 1981 on grounds of conduciveness to the public good.

Rise in Islamophobia and hate crime

In the UK, although crime in general has fallen, the Home Office reported that hate crime rose by 40% from 2016–2017 to 2017–2018, with 52% of all offences aimed at Muslims (Home Office, 2018a). In 2017, the UK agency Tell MAMA recorded a total of 1,201 verified reports of Islamophobia, 70% of which occurred offline, a 30% increase on 2016 (Tell MAMA, 2018).

The US Institute for Social Policy and Understanding reported that in 2017, 61% of US Muslims repeatedly experienced religiously based discrimination compared with less than 30% of other religious groups and the general public (World Economic Forum, 2018). Where Islamophobia is problematised, the problem is conceptualised as the alienation of Muslims as a driver for radicalisation, rather than the effects on its victims.

> Hateful rhetoric and discriminatory policies that target Muslims are morally wrong, factually inaccurate, and genuinely threaten the safety of Muslims in the United States . . . ISIS wants and needs the United States and other Western societies to alienate their Muslim populations . . . This is a stated goal of ISIS leadership. . . ISIS needs the West to alienate and marginalize its Muslim citizens . . . ISIS desperately needs new recruits in order to contend with its massive weakness . . . and its incredible unpopularity among Muslims in Muslim-majority countries . . .This is dangerous and deadly serious. And it must stop. (Gude, 2015)

A Brookings Institute paper on 'the real challenges posed to America by Islam' finds: 'Among these challenges, the most salient is the loyalty of Muslim Americans. This is *not* to suggest that Muslims are actively disloyal. Yet their loyalty to this nation is muddled' (Skerry, 2011). Islamophobia is used to 'explain' right-wing violence as 'reactive co-radicalization', an 'exclusionary reaction to the rising presence of Islam within otherwise secular, albeit nominally Christian, Western European and North American societies' and giving rise to the actions of violent white actors such as Anders Breivik (Pratt, 2015). Through this lens, white violence is seen as reactive and comparatively unproblematic – the 'real' problem is the violence of the 'other'. White violence is often construed variously as understandable if regrettable, perhaps even laudable, or as overreaction, or due to mental illness.

The current security threat

Europe and the UK

The threat is assessed in three categories: the overall threat from international terrorism; and the threat from Northern Ireland-based terrorism, broken down into threats within Northern Ireland and the threat to Great Britain. The threat level from international terrorism and Northern Ireland-based terrorism is considered 'severe' – meaning an attack is highly likely –while the threat to Great Britain is considered 'moderate', which means an attack is possible, but not likely. Although the MI5 account largely focuses on al Qaida and Islamist terrorism, it points out that:

> The majority of terrorist attack plots in this country have been planned by British residents. There are several thousand individuals in the UK who support violent extremism or are engaged in Islamist extremist activity. British nationals who have fought for extremist groups overseas continue to return to the UK, increasing the risk of terrorist attacks. Using skills acquired overseas, they may organise attacks under direction from outside the UK . . . While the majority of returners will not mount attacks in the UK, the large numbers involved mean it is likely that at least some of them will attempt to do so . . . Simple, self-organised attacks by UK-based Islamist extremists have increased and are inherently harder to detect than more complex and ambitious plots. (MI5, 2019)

Notwithstanding the focus on Muslims, MI5 is also concerned with 'domestic extremism', which it describes as 'individuals or groups that carry out criminal acts in pursuit of a larger agenda, such as 'right-wing extremists'. Notably, 'right-wing extremism' is rarely described as terrorism, a point to which we will return. In December 2018, the UK government's counter-radicalisation Prevent programme reported that 45% of those at risk of radicalisation and in need of intervention were referred due to 'Islamism', whereas 44% were referred due to 'right-wing extremism' – a 36% increase for right-wing extremism, while the figures for Islamism were on a downward trend (Home Office, 2018c).

UK police records of the 'ethnic appearance' of arrestees and the Home Office reported that 40% of all arrests connected to terrorism were of white people and 33% were of those of Asian appearance (Home Office, 2018b). The overall number of arrests fell in 2018; the largest decrease was for those of Asian ethnic appearance (46% decrease from the previous year) with a corresponding increase of 21% in the numbers of white people arrested, the second highest for whites since data collection began in 2001. The share of arrests that were white has steadily increased since 2002. Nevertheless, the image of the terrorist suspect persists as that of a brown person, a Muslim.

The US

In January 2019, Dan Coats, US Director of National Intelligence, told the US Congress that 'Terrorism remains a persistent threat and . . . is positioned to increase in 2019' and that ISIS and al Qaida's 'leaders work to strengthen their networks and to encourage attacks against Western interests' (Office of the Director of National Intelligence, 2019).

The data on attacks on US soil belie this assessment. The Anti-Defamation League's (ADL's) Center on Extremism (2019) reported that in 2018, 78% of attacks within the US were due to 'White Supremacy', a further 16% were due to 'anti-government extremism', 4% were due to 'incel extremism'[1] and only 2% were due to 'domestic Islamist extremism' (ADL, 2019). The fifty deaths due to domestic extremists in 2018 were a 'sharp increase' from the thirty-seven in 2017 and were 'overwhelmingly linked to right-wing extremism' and 'White supremacists were responsible for the great majority of the killings, which is typically the case. . . Five of the 17 incidents involved shooting sprees that caused 38 deaths and injured 33 people'. The ADL (2018a) reported that anti-semitic incidents increased by almost 60% in 2017, the largest increase since 1979. Jews (54.2%), followed by Muslims (24.8%), were the victims of these attacks, followed at some distance by Catholics (4.1%) (Federal Bureau of Investigation (FBI), 2017). The Southern Poverty Law Center (SPL) (2018) found that the number of hate groups in the US rose from 917 in 2016 to 953 in 2017 (SPL, 2018). The greatest increase was the 22% growth in neo-Nazi groups.

The 2017 fall semester saw a marked increase on US college campuses of white supremacist propaganda, including both at Ivy League schools and at community colleges. Identity Evropa (IE) was among the most prominent of the organisations involved. IE describes itself as an 'ethno-pluralist' group focused on the preservation of 'white American culture' and promoting white European identity. The ADL estimates that IE was responsible for 158 of the 346 incidents on campuses, or almost half of the total (ADL, 2018b).

The Quartz analysis of the Global Terrorism Database found that almost two-thirds of the terror attacks in the US in 2017 were 'tied to racist, anti-Muslim, homophobic, anti-Semitic, fascist, anti-government, or xenophobic motivations' (Romero, n.d.). Although there had been an overall decline in the number of terrorist attacks from 2014 to 2017, including a 40% decline in the Middle East, attacks in the US had increased from six in 2006 to sixty-five in 2018.

These included an attack on counter-protesters at a right-wing rally, as well as attacks on a gay bar and on mosques (Romero, n.d.).

The growth of the far right

From the end of the Cold War, right-wing movements have been on the rise. Merkl and Weinberg (1997) document how the collapse of Marxism provided the political space for the growth of right-wing movements in Eastern, Central and Western Europe and Africa. A growth in xenophobic tendencies fostered white nationalism, such as neo-Nazi movements in Europe and the US. Within mainstream politics, a corresponding shift to the right led to calls for the reinforcement of borders and the ending of free movement. The UK vote to leave the European Union – BREXIT – and the election of Donald Trump to the US Presidency further emboldened right-wing activists.

But this growth goes back further. In 2005, the FBI reported that right-wing groups articulating racial supremacy, anti-federalism and Christian fundamentalism had formed domestic militias and special interest groups. These had started 'to overtake left-wing extremism as the most dangerous, if not the most prolific, domestic terrorist threat to the country' (FBI, 2005). While roughly two-thirds of terrorism in the US between 1980 and 2001 was conducted by non-Islamic American extremists, it increased by 95% between 2002 and 2005 (FBI, 2005; Masters, 2011).

In the UK, Mark Rowley, the Metropolitan Police's head of anti-terrorism between 2014 and 2018, warned that the UK has not 'woken up' to the threat posed by the far right and pointed to the dangers of underestimating them: 'For the first time since the second world war we have a domestic terrorist group, it's right-wing, it's neo-Nazi, it's proudly white supremacist, portraying a violent and wicked ideology' (Busby, 2018). Earlier still, the West Yorkshire Chief Constable reported in 2009 that 300 weapons and 80 bombs had been recovered from right-wing extremists in two months of that year, the largest seizure of weapons in England since the IRA campaign of the early 1990s (Leppard, 2009).

Frank Gregory (2009) argued that the UK practice of labelling right-wing political violence as 'extremism' rather than terrorism was a 'gap' in the counter-terrorism strategy. It was not until December 2016 that the first far-right group, National Action, became the first to be declared a terrorist organisation in the UK. The UK Government (2015) defined extremism as:

> vocal or active opposition to fundamental British values, including democracy, the rule of law, individual liberty and mutual respect and tolerance of different faiths and beliefs. We also include in our definition of extremism calls for the death of members of our armed forces. (2015, para 7)

It goes on to explain that 'Islamist extremists regard Western intervention in Muslim-majority countries as a "war with Islam", creating a narrative of "them" and "us"' and that they believe 'that people cannot be both Muslim and British' and that they 'purport to identify grievances to which terrorist organisations then claim to have a solution' (UK Government, 2015). Although the threat to Great Britain sits at SUBSTANTIAL, and in Northern Ireland it is SEVERE, the document states that 'Dealing with the threat from Northern Ireland-related terrorism in Northern Ireland is the responsibility of the Secretary of State for Northern Ireland' and 'Most relevant policy areas are the responsibility of the devolved administration in Northern Ireland' (UK Government, 2015). The document mentions white supremacism and 'extreme right-wing terrorist acts', but offers no definitions. The first line of the summary states that 'The most serious [threat] is from Al Qa'ida, its affiliates and like-minded organisations'. When asked why Northern Ireland was not included an official is reported to have said, 'Don't push the issue too far. It is really a counter-Islamic strategy' (Versi, 2017).

In the US, the Patriot Act's 2001 definition of 'terrorism' includes domestic and international terrorism, yet by 2011 law enforcement agencies and the departments of Justice, Homeland Security and Defense used a range of 'sub-terrorist' labels – 'sub-national', 'pre-meditated', 'non-combatant' – to refer to far-right terrorism, while the FBI use the terms 'domestic terrorism' and 'violent extremism' interchangeably (Masters, 2011). This inconsistency in labelling violence resulted in a corresponding inconsistency in disposal of the offences, according to Masters. Agency policy, rather than the facts of the case, determined whether the prosecution was as a terrorist or not, determining whether or not they faced the harsher penalties for terrorism. Although Hoffman (2018) has suggested that this may be due to the higher evidentiary threshold and the consequent prolonged investigation in cases of terrorism, Norris (2017) points to the case of Dylann Roof who killed nine African Americans at a South Carolina church. Roof was not prosecuted as a terrorist, yet he could have been prosecuted as a domestic terrorist under federal law. The failure to prosecute him as a terrorist illustrates the bias in the operation of counter-terrorism.

The politics of minimising far-right terrorism

During the Bush administration, Homeland Security Secretary Janet Napolitano commissioned a Department of Homeland Security report, 'Rightwing Extremism' (Department of Homeland Security, 2009). The report found a political climate that contained 'unique drivers for right-wing radicalization and recruitment' and that 'lone wolves and small terrorist cells embracing violent right-wing extremist ideology are the most dangerous domestic terrorism threat in the

United States'. The report warned that veterans could be targeted by right-wing militias for recruitment.

Mainstream conservatives and veterans groups alleged that the report was an attack on conservative ideologies, on opponents of abortion and immigration, and conservative groups called for Napolitano's resignation. Republican lawmakers and veterans groups were particularly enraged by the passage suggesting that 'The possible passage of new restrictions on firearms and the return of military veterans facing significant challenges reintegrating into their communities could lead to the potential emergence of terrorist groups or lone-wolf extremists capable of carrying out violent attacks' (O'Keefe, 2009). The report was withdrawn.

The effects on countering far-wing extremism were far reaching. Following the report, the work of documenting domestic terror incidents and auditing activities of 'white supremacists' and 'Christian Identity' militants was ended. Two years later, the Department of Homeland Security (DHS) had still not conducted its own intelligence and analysis of home-grown extremism and had cut personnel studying domestic terrorism unrelated to Islam despite rising extremist threats (Smith, 2011). DHS also held back 'nearly a dozen reports' on extremist groups (Smith, 2011). One of the authors of a vilified report remarked that 'Other reports written by DHS about Muslim extremists ... got through without any major problems' (Smith, 2011). A majority of the eighty-six major foiled and executed terrorist plots in the US from 1999 to 2009 were unrelated to Muslim groups.

The DHS was subsequently given the right to veto all reports on domestic terrorism and reports were screened 'for politically sensitive phrases or topics that might be objectionable to certain groups' (Smith, 2011). As a result, far-right extremism and terrorism, largely the prerogative of white people, is not robustly policed, nor is it a focus of counter-terrorism operations.

Smith (2011) attributed these moves to the fact that it is the FBI, not the DHS, that is the lead on domestic terrorism, and to 'worries that aggressive intelligence operations could be seen as civil liberties violations', a worry that does not seem to extend to the civil liberties of Muslims. A DHS official claimed that:

> unlike international terrorism, there are no designated domestic terrorist groups. Subsequently, all the legal actions of an identified extremist group leading up to an act of violence are constitutionally protected and not reported on by DHS. (Smith, 2011)

Veterans

State security personnel in both the military and the police force have access to and are trained in the use of weapons and can use force, including lethal violence, legitimately on behalf of the state. That the police and the armed forces tend to lean to the right politically while possessing this skill-set would suggest their mutual attraction for right-wing groups. Complementing Napolitano's 2009 report pointing to the far right targeting the recruitment of veterans, a 2008 FBI intelligence assessment had found that: 'Some veterans of the conflicts in Iraq and Afghanistan have joined the extremist movement' and their engagement includes 'weapons violations, physical violence, paramilitary training, intelligence collection, drug violations, fraud, threats, and arson' (FBI, 2008). It also reported that:

> A review of FBI white supremacist extremist cases from October 2001 to May 2008 identified 203 individuals with confirmed or claimed military service active in the extremist movement at some time during the reporting period . . . the prestige which the extremist movement bestows upon members with military experience grants them the potential for influence beyond their numbers. Most extremist groups have some members with military experience, and those with military experience often hold positions of authority within the groups to which they belong. (FBI, 2008)

Military members of far-right groups had engaged in criminal behaviour as part of these groups, but:

> they have more often concentrated on recruiting and leadership roles within existing groups. These latter activities have the potential to reinvigorate a movement that has experienced stagnation or decline in recent years. (FBI, 2008)

Former government intelligence analyst Daryl Johnson (2012) reported that right-wing groups focus recruitment efforts on military and law enforcement personnel because of their skills with weapons and explosives and their access to weapons. Of 17,080 military personnel surveyed by the government, 3.5% had been approached to join an extremist organisation and a further 7.1% reported that they knew another soldier who they believed was a member of an extremist organisation (Johnson, 2012).

Similarly, Simi et al. (2013) propose that leaving the military involuntarily, feeling one's military contribution is not recognised or appreciated, may precipitate a shift in some veterans towards far-right extremism and eventually terrorism. Sterman (2013) examined the New America Foundation's dataset on 'homegrown extremists' which includes those indicted or involved in violent activities since 2001 (New America Foundation, 2019). He concluded that, although there is a risk from members of the military becoming jihadis,

> the threat pales in comparison with the threat from right-wing extremists with US military training . . . In contrast to the military-trained jihadist threat, the threat from right wing extremists with military training appears to be growing. About 70 percent of the right-wing extremists who have served in the military were indicted or were involved in an incident since the beginning of 2008 . . . They've committed . . . more than twice as many [attacks] as their jihadist

counterparts . . . About nine out of every ten military-trained right wing extremists obtained weapons . . . right-wing extremists who have served in the military
are by far the best-armed extremists threatening the American people . . . no
group appears to be quite as dangerous as right-wing, military-trained extremists . . . Right-wing extremist violence should be placed at the forefront of any
examination of extremism in the military. (Sterman, 2013)

Yet US counter-terrorism policy and practice remain focused on the Muslim
'other', even when the risk from veteran recruitment by white supremacists and
racists is clearly articulated. To bring attention to the role of veterans in far-right
violence is to run up against political roadblocks in the form of powerful hegemonic nationalist ideology about the role of 'our boys' the armed forces in 'keeping America safe'. Of course, it is within this very nationalist ideology that the
'other' is so easily identified, transformed into a 'suspect' and rendered a subject.
The role of US mainstream politics in protecting rather than policing white
supremacism and racism reinforces Goldberg's (2006) point about the racial
ordering of security, and illustrates how racism and Islamophobia inform that
ordering in both counter-terrorism policy and practice.

UK

Likewise, in 2017 the UK Green Party urged the British government to launch
an inquiry into far-right involvement within the British army following the
arrest of four British soldiers for membership of a banned far-right organisation
(Dearden, 2017). However, the UK Ministry of Defence (MoD) treated the
arrests as an isolated case and did not plan any further inquiries into extremism
within the army (Dearden, 2017). Jonathan Bartley of the Green Party com-
mented that this failure 'suggests it is afraid of what it will find' (Dearden, 2017).
Citing cases of other soldiers' involvement in far-right activities, Bartley said
that the UK government 'cannot bury its head in the sand and hope it will go
away' (Dearden, 2017).

Hope Not Hate, a UK based anti-extremist group, reported claims by a far-
right activist that he had helped ten far-right members infiltrate the British
Army (Hookham and Kerbaj, 2017). The right-wing English Defence League
(EDL) had an 'armed forces division' with a Facebook following in 2018 of over
thirteen thousand, including current or former servicemen and women
(www.facebook.com/edlarmedforcesdivision/). In 2018, during the prosecution
of a soldier recruiting for National Action within the British Army, the lack of
official concern about this trend became apparent. The MOD was unable to say
how many members of the armed forces had been disciplined for involvement in
far-right extremism up to December 2017 because checking the Royal Military
Police database would be prohibitively costly (*Telegraph*, 2018).

Law enforcement

A similar pattern is apparent within the police. As far back as 2006, the FBI warned that 'White supremacist infiltration of law enforcement' represented a significant national threat in the US (FBI, 2006). This history includes the 1990s case where a US District Court found that a neo-Nazi gang composed of members of a Los Angeles sheriff's department habitually terrorised the Black community (Thomas v. City of LA, 978 F.2d 504: 9th Cir. 1992; Tobar, 1991); detective and commander Jon Burge of the Chicago Police Department tortured over 100 Black male suspects in the 1980s; and two sheriff's deputies were found to be recruiting for the Ku Klux Klan (ABC News, 2001).

More recently, around seven San Francisco law enforcement officers were exchanging text messages about 'White Power' and 'lynching African Americans and burning crosses' (Williams, 2015); three correctional officers reported to be Klan members were arrested for conspiring to murder a Black inmate (Chasmar, 2015); and around four Fort Lauderdale police officers were found fantasising about killing Black suspects (Norman, 2015). Jones (2016) concludes that this state of affairs 'rouses ingrained notions of distrust between police and communities of color' and doubts the ability of law enforcement to robustly police far-right groups and individuals.

Likewise in the UK, in 2008 Ellis Hammond resigned as a Police Community Support Officer (PCSO) in London when a package addressed to him was found to contain an illegal Taser gun. Police raids on his home yielded a CS spray, a stun gun, combat knives, a knuckleduster, a replica AK-47, a British National Party (BNP) membership card and far-right literature. Police officers and PCSOs in the UK are banned from joining the BNP. Following his 'strangely lenient' sentence in court, the police were accused of failing to disclose his police links to the court (Foggo, 2008; Gable and Jackson, 2011). In the UK, there is no systematic information about any infiltration of the police by right-wing groups.

Far-right extremists not 'terrorists'?

The Muslim (or Irish) suspect as a colonial 'other' is automatically labelled a 'terrorist', yet the label is rarely – and only relatively recently – applied to right-wing actors. This has implications for those labelled as 'terrorists' since terrorism laws in the UK and the PATRIOT Act in the US specify the treatment of 'terrorist suspects' and more severe penalties for those convicted under such laws. Detention, deportation, removal of citizenship, rendition and house arrest are available for the disposal of 'terrorists' and those suspected of terrorism. By evading the label 'terrorism', white supremacism and far-right violence largely avoids these harsh penalties, which are thus reserved for Muslims and Irish Republicans. White supremacists, such as James Harris Jackson, who stabbed an African American man to death in New York in 2018 in what he claimed openly was the first of his planned acts of terror, is not labelled a 'terrorist' (Richards, 2018). Even when white supremacists and right-wing extremists are charged with terrorist offences, Hasan (2009), citing a range of such cases, found:

> It is as if these crimes had never happened. For most British journalists today, the idea of non-Muslim terrorism perpetrated by non-Irish white folk is inconceivable. Why? Because too many of them reflexively subscribe to the notion that maybe not all Muslims are terrorists, but certainly all terrorists are Muslims. (Hasan, 2009)

After the 2013 Boston Marathon bomb planted by two Chechen White males, before the identity of the bombers was known, American journalist David Sirota (2013) wrote:

> [If] the bomber ends up being a white anti-government extremist, white privilege will likely mean the attack is portrayed as just an isolated incident – one that has no bearing on any larger policy debates . . . (Sirota, 2013)

Sirota (2013) attributes this to 'white privilege at work to not only insulate whites from collective blame, but also to insulate the political debate from any fallout from the attack'. He observes that:

> It will probably be much different if the bomber ends up being a Muslim and/or a foreigner from the developing world . . . when those kind of individuals break laws in such a high-profile way, America often cites them as both proof that entire demographic groups must be targeted. . . (Sirota, 2013)

Mark Steyn (2013) responded by defending the profiling of Muslims, arguing that liberal failure to admit that Muslims are inherently dangerous left society vulnerable and constituted 'anti-white racism'. Watson et al. (2017) argue that this is how liberal multiculturalism is framed as culpable for terrorism within an argument for conservative hard-line approaches to terror attacks (by Muslims). Conservative pundits accuse liberals like Sirota of 'race treachery' and 'suicidal tolerance' in the context of the decline of the white majority in the United States (DiContio, 2013, cited in Watson et al., 2017).

Criminal justice agencies and the labelling of political violence

As right-wing violence and terror has increased with political shifts to the right, acts of terror performed by right-wing actors, usually white folks expressing racist or white supremacist politics, have latterly, in a number of cases, begun to be identified by the law enforcement agencies as terrorism. Law enforcement agencies pay a pivotal role in labelling a violent act as an act of terror and the actor as a terrorist. Practice is driven not merely by the available legal definitions and the agency's knowledge of these, but by the agency staff's level of knowledge and their attitudes and affiliations.

In the US, there is reason to question the ability of certain police departments and the officers within them to dispassionately handle both right-wing and Muslim suspects for three reasons. First, the culture and politics within police departments in relation to race and diversity; second, the links cited above between certain police officers and right-wing extremists; and third, the wider society's perception of brown people, Muslims and 'others' as the 'suspect community' and the primary or exclusive source of risk and danger and white folk as those exclusively threatened. This racialised construction of security is deeply embedded in imperial and settler colonial politics and the cultures of predominantly white police forces (some with far-right affiliations). The hegemonic view of threat emanating from the brown or exotic 'other' while white far-right militants are seen to be 'like us' leads to the far right being treated with undue leniency.

In the UK, there is little or no evidence on the political affiliations of the police, and in spite of the ban on police membership of certain organisations, there is continuing cause for concern about the kind of institutionalised racism and disproportionate policing of certain minority groups found twenty years previously in the Macpherson Report exploring institutional racism in the Metropolitan police, in the wake of Stephen Lawrence's murder and murder inquiry. More recently, the Deputy Chief Constable of the Avon and Somerset Police reported that the police did not have a good knowledge of right-wing groups and individuals, and 'to some extent, [there is] a complacent attitude about the extreme right within the Police service. It was seen as an irritant and not as a significant threat to community cohesion' (Gable and Jackson, 2011).

This complacency and the obstacles to addressing the pattern of proliferation of far-right violence has contributed to the practice of individualising violence by far-right actors. Chermak et al. (2010, p. 1030) examined how state police agencies in the US perceived threats including 'lone-wolf' crimes and concluded that 'far leftists and jihadists were less likely to be considered solely a lone wolf threat compared to far-right extremists and single-issue extremists'. The label 'lone wolf' or 'extremism' signals both a lower level of perceived threat and less serious consequences, a lack of knowledge by the authorities (Gable and Jackson, 2011) and a denial of a political trend towards increasing far-right extremism and violence.

The 'lone' (white) wolf

Spaaij and Hamm (2015) reviewed the academic literature on the 'lone-wolf' labelling of 'terrorists'. Gable and Jackson (2011) point out that far-right attackers are often explained as isolated (McCauley et al., 2013), mentally ill (Gruenewald et al., 2013; Hewitt, 2003), with frustrated ambitions (Rush, 1967) and with family problems rather than dangerous politically motivated actors. Far-right violent actors are seen as sick or misguided, latitude that is not available to the suspect 'other'.

An examination of the manifesto of Anders Behring Breivik, a so-called 'lone wolf' who killed seventy-seven people in two attacks in Norway in 2011, reveals that Breivik, like other 'lone wolves', was inspired by 'far-right' social movements (Berntzen and Sandberg, 2014). Yet it has often been assumed that singletons conducting violent attacks lack political motivation or connection to a cause (see also Pantucci, 2011; and Spaaij, 2011; Spaaij and Hamm, 2015). Gable and Jackson (2011) expose the myth that most far-right racist terrorism is the action of isolated individuals, showing that all the cases they examined had clear and often long-standing involvement with organised groups (see also Schuurman et al., 2017).

This 'lone-wolf' label helps those so-labelled to avoid the severe penalties meted out to 'terrorists'. When in 1986, IRA 'terrorists' were being handed multiple life sentences, extreme rightist Tony Lecomber was sentenced to three years in prison for an attempted bombing of a left-wing target in London (Gable and Jackson, 2011). The lone-wolf label shrinks the apparent size of the threat to one individual, ignoring any larger organisational or international connections, even though far-right politics possess all these features. The suggestion of mental illness portrays the (white) 'lone wolf' as sick – mad, rather than bad, more in need of help than punishment, more to be pitied than blamed, considerations rarely available to 'others'.

Race and the labelling of terrorism

According to Amal Abu-Bakare (2017):

> [T]he alleged unwillingness by state actors and media to unequivocally label a phenotypically white person as a 'terrorist' is historically connected to the global institutionalisation of white privilege, structural and hegemonic conditions of world politics which uphold white privilege. (Abu-Bakare, 2017)

Security, then, is the prerogative of those who deserve to be secured, and understood and managed through processes whereby the 'risk' is to a hegemonic white state and the majority-white population. This is consistent with the historical involvement of Western states in imperialism and colonialism and the set-tler-colonial nature of some more recent states allied to the West. 'Risk' is deemed to originate with the 'other', who is identified through the lens of power and politics, but also of race. 'Security' is not the security of the entire population, but rather the security of the dominant group and of the state itself. The security of minorities or 'others' is dispensable in the interests of this 'greater good'. The inevitability and toleration of the insecurity of the suspect 'other' effectively reinstates the dynamics of racial subordination. The toleration of far-right violence by law enforcement counter-terrorism efforts serves to reinforce this hegemonic racial order and give licence to violent far-right actors.

The suspect community is created in a securitised imagination characterised by hegemonic whiteness (Hughey, 2014). The racialised 'terrorist' suspect 'other' is perceived as a threat to the preciousness, vulnerability and superior entitle-ment to security of that whiteness. In this way, 'terrorism' as a political construct, the way the threat it poses is framed and managed, functions to consolidate and maintain a particular domestic and international order. Hegemonic notions of security replicate and rely on white supremacism and, in turn, white suprema-cism is integrated into common-sense and practitioner notions of security, both in terms of how Muslims are regarded as suspects, how Blacks are policed in the US and how the security of 'others' is exceptionalised.

Conclusions

Suspicion in the public imagination operates to determine which 'category of person' is more likely to be subject to counter-terrorism measures or to be con-sidered as a terrorist suspect. In February 2017, Donald Trump announced the rebranding of the US government programme 'Countering Violent Extremism'. He wished to specify the kind of extremism to be countered: 'Countering Islamic Extremism' or 'Countering Radical Islamic Extremism'. At a time when the vio-lence in the US of the far-right and white supremacists surpasses that from Isla-mism, far-right violence is explicitly not a focus of government intervention (Edwards Ainsley et al., 2017). During the Trump administration, it has become even clearer how contemporary security politics and states of insecurity are deployed in remaking and elaborating tropes of race in the project of ordering the Western military-industrial complex. International politics and world order is not only writ large on maps of the world, but writ smaller on domestic maps of changing national populations at a time when the politics of migration extends foreign wars into domestic relations.

Note

1   'Incel' is an abbreviation of 'involuntary celibate', an online network of largely white
     male heterosexuals, also referred to as the 'manosphere', who are united by their
     inability to find a romantic or sexual partner despite wishing to do so. They express
     entitlement to sex and direct blame at women for their deprivation of it. The
     Southern Poverty Law Center has described them as 'part of the online male
     supremacist ecosystem'. Those with Incel links have been responsible for at least four
     mass murders totaling 45 deaths in North America. Members are radicalised online.

References

Abbas, T., 2018. 'Implementing "Prevent" in countering violent extremism in the UK:
     A left-realist critique, *Critical Social Policy*, 39(3), 396–412.
ABC News, 2001. 'Texas officers fired for membership in KKK', *ABC News*, 20 June.
     Available at http://abcnews.go.com/US/story?id=93046 (19 February 2020).
Abu-Bakare, A., 2017. 'Why race matters: Examining "terrorism" through race in
     International Relations', *E-International Relations*, 9 May. Available at www.e-ir.
     info/2017/05/09/why-race-matters-examining-terrorism-through-race-in-
     international-relations/ (19 February 2020).
Ahmed, S., 2000. *Strange Encounters: Embodied Others in the Post-coloniality*.
     Routledge, London and New York.
Alvi, H., 2014. 'The diffusion of intra-Islamic violence and terrorism: The impact of the
     proliferation of Salafi/Wahhabi ideologies', *Middle East Review of International
     Affairs*, 18(2), 38–50.
Anderson, B., 1991. *Imagined Communities: Reflections on the Origin and Spread of
     Nationalism*. Verso, London.
Anderson, D., 2016. *Supplementary written evidence submitted by David Anderson Q.C.
     (Independent Reviewer of Terrorism Legislation). UK Parliament*. Available at http://
     data.parliament.uk/writtenevidence/committeeevidence.svc/evidencedocument/
     home-affairs-committee/countering-extremism/written/27920.pdf
ADL (Anti-Defamation League), 2018a. 'Anti-semitic incidents surged nearly 60% in
     2017, according to new ADL report'. Available at www.adl.org/news/press-releases/
     anti-semitic-incidents-surged-nearly-60-in-2017-according-to-new-adl-report
ADL (Anti-Defamation League), 2018b. 'ADL finds alarming increase in white
     supremacist propaganda on college campuses across US'. Available at www.adl.org/
     news/press-releases/adl-finds-alarming-increase-in-white-supremacist-propaganda-
     on-college-campuses
ADL (Anti-Defamation League), 2019. 'Murder and extremism in the US in 2018'.
     Available at www.adl.org/media/12480/download
Barton, G., 2018. 'Jihadi-Salafi terrorism and violent extremism in the era of al-Qaeda
     and the Islamic State', in Ireland, J.L., Birch, P. and Ireland, C.A. (eds), *The Routledge
     International Handbook of Human Aggression*. Routledge, London, pp. 376–387.

Berntzen, L.E., Sandberg, S., 2014. 'The collective nature of lone wolf terrorism: Anders Behring Breivik and the anti-Islamic social movement', *Terrorism and Political Violence*, 26(5), 759–779.

Breen-Smyth, M., 2014. 'Theorising the "suspect community": Counterterrorism, security practices and the public imagination', *Critical Studies on Terrorism*, 7(2), 223–240.

Busby, M., 2018. 'UK has not "woken up" to far-right threat, says ex-counter-terror chief', *Guardian*, 18 August. Available at www.theguardian.com/uk-news/2018/ aug/18/former-counter-terrorism-chief-says-uk-has-not-woken-up-to-far-right-threat

Chasmar, J., 2015. 'KKK-affiliated prison guards charged with plot to murder Black prison inmate', *The Washington Times*, 2 April. Available at www.washingtontimes. com/news/2015/apr/2/kkk-affiliated-corrections-officers-charged-with-p/ (accessed 19 February 2020).

Chermak, S.M., Freilich, J.D. and Simone, J. Jr., 2010. 'Surveying state police agencies about lone wolves, far-right criminality and far-right and jihadist criminal collaboration', *Studies in Conflict and Terrorism*, 33, 1019–1041.

Cushing, T., 2013. '"See something, say something" campaign creates massive database of useless info from citizens spying on each other', *Tech Dirt*, 25 September. Available at www.techdirt.com/articles/20130924/10470524637/ documents-obtained-aclu-show-fusion-centers-broad-surveillance-americans-everyday-activities.shtml

Dearden, L., 2017. 'Neo-Nazi arrests: Serving British soldiers held over terror offences as alleged members of National Action', *Independent*, 5 September. Available at www. independent.co.uk/news/uk/crime/neo-nazi-arrests-british-soldiers-army-national-action-terrorism-west-midlands-wales-plot-a7930181.html

Department of Homeland Security, 2009. *Rightwing Extremism: Current Economic and Political Climate Fueling Resurgence in Radicalization and Recruitment*. Available at https://fas.org/irp/eprint/rightwing.pdf

Edwards Ainsley, J., Volz, D. and Cooke, K., 2017. 'Exclusive: Trump to focus counter-extremism program solely on Islam – sources', *Reuters*, 2 February. Available at www.reuters.com/article/us-usa-trump-extremists-program-exclusiv/exclusive-trump-to-focus-counter-extremism-program-solely-on-islam-sources-idUSKBN15G5VO

Federal Bureau of Investigation, 2005. *Terrorism 2002–2005*. Available at www.fbi.gov/ file-repository/stats-services-publications-terrorism-2002–2005-terror02_05.pdf

Federal Bureau of Investigation, 2006. *White Supremacist Infiltration of Law Enforcement*. Available at www.documentcloud.org/documents/3439212-FBI-White-Supremacist-Infiltration-of-Law.html (accessed 19 February 2020).

Federal Bureau of Investigation, 2008. *White Supremacist Recruitment of Military Personnel since 9/11*. Available at https://documents.law.yale.edu/sites/default/files/ White%20Supremacist%20Recruitment%20of%20Military%20Personnel%20 Since%209-11-ocr.pdf

Federal Bureau of Investigation, 2017. *Uniform Crime Report: Hate Crime Statistics*, 2016. Available at https://ucr.fbi.gov/hate-crime/2016/topic-pages/ incidentsandoffenses.pdf

Foggo, D., 2008. 'Armed racist Ellis Hammond's police links "kept from court"', *The Times*, 5 October. Available at https://lancasteruaf.blogspot.com/2008/10/armed-racist-ellis-hammonds-police.html (accessed 19 February 2020).

Fried, R.A., 2015. 'No Irish need deny: Evidence for the historicity of NINA restrictions in advertisements and signs', *Journal of Social History*. Available at doi:10.1093/jsh/shv066 (accessed 19 February 2020).

Gable, G., Jackson, P., 2011. 'Lone wolves: Myth or reality?' *Searchlight*. Available at www.lonewolfproject.org.uk/

Goldberg, D.T., 2006. 'Racial Europeanization', *Ethnic and Racial Studies*, 29(2), 331–364.

Goldberg, D.T., 2009. *The Threat of Race: Reflections on Racial Neoliberalism*. Wiley-Blackwell, Oxford.

Gregory, F., 2009. 'CONTEST (2009): An evaluation of revisions to the UK counter-terrorism strategy with a special focus on the CBRNE threat (ARI)', El Cano Institute. Available at www.realinstitutoelcano.org/wps/portal/rielcano_en/contenido?WCM_GLOBAL_CONTEXT=/elcano/elcano_in/zonas_in/international+terrorism/ari130–2009 (accessed 19 February 2020).

Gruenewald, J., Chermak, S. and Freilich, J.D., 2013. 'Far-right lone wolf homicides in the United States', *Studies in Conflict & Terrorism*, 36(12), 1005–1024.

Gude, K., 2015. 'Anti-Muslim sentiment is a serious threat to American Security', *Center for American Progress*, 25 November. Available at www.americanprogress.org/issues/security/reports/2015/11/25/126350/anti-muslim-sentiment-is-a-serious-threat-to-american-security/

Hasan, M., 2009. 'Know your enemy', *New Statesman*, 9 July. Available at www.newstatesman.com/2009/07/mehdi-hasan-muslim-terrorism-white-british

Hewitt, C., 2003. *Understanding Terrorism in America: From the Klan to al Qaeda*. Routledge, New York.

Hickman, M.J., 1998. 'Reconstructing deconstructing "race": British political discourses about the Irish in Britain', *Ethnic and Racial Studies*, 21(2), 288–307.

Hickman, M., Silvestri, S. and Thomas, L., 2010a. 'A comparative study of representations of "suspect" communities in multi-ethnic Britain and of their impact on Muslim and Irish communities', *Economic and Social Research Council End of Award Report, RES-062-23-1066*. Available at www.esrc.ac.uk/my-esrc/grants/RES-062-23-1066/outputs/read/766adb4e-8698-4ae5-972d-798617a88553 (accessed 1 December 2013).

Hickman, M., Silvestri, S. and Thomas, L., 2010b. 'The construction of suspect communities in Britain 1974–2007: Comparing the impact on Irish and Muslim communities', Interim Report, ISET, London. Available at www.state watch.org/news/2011/may/uk-suspect-communities-first-findings.pdf (accessed 1 December 2013).

Hickman, M., Thomas, L., Nickels, H.C. and Silvestri, S., 2013. 'Social cohesion and the notion of "suspect communities": A study of the experiences and impacts of being "suspect" for Irish communities and Muslim communities in Britain', *Critical Studies on Terrorism*, 5(1), 89–106.

Hillyard, P., 1993. *Suspect Community: People's Experience of the Prevention of Terrorism Acts in Britain*. Pluto Press in association with Liberty/NCCL, London.

Hoffman, B., 2018. 'Mail bombs, hate crimes, and the meaning of terrorism', *Council on Foreign Relations*, 30 October. Available at www.cfr.org/article/mail-bombs-hate-crimes-and-meaning-terrorism

Home Office, 2018a. *Hate Crime, England and Wales, 2017/18, Statistical Bulletin, 20/18*, 16 October. Available at https://assets.publishing.service.gov.uk/government/uploads/system/uploads/attachment_data/file/748598/hate-crime-1718-hosb2018.pdf

Home Office, 2018b. *Operation of Police Powers under the Terrorism Act 2000 and Subsequent Legislation: Arrests, Outcomes, and Stop and Search, Great Britain, Quarterly Update to September 2018, Statistical Bulletin 29/18*, 6 December. Available at https://assets.publishing.service.gov.uk/government/uploads/system/uploads/attachment_data/file/762046/police-powers-terrorism-sep2018-hosb2918.pdf

Home Office, 2018c, December 13. *Individuals Referred to and Supported through the Prevent Programme, April 2017 to March 2018, Statistical Bulletin 31/18*, 13 December. Available at https://assets.publishing.service.gov.uk/government/uploads/system/uploads/attachment_data/file/763254/individuals-referred-supported-prevent-programme-apr2017-mar2018-hosb3118.pdf

Hookham, M., Kerbaj, R. 2017. 'Neo-Nazis on the march as up to 10 extremists infiltrate army', *The Sunday Times*, 10 September. Available at www.thetimes.co.uk/article/neo-nazis-on-the-march-as-up-to-10-extremists-infiltrate-army-h6s5ksjkt

Hughey, M.W., 2014. 'White backlash in the "post-racial" United States', *Ethnic and Racial Studies*, 37(5), 721–730.

Huntingdon, S., 1996. *Clash of Civilizations and the Remaking of World Order*. Simon and Schuster, New York.

Jamal, A.A., Naber, N. (eds), 2008. *Race and Arab Americans before and after 9/11: From Invisible Citizens to Visible Subjects*. Syracuse University Press, Syracuse, NY.

Jarvis, L, Lister, M., 2013. 'Disconnected citizenship? The impacts of anti-terrorism policy on citizenship in the UK', *Political Studies*, 61, 656–675.

Johnson, D., 2012. *Right Wing Resurgence: How a Domestic Terrorist Threat Is Being Ignored*. Rowman & Littlefield Publishers, New York.

Jones, S.V., 2016. Law enforcement and white power: An FBI report unraveled, *Thurgood Marshall Law Review*, 41(1), 99–104.

Kapoor, N., 2013. 'The advancement of racial neoliberalism in Britain', *Ethnic and Racial Studies*, 36(6), 1028–1046.

Leppard, D., 2009. 'Bomb seizures spark far-right terror plot fear', *The Sunday Times*, 5 August.

McCauley, C., Moskalenko, S. and Van Son, B., 2013. 'Characteristics of lone-wolf violent offenders: A comparison of school attackers and assassins', *Perspectives on Terrorism*, 7(1), 4–24.

Mamdani, M., 2002. 'Good Muslim, bad Muslim: A political perspective on culture and terrorism', *American Anthropologist*, 104(3), 766–775.

Masters, J., 2011. 'Militant extremists in the United States', *Council on Foreign Relations*, 7 February. Available at www.cfr.org/backgrounder/militant-extremists-united-states

Merkl, P., Weinberg, L., 1997. *The Revival of Right Wing Extremism in the Nineties*. Routledge, Abingdon.

MI5, 2019. *International Terrorism*. Available at www.mi5.gov.uk/international-terrorism

Mythen, G. and Khan, F., n.d. 'Futurity, governance and the terrorist risk: Exploring the impacts of pre-emptive modes of regulation on young Muslims in the UK'. Available at www.kent.ac.uk/scarr/events/beijingpapers/Mythenppr.pdf (accessed 1 November 2013).

Mythen, G., Walklate, S. and Khan, F., 2009. 'I'm a Muslim, but I am not a terrorist: Victimization, risky identities and the performance of safety', *British Journal of Criminology*, 49, 736–754.

New America Foundation, 2019. *Terrorism in America since 9/11*. Available at www.newamerica.org/in-depth/terrorism-in-america/what-threat-united-states-today/

Nickels, H.C., Thomas, L., Hickman, M.J. and Silvestri, S. 2012. 'Constructing suspect communities and Britishness: Mapping British press coverage of Irish and Muslim communities, 1974–2007', *European Journal of Communication*, 27(2), 135–151.

Norman, B., 2015. 'Girlfriend: Fort Lauderdale police officer idolized 'Django Unchained' slave master', LOCAL 10 NEWS, 24 March. Available at www.local10.com/news/2015/03/24/girlfriend-fort-lauderdale-police-officer-idolized-django-unchained-slave-master/ (accessed 19 February 2020).

Norris, J.J., 2017. 'Why Dylann Roof is a terrorist under Federal Law and why it matters', *Harvard Journal of Law*, 30 March. Available at https://papers.ssrn.com/sol3/Delivery.cfm/SSRN_ID2752517_code1505875.pdf?abstractid=2752517&mirid=1 (accessed 19 February 2020).

O'Keefe, E., 2009. 'Napolitano comments on "right wing extremist" report', *Washington Post*, 15 April. Available at http://voices.washingtonpost.com/federal-eye/2009/04/napolitano_comments_on_right_w.html

Office of the Director of National Intelligence, 2019. *Annual Threat Assessment: Opening Statement*, 29 January. Available at www.dni.gov/files/documents/Newsroom/Testimonies/2019-01-29-ATA-Opening-Statement_Final.pdf

Pantazis, C., Pemberton, S., 2009. 'From the "old" to the "new" suspect community: Examining the impacts of recent UK counter-terrorism legislation', *British Journal of Criminology*, 49, 646–666.

Pantucci, R., 2011. 'What have we learned about lone wolves from Anders Behring Breivik?', *Perspectives on Terrorism*, 5 December 2011. Available at www.terrorismanalysts.com/pt/index.php/pot/article/view/what-we-have-learned/html (accessed 19 February 2020).

Pratt, D., 2015. 'Islamophobia as reactive co-radicalization', *Islam and Christian–Muslim Relations*, 26(2), 205–218.

Richards, K., 2018. 'White supremacist told police he stabbed Timothy Caughman to death as "practice" for larger race terror attack', *Independent*, 21 September. Available at www.independent.co.uk/news/world/americas/james-harris-jackson-timothy-caughman-baltimore-stabbing-ny-times-square-racist-attack-a8549011.html

Romero, L., n.d. 'Attackers in US terror incidents in 2017', *Quartz*. Available at www.theatlas.com/charts/rkN8tZz8m

Rush, G., 1967. 'Status consistency and right-wing extremism', *American Sociological Review*, 32(1), 86–92.

Schuurman, B., Lindekilde, L., Malthaner, S., O'Connor, F., Gill, P. and Bouhana, N., 2017. 'End of the lone wolf: The typology that should not have been', *Studies in Conflict & Terrorism*, 42(8), 771–778.

Shavit, U., Andersen, S., 2016. 'Can Western Muslims be de-radicalized?', *Middle East Quarterly*, Fall 2016. Available at www.meforum.org/MiddleEastForum/media/MEFLibrary/pdf/6272.pdf

Simi, P., Bubolz, B.F. and Hardman, A., 2013. 'Military experience, identity discrepancies, and far right terrorism: An exploratory analysis', *Studies in Conflict & Terrorism*, 36(8), 654–671.

Sirota, D., 2013. 'Let's hope the Boston Marathon bomber is a white American', *Salon Magazine*, 16 April. Available at www.salon.com/2013/04/16/lets_hope_the_boston_marathon_bomber_is_a_white_american/

Skerry, P., 2011. 'The Muslim-American muddle', *Brookings Institute*, 7 September. Available at www.brookings.edu/articles/the-muslim-american-muddle/

Smith, R.J., 2011. 'Homeland Security Department curtails home-grown terror analysis', *Washington Post*, 7 June. Available at www.washingtonpost.com/politics/homeland-security-department-curtails-home-grown-terror-analysis/2011/06/02/AGQEaDLH_story.html?utm_term=.8a3dcf7c0363

Southern Poverty Law Center, 2018. *Hate Groups*. Available at www.splcenter.org/hate-map

Southern Poverty Law Center, 2019. *Hate Groups*. Available at www.splcenter.org/hate-map

Spaaij, R., 2011. *Understanding Lone Wolf Terrorism: Global Patterns, Motivations and Prevention*. Springer, New York.

Spaaij, R., Hamm, M.S., 2015. 'Key issues and research agendas in lone wolf terrorism', *Studies in Conflict & Terrorism*, 38, 167–178.

Sterman, D., 2013. 'The greater danger: Military-trained right-wing extremists', *The Atlantic*, 24 April. Available at www.theatlantic.com/national/archive/2013/04/the-greater-danger-military-trained-right-wing-extremists/275277/

Steyn, M., 2013. 'The "co-exist" bombers', *National Review*, 19 April. Available at www.nationalreview.com/article/346146/co-exist-bombers-mark-steyn

Telegraph, 2018. 'Army veteran worked for neo-Nazi group recruiting active soldiers', 12 November. Available at www.telegraph.co.uk/news/2018/11/12/serving-army-afghan-veteran-recruiter-neo-nazi-terrorists-targeting/

Tell MAMA, 2018. *Beyond the Incident: Outcomes for Victims of Anti-Muslim Prejudice. Annual Report for 2017*. Available at https://tellmamauk.org/wp-content/uploads/2018/07/EXECUTIVE-SUMMARY.pdf

Thomas v. City of LA, 978 F.2d 504 (9th Cir. 1992), *amended* 1993 U.S. App. LEXIS 2165 (9th Cir. 1993).

Tobar, H., 1991. 'Deputies in "neo-Nazi" gang, judge found: Sheriff's department: Many at Lynwood office have engaged in racially motivated violence against Blacks and Latinos, jurist wrote', *Los Angeles Times*, 12 October. Available at http://articles.latimes.com/1991–10–12/local/me-107_1_deputy-county

UK Government, 2011. *Prevent Strategy June 2011*. Available at https://assets.publishing.service.gov.uk/government/uploads/system/uploads/attachment_data/file/97976/prevent-strategy-review.pdf

UK Government, 2015. *Revised Prevent Duty Guidance for England and Wales: Guidance for specified authorities in England and Wales on the duty in the Counter-Terrorism and Security Act 2015 to have due regard to the need to prevent people from*

being drawn into terrorism. Revised 15 July 2015. Available at www.gov.uk/government/
publications/prevent-duty-guidance/revised-prevent-duty-guidance-for-england-
and-wales (accessed 19 February 2020).

Versi, M., 2017. 'The latest Prevent figures show why the strategy needs an independent
review', *Guardian*, 10 November. Available at www.theguardian.com/
commentisfree/2017/nov/10/prevent-strategy-statistics-independent-review-home-
office-muslims

Watson, J., Selod, S. and Kibria, N., 2017. 'Let's hope the Boston Marathon Bomber is a
White American': Racialising Muslims and the politics of white identity', *Identities:
Global Studies in Culture and Power.* Available at https://doi.org/10.1080/10702
89X.2017.1397964 (accessed 19 February 2020).

Williams, T., 2015. 'San Francisco police officers to be dismissed over racist texts',
New York Times, 3 April. Available at www.nytimes.com/2015/04/04/us/san-
francisco-police-officers-to-be-dismissed-over-racist-texts.html (accessed
19 February 2020).

World Economic Forum, 2018. 'Islamophobia is driving more US Muslims to become
politically engaged, suggests report', 10 August. Available at www.weforum.org/
agenda/2018/08/muslims-in-united-states-more-politically-engaged-islamophobia/

5

The personal is political: feminist critiques of countering violent extremism

Jessica Auchter

Introduction

Countering Violent Extremism (CVE) programmes offer an alternative to conventional 'hard' approaches to terrorism prevention, focused on community responsibility for radicalisation, and community engagement as a strategy for law enforcement. Indeed, one of the key differences between CVE and counterterrorism is CVE's focus on the home as the origination site of the terrorist threat. While counter-terrorism refers to a myriad of practices including the use of military force, CVE programmes have as their hallmark a focus on local-level solutions within communities, based on the assumption that extreme ideology can be noticed by communities and thus individuals can be caught before they carry out violent acts, as long as their communities are on the alert for the warning signs of extremist ideology.

Specifically, CVE programmes re-characterise the very idea of threat and its origins. As noted in a recent report on CVE, 'European authorities have begun to describe their efforts using the language of "safeguarding." Radicalisation is presented as a problem like gang recruitment, drugs, or paedophilia – and thus community leaders and teachers have a duty to report cases of young people falling prey to such a social ill' (Vidino and Hughes, 2015, p. 2). US reports similarly use the language of 'support' and invoke the community level of response.[1] Thus, terrorism itself is no longer the threat to be addressed; rather, home-grown ideological extremism that leads to terrorist violence is the threat that needs to be targeted. In this vein, rather than the agency we associate with terrorists, those vulnerable to radicalisation are depicted as sharing characteristics that render them easy prey, thus removing their agency from the radicalisation process. The radicalisation process is often referred to using language that invokes brainwashing, perhaps because it makes 'us' feel better to know that in 'our' communities, there is no rational or political reason to become a terrorist recruit, only social and psychological vulnerabilities. As a result, CVE programmes focus on the components of the personal lives of individuals and communities in ways that are normally outside the purview of traditional security politics.

As an American FBI memo on CVE describes, the programme focuses on 'developing a community-led committee who will share the responsibility to provide an off ramp in order to discourage individuals from going down the path of targeted violence' (Federal Bureau of Investigation, 2015, p. 3). This community focus shifts the location of security operations from the public realm (often foreign lands) to the private realm (the 'homeland' and, even more specifically, the 'home' itself), thus blurring the lines between public and private. As the very idea of public and private realms is a highly gendered notion, paying attention to the gendered dynamics of such a blurring can shed insights on CVE and offer up critiques of its assumptions. Beyond this, as of 2014, women's participation in CVE has been explicitly part of the UN's global counter-terrorism strategy, as well as being taken up by country-level CVE programmes around the world. As described in a recent research report on women in CVE, 'The 2016 Secretary General's UN Action Plan on PVE also importantly included a pillar dedicated to the role of women and girls and gender equality in increasing PVE efforts' (Idris and Abdelaziz, 2017, p. 2). That is, CVE draws both implicitly and explicitly on gendered dynamics, so it is worthwhile examining CVE from a feminist perspective.

Following on the feminist assertion that the personal is political, this chapter uses the focus of CVE programmes on the personal lives of individuals as an opening to offer critiques. Specifically, it argues that CVE programmes are problematic because they are gendered, based on poor evidence, ineffective and self-fulfilling. By focusing on the way CVE instrumentalises the private realm as a realm of security politics and security theatre, I demonstrate how CVE programmes function more broadly as part of the governmentality of society in constructing gendered, liberal subjects. CVE turns the public/private distinction on its head because it is premised on the notion that the security threat derives from the private realm and, indeed, can only be countered there. Since the home has often been considered the purview of women, such discourses place women in the position of responsible actors for ensuring successful counter-radicalisation. I examine this by telling two stories: first, of the way women's liberation exists as a subnarrative of the focus on the home lives of potential Islamic terrorists, and second, in the way CVE focuses on the community, it focuses on countering recruitment strategies, which in the case of female recruits focuses on their vulnerability to potential exploitation. I use these stories to explore the gendered logic of CVE in the way it renders the site of the home subject to security management.

Prevailing understandings of gender and violence

Before unpacking CVE programmes, it bears laying out some of the underlying assumptions that structure the understandings I examine here. Much of the media and policymaking approach to the issue of gender takes the form of the umbrella of the Women, Peace, and Security Agenda (WPS). The components of this agenda focus on women's inclusion in peacebuilding and the 'mounting evidence that women are powerful actors in sustaining peace in their communities and nations'.[2] WPS also draws attention to how 'terrorists and extremist groups manipulate prevailing gender norms and gender stereotypes to advance their agenda and drive recruitment',[3] focusing in a contemporary context on the increased recruitment of foreign terrorist fighters by organisations such as ISIS. That is, the way CVE programmes utilise gender framings is a direct result of their reliance on a larger gendered framework that equates womanhood and peace, masculinity and threat, and tends to label women as victims of men's agency, while men are labelled as the aggressors of violence. While the following two sections illustrate what this looks like in the context of CVE programmes, this section describes some of the theoretical underpinnings at stake here.

Such an agenda relies on understandings from older versions of feminism that sought to argue that women's place at the table could offer a perspective oriented towards peacemaking, and in the 1980s and 1990s even led to arguments that the US should consider drafting women into the military in the interests of peace (Ruddick, 1983). Linda Forcey writes that 'as we all know, the connection between women and peace is ancient' (Forcey, 1994, p. 355). Her argument is also that women's agency is to be found in striving for peace. Some scholars emphasise the peculiar characteristic of women as especially peaceful, and that peace is necessary for women to have their issues recognised (Alonso, 1993; Brock-Utne, 1985; Caldicott, 1984; Ruddick, 1983). Others stress that if women were in power, the world would be more peaceful, essentially delineating peace as a woman's realm while war is a man's, such as Francis Fukuyama's argument that 'as women gain power in these countries, they should become less aggressive, adventurous, competitive, and violent' (Fukuyama, 1998, p. 27). Even Kofi Annan seemed to take this perspective in a speech as UN Secretary General on International Women's Day in 2001. He argued that women should participate fully in the resolution of conflicts, and characterised this as the 'credo for a more peaceful millennium' (Annan, 2001), invoking a causal connection between women's participation and peace.

While women's participation in political processes is a laudable goal, the links drawn between women and peace also naturalise connections between masculinity and violence (Zine, 2006, p. 31). Margaret Randall, for example, states that 'violence, like all other human interaction, is gendered: women and children are most often its victims, men or male-controlled states their victimisers' (Randall, 1993, p. 1). Cynthia Enloe has offered a critique of the naturalisation of this perspective, noting that 'Men are just naturally those who wield violence, whether that violence is organised by the state or by non or anti-state actors. . . "naturally" is a powerful and dangerous notion. It informs a lot of political narrative building when men are the actors' (Enloe, 2006, p. viii). Some of this argument draws on biological dimensions: Brigitte Nacos describes a study published in an American news magazine which linked terrorism to male hormones. The study stated that testosterone has a lot to do with terrorism (Nacos, 2005, p. 435). As a result of this, two focal points emerge: first, the inability to conceptualise female terrorists as agents of their own decisions, and second, the focus on women as the community solution to radicalisation, which I take up in the remainder of the chapter.

To briefly discuss the first component, terrorist groups, especially Islamic ones, are often described as male institutions driven by masculine aggressiveness. This perspective argues that institutions of violence are the institutions of men, and epiphenomenal to their agency. Militarism is equated with patriarchy, therefore linking any military action with male-ness. This excludes the possibility of women participating in the military or in violent action without having been seduced or brainwashed into it, contextualising in advance our understandings of recruitment and extremism. The extreme of this logic is exemplified by the response Carolyn Nordstrom encountered when she presented her research on the participation of women in violence: 'People from the audience stood up, incensed, to challenge my data. "How can you say that women were involved in violence?". . . "Females don't join mobs, they are only assaulted by them!". . . It did not matter that I had witnessed these events personally, talked to the people involved' (Nordstrom, 2005, p. 400).

Female terrorists, then, are viewed as interlopers in a male domain, a mechanism of justification for the fact that we cannot fit their participation in a linear correlation between gender and terrorist violence. As Brigitte Nacos argues, female terrorists are framed in a similar manner as women politicians. Stereotypes, essentially discourses of what is normal, are similar in the depiction of both female legitimate political actors (politicians) and female illegitimate political actors (terrorists). Women are framed in the media according to the way they look, in striking contrast to their actions, as if we cannot conceive of a beautiful woman engaging in violence. She argues that perception of terrorism as the domain of men and the pattern of social gender stereotypes which leads us to be surprised when women participate in terrorism limit our understanding of the topic (Nacos, 2005). As I have noted elsewhere (Auchter, 2012), when it comes to terrorism, media and scholarship tend to portray women as victims of the male-dominated system of terrorism and violence in general.

Such gendered understandings of violence, terrorism and extremism can be found in CVE programmes; this is the basis of the critique I pose here. As an Organization for Security and Co-operation in Europe (OSCE) report from 2013 (p. 5) notes, 'the misconception that women are not involved in violent extremism or terrorist radicalisation has often shaped counter-terrorism strategies, exacerbating women's exclusion from decision making processes and their significant underrepresentation among law enforcement officers and security personnel'. The remainder of the chapter draws on this elaboration of gender essentialisms to examine how they circulate in rhetoric about security and countering extremisms in CVE programmes.

CVE as a means to women's liberation

In 2015, the UN Security Council passed Resolution 2242, which focused on the importance of women and youth in CVE. It calls on member states 'to ensure the participation and leadership of women and women's organisations in developing strategies to counter terrorism and violent extremism'.[4] The specificity of calls for women's involvement invokes a discourse of women's empowerment associated with CVE programmes. In short, women's liberation forms an undercurrent to the techniques of CVE regimes. That is, extremists and extremism are posited as threats not only because of the possibility of violence, but threats to cultural identity via 'antiquated and primitive' views on gender roles, and threats to Muslim women within their own households. Thus, identifying and arresting extremists becomes necessary for the liberation of 'their' women as well, a narrative that Gayatri Spivak has referred to as white men (and women) saving brown women from brown men (Spivak, 1993, p. 93).

This section seeks to illustrate two things in turn: first, how women's empowerment has become part and parcel of CVE programmes and their design, and second, how CVE programmes equate womanhood with peacemaking, in the model of the narratives I explored in the previous section. In illustrating these processes, it seeks to draw attention to the way in which CVE programmes draw on gender essentialisms that label the home as a feminine site to reinforce women's roles in their own communities to be peacemakers.

The focus on the need for women's participation in CVE programmes reinforces the division between hard and soft counter-terrorism and seems to imply that now that counter-terrorism is adopting soft, community-oriented methods that operate in the private realm, the spaces have opened for women's participation. That is, the call for women's participation draws on gender essentialisms that equate women and the home. This is a problematic reification of the gendered nature of the public/private distinction, which holds women responsible for their communities because of a presumed maternal inclination towards care at the community level.

Women's empowerment in CVE

In addition to the aforementioned UN Security Council Resolution, international organisations, states and research centres almost unanimously call for women's participation in CVE programmes specifically. In 2013, an OSCE report noted women's 'special potential' in countering extremism (OSCE, 2013, p. 3). As another example, the Global Center on Cooperative Security in 2016 issued a report entitled 'A Man's World? Exploring the Roles of Women in Countering Terrorism and Violent Extremism' (Chowdhury et al., 2016). With sections titled 'A New Security Architecture: Mothers Included!' and 'Preventing and Countering Violent Extremism (CVE): The Role of Women and Women's Organisations', the report clearly focuses on how women are uniquely positioned for involvement with CVE programmes.

That is, women's empowerment and discourses about women's rights are entangled with CVE programmes, as CVE discourses note the unique potential of women's empowerment for countering extremism in their own communities. In this same narrative, women's rights act as an undercurrent for tactics for identifying extremist ideology in CVE programmes, sustaining a narrative that Islamic extremists don't respect women's rights and systematically disempower women through their religious ideology, while the societies from which CVE programmes emerge are engaged in the promotion of women's rights and women's empowerment.

As a Global Counterterrorism Forum (GCTF) best-practices document outlines, 'the promotion and protection of women's rights and gender equality needs to underlie CVE programs and strategies' (GCTF, 2016, p. 2). The report notes that in order to integrate women and girls practically into CVE programmes, there must be a larger context of 'broader guarantees of the human rights of women and girls in particular' (GCTF, 2016, p. 2). Indeed, much of CVE programming has the underlying message of women's empowerment.

General John Allen, for example, notes that empowering women makes 'them a force to reduce the reality of radicalisation', and calls attention to the education programmes for women that the US ran in Afghanistan as part of its fight against the Taliban (Council on Foreign Relations, 2016). Indeed, a common CVE programme overseas involves teaching women English. As McCants and Watts (2012) note, this may be a worthy action, but there is no evidence that it has any impact on support for terrorism. Beyond this, there is a concern that if women's rights and empowerment are viewed as a means to the end of national security via a CVE framework, that makes them 'amenable to bartering', according to Jayne Huckerby (Council on Foreign Relations, 2016). This has been one of the concerns related to the Afghan government negotiating with the Taliban: that women's rights will be sacrificed for political considerations.

That is, while women's empowerment is an underlying narrative of CVE programmes, there is a complex narrative at work here. First of all, this narrative succeeds largely because of the base assumption that in communities vulnerable to radicalisation, women are not already agents and are not considered equals. This appears, as one example, in discussion of the prevalence of domestic violence backgrounds in lone-wolf attackers, with the idea that conflict is a manifestation of unequal power relations and gender inequality.[5] While it is worth paying attention to connections between domestic violence and other forms of violence, the way these connections are presented seemingly naturalises an assumption that perpetrators of terrorism have backwards ideas of gender equality. The idea that CVE programmes can empower women rests on the notion that within their communities currently they are powerless to resist the forces of radicalisation. In many cases, women and men both are already attempting to resist recruitment and radicalisation, whether the communities be in the US, Europe, Afghanistan or elsewhere.

The focus on women's empowerment is based on numerous studies that indicate the importance of gender equality in resisting extremism. As Phumzile Mlambo-Ngcuka and Radhika Coomaraswamy (2015) note,

> overwhelming evidence from around the world shows that women's empowerment is a powerful force for economic growth, social and political stability, and sustainable peace. Gender equality and women's participation in the workforce and income generation are linked to higher GDP per capita; equal access to land and other agricultural inputs can increase agricultural productivity and slash world hunger; and involving women in peacebuilding strongly increases the probability that violence will end. It is no coincidence that in societies and communities where gender equality indicators are higher, women are less vulnerable to the impacts of violent extremism.

The issue becomes when such evidence is utilised to reinforce assumptions about Muslim communities in particular being more prone to gender inequality, or when women's empowerment becomes simply a mechanism for advancing larger security goals. Under this narrative, Muslim communities are targeted for CVE programmes because they are viewed as vulnerable to radicalisation, but defending Islam against those who view it as mistreating women can itself identify one as a potential extremist.

As an example, Katerina Papatheodorou (2018) tells a story of what she refers to as the successful outcomes of a CVE-type programme in Denmark:

> Jamal was suspended from school following a fight with a classmate who said that Islam mistreats women and terrorises Westerners. During his suspension, Jamal's mother passed away, something he attributed to the anxiety induced by the investigation. After her death, Jamal began associating with a group of Anwar al-Awlaki fans who spent their days fantasising about jihad and planning their trip to Syria. A police officer working for the municipality's prevention program contacted Jamal who, though initially resistant, eventually agreed to join the program. Now, Jamal credits the program with saving his life and helping him feel more Danish, declaring: 'I'm lucky I got that phone call'.

There are several interesting narratives at play here. First, the very reason why Jamal was identified in the first place was that he argued that Islam does not mistreat women. Thus, standing up for women's equality within the context of his own religion, because it was a defence of Islam, led Jamal to be viewed as suspicious, even though he was advancing the very same ideas of women's empowerment that CVE programmes seek to cultivate. Second, it seems as though it is precisely the investigation into his potential extreme ideologies that led Jamal to become radicalised in the first place, one of the key critiques of CVE. In this sense, CVE has a self-fulfilling character in producing the radical. Third, and relevant for my purposes here in this chapter, is how the story relies on an undercurrent of women's liberation and on Jamal's vulnerability precisely because he did not have his mother as a moderating effect after she passed away. This invokes gender essentialisms that presume connections between men and violence and women and peacemaking. Beyond this, community care is equated with nationalism and national identity, where if only mothers taught their children how to 'feel Danish', and community leaders stepped in where mothers were not present, extremism would no longer be an issue.

It should also be noted that the emphasis on women's empowerment that we see in CVE discourses focuses on a particular type of woman: woman-as-moderate and woman-as-moderating. In this vein, Jamal is in need of moderating because of the lack of maternal influence in his life. But, also, the woman who is posited as key to countering extremism is the 'moderate woman'. The invocation of this figuration relies on patriarchal norms that posit inherent links between women and peace, but that also posit a particular type of women's empowerment. Women are not empowered to lead, but rather empowered to solve problems only in their own communities, reifying the public/private distinction that feminists have pointed to as problematic. In this vein, women's empowerment becomes part and parcel of the construction of moderate liberal democracy, in which women still reside in the private realm. CVE's focus on women's empowerment masks the inequality inherent in this notion that women should be empowered to fix problems in their own home and communities through their role as moderates and moderating influences.

The stereotype of peaceful women

CVE focuses on women's agency only insofar as it equates womanhood with peacemaking. As Szmania (2015) notes,

> policymakers and practitioners involved in countering violent extremism (CVE) have taken great interest in better understanding the role that women play in terrorism prevention. However, this singular focus, usually on women as peacemakers, overlooks the range of activities that women are engaged in, from active participation in terrorism networks to a wide range of creative and effective intervention, prevention and advocacy roles.

As noted above, women's empowerment is widely invoked in CVE programmes, and this is precisely because women are viewed as the purveyors of identity and community in the private realm, and as inherently peaceful because of their womanhood.

Women are depicted both as victims of community extremism, and as agents of solving it, as in the calls that are often made for the inclusion of 'mothers' in community engagement as part of CVE (Calfas, 2016; Majoran, 2015; Schlaffer and Kropiunigg, 2015). Adnan Khifayat, Co-Chair of the US Homeland Security Advisory Committee's Countering Violent Extremism Subcommittee, noted, 'we should never forget as a guiding principle that even the men who are recruited were once boys, were once children, and were connected to a female figure' (Council on Foreign Relations, 2016). UK counter-terrorism expert Robert Milton, as another example, notes that 'family is at the heart of this. We need to reach out to families, mothers, and empower women to help them identify when changing behavior might lead to radicalisation' (Owen, 2017). It has also been noted that 'A number of organisations worldwide such as Women Without Borders and PAIMAN Alumni Trust are utilising the strategic role of mothers and matriarchs to build early warning systems when they suspect their husbands, sons, or daughters may be involved with extremist groups' (Mlambo-Ngcuka and Coomaraswamy, 2015).

Additionally, groups such as Mothers for Life and The Mother's School focus on empowering women to safeguard their families against extremism, as does the film 'Your Mother', about the families of those who have chosen to commit extremist acts.[6] That is, women's empowerment becomes the solution for starting 'interventions before violent attacks occur' (Owen, 2017). As Jennifer Eggert has noted, 'this discourse is problematic as it focuses on the women and puts blame on families as bearers of "extremist culture" rather than seeing radicalisation and extremism as the multi-causal phenomenon they are in reality' (Eggert, 2017). Beyond this, focusing on women's potential for CVE related solely to the family renders them one-dimensional actors in CVE, rather than considering them as actors who can serve in security forces, develop programming and work with government agencies and NGOs (Idris and Abdelaziz, 2017, p. 2).

This is integral to the work of constructing the liberal, gendered subject. The governmentality associated with CVE is not solely evident as the obvious level of the governance of subjectivity related to radicalisation, it can also be seen in the way the roles of mothers, fathers, families and communities are constructed and reinforced by CVE discourses. Motherhood then becomes a tool of counter-radicalisation, and mothers themselves are expected to do political work in the home, rendering the home a key site of the production of liberal subjects.

Vulnerability: gendering CVE

Under CVE, everyone is a potential recruit for terrorists. Still, the programmes focus on providing characteristics that those vulnerable to recruitment share. I argue that such vulnerability is gendered, and that potential male recruits are perceived as threatening both to their own communities and to the larger state, while potential female recruits are perceived as passive instruments of men's agency. CVE programmes rely on gender stereotypes that paint radicalisation as a men's issue, that can then be solved by women. Such rhetoric invokes gender essentialisms that ultimately have the effect of minimising the threat of women's recruitment while painting young men as a naturalised extremist threat.

As illustrated earlier in the chapter, assumptions about the innate connections between masculinity and violence structure our perceptions of such violence. One of the effects, discussed above, is the assumption that women leaders of the community are the solutions to extremism. Yet another effect, though, is the very different perception of potential or actual female recruits to terrorist organisations compared with male recruits. The naturalisation of masculinity and violence, intimately connected with the assumption linking women and peace, disables CVE programmes from being able to deal with vulnerable men.

That is, assuming that female recruits are the victims of brainwashing, assuming their vulnerability, means that men who are also vulnerable to such processes are often prosecuted rather than receiving the community reintegration their cases may instead merit. Charli Carpenter has drawn attention to a similar problem in the case of non-combatant immunity prior to the Srebrenica massacre. She illustrates how, at Srebrenica, women, children and the elderly were feminised, and thus associated with the status of non-combatants, and were granted the immunity therein entailed. The military-aged men were considered to be combatants simply by virtue of their gender, and the characteristics usually associated with it, including the ability to defend oneself. As a result, they were not given the immunity given to non-combatants, despite their legal status as civilians and non-combatants, despite the fact that they were just as helpless as those who were evacuated, as was made evident when they were massacred two years later. The terms women and children were conflated with that of non-combatant, as Carpenter demonstrates, while masculinity seemed to preclude one from being a non-combatant, perhaps due simply to the potentiality of military-age men to successfully engage in violence. She argues that

> 'protection of civilians' as an international norm has been framed in such a way as to reproduce the traditional notion that 'women and children' (but not adult men) are 'innocent' and 'vulnerable.' Through this process, the 'civilians frame' has been distorted by reliance on a proxy – 'women and children' – that both encompasses some combatants (female and child soldiers) and excludes some non-combatants (adult civilian men). (Carpenter, 2005, p. 296)

The problem with this distortion of the frame is that it renders civilian men legitimately targetable and represents a failure to respond to the vulnerabilities of male non-combatants. Carpenter recounts a conversation between UNPRO-FOR General Morrillon and UNHCR official Hollingworth, where the former says to the latter in reference to the evacuation at Srebrenica in 1993, 'No men under sixty, ok?' (Carpenter, 2003, p. 661). The notion that these men do not count as civilians, regardless of the fact that they were not engaged in fighting, reinforces gender essentialisms that naturalise a link between men and violence. This case illustrates the way in which gender essentialisms limit our ability to properly conceptualise vulnerability, one of the problems with assuming that women are always the victims of violence (Auchter, 2012, 2017; Carpenter, 2003, 2005, 2006; Sjoberg and Gentry, 2007). The remainder of this section describes some of the issues this presents with regards to CVE programmes.

When it comes to extremism in particular, these same understandings circulate. As Jennifer Eggert has noted,

> Simplified gender stereotypes (according to which men are perpetrators and supporters of violence and women are either victims of extremism or peacemakers) continue to dominate in large parts of our societies. These biased views of the roles of men and women in (violent) extremism are highly problematic, as they prevent us from seeing how violent extremist movements really work. (Eggert, 2018, n.p.)

Following on what I noted in the previous section about women's empowerment as a solution to extremism, there is a second part to this story, which involves gendered understandings of threat, where women are simply posited as less threatening than men.

It is also worth noting here that, as Carpenter demonstrates with the Srebrenica case, very young men and very old men are typically emasculated by such assumptions. In that sense, though women are typically painted as vulnerable while men are depicted as invulnerable (and thus threatening), the dynamics are slightly more complex for young men. In some cases, adolescent boys or young men are depicted as being vulnerable to terrorist recruitment as a function of their youth. This still fits with the gender essentialism paradigms I have outlined here, because in these particular instances, these boys or young men are not considered to be 'men'. Cynthia Enloe gets at this with her discussion of the uses of the phrase 'womenandchildren' to describe those vulnerable in global politics (Enloe, 1993, pp. 166–167), and Carpenter illustrates this as well in the Srebrenica case. In short, gender essentialisms limit our ability to understand the complexities associated with vulnerability to radicalisation. Let me explain further.

A 2017 EU Parliament Report notes that women are often recruited by terrorist organisations precisely because security apparatuses are less likely to consider women as a threat:

> Women are often not expected to carry out acts of violence, which provides women with a 'natural cover'. Furthermore, attractive women have been known to distract surveillance and security teams. In addition, violent women attract more media-attention than violent men. The perceived juxtaposition of violent women similarly sends a powerful message of intimidation. Combatants and civilians of the target population are not safe anywhere if even women can carry out violent attacks. It also underlines the seriousness of the cause if there is the perception that 'even women' are prepared to engage in violence. Also, including women in militant operations can serve as a catalyst for men to take up arms, shaming them for letting women do the fighting.[7]

Several important pieces can be found in this quotation. First, despite frequent involvement by women in terrorist attacks, counter-terrorism programmes have still been unable to come to terms with the idea of violent women. This very disjuncture and rupture of our preconceived notions about who participates in violence seems to only reinforce the extreme nature of extremists, in the invocation of the 'even women' refrain, which only serves to reify preexisting notions about women's participation in violence.

A 2013 report by the OSCE notes:

> As violent extremism and terrorist radicalisation are still often considered a male issue, the question of women terrorist radicalisation is characterised by bias and misconceptions. In situations of conflict and violence, women are often seen as passive, victims, helpless, subordinate and maternal. Such assumptions reinforce gender stereotypes. As a result, women are neither considered to be potential terrorists, nor perceived to be as dangerous as their male counterparts

if they were to be involved in terrorism. However, a woman should not be assumed to be more or less dangerous, nor more prone to peace, dialogue, non-violence and co-operation than a man. In fact, the very image of the peaceful woman has been used by terrorist groups to recruit women and to claim an innocent and nonviolent character by highlighting the involvement of women in their organisations. (OSCE, 2013, p. 3)

That is, when women do participate in terrorism, their motives are often attributed to causal factors stemming from men. As a result, their radicalisation is viewed differently: female recruits, especially foreign ones, are seen to have been 'groomed or brainwashed' and gender expectations lead to the assumption that women are predominantly passive in their radicalisation (Pearson and Winterbotham, 2017).

This can lead to shorter sentences when women are prosecuted for terrorism-related offenses, or to reintegration into the community without any prosecution at all. Speckhard and Shajkovci (2017) note that

most countries accept their female returnees from Iraq and Syria and many countries do not prosecute these women – or if they do, they receive lighter sentences. This is due to the notion that they only followed their men as a result of being tricked or coerced, which often is not the case. In the Balkans and Central Asia, we were told by intelligence and law enforcement that women are 'zombies' (following their men and controlled by their men). But our research shows that ISIS women often followed their men willingly into Syria and Iraq, and in some cases willingly joined them in homegrown terrorist attacks.

Sentences are fairly rare for female foreigners who leave to join terrorist organisations:

The EUISS reports that women returning from Syria or Iraq have been punished with comparatively soft measures, such as the confiscation of their passports or limitations on access to social benefits, or they have been acquitted. If women are convicted at all, it is usually for child abuse (because they took their children to a war zone) rather than for supporting a terrorist organisation.[8]

There are a few cases of prison sentences for returnees, such as up to fifteen years in the UK for several women prosecuted for endangering their children, providing material support to a terrorist organisation and proselytisation, and in Belgium, where, in 2015, seven women were convicted for supporting ISIS and recruiting women to travel to Syria and marry ISIS fighters; four of the seven were given five year sentences in absentia, while the three women who were present received 20–30 month prison sentences for facilitating ISIS recruitment.[9] I am not arguing here that women should receive harsher sentences to render them equal with male recruits. Rather, these short sentences tell us something about how we conceptualise threat. Indeed, punishment in general is at odds with the very spirit of CVE: that radicalisation can be prevented, countered, managed and even treated, as if it was a mental health matter. In fact, more than forty countries have developed de-radicalisation programmes to rehabilitate prisoners found guilty of extremist violence, which also reduces the likelihood that younger prisoners will become further radicalised in prison, the way Cherif Kouachi, the Charlie Hebdo killer, was (Khan, 2015).

In this sense, the problem is that CVE is unevenly applied to women and men not as a result of risk assessment or legal mechanisms, but solely on the basis of gender essentialisms, assumptions that equate masculinity and violence. This disables CVE frameworks from being able to properly reckon with the mechanisms of recruitment mobilised by terrorist organisations. In this vein, while I have posited a feminist critique of CVE here, such an argument follows with the calls made by Jossif Ezekilov (2017) to 'men-stream' CVE by better understanding the way ISIS and other organisations rely on assumptions about masculinity to target vulnerable young men for recruitment.

In this sense, CVE offers up a stereotypical depiction of gender roles, in which men are always potentially violent actors who need to be contained, while women are potential victims, passive instruments of men's agency, who can, in specific roles as mothers or wives, contain the potential radicalisation of their male counterparts. Part of the struggle may be that CVE functions as a mechanism of 'soft' counter-terrorism, examining discourses of radicalisation, yet without attention to wider social discourses and how they are gendered, an incomplete picture is painted.

Conclusion

As a 2013 OSCE report notes, in the context of terrorism and violence, women are often viewed as passive and *maternal*. This is interesting precisely because, as noted earlier in this chapter, CVE programmes highlight the potential for women-as-mothers to have a significant impact in their communities, mirroring the very same rhetoric utilised by ISIS recruiters, who draw on notions about women's roles as mothers of future ISIS fighters. Umm Ubaydah, who is active on social media to recruit women to join ISIS, writes, 'The best thing a man can do is jihad, and the best thing for a woman is to be a righteous wife and to raise righteous children' (Hoyle et al., 2015, pp. 31–32). A Carter Center study (2017, p. 5) examining ISIS recruitment strategies demonstrates how ISIS portrays Western feminism as 'an exclusionary model of emancipation for elite white women at the expense of minority women groups'. Thus, both CVE and the extremism it targets rely on gender essentialisms that depict women as powerful actors precisely because of their status as wives and mothers.

This chapter has sought to demonstrate that the very notion of community prevention called upon by CVE programmes relies on gendered notions of threat. While CVE programmes often seek to empower women as a means to resist extremism in their own communities, there is still room to be cautious: 'gender equality and women's empowerment should not be valued only to the extent that it helps national security and counter-terrorism. Gender equality should be promoted in its own right and women should be empowered to participate fully in society, not be instrumentalised to "spy" on their communities' (OSCE, 2013, p. 5). In this vein, many CVE programmes simply reify the same perceptions of women as maternal, leading to an inability to properly conceive of their role in their communities and of the reasons for women's radicalisation. While CVE programmes themselves seem to focus on women's empowerment via education (particularly throughout the Middle East) and via their role as safeguards within their own communities (particularly within Western countries), much of the scholarship on gender and CVE has focused on the reasons for women's radicalisation. Thus, while there is a lot of discussion about gender, it seems to be working at cross-purposes. This chapter has sought to provide a framework for thinking about feminist critiques of CVE, particularly the way in which the programmes reinforce the placement of women in the private realm, even as the private realm itself becomes more securitised in the era of modern CVE.

Notes

1 See, for example, the US 2016 report on the subject at www.brennancenter.org/sites/default/files/2016_strategic_implementation_plan_empowering_local_partners_prev%20(2).pdf (accessed 17 February 2020).
2 www.unwomen.org/en/news/in-focus/women-peace-security (accessed 17 February 2020).
3 www.unwomen.org/en/news/in-focus/women-peace-security
4 www.un.org/sc/ctc/focus-areas/countering-violent-extremism/ (accessed 17 February 2020).
5 See for example, www.international-alert.org/blog/ask-right-questions-about-gender-and-violent-extremism (accessed 17 February 2020).
6 www.europarl.europa.eu/RegData/etudes/STUD/2017/596838/IPOL_STU(2017)596838_EN.pdf, pp. 36–37 (accessed 17 February 2020).
7 www.europarl.europa.eu/RegData/etudes/STUD/2017/596838/IPOL_STU(2017)596838_EN.pdf, p. 14.
8 www.europarl.europa.eu/RegData/etudes/STUD/2017/596838/IPOL_STU(2017)596838_EN.pdf, p. 19.
9 www.europarl.europa.eu/RegData/etudes/STUD/2017/596838/IPOL_STU(2017)596838_EN.pdf, p. 19.

References

Alonso, H., 1993. *Peace as a Women's Issue: A History of the US Movement for World Peace and Women's Rights*. Syracuse University Press, Syracuse, NY.

Annan, K., 2001. 'Daily life for majority of world's women remains difficult struggle', 8 March. Available at www.un.org/press/en/2001/sgsm7726.doc.htm (accessed 17 February 2020).

Auchter, J., 2012. 'Gendering terror: Discourses of terrorism and writing woman-as-agent', *International Feminist Journal of Politics*, 14(1), 121–140.

Auchter, J., 2017. 'Forced male circumcision: Gender-based violence in Kenya', *International Affairs*, 93(6), 1339–1356.

Brock-Utne, B., 1985. *Educating for Peace: A Feminist Perspective*. Pergamon, Oxford.

Caldicott, H., 1984. *Missile Envy: The Arms Race and Nuclear War*. William Morrow and Company, New York.

Calfas, A., 2016. *Why Women are the Missing Link in Countering Extremism*. Fair Observer, 27 October. Available at www.fairobserver.com/region/middle_east_north_africa/women-counter-extremism-middle-east-north-africa-99121/ (accessed 17 February 2020).

Carpenter, C., 2003. '"Women and children first": Gender, norms, and humanitarian evacuation in the Balkans 1991–95', *International Organisation*, 57(4), 661–694.

Carpenter, C., 2005. '"Women, children and other vulnerable groups": Gender, strategic frames and the protection of civilians as a transnational issue', *International Studies Quarterly*, 49(2), 295–334.

Carpenter, C., 2006. *'Innocent Women and Children': Gender, Norms, and the Protection of Civilians*. Ashgate, London.

Carter Center, 2017. *The Women in Daesh: Deconstructing Complex Gender Dynamics in Daesh Recruitment and Propaganda*. Available at www.cartercenter.org/resources/pdfs/peace/conflict_resolution/countering-isis/women-in-daesh.pdf (accessed 17 February 2020).

Chowdhury Fink, N., Zeiger, S. and Bulai, R., 2016. 'A man's world? Exploring the roles of women in countering terrorism and violent extremism', Global Center on Cooperative Security. Available at www.globalcenter.org/publications/a-mans-world-exploring-the-roles-of-women-in-countering-terrorism-and-violent-extremism/ (accessed 17 February 2020).

Council on Foreign Relations, 2016. 'Countering violent extremism by engaging women', 7 December. Available at www.cfr.org/event/countering-violent-extremism-engaging-women (accessed 17 February 2020).

Eggert, J.P., 2017. 'Mothers, bombs, and a whole lot of gender cliches', *LSE Blog*, 29 June. Available at http://blogs.lse.ac.uk/gender/2017/06/29/mothers-bombs-and-a-whole-lot-of-gender-cliches/ (accessed 17 February 2020).

Eggert, J.P., 2018. 'Counterextremism, communities, and gender', *Connect Futures*, 29 April. Available at www.connectfutures.org/counterextremism-communities-and-gender/ (accessed 17 February 2020).

Enloe, C., 1993. *The Morning After: Sexual Politics at the end of the Cold War*. University of California Press, Berkeley.

Enloe, C., 2006. 'Foreword', in Hunt, K. and Rygiel, K. (eds), *(En)gendering the War on Terror: War Stories and Camouflaged Politics*. Ashgate, Burlington, VT, pp. vii–x.

Ezekilov, J., 2017. 'Gender men-streaming CVE: Countering violent extremism by focusing on addressing masculinities issues', *Reconsidering Development*, 5(1). Available at https://pubs.lib.umn.edu/index.php/reconsidering/article/view/908 (accessed 17 February 2020).

Federal Bureau of Investigation, 2015. 'ASAC Conference – Countering Violent Extremism Training', *Electronic Communication*, 13 August. Available at www.brennancenter.org/sites/default/files/9D189AFA9E878DF18145FA7D70DE4A5B36CFB1E.pdf (accessed 17 February 2020).

Forcey, L., 1994. 'Feminist perspectives on mothering and peace', in Glenn, E., Chang, G. and Forcey, L. (eds), *Mothering: Ideology, Experience and Agency*. Routledge, New York, 355–375.

Fukuyama, F., 1998. 'Women and the evolution of world politics', *Foreign Affairs*, 77(5), 24–40.

GCTF, 2016. 'Good practices on women and countering violent extremism', Global Counterterrorism Forum. Available at www.thegctf.org/Portals/1/Documents/Framework%20Documents/2016%20and%20before/GCTF-Good-Practices-on-Women-and-CVE.pdf?ver=2016-09-09-112914-837 (accessed 17 February 2020.

Hoyle, C., Bradford, A. and Frenett, R., 2015. *Becoming Mulan? Female Western Migrants to ISIS.*, Institute for Strategic Dialogue. Available at www.isdglobal.org/wp-content/uploads/2016/02/ISDJ2969_Becoming_Mulan_01.15_WEB.pdf (accessed 17 February 2020).

Idris, I., Abdelaziz, A., 2017. 'Women and countering violent extremism', *GSDRC Report*, 5 April. Available at www.gsdrc.org/wp-content/uploads/2017/05/HDR_1408.pdf (accessed 17 February 2020).

Khan, H., 2015. 'Why countering extremism fails', *Foreign Affairs*, 18 February. Available at www.foreignaffairs.com/articles/united-states/2015-02-18/why-countering-extremism-fails (accessed 17 February 2020).

Majoran, A., 2015. *Mothers & Wives: Women's Political Role in Countering Violent Extremism*. The Mackenzie Institute. Available at www.quilliaminternational.com/mothers-wives-womens-potential-role-in-countering-violent-extremism/ (accessed 17 February 2020).

McCants, W., Watts, C., 2012. 'US strategy for countering violent extremism: An assessment', *Foreign Policy Research Institute*. Available at www.fpri.org/docs/media/McCants_Watts_-_Countering_Violent_Extremism.pdf (accessed 17 February 2020).

Mlambo-Ngcuka, P., Coomaraswamy, R., 2015. 'Women are the best weapon in the war against terrorism', *Foreign Policy*, 10 February. Available at http://foreignpolicy.com/2015/02/10/women-are-the-best-weapon-in-the-war-against-terrorism/ (accessed 17 February 2020).

Nacos, B., 2005. 'The portrayal of female terrorists in the media: Similar framing patterns in the news coverage of women in politics and in terrorism', *Studies in Conflict and Terrorism*, 28(5), 435–451.

Nordstrom, C., 2005. '(Gendered) war', *Studies in Conflict and Terrorism*, 28(5), 399–411.

Organization for Security and Co-operation in Europe, 2013. *Women and Terrorist radicalisation: Final Report*. Available at www.osce.org/secretariat/99919? download=true (accessed 17 February 2020).

Owen, P., 2017. 'Expert says mothers at heart of terrorism prevention', *The Telegram*, 6 April. Available at www.telegram.com/news/20170406/expert-says-mothers-at-heart-of-terrorism-prevention (accessed 17 February 2020).

Papatheodorou, K., 2018. 'Preventing, not just countering, violent extremism', *Lawfare*, 29 April. Available at https://lawfareblog.com/preventing-not-just-countering-violent-extremism (accessed 17 February 2020).

Pearson, E., Winterbotham, E., 2017. 'Women, gender and Daesh radicalisation', *The RUSI Journal*, 162(3), 60–72.

Randall, M., 1993. *When I Look into the Mirror and See You: Women, Terror, and Resistance*. Rutgers University Press, New Brunswick, NJ.

Ruddick, S., 1983. 'Pacifying the forces: Drafting women in the interests of peace', *Signs*, 8(3), 471–489.

Schlaffer, E., Kropiunigg, U., 2015. *Can Mothers Challenge Violent Extremism? Mothers' Perceptions and Attitudes of Violent Extremism and Radicalisation*, Women Without Borders. Available at https://wwb.org/activity/can-mothers-challenge-extremism/ (accessed 17 February 2020).

Sjoberg, L., Gentry, C., 2007. *Mothers, Monsters, Whores: Women's Violence in Global Politics*. Zed Books, London.

Speckhard, A., Shajkovci, A., 2017. 'Beware the women of ISIS: There are many, and they may be more dangerous than the men', *The Daily Beast*, 21 August. Available at www.thedailybeast.com/beware-the-women-of-isis-there-are-many-and-they-may-be-more-dangerous-than-the-men (accessed 17 February 2020).

Spivak, G., 1993. 'Can the subaltern speak?', in Williams, P. and Chrisman, L. (eds), *Colonial Discourse and Post-Colonial Theory: A Reader*. Harvester, Hemel Hempstead, pp. 66–111.

Szmania, S., 2015. 'Broadening the discussion about women and violent extremism', *START*, 30 June. Available at www.start.umd.edu/news/broadening-discussion-about-women-and-violent-extremism (accessed 17 February 2020).

Vidino, L., Hughes, S., 2015. 'Countering violent extremism in America', Program on Extremism, George Washington University. Available at https://extremism.gwu.edu/sites/g/files/zaxdzs2191/f/downloads/CVE%20in%20America.pdf (accessed 17 February 2020).

Zine, J., 2006. 'Between Orientalism and fundamentalism: Muslim women and feminist engagement', in Hunt, K. and Rygiel, K. (eds), *(En)Gendering the War on Terror: War Stories and Camouflaged Politics*. Ashgate, Burlington, VT, pp. 27–50.

6

A peace studies approach to countering extremism: do counter-extremism strategies produce peace?

Kieran Ford

Introduction

Once extremism has been countered, what will the world look like?

This is, obviously, an important question. That a counter-extremism strategy should know exactly what it is hoping to achieve – the kind of world it is attempting to build – appears common sense. Yet, interestingly, while counter-extremism strategies proliferate around the world, it is fascinating to note how poorly defined both extremism and counter-extremism remain. If one cannot define what one is attempting to counter, how can one claim to have succeeded? Two years after committing to 'defeat extremism' (Her Majesty's Government, 2015, p. 6), the UK government admitted it was still searching for a clear definition of extremism that could stand up in court (Hooper, 2017). While the question of what counter-extremism is hoping to achieve becomes ever more important, the answer remains elusive. This chapter hopes to offer a critical framework to evaluate counter-extremism strategies, borrowed from the realm of peace studies, in order to offer a way to answer this question. Answering this question is of profound importance. If counter-extremism engenders violence, then current approaches are far from likely to contribute to a sustainable peace.

Peace scholars have for the past fifty years debated various typologies of peace and violence, exploring multiple understandings of what peace looks like and the various forms of violence that such peace(s) both address and allow to persist. Peace has been defined both negatively (in terms of a pause in active hostilities between actors) and positively (in terms of conflict transformation and the addressing of grievances). Moreover, criticism regarding the so-called 'liberal peace' has revealed a further set of debates regarding the imposition of Eurocentric values in peacebuilding, the centrality of military violence to the liberal peace model and the use of coercion in the imposition of peace (Jackson, 2018;

Richmond, 2009). Violence has been understood to encompass not just the harm caused by one actor to another, but the harm caused by more systemic or structural forces which, though still constructed by human society, do not have such an easily identifiable actor. By examining the many different types of peace and violence, one can ask the question of what kind of peace is being achieved in countering extremism, and what kinds of violence are perhaps being perpetrated. Interactions between the field of peace studies and terrorism studies have been few and far between (Ford, 2019; Jackson, 2017; Toros and Tellidis, 2013). Furthermore, such interactions have tended to focus on the lessons terrorism studies can learn from peacemaking, and questions around negotiations and peace settlements (Toros and Tellidis, 2013), rather than on building a culture of peace. This chapter builds on Jackson's (2017) call for research on non-violence and terrorism, and Lindahl's (2017) examination of a non-violent, *critical* model of counter-terrorism, with a particular emphasis here on the context of extremism.

Through using the British *Prevent* counter-extremism strategy as an illustrative example, the chapter argues that contemporary approaches to counter-extremism, while attempting to achieve some sort of peace, engage in multiple forms of violence. In particular, the chapter emphasises the way in which counter-extremism seeks to build a consensus around liberal democratic values, and the problematic practices that such consensus-building engenders (see also Cuadro, this volume; Martini, this volume). From this point of criticism, the chapter is then able to offer constructive directions as to how a more peaceful approach to countering extremism could be envisaged. Jackson (2017) highlights the lack of attention that has been given by critical terrorism scholars to the question of non-violent responses to terrorism. Critical terrorism scholars have built an established field of criticism, understanding the implications of contemporary counter-terrorism strategies. The next step is to offer peaceful alternatives. Countering extremism, this chapter argues, is so often conceptualised within a framework which proclaims: once we rid the world of extremism, there will be peace. This chapter begins to examine how countering extremism could be framed differently – as something to manage, and to engage with, not as something to expunge from society. Extremism need not be *countered,* if opportunities and frameworks are offered for extremism to be *encountered.*

A peace studies framework of peace and violence

The field of peace studies is, of course, multifaceted and complex with peace scholars drawing from many perspectives while searching for solutions to the many conflicts around the world. A small component of peace studies examines definitions and typologies of peace and violence. It is through exploring these typologies that this chapter argues peace studies offers a helpful framework with which to examine the relative merits of contemporary approaches to countering extremism.

That violence should be considered more nuanced than simply the act of one individual physically harming another has become common knowledge across political studies. Slavoj Žižek (2008), for example, distinguishes between a physical, individual *subjective* violence and a systemic *objective* violence. Žižek's distinction – albeit leaning far more heavily on a specific critique of the objective violence of capitalism – is reminiscent of Galtung's (1969) earlier distinction between direct and indirect violence. Direct violence is the harm one actor does to another. Indirect, or structural violence, is an actor-less, though still caused and avoidable, violence. It might, for instance, refer to starvation, or as Galtung writes, 'We shall sometimes refer to the condition of structural violence as *social injustice*' (1969, p. 171). Some years later, 'cultural violence' was added by Galtung: 'those aspects of culture, the symbolic sphere of our existence. . . that can be used to justify or legitimise direct or structural violence' (1990, p. 291). For example, this might include violent films or television programmes.

Peace, then, is the absence of violence; the absence of direct violence being negative peace, the absence of structural and cultural violence being positive peace (Galtung, 1969). Yet, aside from definitions of positive peace that focus on what it is *not* – emphasising an *absence* of violence – positive peace remains the source of much conceptual contestation, leaving practitioners somewhat paralysed in their hope to engender peace and eliminate violence. Galtung's attempt to define positive peace is particularly vague:

> The reason for the use of the terms 'negative' and 'positive' is easily seen: the absence of personal violence does not lead to a positively defined condition, whereas the absence of structural violence is what we have referred to as social justice, which is a positively defined condition (egalitarian distribution of power and resources). (Galtung, 1969, p. 183)

There appears little doubt that much contestation exists as to what such an 'egalitarian distribution' might look like. Žižek (2008), for instance, suggests that capitalism itself is a source of objective violence, setting positive peace the gargantuan task of addressing the violence of capitalism. Many scholars, however, would not see capitalism as inimical to peace.

Moreover, the very notion of positive peace has come under scrutiny. Ilan Gur-Ze'ev (2001) offers what he refers to as a 'postmodern' critique of peace, exploring its epistemological foundations. Gur-Ze'ev argues peace has become synonymous with homogeneity: once everyone agrees, there will be peace. Gur-Ze'ev challenges the ethnocentrism of peace that fails to encounter 'the violence that produces their yardsticks and conceptions of knowledge, values, aims and imagination, as well as their own identity' (Gur-Ze'ev, 2001, p. 316). Critics of the liberal peace also examine the suppression of difference at the heart of peace. Jackson argues, 'liberal peace(state)building can be seen as a continuation of longer historical processes of imperialism, neo-colonialism and Westernisation' (2018, p. 3). As Richmond notes, a liberal peace is 'a disciplinary framework that often rests on coercion, a lack of consent, conditionality, and the prioritisation of elites over the interests of the many' (2009, p. 561).

Peace education, which Gur-Ze'ev refers to as 'normalising education' (2001, p. 322), is a key tool in this homogenisation process. It is this that Gur-Ze'ev claims ensures that peace education entails 'epistemic violence', adding a further form of violence to the conceptual framework:

> Epistemic violence is realised in the formation of conceptual apparatuses, knowledge, consciousness, ideological orientations, and consensus or self-evidence; it is the aim of normalising education, in the service of the self-evident and hegemonic order of things. (Gur-Ze'ev, 2001, p. 331)

'Modern' concepts of peace, including positive peace, as Cremin notes, 'promote suffocating homogeneity, security, assimilation, false ideals and limited horizons' (Cremin, 2016, p. 3). The ethnocentricity of dominant conceptualisations of peace rely upon the notion of consensual agreement, and dismiss diversity, to the extent that for peace to be achieved, a process of epistemic violence is necessary. These critiques thus muddy the waters regarding the positivity of positive peace if the very term 'peace' is imbued with a level of violence. What 'peace' is there in oppressing others with one unitary vision of a positively peaceful future?

Defining positive peace is thus immensely challenging. However, and indeed helpfully, a third dimension of peace is at hand: agonistic peace. While Gur-Ze'ev's critique of positive peace, and exploration of epistemic violence, suggests positive peace might impose a peace onto a population, agonistic peace begins from the premise, which Shinko characterises, as resisting 'the trap wherein peace emerges as just another tactic for reinscribing hegemonic structures of domination, exclusion and marginalisation' (2008, p. 488).

Agonistic peace begins from the premise that contestation and conflict are ubiquitous, and thus peace should not envision a space where conflict is eliminated, but a space in which conflict can be deliberated (Ramsbotham, 2010; Shinko, 2008) and pluralist approaches to difference embraced (Mouffe, 2005). As Chantal Mouffe writes, 'It is not in our power to eliminate conflicts and escape our human condition, but it is in our power to create the practices, discourses and institutions that would allow these conflicts to take an agonistic form' (2005, p. 130). Agonism is deployed by a diverse set of voices who converge on the idea of embracing rather than suppressing what Ramsbotham (2010) calls 'radical disagreements'. Placing such disagreements

Table 6.1   Types of peace and violence

Types of peace	Types of violence
Negative peace	Direct violence
Positive peace	Structural/indirect violence
Agonistic peace	Cultural violence
	Epistemic violence

centre stage, agonistic politics seeks not to replace disagreement with a consensus (and thus risk engendering epistemic violence), but instead provide spaces and institutions such that the Other may no longer be seen as an 'enemy' but as an adversary (Mouffe, 2005). Agonistic spaces must be ones in which ideas can be argued and, importantly, respect for the other can be developed. As Shinko writes, these spaces 'offer the possibility of replacing enmity with adversarial positionality' (2008, p. 477). Agonistic peace therefore takes the challenge that Gur-Ze'ev lays down to positive peace and rejects the possibility of imposing a particular form of positive peace, and repressing inevitable conflict over that peace.

The concepts of peace and violence, as this section has demonstrated, are far from simple ideas. The chapter has examined three types of peace and four types of violence (Table 6.1).

Yet, through this contestation, the question 'what *kind* of peace is being envisaged?' emerges as a helpful mode of critical evaluation, particularly considering the types of violence that some types of peace leave unaddressed. Examining these typologies of peace and violence thus allows for critical analysis of the implications and consequences of counter-extremism strategies. The chapter now turns to the topic of extremism and counter-extremism. It explores how these two concepts have been defined within academic and policy literatures, and from there deploys this critical framework of peace and violence to examine the kind of 'post-extremist peace' counter-extremism attempts to engender.

Defining extremism and counter-extremism

Definitions of counter-extremism are difficult to unearth in academic and practitioner literatures alike. For instance, in a British context, policy documents speak of protecting people from extremism, defeating extremism (Her Majesty's Government, 2015) or 'dealing with extremism' (Balls, 2008, p. 3). Yet a specific definition of counter-extremism is not put forward – even in instances where definitions of extremism, radicalisation and counter-radicalisation are all offered (Her Majesty's Government, 2011, p. 107). Harris-Hogan et al. argue similarly that 'many CVE [countering violent extremism] approaches cannot define the specifics of what they are preventing, let alone how or whether they have prevented it' (Harris-Hogan et al., 2016, p. 6). Counter-extremism eludes definition. To achieve the present examination therefore, understandings of counter-extremism must be pieced together by exploring definitions of extremism and examining their opposite.

In order to evaluate the peace envisioned within counter-extremism, this section will critically deconstruct the term extremism, arguing that there are three dominant definitions or iterations of extremism, and thus three aspects to countering extremism. Counter-extremism is defined in terms of promoting centrist 'moderate' values, pluralism in the face of absolutism, and non-violent methods of political participation in the face of violence (Ford, 2017a, 2019). Examples from the author's research into countering extremism in British schools will be used to illustrate these strategies. Through exploring how these three definitions operate together, an understanding of the peace, which counter-extremism seeks to engender, will begin to emerge.

Promoting moderate values

The Oxford English Dictionary defines extremism as 'the holding of extreme political or religious views; fanaticism' (Oxford Dictionaries, n.d.). Such a definition encompasses the first two of three deployments of the term 'extremism' examined within this chapter. Fanaticism will be dealt with below. First, the somewhat tautological understanding of extremism as holding onto extreme views should be explored. Such an understanding of extremism is widespread, with authors depicting bell curves demonstrating a popular 'moderate' centre in contrast to less popular 'extreme' fringes (Bartlett and Miller, 2012; Borum, 2011; Lake, 2002). Furthermore, the dictionary stipulates that extremism exists within political and religious realms. As I have written elsewhere, 'Such an understanding of extremism cements hegemonic liberal attitudes at the centre of understandings of what constitute legitimate attitudes' (Ford, 2017b, p. 128) and as such constructs the extreme as its opposite. This moderate/extremist binary may also be depicted as a spectrum which 'has, at one end, moderates who advocate democracy and tolerance and reject violence as a means to attain political goals and, at the other end, radicals who oppose democratic and pluralistic values and embrace violence' (Rabasa, 2005, p. 2). Such an understanding is perhaps most commonly deployed in discourses surrounding the contrast between moderate and extreme Islam (Aly and Green, 2008). Of course, one elephant in the room regarding this definition is the centrality of state violence to liberal 'moderation'. Such a definition of extremism is thus only a partial rejection of violence.

If extremism is depicted as the tail of a bell curve of political opinion, counter-extremism would entail a process of reducing the population at the tail and increasing the population at the centre. Such a process of counter-extremism would involve promoting moderate views, and, perhaps uncomfortably for a democracy, reducing the overall diversity in political opinion. Some authors have raised concerns regarding how this first iteration of extremism is in danger of including all political ideas that are divergent or unpopular (Jackson, 2012). Moreover, as explored in more depth below, concerns are raised regarding who is deemed to sit outside of these curated fences of permissible values, and what experiences they face from those who deem them to be threatening. It is these consequences of consensus-based counter-extremism that the chapter highlights as necessitating a re-conceptualisation of extremism.

One arena in which to witness this understanding of extremism playing out is within the UK's strategy to counter extremism in schools. Such a facet of counter-extremism materialises in the promotion of 'fundamental British values'. In 2011, the UK government reviewed its *Prevent* counter-extremism strategy and defined extremism as 'vocal or active opposition to fundamental British values, including democracy, the rule of law, individual liberty and mutual respect and tolerance of different faiths and beliefs' (Her Majesty's Government, 2011, p. 107). These four 'included' values soon became the *de facto* fixed set of values that the strategy considers fundamentally British. Schools must actively promote these values, and their ability to promote them is evaluated by the schools' inspectorate (Office for Standards in Education, 2015). Moreover, promoting these values is considered a component of teacher professional standards (Department for Education, 2011). Countering extremism entails a process of moderate values promotion – attempting to increase the population at the centre of the curve.

Countering absolutism with pluralism

As mentioned above, the Oxford Dictionary also mentions 'fanaticism' within its definition of extremism. This understanding – alongside similar terms like fundamentalism or absolutism – is common within the literature on extremism. Davies isolates one feature of extremism as 'an uncritical acceptance of single truths' (Davies, 2008, p. 2). Some decades earlier, Robert Kennedy writes, 'what is objectionable, what is dangerous about extremists is not that they are extreme, but that they are intolerant. The evil is not what they say about their cause, but what they say about their opponents' (Kennedy, 1965, pp. 68–69). This understanding of extremism is matched by practitioners, such as the then head of MI5 who suggested 'the ideology underlying Al Qaida and other violent groups is extreme. It does not accept the legitimacy of other viewpoints. It is intolerant' (Evans, 2007).

This emphasis on fundamentalism and rigid modes of thinking ensures that the term 'ideology' gains currency when discussing extremist threats, as the then UK Prime Minister David Cameron made clear: 'The root cause of the threat we face is the extremist ideology itself' (Cameron, 2015). Cameron's emphasis that the threat comes from an ideology – as opposed to a threat from the use of violence as political strategy – is mirrored elsewhere. Research has been conducted that attempts to understand the precise nature of extremist ideology or narrative (Bartlett and Miller, 2012; Schmid, 2014). Scholars cling to the explanatory power of ideology despite the lack of evidence: 'There is no doubt that ideology, including global neo-jihadi ideology, is an important part of any explanation in the turn to political violence, but we still don't understand how' (Sageman, 2014, p. 567).

If extremism is synonymous with absolutism, counter-extremism must be synonymous with pluralism. Counter-extremism often promotes pluralism through, for instance, the inclusion of 'tolerance' as one of the fundamental British values. Yet, if extremism is an ideology, then counter-extremism must also involve a counter-ideology – both in terms of a set of values that counter extremist values and in terms of skills to enable individuals to counter extremist ideas themselves. In the face of an extremist ideology that promotes fundamentalist and absolutist adherence to its values and narratives, critical thinking skills gain a great deal of currency as an effective tool in countering extremism from numerous actors at a political and policy level. UNESCO hopes educators will 'help learners develop their critical thinking to investigate claims, verify rumours and question the legitimacy and appeal of extremist beliefs' (UNESCO, 2016, p. 15). The European Commission's Radicalisation Awareness Network (RAN) argues, 'Critical thinking is a key element in building resilience against extremism' (RAN, 2017, p. 230). The document *Learning to be Safe*, written by the then UK Labour government, asks schools to provide learning opportunities 'which explore controversial issues in a way which promotes critical analysis and pro-social values' (Department for Children, Schools and Families, 2008, p. 9).

Such arguments in favour of critical thinking to prevent extremism are supported by academic literature on the topic. It is, however, somewhat unclear what critical thinking entails, with concise and comprehensive definitions a rarity within the literature, though certain themes emerge: practising reflection (Sieckelinck and de Ruyter, 2009, p. 193), acknowledgement of plural viewpoints (Davies, 2008, p. 33) or open dialogue (O'Donnell, 2016, p. 63). Lynn Davies, author of the key text on this subject, *Educating against Extremism*, argues: 'Cognitive dissonance is essential in learning, whether about religion or anything else. Comparing what one thought one knew against new and different information or ideas is the essence of education – that's what it's for' (Davies, 2008, p. 134). The challenge for counter-extremism comes, however, when critical thinking is deployed to promote a fixed set of values: 'what value is there' as I have argued, 'in "critically" approaching this predetermined answer?' (Ford, 2017a, p. 150).

Violent extremism

Lastly, extremism is often defined in relation to violence. This may be through the use of terms such as 'violent extremism' and 'countering violent extremism' or through arguments that suggest that extremism is inherently violent. Often these theories suggest that extremists might see violence as an end in itself, not a means to an end (Selma-Gregg, 2016). While this argument appears to negate other explanations for political violence – theories that might examine political grievances (Baker-Beall et al., 2015) or look at group dynamics (Della Porta, 1992), the popularity of discourses regarding violent extremism and violent extremist ideology cannot be dismissed. The threat of violence extends even beyond those extremists deemed to pose an immediate violent threat. The categorisation of 'non-violent extremists' defines those who provide ideological support to violent extremists and thus are in need of being countered themselves (Maher and Frampton, 2009). The UK government makes such an argument: 'some terrorist ideologies draw on and make use of extremist ideas which are espoused by apparently non-violent organisations very often operating within the law' (Her Majesty's Government, 2011, p. 50). Even if you do not promote (non-state) violence yourself, if your extreme ideas might be used by those who are willing to use violence, then you pose a violent threat.

Countering the violence of extremism thus requires counter-extremism to promote non-violence, and in particular, non-violent modes of political participation. The UK's Department for Education encourages citizenship education: 'In Citizenship, pupils learn about democracy, government and how laws are made and upheld' (Department for Education, 2015, p. 8). Davies justifies this as 'about opening up, presenting alternatives to understandings and actions' (Davies, 2008, p. 60). Sieckelinck and de Ruyter (2009) frame counter-extremism in terms of offering alternative modes through which people can attempt to achieve their political change. Counter-extremism focuses on providing students with the knowledge to counter the arguments made by extremist narratives regarding the legitimacy of violence, as well as the knowledge of the various channels through which members of the public can influence political and legislative processes. It is a strategy that promotes non-violent modes of political participation, not a strategy that promotes non-violence, leaving certain violent norms such as the legitimacy of state violence in place.

In combination, counter-extremism strategies and practices therefore appear to appropriate these three strands of understanding expressed here: the promotion of hegemonic values, pluralism and tolerance, and non-violent political partici-pation. The question guiding this chapter concerns what kind of peace is being produced through such a mode of countering extremism.

The peace and violence of counter-extremism

This section will take Britain's counter-extremism strategy as an example case and evaluate it from the perspective of the critical framework of peace and violence explored above. To do so, a matrix of peace and violence can be used (Table 6.2). Built on a similar matrix developed by Cremin (2016), this matrix visualises the ways in which each type of peace addresses certain forms of violence and leaves others unchallenged. Furthermore, it explores how this peace or vio-lence might materialise in the context of extremism.

In the first column, the four types of violence discussed in the chapter are listed. Moving horizontally across the matrix, the table lists how that violence might appear in various states of peace. The matrix is shaded grey where vio-lence remains, and white where the violence is addressed. For example, while

Table 6.2   *A matrix of peace and violence*

	No peace	Negative peace	Positive peace	Agonistic peace
Direct violence	Terrorism, hate crimes, violent counter-terrorism	No terrorism, hate crimes or other direct violence	No terrorism, hate crimes or other direct violence	No terrorism, hate crimes or other direct violence
Structural violence	Political grievances such as economic inequality, avoidable death by disease	Political grievances such as economic inequality, avoidable death by disease	Social justice addressing political grievances	Social justice addressing political grievances
Cultural violence	Discourses that legitimate discrimi-natory practices based on racialised categories of suspicion	Discourses that legitimate discriminatory practices based on racialised catego-ries of suspicion	Discourses of anti-racism	Discourses of anti-racism
Epistemic violence	Ideological counter-extremism programme demanding consensus based around Eurocentric, hegemonic values	Ideological counter-extremism programme demanding consen-sus based around Eurocentric, hegemonic values	Ideological counter-extremism programme demanding consen-sus based around Eurocentric, hegemonic values	Dialogic space for multiple peaces to co-exist

in a form of negative post-extremist peace there would be no terrorism, hate crime or other forms of direct violence, it is evident that counter-extremism is not addressing other forms of violence, but leaving them unchallenged. The matrix then goes on to begin to imagine what a more peaceful form of counter-extremism could entail. For instance, if counter-extremism strategies sought to achieve a positive peace, then they would need to address the structurally violent inequalities and discriminatory practices of cultural violence, alongside the direct violence.

Initially, it can be argued that Britain's counter-extremism strategy, and counter-extremism more broadly, attempts to achieve a negative peace. According to the matrix developed above, it fulfils the criteria of preventing forms of direct violence that might emerge from extremist groups or individuals such as terrorism or hate crimes. It does this through both promoting non-violent forms of political participation and promoting a fixed set of values – parameters within which, were the entire population to be located, the need for political violence would be eliminated. In layman's terms, it is a strategy that attempts to remove conflict by getting everyone to agree.

It is important to note, however, that achieving negative peace leaves structural, cultural and epistemic violence unaddressed (Cremin, 2016). Moreover, and as will become clearer within this section of the chapter, the process of achieving this form of negative peace *itself constitutes these forms of violence*. This section of the chapter will argue that Britain's counter-extremism strategy thus sits within the negative peace column of the matrix.

As has been explored above, the UK government currently defines extremism in opposition to what it terms 'fundamental British values'. Counter-extremism thus becomes a strategy of promoting these fixed values. While the promotion of shared values as a tactic to reduce the likelihood of political violence relies on unstable or non-existent empirical evidence (Edyvane, 2011; Kundnani, 2007), it remains a popular strategy. In particular, this strategy rose to prominence to face the threat of so-called 'home-grown terrorism' – terrorist threats not from abroad, but from those who have grown up to attack their own country. In the UK, the attacks on the London transport network in 2005 by four young British Muslims catalysed attempts to understand why someone would decide to attack their own country, and the attackers' faith and ethnicity were scrutinised. A lack of shared values and the failure of multiculturalism shouldered the blame. Meer and Modood note this trend, arguing it is the 'coupling of diversity and anti-terrorism agendas that has implicated contemporary British multiculturalism as the culprit of Britain's security woes' (2009, p. 481). Multiculturalism had failed, and a new approach to security and diversity was needed – and shared values fitted the bill.

The challenge, however, with seeing shared values as a solution to a problem of multiculturalism is that, with multiculturalism's implicit subjectivities of 'host' and 'new arrival', it is implied that some people *always already* hold onto these values, whereas others need to learn them. Hage's critique of the political dynamics of multiculturalism helps to reveal how multiculturalism builds these subjects:

> Both the 'racists' and the 'multiculturalists' shared in the conviction that they were, in one way or another, masters of national space, and that it was up to them to decide who stayed in and who ought to be kept out of that space. (Hage, 2000, p. 17)

That this discourse of fundamental values constructs these two groups is evident. David Cameron, then UK Prime Minister, argued that the fundamental British values 'are Christian values and they should give us the confidence to say yes, we are a Christian country and we are proud of it' (2016). In the context of a political fear of so-called Islamic extremism, the emphasis was placed on ethnic minorities to take on these Christian, white values (Keddie, 2014; Lander, 2016; Maylor, 2016). White Britons, contrarily, have no need to prove their adherence to the values. Multicultural pluralism has shifted into assimilationism. One can see this in practice in a school context in Sian's (2015) research, which included an example of two neighbouring schools. Only one of these schools undertook training for its staff in countering extremism, and it was only the school with a majority of Black and ethnic minority students.

It is in this sense, then, that I argue that the promotion of fundamental British values is a form of both cultural and epistemic violence. Cultural violence refers to the symbolic and discursive markers that allow for other forms of violence to occur. This values promotion is a form of cultural violence in that the discourse regarding fundamental British values perpetuates a discourse of cultural incompatibility that must be addressed through values-promotion education.

One form of violence it precipitates through values education is epistemic violence. To borrow Gur-Ze'ev's words, this values promotion entails promoting 'homogeneity and ethnocentristic-oriented cohesion' (2011, p. 104). It places an uneven burden on some and not on others. In an educational setting, some researchers have found that teachers have experienced the promotion of these values akin to 'propaganda-like messages' (Jerome and Clemitshaw, 2012, p. 38). This seems profoundly concerning. In Cremin's words, 'when peace is grounded in hegemonic practices and a lack of concern for diversity, it becomes the very opposite of itself' (Cremin, 2016, p. 3).

These concerns of epistemic violence continue when examining the second iteration of counter-extremism, the promotion of pluralism and tolerance. While on one level it appears that this promotion of pluralism challenges the above criticism of promoting homogeneity, the presence of political power within the idea of tolerance offers a strong rebuttal to this. As Wendy Brown notes, 'Despite its pacific demeanour, tolerance is an internally unharmonious term, blending together goodness, capaciousness, and conciliation with discomfort, judgement, and aversion' (2006, p. 25).

While tolerance-promotion as a mode of countering extremism appears to promote tolerance of others, it also clearly delineates that which it does not tolerate. In particular, it evidently does not tolerate extremists (Ford, 2017b). Yet, moreover, it creates the power dynamic of producing those that do the *tolerating* and those who are deemed to be *(in)tolerable* (Brown, 2006). In Wemyss' words, it creates a 'hierarchy of belonging' where 'those at the top of the hierarchy of belonging have the power to grant or withhold tolerance from those at the bottom' (2006, p. 235). Furthermore, in the racialised context of fundamental British values and the global war on terror more broadly, this creates a hierarchy of belonging along racialised lines.

Scholars have been quick to note the lack of tolerance evident within discourses and practices that appear to promote tolerance. Brown notes that 'tolerance regulates the presence of the Other both inside and outside the liberal democratic nation-state, and often it forms a circuit between them that legitimates the most illiberal actions' (2006, p. 8). Žižek makes a similar point (and one that ties closely to critics of the liberal peace): 'Liberalist multiculturalism preaches tolerance between cultures while making it clear that true tolerance is fully possible only in individualist Western culture and thus legitimating even military interventions as an extreme mode of fighting the other's intolerance' (Žižek, 2008, p. 992, see also Ford, 2017b; Jackson, 2018). As such, here the material implications of epistemic violence become apparent – the moments in which the epistemic violence of the construction of a realm of legitimate values and beliefs transforms into direct violence enacted against those that stray into the realm of the impermissible. In this sense, it could therefore be argued that the apparent negative peace of counter-extremism masks the fact that it does not in fact produce any peace at all.

This direct violence may not necessarily emerge in the most brutal of contexts – in the drone strike or the deadly shooting of individuals like Jean Charles de Menezes – but occurs also in more subtle ways. In British schools, teachers are by law required to fulfil what is known as the 'Prevent duty' – a responsibility to inform the police or child protection agencies of any students they think might be at risk of radicalisation. Such a policy has led to that line that delineates the tolerable from the intolerable being rendered plainly visible. Human rights organisations have filed reports with numerous case studies where young Muslims have displayed behaviours that, due to their faith or ethnicity drawing them into a 'suspect category' (Breen-Smyth, 2014), have been categorised as 'extreme'. Police have interviewed students for displaying signs of greater religiosity (Open Society Justice Initiative, 2016) or for wearing a pro-Palestinian badge

(Rights Watch UK, 2016). Galtung defined violence as 'the cause of the difference between the potential and the actual' (1969, p. 168). When one considers the social and psychological impact of interactions with police and counterterrorism officers, one can begin to see how the impact on someone's potential that might emerge from this experience is a form of violence. In one case of a nine-year-old boy interviewed by school leaders for making a joke about a bomb, a report notes that 'this incident caused great distress to the entire family' (Rights Watch UK, 2016, p. 71), with the father in hospital with angina, the mother receiving treatment for psychological trauma and the boy himself scared to speak up in school. The promotion of a carefully curated sphere of permissible pluralism within the realm of ethnocentric, hegemonic values necessitates violence to retain the inside/outside borders.

In this sense, this chapter argues that current forms of counter-extremism appear to create a form of negative, liberal peace. It follows a logic that suggests once extremism has been removed and consensus imposed, then there can be peace. Yet the removal of extremism is evidently a very violent process, and one that also further embeds certain modalities of violence into the negative peace it produces. The question thus then emerges of how else could peace in the context of extremism be envisaged.

Positive peace, as was argued earlier in the chapter, addresses direct, structural and cultural violence. Yet, potentially too embedded in notions of consensus, a positive peace approach could entail the perpetuation of epistemic violence. Thus, the ultimate challenge here for a peace approach to countering extremism is to begin to envisage how to engender agonistic peace, and for this it is argued that what may be required is an approach that creates agonistic, dialogic spaces.

Conclusion: a counter-extremism strategy for agonistic peace?

In this concluding section, the chapter turns to the other end of the peace/violence matrix, and asks what a counter-extremism for agonistic peace may look like. The matrix suggests that agonistic peace offers a mode, through the production of dialogic, agonistic spaces, where all forms of violence – direct, structural, cultural and epistemic – can be addressed. Here, the chapter will conclude by exploring how extremism could be re-conceptualised, allowing for a revision of countering extremism through producing dialogic spaces in which multiple forms of peace can be debated.

Overall, the chapter has attempted to challenge the level to which counterextremism appears to be based on a notion of consensus, and particularly a consensus of liberal democratic values and political institutions. It has argued that this demand for liberal democratic consensus denies counter-extremism the opportunity to reduce certain forms of violence.

Interestingly, in Chantal Mouffe's (2005) *On the Political*, her work that lays a foundation for an understanding of agonism, a similar framing of liberal democratic consensus is depicted. Mouffe labels the contemporary political climate – in which liberal democratic bureaucratic institutions are presented as the universal and common-sensical norm for political organisation – as a *post-political* climate. Mouffe's argument is that *politics* – these bureaucratic mechanisms – are suppressing *the political* – the realm of contestation, debate and disagreement which perpetuates throughout human existence. Mouffe challenges this post-political setting, arguing it is contrary to the values of radical democracy. Furthermore, through the process of excluding those who do not conform to the liberal democratic consensus from democratic spaces, Mouffe argues that the post-political promotes the use of violence by those whose opportunities for political participation are restricted to the realm outside of the democratic sphere.

Counter-extremism appears in much the same post-political boat. It is a strategy which imposes a liberal democratic consensus, demanding that everyone sign up to the moderate centre values. Moreover, akin to Mouffe's criticism of post-political democracy, this form of counter-extremism appears to endanger the very values it is hoping to defend – defending democracy through anti-democratic means. It promotes intolerance as much as tolerance, and the violence experienced by those that stray too far from permissible ideas suggests that it is far from embracing a democratic ideal. If the goal of counter-extremism is a negative peace, this may not prove problematic to read. If, however, as peace studies allows us to do, our goal is to embrace a more nuanced understanding of positive peace, then counter-extremism needs to go beyond this remit.

Contrarily, an agonistic counter-extremism strategy could approach this problem of extremism very differently. Agonism, as mentioned above, begins from the premise that conflict is a perennial element of human existence, and that peace should envision a space in which such conflict can be deliberated and managed (rather than removed) in non-violent ways. Returning to the analogy of a bell curve drawn out earlier in the chapter, if instead of counter-extremism having as its goal the removal of contestation through the promotion of hegemony, counter-extremism could acknowledge the permanence of a spectrum of beliefs or values, and instead promote non-violent, pluralist ways for that disagreement to play out. Agonistic peace requires then the promotion of spaces for, what Shinko refers to as, 'Pluralistic contestation within a democratic political framework' (2008, p. 478). Instead of attempting to increase the population at the bell curve's middle, counter-extremism should accept that the curve of belief is here to stay.

Yet this notion is a lot easier said than done. In particular, the idea stumbles when facing the third dominant iteration of extremism, which emphasises a violent ideology. While it was argued above that there are a number of problems with such an understanding of extremism, the violent threat of extremists persists in the extremism discourse. The idea of attempting to adopt a non-violent approach to address the violence of extremists seems at the outset fatally flawed. It is here then that the foundational work for an agonistic approach to countering extremism must begin – unpicking this relationship between ideology and violence that currently dominates the field.

The synergy between extremist ideology and violence, though popular in discourse, in fact relies on very shaky foundations. These foundations appear to have two prominent departure points. One is a discourse which denies the legitimacy of political grievances of non-state actors (Baker-Beall et al., 2015). The political grievances of extremists are often downplayed (e.g., Cameron, 2015), denying the political nature of these violent situations. For example, the murder of Lee Rigby, a British soldier killed in the UK, was justified by the killer, recorded on video moments after the attack arguing: 'The only reason we have done this is because Muslims are dying every day' (Dodd and Halliday, 2013). The response by Boris Johnson, then Mayor of London, was clear: 'It is certainly not a question of blaming any aspect of British foreign policy or what British troops do in operations abroad when they risk our [sic] lives on behalf of all of us' (Channel 4 News, 2013). If violence cannot have a political cause, it comes to be seen as an end in itself.

The second departure point for the conflation of ideology and violence lies within discourses of radicalisation. Here, terrorists are portrayed as having gone on 'journeys' to terrorism, and along the way passed through a series of stages – non-violent extremism, violent extremism and terrorism (Baker-Beall et al., 2015; Borum, 2011). Such a mode of thinking, while popular, remains without strong empirical support. Yet this logic leads to what might be termed an 'upstreaming' approach to countering terrorism which seeks out the 'source' of the radicalisation journey (Sewall, 2017). This process inevitably produces a causation pattern between 'ideology' and 'violence' – with ideology being a key domino causing violence to occur.

Such conflation between these two ideas of ideology and violence has direct impact on people's lives. When extremism is imagined on a bell curve, clear lines become drawn at the point at which someone goes 'too far' from the centre, delineating the permissible and the impermissible. Ideas that do not in themselves threaten violence – but through conflation of ideas and the threat of violence – become seen to be impermissible.

It is this depiction of ideas as in and of themselves threatening that posits the greatest barrier to agonistic peace emerging in the context of extremism, as this mode of thinking promotes the exclusion rather than inclusion of such ideas. Through decoupling these two concepts, each concept can then merit its own response. An agonistic, democratic counter-extremism strategy could allow for the ideas behind extremism to be tackled and approached rather than excluded, while modes of non-violent political participation could be promoted. Yet it is here also that the biggest barrier to agonistic peace in the context of extremism emerges: the centrality of a distinction between legitimate and illegitimate violence within discourses of extremism. A pluralistic, agonistic space in which ideas, once deemed 'extreme' or 'moderate', can engage with one another as political ideas, requires also a pluralistic approach to the question of the legitimacy of violence. The question of violence therefore must no longer be limited to 'extremist' violence, but instead widened to encompass all forms of violence, including military and other forms of normalised violence. Non-violence can be promoted to the moderates as much as to the 'extremists'. The question of competing ideologies can then be tackled as what they are: ideas.

This chapter has attempted to argue that agonistic spaces can emerge in which the profound and complex questions that are thrown into the air within contemporary debates around extremism(s) can be explored. It is not possible in a chapter of this length to address all the issues at stake in such a claim, but instead the chapter has laid out the debates underpinning this claim. Fundamentally the chapter suggests that without addressing the elephant in the room in orthodox extremism discourses – the need to normalise and mask the 'legitimate' violence of the moderate – agonistic counter-extremism remains impossible.

References

Aly, A., Green, L., 2008. '"Moderate Islam": Defining the good citizen', *M/C Journal*, 11(1). Available at www.journal.media-culture.org.au/index.php/mcjournal/article/view/28/0 (accessed 27 February 2018).

Baker-Beall, C., Heath-Kelly, C. and Jarvis, L., 2015. 'Introduction', in Baker-Beall, C., Heath-Kelly, C. and Jarvis, L. (eds), *Counter-Radicalisation: Critical Perspectives*. Routledge, Abingdon, pp. 1–13.

Balls, E., 2008. 'Introduction', in Department for Children, Schools and Families (DCSF), *Learning Together to Be Safe: A Toolkit to Help Schools Contribute to the Prevention of Violent Extremism*. DCSF Publications, Nottingham, pp. 3–4.

Bartlett, J., Miller, C., 2012. 'The edge of violence: Towards telling the difference between violent and non-violent radicalization', *Terrorism and Political Violence*, 24(1), 1–21.

Borum, R., 2011. 'Radicalization into violent extremism I: A review of social science theories', *Journal of Strategic Security*, 4(4), 7–36.

Breen-Smyth, M., 2014. 'Theorising the "suspect community": Counterterrorism, security practices and the public imagination', *Critical Studies on Terrorism*, 7(2), 223–240.

Brown, W., 2006. *Regulating Aversion: Tolerance in the Age of Identity and Empire.* Princeton University Press, Princeton, NJ.

Cameron, D., 2015. 'Extremism: PM speech'. Available at www.gov.uk/government/ speeches/extremism-pm-speech (accessed 27 February 2018).

Cameron, D., 2016. 'Easter 2016: David Cameron's message'. Available at www.gov.uk/ government/news/easter-2016-david-camerons-message (accessed 28 February 2018).

Channel 4 News, 2013. 'Boris Johnson on Woolwich attack', 23 May. Available at www. youtube.com/watch?v=tQj-n90rNVU (accessed 28 February 2018).

Cremin, H., 2016. 'Peace education research in the twenty-first century: Three concepts facing crisis or opportunity?', *Journal of Peace Education*, 13(1), 1–17.

Davies, L., 2008. *Educating against Extremism.* Trentham Books, Stoke-on-Trent.

Department for Children, Schools and Families, 2008. *Learning Together to Be Safe: A Toolkit to Help Schools Contribute to the Prevention of Violent Extremism.* DCSF Publications, Nottingham.

Della Porta, D. (ed.), 1992. *Social Movements and Violence: Participation in Underground Organisations.* Emerald Group Publishing Limited, Bingley.

Department for Education, 2011. *Teachers' Standards: Guidance for School Leaders, School Staff and Governing Bodies.* Crown Copyright, London.

Department for Education, 2015. *The Prevent Duty: Departmental Advice for Schools and Childcare Providers.* Available at https://assets.publishing.service.gov.uk/ government/uploads/system/uploads/attachment_data/file/439598/prevent-duty-departmental-advice-v6.pdf (accessed 24 March 2020).

Dodd, V., Halliday, J., 2013. 'Lee Rigby killing: Two British Muslim converts convicted of murder', *Guardian*, 19 December. Available at www.theguardian. com/uk-news/2013/dec/19/lee-rigby-killing-woolwich-verdict-convicted-murder (accessed 31 October 2019).

Edyvane, D., 2011. 'Britishness, belonging and the ideology of conflict: Lessons from the Polis', *Journal of Philosophy of Education*, 45(1), 75–93.

European Commission Radicalisation Awareness Network, 2017. *Preventing Radicalisation to Terrorism and Violent Extremism: Approaches and Practices.* Available at https://ec.europa.eu/home-affairs/sites/homeaffairs/files/what-we-do/ networks/radicalisation_awareness_network/ran-best-practices/docs/ran_ collection-approaches_and_practices_en.pdf (accessed 27 February 2018).

Evans, J., 2007. 'Intelligence, counter-terrorism and trust'. Available at www.mi5.gov.uk/ news/intelligence-counter-terrorism-and-trust (accessed 27 February 2018).

Ford, K., 2017a. 'Developing a peace perspective on counter-extremist education', *Peace Review*, 29(2), 144–152.

Ford, K., 2017b. 'The insecurities of weaponised education: A critical discourse analysis of the securitised education discourse in North-West Pakistan', *Conflict, Security & Development*, 17(2), 117–139.

Ford, K., 2019. 'Defending a castle under siege: A critical examination of the British counter-extremism in schools strategy' (Thesis, Doctor of Philosophy). University of Otago. Available at http://hdl.handle.net/10523/9420 (accessed 17 February 2020).

Galtung, J., 1969. 'Violence, peace, and peace research', *Journal of Peace Research*, 6(3), 167–191.

Galtung, J., 1990. 'Cultural violence', *Journal of Peace Research*, 27(3), 291–305.

Gur-Ze'ev, I., 2001. 'Philosophy of peace education in a postmodern era', *Educational Theory*, 51(3), 315–336.

Gur-Ze'ev, I., 2011. 'Improvisation, violence and peace education', *Critical Issues in Peace and Education*, 42, 104–120.

Hage, G., 2000. *White Nation: Fantasies of White Supremacy in a Multicultural Society*. Routledge, London and New York.

Harris-Hogan, S., Barrelle, K. and Zammit, A., 2016. 'What is countering violent extremism? Exploring CVE policy and practice in Australia', *Behavioral Sciences of Terrorism and Political Aggression*, 8(1), 6–24.

Her Majesty's Government, 2011. *Prevent Strategy*. Crown Copyright, London.

Her Majesty's Government, 2015. *Counter-Extremism Strategy*. Crown Copyright, London.

Hooper, S., 2017, March 2. 'What is an extremist? UK Government admits it still doesn't know', *Middle East Eye*, 2 March. Available at www.middleeasteye.net/news/ exclusive-uk-government-still-considering-definition-extremism-1299352943 (accessed 26 February 2018).

Jackson, R., 2017. 'CTS, counterterrorism and non-violence', *Critical Studies on Terrorism*, 10(2), 357–369.

Jackson, R., 2018. 'Post-liberal peacebuilding and the pacifist state', *Peacebuilding*, 6(1), 1–16.

Jackson, W., 2012. 'Countering extremism in the name of security: Criminalizing alternative politics', in Taylor, E., Darlington, J. and Cookney, D. (eds), *Extremity and Excess*. University of Salford Press, Salford.

Jerome, L., Clemitshaw, G., 2012. 'Teaching (about) Britishness? An investigation into trainee teachers' understanding of Britishness in relation to citizenship and the discourse of civic nationalism', *Curriculum Journal*, 23(1), 19–41.

Keddie, A., 2014. 'The politics of Britishness: Multiculturalism, schooling and social cohesion', *British Educational Research Journal*, 40(3), 539–554.

Kennedy, R.F., 1965. *The Pursuit of Justice, etc.* Hamish Hamilton, Scranton, PA, London.

Kundnani, A., 2007. 'Integrationism: The politics of anti-Muslim racism', *Race & Class*, 48(4), 24–44.

Lake, D.A., 2002. 'Rational extremism: Understanding terrorism in the twenty-first century', *Dialogue IO*, 1(1), 15–28.

Lander, V., 2016. 'Introduction to fundamental British values', *Journal of Education for Teaching*, 42(3), 274–279.

Lindahl, S., 2017. 'A CTS model of counterterrorism', *Critical Studies on Terrorism*, 10(3), 523–541.

Maher, S., Frampton, M., 2009. *Choosing our Friends Wisely*. Policy Exchange, London.

Maylor, U., 2016. '"I'd worry about how to teach it": British values in English classrooms', *Journal of Education for Teaching*, 42(3), 314–328.

Meer, N., Modood, T., 2009. 'The multicultural state we're in: Muslims, "multiculture" and the "civic re-balancing" of British multiculturalism', *Political Studies*, 57(3), 473–497.

Mouffe, C., 2005. *On the Political*. Routledge, Abingdon.

O'Donnell, A., 2016. 'Securitisation, counterterrorism and the silencing of dissent: The educational implications of Prevent', *British Journal of Educational Studies*, 64(1), 53–76.

Office for Standards in Education, 2015. *School Inspection Handbook*. Ofsted, Manchester.

Open Society Justice Initiative, 2016. *Eroding Trust: The UK's Prevent Counter-Extremism Strategy in Health and Education*. Open Society Foundations, New York.

Oxford Dictionaries, n.d. Definition of extremism. *Oxford English Dictionaries*. Available at https://en.oxforddictionaries.com/definition/extremism (accessed 27 February 2018).

Rabasa, A., 2005. *Moderate and Radical Islam*. Testimony presented before the House Armed Services Committee Defense Review Terrorism and Radical Islam Gap Panel on November 3, 2005. Available at www.rand.org/content/dam/rand/pubs/testimonies/2005/RAND_CT251.pdf (accessed 27 February 2018).

Ramsbotham, O., 2010. *Transforming Violent Conflict: Radical Disagreement, Dialogue and Survival*. Routledge, London.

Richmond, O.P., 2009. 'A post-liberal peace: Eirenism and the everyday', *Review of International Studies*, 35(3), 557–580.

Rights Watch UK, 2016. *Preventing Education? Human Rights and UK Counter-terrorism Policy in Schools*. Available at http://rwuk.org/wp-content/uploads/2016/07/preventing-education-final-to-print-3.compressed-1.pdf (accessed 28 February 2018).

Sageman, M., 2014. 'The stagnation in terrorism research', *Terrorism and Political Violence*, 26(4), 565–580.

Schmid, A.P., 2014. *Al-Qaeda's 'Single Narrative' and Attempts to Develop Counter-Narratives: The State of Knowledge*. ICCT, The Hague.

Selma-Gregg, H., 2016. 'Three theories of religious activism and violence: Social movements, fundamentalists, and apocalyptic warriors', *Terrorism and Political Violence*, 28(2), 338–360.

Sewall, S., 2017. 'Looking upstream: Taking a hybrid approach to prevent violent extremism', *Fletcher Forum of World Affairs*, 41(1), 137–142.

Shinko, R.E., 2008. 'Agonistic peace: A postmodern reading', *Millennium: Journal of International Studies*, 36(3), 473–491.

Sian, K.P., 2015. 'Spies, surveillance and stakeouts: Monitoring Muslim moves in British state schools', *Race Ethnicity and Education*, 18(2), 183–201.

Sieckelinck, S., De Ruyter, D.J., 2009. 'Mad about ideals? Educating children to become reasonably passionate', *Educational Theory*, 59(2), 181–196.

Toros, H., Tellidis, I., 2013. 'Editor's introduction: Terrorism and peace and conflict studies: Investigating the crossroad', *Critical Studies on Terrorism*, 6(1), 1–12.

UNESCO, 2016. *A Teacher's Guide to the Prevention of Violent Extremism*. UNESCO, Paris.

Wemyss, G., 2006. 'The power to tolerate: Contests over Britishness and belonging in East London', *Patterns of Prejudice*, 40(3), 215–236.

Žižek, S., 2008. *Violence: Six Sideways Reflections*. Verso Books, London.

7

What is an educational response to extreme and radical ideas and why does it matter?

Aislinn O'Donnell

Introduction

Why should educators need to know about policies aimed at countering terrorism, radicalisation and (violent) extremism, and how do these policies shape educational practice? The UK's 'Four P' (Protect, Prevent, Pursue, Prepare) conceptualisation of the work-strands of the counter-terrorist strategy (CONTEST), together with the Dutch Information House's development of countering violent extremism (CVE) as 'soft interventionism' (Kundnani and Hayes, 2018, p. 6), have shaped wider European and global landscapes in respect of countering (violent) extremism, countering radicalisation and countering terrorism policies. One example of this is the European Commission's Radicalisation Awareness Network (RAN). However, the concept of 'extremism' is poorly defined in the policy literature, and although operational approaches and strategies to prevent and counter extremism and radicalisation are usually comprehensively described, as a general rule they fail to offer with any clarity or legal certainty the meaning and extension of central terms and concepts, like extremism and radicalisation, that provoke such strategies, shape their intent and presumably inform their enactment. Even the UN General Assembly's 2015 *Plan of Action to Prevent Violent Extremism* begins with an admission that, despite offering a more limited formulation of extremism, the term still eludes definition (Shepherd, 2017, p. 69). Nonetheless, extremism, including non-violent extremism, has been flagged as a security concern for educators, even if some states, like Germany, do not approach the question of extremism through a framework of counter-terrorism (Christodolou and Szakács, 2018).

This chapter addresses the question of non-violent extremism in the context of wider preventative and pre-emptive counter-terrorist policies, mobilising the example of the UK's influential Prevent strategy. It aims to articulate what an educational response, as distinct from a security response, to extreme and radical ideas involves and why it matters. For educational reasons, the terms 'radical' and 'extreme' ideas are favoured over the terms 'extremism' and 'radicalisation'. Extremism and radicalisation suggest identity or ideological positions (the extremist, the person who is radicalised or at risk of radicalisation). By focusing on 'extreme' ideas rather than 'extremism', this invites enquiry into the ideas, beliefs, values and positions 'on the table', so to speak, rather than focusing primarily on the one *who* is holding such ideas. This also allows for greater sensitivity to *how* ideas, values and beliefs are held and the potential responses to these ideas, including those that are intolerant, hateful or advocate violence. Panjwani et al. write in this regard,

> Ultimately, the central problem relating to extremism may not be the beliefs held, but rather the ways in which they are held: intolerant, closed to scrutiny and fixed. This intolerance, combined with other factors, can develop into violence. The will to impose and not the will to believe seems perhaps to be the underlying problem in extremism. (2018, p. 2)

The ways in which ideas are held is an issue for educators and is at the heart of educational practice. A more finely grained educational approach which pays attention to the contexts in which ideas circulate, including the space, time, place, bodies, traditions and histories, and that is attentive to the ways in which risk is perceived and conceptualised in educational spaces, is suggested in this chapter.

Education takes place in wider societal and political contexts. Climates of fear or insecurity affect both educational and political life. Educators are not immune from discourses of catastrophic risk and this can impact their capabilities to exercise judgement about risk in educational spaces. When pre-emptive logics are privileged even and particularly if there is no suggestion that risk can be completely eliminated, this shapes how risk is perceived. The original architect of CONTEST, David Omand, accepts and communicates to the public that risk cannot be completely eliminated, arguing that it is essential to ensure that the pursuit of security does not undermine human rights, freedom of movement and free speech, and that freedom and liberty must not be opposed to security. He acknowledges that it is important to be cognisant of the

> inter-relationship between our security efforts, their direct effect on the risks we face and the indirect effects on the rule of law, civil liberties, human rights and thus civic harmony or 'Civitas' – the public value of harmony in the community based on a shared sense of place, of belonging, regardless of ethnic roots or religious difference. The choice of security strategy is of course crucial to getting that thermodynamic judgment right. (Omand, 2012, p. 2)

He suggests that a pre-emptive approach to intelligence, described as the 'thermodynamics of counter-terrorism' (2015, p. 16), aids this balance in that it resists overreaction to acts of terrorism by privileging approaches that manage and provide strategic notice of risk. He argues nonetheless that 'The formal aim of CONTEST – which *is* being achieved – is [. . .] to reduce the risk from terrorism so that people can go about their normal life freely (that is, with the rule of law upheld and without the authorities having to interfere with individual rights and liberties) and with confidence' (2015, p. 16). Reducing (violent) radicalisation and extremism arguably modernises classic counter-insurgency doctrine.

However, Omand emphasises that CONTEST was originally conceived in such a way as to clearly separate the issue of violent extremism from questions of integration and social and community cohesion. He says, commenting on the introduction of fundamental British values and the policy and legislative turn to issues of non-violent extremism, 'We did think [in the original version of Prevent that] the priority was to prevent violent extremism. Once you get into being accused of policing different ways of living and "thought crime" over controversial areas such as foreign policy you enter a difficult area' (Open Society Justice Initiative, 2016, p. 36). In the original iterations of Prevent, there was no clear operational distinction between the integration and cohesion roles of the Department of Community and Local Government. One senior civil servant interviewee from the Office for Security and Counter Terrorism admits in O'Toole et al.'s study that, 'Because we arrived in a rather security-like way with a very determined delivery plan, occasionally people were just run off the court. They didn't have as much money. They didn't, frankly, have as much drive. They didn't quite know what they were doing. And it was hard. So what happened was Prevent took over Cohesion' (O'Toole et al., 2016, p. 168). Indeed, Omand himself suggests that it may also have been unwise to put the Prevent duty on a statutory footing in 2015 because teachers may feel obligated to report to authorities rather than deal with problems pragmatically, especially given adverse consequences of not doing so.

The chapter shares Omand's concern at the shift to non-violent extremism in counter-terrorism strategy, but unlike him it also looks at the wider implications and unintended consequences of pre-emptive approaches in counter-terrorism policy for addressing extreme and radical ideas in education. It focuses on three primary issues that have significant implications for educational practice and policy: (1) developments in European law and policy to regulate and address extremism; (2) the privileging of pre-emptive and anticipatory risk logics in an expanding field of counter-terrorist strategy; and (3) the adoption of the language of safeguarding against the risk of radicalisation and extremism. It explains why developing educational responses to extreme and radical ideas is important, how such responses differ from both political and security responses, how to distinguish between the different norms governing educational, political and security spaces, and why the shift to pre-emptive logics in counter-terrorism policies and non-violent extremism is problematic for education. It explains why it is important to engage with a wide range of ideas, values, traditions and dispositions in educational spaces and how counter-terrorist policies risk undermining educational practice. Finally, it offers a description of the norms, practices and values that govern educational spaces and pedagogical practices.

The implications of lack of clarity in the definition of extremism

Like the concept of radicalisation, the concept of extremism has been at the heart of global counter-terrorism strategies once the terrain shifted to the 'battle of ideas'. Extremism is, however, an imprecise and generically extended concept whose normative force trades on the implication that it *may* lead to violence and terrorism. There is no reason why extreme and radical ideas should be associated with violence, intolerance and hatred. Extremism is a relative and formal concept that requires context to give it substance and meaning. This vagueness explains why it eludes definition, enabling it to be deployed in multiple ways. It simply describes X distance from whatever Y at time T happens to constitute the mainstream M. This need not involve a normative judgement but can just describe a state of affairs. There is no evidence of direct causal connections between extreme ideas and violence.

Extremism in counter-terrorism policies has tended to be framed in one of two ways. Either extremism is the kind of speech used by the extremist who is, by his or her nature, hostile to society's norms and values, and consequently at risk of condoning, inciting or engaging in violence; *or* extremism is presented in virological or epidemiological language that claims that vulnerable people can be 'exposed to' extremist ideas that may put them at risk of radicalisation (to violence) if they are susceptible. The language of contagion communicates how such ideas are seen to spread through vulnerable populations (O'Donnell, 2018a). An example of the former is found in the latest iteration of the UK's CONTEST strategy, which states

> extremists *of all kinds* use malevolent narratives to justify behaviour that contradicts and undermines the values that are the foundation of our society. If left unchallenged, these narratives fragment and divide our communities. We protect the values of our society – the rule of law, individual liberty, democracy, mutual respect, tolerance, and understanding of different faiths and beliefs – by tackling extremism in all its forms. (HM Government, 2018, p. 23, my italics)

The European Commission (2015) has also described how the effect of attacks gives 'rise to increasingly reactionary and extremist views in other parts of society, which contributes to a breeding ground for extremism, perpetuating a vicious circle of radicalisation, aggression and polarised responses' (2015, p. 2). This risk of binary and polarised logics may also be exacerbated by unreflective and monolithic appeals to core, shared or fundamental values, in particular when expressed by states or other international bodies and institutions (O'Donnell et al., 2019).

An example of the virological image can be found in the title of this note from the UK : *Community Safety Board's Practice Guidance Note: Safeguarding Adults Exposed to Extremist Ideology (radicalisation)* (South Tyneside Community Safety Board, 2016, my emphasis). The note states that its aim is to ensure that staff understand what radicalisation means, why people may be vulnerable to being drawn into terrorism as a consequence, what the [UK] government means by 'extremism', the relationship between it and terrorism and the importance of challenging the extremist ideology associated with terrorism. These terms are all described in terms of vulnerability to exploitation and grooming. Questioning this kind of approach, the Royal College of Psychiatrists (2016) has issued a position statement in which it challenged the idea that there is a 'generally identifiable path to radicalisation', rejecting the suggestion that radicalisation is a mental illness. It stated that it is important 'to distinguish the role and expertise of psychiatrists in treating psychiatric disorders from the task of altering "extremist" views' (2016, p. 5). Finally, it underlined that there is no valid risk assessment instrument to predict radicalisation, primarily because of the enormous difficulty of predicting events that are extremely rare, an important issue to which we will return later.

Nonetheless, Amy Shepherd notes that 'numerous States have bolstered, enacted or proposed to enact laws focused on outlawing so-called extremist speech, drawing, whether explicitly or implicitly, a direct line from people publicly expressing "extreme" views to their committing acts of terrorist violence' (2017, p. 62). This is in spite of the enshrinement of the right to freedom of expression in the Universal Declaration of Human Rights, International Covenant on Civil and Political Rights (ICCPR) and a range of other conventions. Freedom of expression includes the right to express views that are unpalatable and controversial within limits of hate speech legislation and legislation which criminalises incitement to violence in a number of countries. These initiatives to outlaw extremist speech also challenge international law which requires that 'laws must be clear, accessible and formulated with sufficient precision to enable individuals to regulate their conduct accordingly' (Shepherd, 2017, p. 65). In fact, the European Court of Human Rights has made clear that to count as incitement, there must be positive intention to solicit and encourage others to engage in discrimination and violence. Simply expressing 'a hostile, discriminatory or violent worldview' will not necessarily meet that threshold (Shepherd, 2017, p. 66).

The Joint Committee on Human Rights (2016) in the UK also makes clear that extremism is not a clear-cut criminal offence. It questions the language of safeguarding in the 2015 Counter-Extremism and Safeguarding Bill because there is 'no consensus or shared definition of what children would be safeguarded from in the case of so-called radicalisation' (2016, p. 5), unlike in cases of physical abuse, sexual abuse or neglect of children. It voiced its concern about the proposed use of civil orders and underlined that no definition has been offered of non-violent extremism or British values that offers the legal certainty required in such a bill. The recent appointment of a Commission for Countering Extremism can be seen as an effort to provide such certainty. This issue is also addressed in the Office of the United Nations High Commissioner for Human Rights (OHCHR) Report of the Special Rapporteur (2016) on the promotion and protection of human rights and fundamental freedoms while countering terrorism (A/HRC/31/65), which states the crucial importance of legal certainty in respect of violent extremism. He describes the shift towards CVE approaches in counter-terrorist strategies globally, and explains how, despite numerous initiatives to prevent or counter violent extremism, there is still no generally accepted definition of violent extremism (OHCHR, 2016, pp. 5–6). Nor is there a clear conceptual distinction between terrorism and violent extremism. Additionally, he argues that the process of radicalisation is still presented in far too simple a manner, relying on supposedly causative factors or drivers like ideology.

A further danger is that overly expansive concepts of extremism can be mobilised to eliminate political or religious dissent under the aegis of counter-radicalisation should states choose to try to justify their actions using these wider counter-terrorist frameworks. Of particular concern is the use of the term 'extremism' as an offence in itself. Responding to the adoption of Resolution A/HRC/30/15 by the Human Rights Council in 2015, the Special Rapporteur comments on the *lack* of a requirement that activities should involve the use of violence if they are to be included in the description of violent extremism, as to exclude the question of use of violence constitutes a considerable risk for human rights abuses because it may lead to governments qualifying even non-violent actions that are critical of them as 'violent extremism'. He notes that 'this is compounded by the resolution's reference to "extremist ideologies or intolerance" without any reference to violence and the use of the vague expression "supporters" of violent extremists' (OHCHR, 2016, p. 12).

The Special Rapporteur explains the impact on human rights of those measures that target particular individuals or groups in seeking to counter and prevent extremism on the basis that they are 'at risk' of violent extremism. He argues that such 'inchoate offences far removed from the commission of acts of violence can violate freedom of expression, thought, conscience, religion and belief, while freedom of assembly and association can be impacted by measures to curb "extremist" NGOS' (OHCHR, 2016, p. 14), as well as impacting on the right to education and academic freedom. He comments on the implications of statutory duties to prevent extremism and radicalisation for the exercise of professional functions by those staff in public bodies as well as the capacity for the child to exercise his or her rights in educational settings. This wider context of global counter-terrorism policies indicates some of the (unintended) consequences of initiatives to counter non-violent extremism and may explain Prevent's recent reframing as safeguarding. How then ought education respond to the question of extremism?

Educational responses to extreme and radical ideas

It is understandable to be deeply concerned about a rise in identitarian politics, hostility to pluralism, anti-democratic sentiments, authoritarianisms and populisms, polarisation, intolerant and hateful extremisms and the presence of discourses of ethno-national purity in mainstream political discourse. Bart Brandsma's (2017) work on polarisation explains what happens in oppositional dynamics that fuel reciprocal counter-reactions, rather than creating the conditions for dialogue and engagement. However, when ideas seen as radical and extreme are automatically associated with terrorism and violence, this has implications for education and politics as it suggests that such ideas are potentially dangerous or suspect. As noted above, given the imprecision and lack of legal certainty of the definition of extremism, this may be used by states to justify silencing dissenting positions positioned as 'extreme' or 'radical' as *a priori* dangerous in both political and educational spaces (O'Donnell, 2018a). This is not to suggest that as an educator one ought not respond to those ideas that try to legitimate dehumanisation, violence and hatred or refuse to try to understand and indeed interrogate them.

There is, however, no necessary correlation between ideas that are radical or extreme and acts of violence. Extreme and radical ideas often simply describe those ideas that are different from the dominant norms and values of a given society at a given time. Reflective citizens and students will also be aware that accepted dominant norms and values, including those of states, may be not only neither right nor just but may be cruel and violent or even 'extremist', if we take seriously some of the policy language describing extremism. The disenfranchisement of voters, subordination of women, imperialism, institutionalised forms of racism and slavery reveal the pernicious nature of what were once dominant norms and the ways in which dissenting positions were viewed as extreme or radical (Wolton, 2019).

In this regard, Enrique Dussel (1999) explains how critical moments stemming from the 'outside' of a system may rather serve to mark what is intolerable and show what needs to be transformed in a system. What really matters is not whether or not ideas are extreme or radical but rather whether they promote and advocate violence, encourage hatred and intolerance, dehumanise others and seek to annihilate difference. It is only when the threat of violence arises that a security response or legal response may be required. Holding certain kinds of extreme or radical ideas, such as white supremacist views, is often accompanied by a set of traits and dispositions that undermine epistemic virtues: an inability to listen to alternative perspectives, the refusal of pluralism, the exhibition of dogmatic certainty and the tendency to select only 'evidence' that consolidates one's own position, as well as the desire to adopt an affective framework that dehumanises or silences others.

But some positions of dogmatic certainty, for example fundamentalist religious views, do not necessarily indicate tolerance of violence or even hatred. Some of the traits associated with extremism may also be found in those who claim to hold liberal or progressive positions if they are unable to listen to others or imagine the world from the perspective of another. And none of this means extreme or radical ideas *qua* ideas cannot be engaged with educationally. Even noxious ideas can be engaged with in educational ways, including through dialogue and listening. For example, in the context of a set of reflections about school shootings and gun violence, I have written of the importance of developing curricula and diverse pedagogical approaches that allow for conversations about violence, the genealogies of violence, the persistence in the contemporary world of a variety of kinds of violence, including state violence, in the context of reflecting on the vulnerability of the human condition (O'Donnell, 2015). Gereluk and Titus (2018) think that this kind of approach to curriculum is important for engaging with the violent radicalisation of youth.

Educational spaces are complicated spaces. They are thinking spaces in which very different kinds of knowledge, concepts, ideas, beliefs, disciplines, traditions and values circulate and are interrogated, explored and questioned or blocked and silenced. They are affective spaces in which different kinds of felt emotions, imaginaries and commitments circulate or get stuck from anger, resistance and fear to joy, surprise and solidarity. They are aesthetic spaces in which different bodies, stories, objects, gestures and movements are read and received in different ways at different times. They are ethical spaces of encounters with others who hold different values, perspective, beliefs, worldviews and ideas. Educational spaces are pluralistic spaces by virtue of the diverse knowledges encountered, the pedagogies that express, create and communicate ideas, knowledge and experience, and because of the people within them. They are governed by sets of norms and values that aim at creating the conditions for *educational* experiences and encounters (O'Donnell, 2018b). This involves orienting students from a focus on self towards our common world to those matters on the 'educational or studying table' (Masschelein and Simons, 2013; O'Donnell et al., 2019).

A classroom or study space might broach extreme ideas through an examination of historical archives, podcasts, forum theatre, opera, literature, philosophical reasoning or absent memorialisation, and the subject matter and pedagogical approach will frame the space through norms agreed, implicitly or explicitly, by teachers and students. Pedagogical parameters are often made explicit and operate as immanent sets of rules that change with different exercises devised to open up different educational experiences and encounters with knowledge. A useful analogy here is the rules and norms of a game. How rules and norms are devised and play out in educational spaces differs in one significant way from the approach in a political space because the latter is a community of political equals (at least in principle). In political spaces, engagement with extreme ideas might involve a variety of forms of manifestation or dialogue: a protest, manifesto, discussion or debate.

The nature of the norms that govern educational spaces also help students and teachers to grapple with difficult questions with the help of thoughtful, creative pedagogies, including reflecting on those aspects of life that deal with the existential quest for purpose and meaning, the desire for 'sacred values' (Atran, 2011) and the political quest for justice, but they do so in an *educational* way. This might involve engaging with positions self-described as extremist or radical, and re-interrogating and re-appropriating these terms for contemporary times, for example discussing Extinction Rebellion. Historical examples might include Martin Luther King stating that he is an extremist for love, Myles Horton in his auto-biography *The Long Haul* writing of the moment when he was 'radicalised' and young male and female foreign fighters, like George Orwell and Simone Weil, who once travelled to Spain to fight in the Spanish Civil War.

Thinking about *educational* responses to extreme and radical ideas involves attunement to the ways in which educational conversations and questions differ from security conversations and even political conversations. The importance of developing educational responses to difficult and controversial ideas, positions and questions in resistance to securitisation has been articulated by a number of scholars and researchers (Jerome and Elwick, 2019; Mattsson and Säljö, 2018; Ragazzi, 2018; Ruitenberg, 2017; Sieckelinck et al., 2015). Educational spaces, at least in theory, are spaces of plurality in which students in their very plurality gather in order to encounter the rich stories of humankind and to learn of worlds beyond their personal experience, private concerns, and faith and philosophical traditions. They create the conditions for engagement with complex stories of our common world. Pedagogical encounters with knowledges and ideas of all kinds are the means by which humans pass on the complex stories of our world to the next generation. Educators foster depth of understanding by supporting the genesis of students' 'enlarged mentality', that is, their ability to cultivate situated impartiality. This can enable students to hold together plural, even contradictory, epistemological approaches and ways of being without always seeking out consensus or refusing difference. In these ways, students come to form their own opinions, ideas, judgements, values and sense of purpose.

Educational spaces share with political spaces the potentials for activation of collective modes of engagement and enquiry that foster critical thinking, dialogue, deep listening, a taste for pluralism and intellectual humility. They help students and teachers understand how and when *parrhesia*, or fearless speech, may be necessary, and to understand why, like political speech, educational speech involves shouldering the responsibilities of speaking responsibly in public, including in classroom spaces (Ruitenberg, 2017). Educational spaces also require students and teachers to try out and test different ideas, to take on different standpoints and to train the imagination to go visiting.

Some differences between educational spaces and political spaces include the different ways in which their respective subject matters are put on the table, the different ways in which freedom is understood and enacted, the ways they approach the question of values, the different expectations for, and responsibilities of, students, persons and citizens in particular in relation to free speech, and the different norms that govern these different spaces. Extreme or radical ideas will be dealt with in one way in a political space, another way in a security space, another in a domestic space and in yet another way in an educational space. There may also be democratic moments, security moments, pastoral moments and moments for free speech in educational spaces, just as there are sometimes pedagogical moments in political or security spaces, even if the norms that govern each of those spaces are distinct.

The norms that govern educational spaces aim to preclude the domination or imposition of a single perspective or voice, be it of teacher or student, on *educational* grounds. As part of this practice, an important role of the educator is not just to put something on the table but also to take it off the table, at least temporarily, as an act of professional judgement. This might involve suspending a heated debate or flagging that a student's hateful comment will be addressed later. Sensitive and thoughtful educators will treat the subject matter of extremism as a curricular issue using multiple lenses that enable diverse kinds of educational experiences – at one moment, poetry from Guantanamo Bay, at another, Plato's philosophical argument against democracy, or historical accounts of the genesis of racialised slavery, or Fanon's acerbic furious first lines of *Black Skin, White Masks*. This is what good pedagogy involves. It refuses a 'single vision' (O'Donnell, 2015).

It is difficult for educators to countenance the idea that when engaging with extremism, the task ought to be simply to 'challenge' and 'counter' certain ideas. This negates the educator's educational responsibilities to students, unless such challenges are part of a particular pedagogical strategy. Of course, certain statements uttered publicly in class may need to be challenged or explored, but how and when is a matter of professional judgement. Educators constantly make judgements and should be supported professionally in making distinctions between pedagogical, pastoral and judicial moments in their classrooms, with appropriate awareness of a range of different kinds of phronetic or epistemic risks that arise in assessing evidence. Some will need further support to develop culturally responsive pedagogies that welcome the life worlds of the child or young person and their families and carers into the educational space.

This is particularly important given the racialisation of risk perception, not only in the domain of counter-terrorism. Unfortunately, when interventions seek to pre-empt or anticipate the potential or possible risk of extremism (or terrorism), it renders it unclear which norms are governing which spaces and when they are doing so. It also does not explain how educators can manage epistemic and phronetic risks in order to ensure objectivity in their judgements (Burch and Furman, 2019). Such judgements are being made in a context where the pre-emptive logics of catastrophic risk intensify urgency of correct assessment, given the implications of failing to notice whether a student is 'at risk of radicalisation'.

How the shift from prevention to pre-emption in counter-terrorist policies affects educational practice

> The norm is no longer explicit, and is not as explicit as a law and it is no longer contestable. It is no longer contestable in court since there is no longer disobedience and thus it no longer needs to be interpreted. This is called pre-emption. This is pre-emption and not prevention. [..] It is not prediction either. It is a regime of action on the future which is absolutely new, in my opinion. (Antoinette Rouvroy in Rouvroy and Stiegler, 2016, p. 15)

It is troubling when educators are asked to *challenge* non-violent extremism as a duty under counter-terrorist policies, or to see 'extremist ideas', including their aesthetic manifestation in public spaces, as first and foremost a safeguarding concern that involves managing risk by providing 'support' to a vulnerable person, rather than an educational opportunity for learning and thinking.

Nikolas Rose (2000) describes how risk management approaches traverse a range of domains and institutions, saying that it is a style of thinking that tries to tame uncertainty by expertise. The application of a criminological lens to counter-terrorism led to the emergence of a range of new counter-terrorist functions including identifying suspicious behaviour, challenging extremist narratives and deploying an increasingly nebulous discourse of resilience. Risk-based and anticipatory approaches rely less on knowledge than suspicion, resting on expert professionals' readings of what is deemed 'normal' for their sphere of practice, with an emphasis on 'gut feeling'. This can make sense in schools when reflecting on issues of child protection and abuse. However, the development of gut feeling or abduction requires significant experience when it comes to predicting 'potential terrorists', given how rare such cases are in the general population. It has proven extremely difficult, if not impossible, for experienced practitioners, including those from security, policing and intelligence, to predict risk of violent radicalisation. Gut feeling is not a reliable approach to risk assessment, in particular for non-experts such as educators operating in a context of pre-emptive counter-terrorism within racialised framings of terrorism.

This is compounded by a shift from an approach to risk that aims to *predict* the future based on some, however imperfect, engagement with evidence, to the anticipation and pre-mediation of multiple *possible* futures such that immediate pre-emptive security action can be taken. Contemporary apparatuses of security are now oriented towards the incalculable and unpredictable rather than making judgements on the basis of evidence (De Goede et al., 2014). Pre-emption is here described in terms of security practices that aim to act on threats that are both unknown and recognised to be unknowable, yet are also deemed potentially catastrophic, such that they require security intervention at the earliest possible stage (De Goede et al., 2014, p. 412). François Ewald contends that 'the precautionary principle invites one to anticipate what one does not yet know, to take into account doubtful hypotheses and simple suspicions. It invites one to take the most far-fetched forecasts seriously, predictions by prophets, whether true or false' (2002, p. 288). This has created techniques of governmentality that make it possible to prosecute an individual before an act is committed or even planned, enabling security interventions to work from *any* possible, without reference to reasonable suspicion based on evidence or even inductive probabilistic methods of analysis.

The logics of pre-emption and pre-caution work because they are intensified by the claims to urgency, in particular the always imminent threat of possible catastrophe or disaster, and not because their conclusions and claims can be contested or checked. These logics produce decisions that cannot be bound by evidence, that are not subject to criteria of effectiveness and that can never be shown to be either true or false. They are performative, producing new realities without taking responsibility for them. Brian Massumi, reflecting on this phenomenon, says, 'The exercise of [pre-emptive] power is incitatory. It contributes to the actual emergence of the threat' (2007, p. 216) in that the purpose of its operative functioning is to *test* possibles, rather than reacting to or deterring real threats or situations. In order to test the threat, one does not wait; one moves and acts. The possible and the speculative here exceed the probable, as experience becomes over-burdened with potential or possible significance, including the threat of disaster. By operating proto-formally in a space of possible catastrophe, and by putting into abeyance questions of evidence or intelligence, the predominant affective responses provoked are fear and insecurity. Pre-emptive interventions initiate performative feedback loops that act from possible futures to the present. They are thus different from probabilistic logics of induction that rely in however minimal a fashion on some provision of evidence, data or knowledge for inductive reasoning and prediction.

The activation of the concept 'risk of radicalisation', and the introduction of safeguarding measures and duties in response to this risk in the European context and beyond, exemplify how elements of this logic of pre-emption has now crept into the heart of a number of public institutions through counter-terrorism policies, primarily because of the lack of clarity of definition of central terms like extremism and radicalisation. However, this shift from probabilistic logics to pre-emptive logics need not only target susceptible populations; instead it can take a global approach to gathering data. Those algorithms that work on that data may subsequently generate further intensive focus on specific, often racialised, populations, as predictive algorithms in sentencing has shown in the US. With algorithmic governance, accountability becomes difficult because there is no recourse to contest judgements due to the proprietorial ownership of algorithms used in sentencing practices. Indeed, with the shift from big data to machine learning, 'false positive' cases, like 95% of referrals to Prevent in the UK which are subsequently rejected, could constitute very useful data, enabling previously unknown connections of variables to be identified as part of a pre-crime, pre-emptive strategy. These would presumably then be mobilised in new knowledge applications and inform further interventions into other spaces, like the educational space.

A potential further problem with the pre-emptive logics of security is the way in which the subject of Big Data and machine learning is understood to be an abstract subject and not a living human being. This abstract subject is privileged over the sentient, embodied subject who, according to the logic of algorithmic governmentality, does not know him or herself or others sufficiently well to be trusted in either self-appraisal or the evaluation of others. Although algorithms that govern data require verification, this is only in order that they can be operationalised. The algorithmic, abstract subject remains unknowable, like a black box. Even if this is true, it means that human subjects are rendered superfluous, powerless and speechless in the face of 'expertise' that exceeds human cognition. In this regard, Rouvroy cites Hannah Arendt's letter to her mentor Karl Jaspers:

> What radical evil is I don't know, but it seems to me it somehow has to do with the following phenomenon: making human beings as human beings superfluous – not using them as means, that does not infringe upon their humanity but merely upon their dignity of human beings, but rendering them superfluous despite their quality of being human. This happens as soon as unpredictability – which, in human beings, is the equivalent of spontaneity – is eliminated. (Rouvroy, 2016, p. 82)

This raises significant difficulties for educators who wish to exercise phronetic judgement on a case-by-case basis and provides an important context for understanding the ways in which extremism and radicalisation are conceptualised in educational spaces and the prospects for the future of the extension of these pre-emptive logics.

Why does this matter for education? By presenting radicalisation and extreme ideas and views as, for example, a 'safeguarding' issue akin to other kinds of safeguarding against abuse, this version of safeguarding is presented as just another element on a continuum of care or support for the vulnerable. There is no acknowledgement of the wider context of the pre-emptive logics of catastrophic risk that drives the move to safeguard those at 'risk of radicalisation'. It is not even clear *what* one is being safeguarded from. Moreover, to suggest that an encounter with or exposure to extremist views can constitute abuse is deeply worrying, from both an educational perspective and a democratic perspective. What really matters is *how* extreme and radical ideas are engaged with.

Of course, given educational spaces are sites for the exchange of knowledge and engagement in collective enquiry, educators do have heightened responsibility for the circulation of speech in those settings marked as educational (Ruitenberg, 2017). Claudia Ruitenberg is clear that 'part of a teacher's educational responsibility is to model that we cannot just scatter words in social space willy-nilly any more than we can scatter seeds in a field without informing ourselves whether some of them might be invasive weeds' (2017, p. 220). Students should come to understand the duties and responsibilities involved in educational speech and to do so they must develop their skills of analysis, evaluation and comprehension. This will include addressing in classrooms the perlocutionary effects of speech acts that express hatred and intolerance, and the ways in which silence can be seen as accommodation and encouragement of such views.

The importance of preserving the integrity of educational spaces

We have seen what happens when extreme and radical ideas are understood and framed under a 'security umbrella' as extremism and radicalisation. One example of this 'security umbrella' was the way in which preventative counter-terrorism was re-framed as safeguarding under Prevent and having due regard to the need to prevent people from being drawn into terrorism was made a legal duty for all frontline public sector workers. Once security objectives are privileged above, or set the context for, educational experiences, judgements and purposes, this changes educational relationships and the educational engagement with ideas. Certainly, policies like Prevent may have a limited role in addressing those real security issues that arise, albeit rarely, and those who risk engaging in political violence, but it should not have a global remit that encompasses all students. I have outlined a number of reasons why the pre-criminal space of pre-emption ought not be brought into educational spaces as a matter of policy. Educators and institutions should be trusted and supported to take care of these difficult topics, a significant task, no doubt, when many governments also promote narrow measures of educational success and cultures of performativity and surveillance of both staff and students.

We have learned that safeguarding against radicalisation is not the same as the broader societal responsibility and commitment to safeguard children, young people and vulnerable adults (Royal College of Psychiatrists, 2016). First, the person in question is, in such cases, not only seen as 'at risk' but also is viewed as potentially constituting a real and serious threat to wider society such that society in turn must be safeguarded from that person. Second, the nature of that risk or threat is often loosely construed within pre-emptive logics, unlike other forms of safeguarding that are more explicitly oriented towards prevention than pre-emption, requiring clear grounds for intervention and opportunities for verification. Third, appealing to the possibility of a (catastrophic) exception in order to justify pre-emptive and precautionary interventions against the 'risk of radicalisation or extremism' under the aegis of safeguarding shifts the educational terrain in ways that may not be fully understood by non-educators, that is, by professionals whose primary focus is security, policing or intelligence. It is not clear that safeguarding against the 'risk of radicalisation' responds to verifiable threats supported by evidence. It risks operating in the speculative realm of possible futures, or at least being framed as such by practitioners keen to avoid catastrophic risk. It may be simply unclear to educators and students which speech acts and ideas ought to be treated as a matter for safeguarding and which a topic for educational enquiry.

When safeguarding language is applied to 'non-violent extremism', it suggests that extreme ideas and views ought to be addressed *a priori* in a securitised manner, even if it is also claimed that it is important to discuss sensitive and difficult issues in schools. Ambiguity in this regard is problematic in education. It undermines the exercise of professional judgement and precludes the cultivation of epistemic virtues. Educational and pedagogical practice involves complicating and enquiring into ideas and questions rather than simply 'challenging' them. To only respond to extreme ideas by challenging them not only risks pushing a student into an entrenched position, it also tends to be counter-productive educationally and pastorally by not attending to *how* such views are held or exploring how one might work with pedagogical strategies and educational norms to engage with these ideas. This is not to suggest that educational spaces ought merely to be unregulated spaces for 'free speech', sometimes understood by students as the right to voice opinions without corresponding duties. Nor should they be policed spaces in which difficult conversations are avoided or silenced. Skilful educational facilitators can open up most topics for thoughtful engagement.

In his report (OHCHR, 2016), the Special Rapporteur rightly emphasised the importance of freedom of expression, also highlighted by the Human Rights Committee's comments on Article 19 of the ICCPR. However, freedom of expression is understood differently in the political domain from the educational domain. Educational freedom involves fostering the capacity and curiosity for intellectual enquiry, exploration of values and purposes and the activation of the imagination as students come to more deeply understand and engage with the pluralistic nature of the human condition in our common world. Educational spaces, like political spaces, are spaces where one comes to form or develop one's opinions and ideas about matters of common concern, but unlike political spaces, this formation occurs not solely through listening and testing their ideas against those of other citizens and developing the capacity for responsible speech, but by also developing a deeper understanding of the world and by being explicitly asked to look at the world through multiple lenses. The world in education is the subject matter that is put on the table.

The educational act of putting something on the table also demands a sense of perspective and humility – the world long preceded us and it will long outlast us. Part of educational experience and training involves testing and examining different ideas, theories and stories, weighing up evidence and argument and actively engaging in scrutiny of one's ideas and commitments with sufficient humility and a sense of fallibility. It involves developing the capacity for perspective taking and listening, the ability to change one's mind if the facts, arguments or evidence require such, and to recognise one might be wrong, as well as to have the intellectual courage to formulate positions and arguments and articulate one's commitments, principles and values in public spaces. The responsibility of education is also to our common world and the next generation, as well as to one another. This entails creating spaces of cultural safety that allow for critical, sensitive and thoughtful interrogation of values and ideas in educational spaces. This means that the lifeworld and traditions of the student are not left at the door but rather become part of the fabric of educational encounter.

If education spaces are understood to be equivalent to political spaces of 'free speech' or if they are modelled on deliberative democracy, their educational function is undermined. Educational spaces nonetheless retain affinities with the public sphere of politics, stemming from a shared understanding that our common world discloses itself differently to each of us, that it will not yield to our will and that facts are fragile and readily destroyed by power. In both politics and education, as we listen to others, we come to develop an enlarged and representative mentality. To seek to impose one's view without listening to others is coercive and destroys the conditions for political and educational engagement. In both spaces, matters of common concern are put on the table, though in different ways, and educational spaces preserve relations of authority between teacher and student for the sake of the world. Educational spaces at their best foster deep attention, dialogue, enquiry and listening, fostering the capacity to deal with complexity, uncertainty and ambiguity, and asking students to enter into the traditions and conversations that have shaped the subject matter at hand (O'Donnell, 2015). Part of the educational task also involves being able to come to think about those positions that one finds most difficult, challenging or even intolerable in order to learn to judge and think 'without a banister', and engage in dialogue with others with whom we disagree.

Soft-power approaches to counter-terrorism are motivated by many reasons including the concern that the circulation of certain beliefs and ideas may serve to create an atmosphere conducive to violence and terrorism. An additional concern is that silence of bystanders in the public domain, in respect of the circulation of extremist speech, implicitly accommodates, sanctions and even encourages speech acts that promote hate, risking the perception of legitimacy for the use of violence against target groups. It is, as we have seen, tempting to imagine that direct, pre-emptive and active engagement in the sphere of ideas will proactively shift the beliefs, ideas and mind-sets of those who may be 'at risk of radicalisation', thus reducing the prospect of violence and terrorism. However, such actions also risk undermining and impoverishing the pluralism of the public domain. This may be by sanctioning only one version of individualist and secular liberalism, which can result in a coercively uniform set of ideologically driven values (Rivers, 2018) and an intolerant, even illiberal, liberalism. Indeed, the nature of democracy is such that it requires the endless vital agonism of the political sphere to renew it and keep it alive. Coming to understand these values and priorities in a multiplicity of ways shapes the democratic experience, exemplifying the pluralism of the human condition and giving space for the ongoing contestation of what Jacques Rancière (2004) calls 'the part that has no part' that struggles to visibility and audibility. In educational spaces, as in political spaces, sustaining pluralism is essential.

Educational spaces, like political spaces, are spaces committed to truth, in their own way, and they are grounded in facts, again in their own way. While education's attention is focused on the 'objective' world and the pasts that we inherit and renew with each generation, the world of political spaces arises each time we weave together the invisible web of pluralistic opinions, or *doxa*, in attending to matters of common concern, and vanishes once we leave. Opinions are not opportunities for monologues of self-expression, they are not 'human rights' and they cannot be reduced to the mere manifestation of immutable psychological traits. Unlike some popular misconceptions of liberalism none of us is simply 'entitled' to our opinions without challenge. Such a position would undo and negate the plurality of the human condition.

Instead, as one begins to form one's thinking at the outset of a dialogical encounter, opinions are only in their genesis, embryonic and in process. Through acts of seeking out encounters with the perspectives of others, one comes to eventually form one's own opinion, however provisional. The criterion of validity by which this can be evaluated is only introduced at the point of conclusion when it can be seen whether that opinion has taken into account a plurality of perspectives by engaging in 'representative' thinking. Lisa Disch describes this as 'situated rather than abstract impartiality', saying that 'training one's imagination to go visiting [. . .] involves evoking or telling yourself the multiple stories from the plurality of conflicting perspectives that constitutes it' (1993, p. 686). All kinds of perspectives and interpretations constitute the tapestries of stories in education and although not all are of equal merit and equal value, they ought to be put on the table for examination. This is done with the help of thoughtful pedagogies that sustain commitment to cultivating, creating and conserving the pluralism of the human condition and our common world.

Truthfulness matters in the political domain just as it does in the educational domain; one cannot fabricate 'facts' as one wishes. In 'Truth and Politics', Arendt says that 'even if we admit that every generation has the right to write its own history, we admit no more than that it has the right to rearrange the facts in accordance with its own perspective; we don't admit the right to touch the factual matter itself' (1996, pp. 237–238). What interested Arendt about the public space was that it helps to create the conditions to enable one to *find* the truth in one's opinion, rather than to speak a truth one already knows (Zerilli, 2012, p. 65). This is as part of a 'broader process of critical thinking and judging' (Zerilli, 2012, p. 68).

The kind of truth with which politics is concerned requires publicity in order that representative thinking can be activated, and this has affinity to the ways in which educational spaces operate. By taking responsibility as educators to introduce students to the common world, in all its horrors and its beauty, we can come to reconcile ourselves to reality, and in so doing we open to the creation of new futures. This is why students must not be 'protected' or 'safeguarded' from extremist ideas, and these must not be presented as an indicator of 'risk of radicalisation' or provide reasons for safeguarding. Rather, all ideas, including extreme and radical ideas, should be put on the 'educational table' and studied and discussed according to the norms that govern educational spaces while remaining committed to the pluralism at the heart of the human condition and democratic life.

References

Arendt, H., 1996. *Between Past and Future*, Penguin, London.

Atran, S., 2011. *Talking to the Enemy: Sacred Values, Violent Extremism, and What it Means to Be Human.* Penguin, London.

Brandsma, B., 2017. *Polarisation: Understanding the Dynamic of Us versus Them.* BB in Media, Amsterdam.

Burch, M., Furman, K., 2019. 'Objectivity in science and law: A shared rescue strategy', *International Journal of Law and Psychiatry*, 64, 60–70.

Christodolou, E., Szakács, S., 2018. *Preventing Violent Extremism through Education: International and German Approaches.* Georg Eckert Institute, Braunschweig: and young people in Britain', *Children and Society*, 28, 242–256.

De Goede, M., Simon, S. and Hoijtink, M., 2014. 'Performing pre-emption', *Security Dialogue*, 45(5), 411–422.

Disch, L., 1993. 'More truth than fact: Storytelling as critical understanding in the writings of Hannah Arendt', *Political Theory*, 21(4), 665–694.

Dussel, E., 1999. 'Six theses toward a critique of political reason: The citizens as political agent', *Radical Philosophy Review*, 2(2), 79–95.

European Commission, 2015. *Preventing Radicalisation to Terrorism and Violent Extremism: Strengthening the EU's Response.* European Commission, Brussels. Available at www.interior.gob.es/documents/642012/5179146/RAN+Collection+-+Preventing+Radicalisation+to+Terrorism+and+Violent+Extremism. pdf/12527573-50b0-4126-aa68-5ddcbed01ca5 (accessed 15 February 2020).

Ewald, F., 2002. 'The return of Descartes' malicious demon: An outline of a philosophy of precaution', in Baker, T. and Simon, J. (eds), *Embracing Risk: The Changing Culture of Insurance and Responsibility.* University of Chicago Press, Chicago, pp. 273–302.

Gereluk, D., Titus, C.-A., 2018. 'How schools can reduce youth radicalization', *Šolsko Polje*, 5(6), 33–50.

HM Government, 2018. *CONTEST: The United Kingdom's Strategy for Countering Terrorism.* Crown Copyright, London.

Home Office, 2018. *Individuals Referred to and Supported by the Prevent Programme: April 2016–March 2017*. Crown Copyright, London.

Jerome, L., Elwick, A., 2019. 'Identifying an educational response to the Prevent policy: Student perspectives on learning about terrorism, extremism and radicalisation', *British Journal of Educational Studies*, 67(1), 97–114.

Joint Committee on Human Rights, 2016. *Counter-Extremism: Second Report 2016–2017 (HL 39 and HC 105)*. Crown Copyright, London.

Kundnani, A., Hayes, B., 2018. *The Globalization of Countering-Extremism Policies*. Transnational Institute, New York.

Masschelein, J., Simons, M., 2013. *In Defence of the School: A Public Issue*. Education, Culture and Society Publishers, Leuven.

Massumi, B., 2007. 'Potential politics and the primacy of preemption', *Theory and Event*, 10(2).

Mattsson, C., Säljö, R., 2018. 'Violent extremism, national security and prevention: Institutional discourses and their implications for schooling', *British Journal of Educational Studies*, 66(1), 109–125.

O'Donnell, A., 2015. 'Curriculum as conversation: Vulnerability, violence and pedagogy in prison', *Education Theory*, 65(4), 475–490.

O'Donnell, A., 2018a. 'Contagious ideas: Vulnerability, epistemic injustice and counter-terrorism in education', *Educational Philosophy and Theory*, 50(10), 981–997.

O'Donnell, A., 2018b. 'Experimentation in institutions: Ethics, creativity and existential competence', *Studies in Philosophy and Education*, 37(1), 31–46.

O'Donnell, A., Kieran, P., Bergdahl, L. and Cherouvis, S., 2019. *The Enquiring Classroom*. Available at www.enquiring-project.eu/project-outputs.html (accessed 15 February 2020).

Office of the United Nations High Commissioner for Human Rights (OHCHR), 2016. *Report of the Special Rapporteur on the Promotion and Protection of Human Rights and Fundamental Freedoms while Countering Terrorism, 22 February*. OHCHR, Geneva.

Omand, D., 2012. 'Securing the state: National security in contemporary times', *RSIS Working Paper,* 6 November. S. Rajaratnam School of International Studies, Singapore.

Omand, D., 2015. 'Securing the state', *Prism*, 4(3), 14–27.

Open Society Justice Initiative, 2016. *Eroding Trust*. Open Society Foundations, New York.

O'Toole, T., Meer, N., DeHanas, D.N., Jones, S.H. and Modood, T., 2016. 'Governing through Prevent? Regulation and contested practice in state-Muslim engagement', *Sociology*, 50(1), 160–177.

Panjwani, F., Revell, L., Gholami, R. and Diboll, M., 2018. *Education and Extremism: Rethinking Liberal Pedagogies in the Contemporary World*. Routledge, London.

Ragazzi, F., 2018. *Students as Suspects?: The Challenges of Developing Counter-radicalisation Policies in Education in Council of Europe Member States*. DGII/EDU/CCY-2017–8, Interim Report. Council of Europe, Brussels.

Ranciére, J., 2004. *The Politics of Aesthetics: The Distribution of the Sensible*. Continuum, London.

Rivers, J., 2018. 'Counter-extremism, fundamental values and the betrayal of liberal-democratic constitutionalism', *German Law Journal*, 19(2), 167–299.

Rose, N., 2000. 'Government and control', *The British Journal of Criminology*, 40(2), 321–339.

Rouvroy, A., 2016. '"Of data and men": Fundamental rights and freedoms in a world of Big Data', T-PD-BUR(2015)09REV. Council of Europe, Strasbourg.

Rouvroy, A., Stiegler, B., 2016. 'The digital regime of truth: From the algorithmic governmentality to a new rule of law', *La Deleuziana*, 3, 6–29.

Royal College of Psychiatrists, 2016. *Counter-terrorism and Psychiatry: Position Statement*. London.

Ruitenberg, C., 2017. 'Location, location, locution: Where it matters where we say what we say', *Philosophical Inquiry in Education*, 24(3), 211–222.

Shepherd, A., 2017. 'Extremism, free speech and the rule of law: Evaluating the compliance of legislation restricting extremist expressions with article 19 ICCPR', *Utrecht Journal of International and European Law*, 33(85), 62–83.

Sieckelinck, S., Kaulingfreks, F. and de Winter, M., 2015. 'Neither villains nor victims: An educational response to radicalisation', *British Journal of Educational Studies*, 63(3), 329–343.

South Tyneside Community Safety Board, 2016. *Safeguarding Adults Exposed to Extremist Ideology (Radicalisation): Practice Guidance Note*. Available at www.google.com/url?sa=t&rct=j&q=&esrc=s&source=web&cd=1&ved= 2ahUKEwjjx8v1lernAhVGi1wKHSm7D9cQFjAAegQIBBAB&url= https%3A%2F%2Fwww.southtyneside.gov.uk%2Fmedia%2F30284%2FSafe guarding-Adults-at-Risk-Exposed-to-Extremist-Ideology%2Fpdf%2FSafeguarding_ Adults_at_Risk_Exposed_to_Extremist_Ideology_&usg=AOvVaw0aXk- aznZkc9Jgj_DKhCQz (accessed 15 February 2020).

Wolton, S., 2019. 'Are biased media bad for democracy?', *American Journal of Political Science*, 63(3), 548–562.

Zerilli, L., 2012. 'Truth and politics', in Elkins, J. and Norris, A. (eds), *Truth and Politics*. University of Pennsylvania Press, Philadelphia.

Part II

Extremism, countering extremism and preventing extremism: from theory to international and local challenges

8

Legitimising countering extremism at an international level: the role of the United Nations Security Council

Alice Martini

Introduction

Counter-terrorism has undergone a significant shift since its 'post-9/11' inception. In the last decade, the language and the policies of the 'war on terrorism' started losing legitimacy. Maintaining this discursive structure and its practices meant that the discourse had to be reformulated against new challenges. The discourse on terrorism is now replete with references to radicalisation and extremism. These categories have become central in fighting terrorism but do not present a lesser grade of incongruency than their predecessors. Despite their problematic nature, a new language based on these terms found its way into various policy, legal and political settings and it now represents the core of counter-terrorism activity, to the point that 'extremism' has somehow become synonymous with 'terrorism'.

Whereas at the beginning this was more related to single initiatives by states, this new language of 'extremism' has become standardised at an international level. This chapter focuses on the role of the UN Security Council (UNSC) in this discursive shift. This body represents the main legal and political inter-state institution at a global level, tasked with the legal capacity to produce, shape and enforce international norms on states.

By focusing on the Security Council as a context of (global) knowledge and (legal) norms production, this chapter highlights how the organ had a central role in the internationalisation of the discourse and practices to counter extremism. The fact that it adopted and reproduced the new language of extremism unproblematically had several consequences. First, the UN body gave a further impetus to this shift in the discourse providing international legitimacy to the implementation of this concept and states' deriving (abusive) practices.

Second, the Council not only had a role in the reproduction and legitimisation of the discourse, but it also led its legal standardisation at a global level, what Kundnani and Hayes named 'the globalisation of countering violent extremism policies' (Kundnani and Hayes, 2018). In virtue of its international legal powers, the organ imposed on states various binding measures to combat extremism forcing and, at the same time, providing governments with the legitimacy to widen the range of methods used to counter terrorism both domestically and internationally.

Based mainly on Critical Discourse Analysis (CDA), the chapter examines the Council's discourses and practices in relation to extremism. The study focused on the body's stream of meetings entitled 'threats to international peace and security caused by terrorist acts' in a timeframe that goes from 1998 to 2018. It encompassed and examined all the material produced in relation to this matter – for example, debates, Resolutions, Presidential Statements, etc. Driven by the observation that a shift took place in the Council's language and practice, the research was guided by the interest in understanding how extremism was discursively constructed in this specific context, how this shift was legitimised and what were its consequences.

The Council's specific discursive construction of 'extremism' legitimised the broadening of the discourse to various material and ideological aspects. The UNSC rendered 'extremism' an 'umbrella-term' that encompassed and securitised anything that could be related to terrorism, from real violent behaviours to ideologies and ideas considered 'risky' by policymakers (see, for example, Heath-Kelly, 2013). The blurred meaning of extremism permitted not only the dichotomic interpretation of this as both a physical and abstract threat but also as a domestic and international menace. This understanding resulted in all-encompassing securitisation which merged the domestic and private sphere with the international domain. It is in this process that the Council, a producer of international legislation with domestic repercussions, becomes an important context of analysis.

Because discourse and practices are strictly intertwined, this chapter also describes some of the Council's new institutions, legal norms and practices implemented in relation to 'extremism'. Therefore, this research is not merely an analysis of the UNSC's discourse, but it is a study of the deployment of a holistic Foucauldian *dispositif* (Ditrych, 2013, 2014) of extremism, a term encompassing discourses and practices. It was through this *dispositif* that the Council was able to standardise, legitimise and enforce an internationalised governmentality (Baker-Beall et al., 2015; Ditrych, 2013). This was implemented in the name of fighting this threat at an international level and allowed the control of populations at home and the global domestic governance of dissent, legitimised by the Council.

The chapter will first provide a brief background on the conditions of possibility for the shift in the discourse. It will then highlight why a study of the Security Council as an international body is important and how the analysis has been carried out. Subsequently, it will detail the results of the study, focusing specifically on the two meanings of 'extremism' identified in the discourse. Lastly, it will reflect on the consequences of this dichotomic construction of 'extremism' and on the discursive process used to link the domestic and the international in the name of deploying a comprehensive *dispositif* of extremism central to the process of global governmentality.

From counter-terrorism to counter-extremism: the evolving regime of governing through fear

Experts and scholars had always considered terrorism as being driven by extreme ideology and the relation between this and violence had long been examined (Townshend, 2011). Within the UNSC, the idea that extremism led to terrorism was present since the inception of the discourse on 'international terrorism'. In the official documents analysed, this causation was first made explicit in Resolution 1373 (2001). Nevertheless, the focus on the ideology supposedly driving terrorism received further impetus after the 2004 Madrid and 2005 London bombings. These events catalysed a shift in the Council's understanding of terrorism. They led to a reformulation of the by-then hegemonic narrative of the 'root causes' which considered underdevelopment and poverty as the primary drivers of terrorism (Ditrych, 2013; Huesmann and Huesmann, 2012).

These attacks had been perpetrated by (Muslim) Westerners who were somehow linked to the countries they targeted. The fact that the 'terrorists' were nationals of these 'developed countries' rendered explanations related to poverty and underdevelopment obsolete. Experts thus focused on what they defined 'homegrown terrorism' (Schmid, 2013), international terrorism taking place domestically. The discourse shifted towards new understandings of the causes of terrorism and focused on the ideology behind terrorism – extremism – emphasising the need to counter it by winning 'hearts and minds' through narratives. The causes of terrorism were not considered to be structural anymore, and the focus shifted to ideological elements producing a further depoliticisation of this violence (Baker-Beall et al., 2015; Heath-Kelly, 2013).

In the Council, this change started taking place in the late 2000s, but it was after 2014 that it reached its climax. ISIL's Caliphate, the phenomenon of 'foreign fighters' and, above all, the impossibility of explaining these individuals' recruitment consolidated the focus on 'extremism'. Countering terrorism started including references to countering extremism and eventually shifted almost completely towards it. Remarkably, all this took place despite the lack of an international definition of this term, which the Council never provided.

The Security Council as a locus of knowledge production and norms legitimisation

The United Nations is the main global political arena and the organisation tasked with the promotion of international cooperation and maintenance of peace and security. The UN has always been a central organisation in the international activities on countering terrorism (Boulden and Weiss, 2004; Brulin, 2011; Comras, 2010; Ditrych, 2014; Hegemann, 2014). It thus represents a fascinating example of the global construction of the 'international discourse on terrorism' and of the (re)formulation and evolution of the fight against terrorism. This process was accompanied by a shift in its internal dynamics, significant to the new importance 'international terrorism' will achieve in the 2000s.

In 2001, the Security Council became the main body to be tasked with countering terrorism. Sometimes named the 'hard ONU' (Saul, 2005), the Council is the organ that can adopt and enforce binding Resolutions. Moreover, the charter confers it the authority to determine what constitutes a threat to international peace and security. In virtue of its power, terrorism stopped being a lower-order matter and became among the most important matters on the UN agenda – the agenda representing global issues for the whole international community.

It is significant that the body named the stream of meetings under analysis 'threats to international peace and security constituted by terrorist acts'. This phrasing is particularly relevant as it recalls the special powers the Council receives from Article VII of the UN Charter. This article empowers the UNSC to determine what acts constitute a 'threat to international peace and security'. It thus tasks it with deciding when and how to activate collective security and apply exceptional measures that could include economic sanctions, the use of military force or the imposition of new legislation on member states (Imber, 2006, p. 330).

The Council represents an important case study to analyse the international standardisation of the discourse on terrorism and its evolution into extremism. The body is representative of states' global discourse on terrorism because of its international composition. However, the Council is not only reflecting these aspects, it is creating legal norms and practices imposing international standardised, exceptional legislation on all members and, at the same time, legitimising their exceptional measures – and thus their sovereign powers. In other words, the UNSC is an institution belonging to the 'terrorism industry' (Herman and O'Sullivan, 1989). Its discourse on terrorism is both a construction and a constructor of the narratives on terrorism and should be understood as in a mutually constitutive relation with those present in other societal and political spheres.

At a global level, the organ contributed to the co-constitution of the discourse on international terrorism and its evolution towards extremism. However, the UNSC did not only (re)produce the discourse on the threat. As seen, the body has the power to create international legal norms and rules and global institutions, such as committees and working groups to deal with extremism. Moreover, as an international political arena of confrontation, debate and negotiation, the UNSC (re)produced and legitimised ideas, behaviours and conducts in relation to this concept. Therefore, the relation between discourse and practices analysed here is better conceptualised as a Foucauldian *dispositif* on extremism.

Taking from Foucault (1980, p. 194), a *dispositif* is understood as 'a thoroughly heterogeneous ensemble consisting of discourses, institutions, architectural forms, regulatory decisions, laws, administrative measures, scientific statements, philosophical, moral and philanthropic propositions'. The Council's discursive construction of extremism affected all these spheres, constituting discourses and institutions, producing legal norms and affecting behaviours, ideas and understanding of extremism. It, therefore, constituted a Foucauldian *dispositif*.

Influencing states' but also their populations' behaviours, this *dispositif* was bearer of standardised global governmentality. This may be understood as 'a technique of sovereign power that produces certain sorts of subjects and involves oppression, regulation, violence, control, policing and surveillance of life itself' (Stern and Öjendal, 2010, p. 41), the sovereign power in this case being the Security Council, but also the states implementing these new measures. The body's *dispositif* can thus be interpreted as a technique of 'ordering and organising' the international and domestic sphere (Stump and Dixit, 2013, p. 21).

Methodology: studying discourse at an international level

This chapter is founded on a discursive and constructivist view of reality and therefore assumes that, paraphrasing Onuf (2009), we all make 'extremism' what we say it is. In this sense, language – as constitutive of discourse – is given a central role in this analysis. The goal of the present work is to question the ontological nature and the epistemological status of the word 'extremism' as discursively constructed by the Security Council. This has been done mainly through the application of CDA as postulated by Fairclough (1992) and then applied in Critical Terrorism Studies mainly by Richard Jackson (Jackson, 2005, 2016). This depends on the fact that the present analysis aims at problematising how language has been deployed to construct specific realities (Stump and Dixit, 2013).

Because of the nature of the United Nations, and of the Security Council, the study has analysed a wide array of actor' speeches, observing how each of them played a role in the construction of the discourse. These were mainly state representatives, but briefings by experts, the Secretary-General's statements and official documents produced – for example, Resolutions and Presidential Statements – have also been included.

The research has been driven by the following question: 'How was extremism discursively constructed in the UNSC and what are the consequences of this construction?'. Centred on the stream named 'Threats to international peace and security by terrorist acts,'[1] the corpus included the debates and the documents produced between and including 1998, when the first meeting took place, and 2018, as it was in this timeframe when significant UN counter-terrorism activity took place.

Lastly, because 'language and practice [. . .] are inextricably linked [. . .] (and) they mutually reinforce each other' (Jackson, 2005, p. 9), Resolutions have also been considered as part of the norms and laws production activity of the Council. Therefore, the constitution of new bodies and committees – which in the UNSC is created through Resolutions – has also been analysed. As Jackson (2016) states, all these institutions are based on the language – and therefore the knowledge – produced in the discourse. In other words, they represent the 'tangible' part of the deployment of the *dispositif*.

From terrorism to extremism: the evolution of the Security Council's discourse

The use of the concept of extremism in the UNSC goes back to the beginning of the formation of the discourse on international terrorism 'post-9/11'. Extreme ideologies had long been considered the ideational cause of terrorism (Townshend, 2011) and the Security Council reflected this belief. 'Extremism' and mentions to its link to terrorism entered the debates in 2001. Here, the concept was mentioned in Resolution 1373 (2001), where the UNSC called on states to focus on 'acts of terrorism motivated by intolerance or extremism' (p. 2). As this quotation shows, the discourse was, from the very beginning, linking 'extremism' and 'terrorist acts'. Although major concerns about extremism had arisen already in 2004–2005, it was between 2014 and 2016 that extremism managed to establish itself at the core of the Council's discourse. The idea that 'to be effective in fighting terrorism, [it is important] to fight extremism,'[2] shifted the focus of the discourse – and of the deriving counter-measures – on this second matter. Gradually, the Council started being concerned with 'developing strategies to counter terrorism and violent extremism' (Resolution 2195, 2014).

Symbolic of the new importance this matter would receive, some meetings started mentioning the word extremism in their title. For example, the 7,316[th] (2014) was named 'Threats to international peace and security caused by terrorist acts. International Cooperation on Combating Terrorism and Violent Extremism'. Eventually, countering extremism became central to the UNSC's counter-terrorism and the main focus was shifted to 'countering violent extremism in order to prevent terrorism' (Resolution 2170, 2014).

Overall, and similarly to 'terrorism', the Council was never clear about the meaning of 'extremism', despite its wide usage. It is probably because of this lack of specificity that the same relation of extremism to terrorism is not clear. The linguistic analysis of the UNSC's discourse reflected this semantic confusion. Here, it was argued that the 'root causes of terrorism [. . .] (are) economic and political injustice, foreign occupation, poverty and extremism'.[3] In some other instances, however, this causal connection was denied, and it was argued that 'Terrorism is often' – therefore, not always – 'accompanied by the spread of separatism, extremism, violent hatred and intolerance'.[4] In some other instances, emphasising the importance of 'dealing with all forms of extremism, including terrorism',[5] 'terrorism' was constructed as a possible manifestation of 'extremism'.

The Council's use of extremism, thus, displayed a lack of clarity that allowed the reformulation of the discourse. Nevertheless, the lack of specificity did not prevent the Council and its members from eventually centring the discourse and their measures on 'extremism'. This, however, rendered it a category even emptier than terrorism, an ambiguity of meaning which proved very useful in the construction of a dichotomic phenomenon, as shown in the following section.

Extremism: an ideological or a material threat?

Constructed through a 'conceptual back-formation' (Githens-Mazer, 2012, p. 558) and on a lack of clarity, extremism came to identify two main elements. On the one hand, through a process of strict causation and, at the same time, semantic confusion, extremism became a synonym of terrorism. Inconsistently, sometimes the adjective 'violent' was added to the word (Richards, 2015; Schmid, 2014), a division that was fictional, given the Council's inconsistent application of this word. On the other hand, and more abstractly, it represented possible ideologies, ideas and beliefs considered dangerous and risky because they may bring an individual to embrace violence.

Discursively, 'extremism' was constructed around a clear ambiguity that allowed the encompassing both of ideas, ideologies and thoughts and terrorist violence within the same concept. Therefore, the strict relation created discursively between ideas and terrorism merged the two and 'materialised' the threat of 'extremism'. Tautologically, extremism came to be used to refer to terrorist actions perpetrated by individuals with 'extreme' views but also to the same 'extreme' views. The merging of the two concepts was so strong that it became difficult to differentiate and identify the exact relation between violent extremism and other forms of political violence (Nasser-Eddine et al., 2011).

This was a dangerous conflation of ideas and violence that not only constructed a linear relation between ideology and violence but had the consequence of criminalising the former in the name of fighting the latter. To achieve this ambiguous discursive use of the word, extremism was emptied of any meaning. Therefore, its signification started depending on the context of appearance and was constantly (re)produced within the discourse. This allowed identifying, securitising and criminalising anything from violence to behaviours, ideas and beliefs – a process that was key in linking international and domestic counter-extremism. However, before discussing these matters, the next sections will describe the different discursive contexts that created this dual meaning of 'extremism'.

Materialising ideology: how extremism became a synonym of terrorism

The 'materialisation' of extremism is symbolic of a strong and deep discursive process that merged this issue with terrorism. This process took place mainly through the repeated association of the two concepts. In the first place, actors started mentioning both threats together. They referred unproblematically to 'any manifestation of violent extremism or terrorism'[6] and to 'acts of terrorism and violent extremism'.[7] References were also made to 'the impact of terrorism or violent extremism'[8] and to the 'human cost of terrorist attacks and violent extremism'.[9]

The juxtaposition of the two concepts constructed them as 'twin cancers'[10] and as deserving the same degree of concern. In this sense, the first step in this construction consisted of criminalising both the violent terrorist action and the ideas behind it.

Extremism evolved from being a category representative of the risk of the terrorist threat into being considered the threat itself. Gradually, the 'scourge afflicting modern times' became 'violent extremism and its corollary, terrorism'.[11] Symbolic of a second step in the construction of the threat and of the merging of the concepts, actors started referring to the two issues using a singular noun. 'Terrorism and violent extremism' became 'unquestionably one of the worst scourges of our time',[12] or, in other words, a single threat. Therefore, the initial juxtaposition eventually merged the menaces.

The consequence of this discursive fusion was the 'materialisation' of extremism. Eventually, the term, originally identifying abstract phenomena, started being used as a synonym of 'terrorism', tangible physical violence. It was argued that 'we are confronting extremism with military force'[13] and that actors had to launch a 'war against terrorism and extremism'.[14] Even past terrorist attacks such as the 2008 Mumbai bombings were retrospectively interpreted as the result of the previous 'waves of violent extremism'.[15] Eventually, actors even used this word to refer to 'ISIL and other extremist organizations',[16] further materialising extremism.

The process of juxtaposition of the terms 'terrorism' and 'extremism' peaked in 2014 and 2016. Again, historical events shaped this construction and described it as unprecedented and exceptional. ISIL and its dynamics of recruitment, among other international aspects, played a central role in the development of the international *dispositif*. This started gradually to encompass measures related to international extremism and widened the discourse to this 'new phenomenon'. Renewing the 'international enemy' was, again, giving legitimacy to the 'international community' but also providing its members with a wider set of actions – a renewed international governmentality.

This was wider than the previous *dispositif* implemented in the name of fighting terrorism. The inconsistency of the category allowed a broadening process that, as seen, permitted states to encompass different aspects. Despite its use to refer to violence, the ideological content of 'extremism' was also still present in the discourse. Grounded in the 'materialisation of extremism', the merge of the threat and the equivalence of extremism with terrorism allowed the criminalisation of ideas and ideologies.

Countering terrorism or homogenising thoughts? Countering extremism and 'thought-crime'

Used also to refer to abstract processes, the term retained its original, tautological signification of having 'extreme ideas'. The same word was, thus, used to name two different things – although strictly related by a fictional, causal relation discursively constructed (O'Donnell, 2016) which, eventually, merged the threats. Through its evolution into countering extremism, counter-terrorism was rendered a 'struggle in the field of ideas'[17] and a 'battle for the hearts and minds of potential terrorists'.[18] States were concerned with the 'violent extremist ideologies that underpin the terrorist narrative'.[19]

The main focus became finding the 'best narrative to counter violent extremism'[20] in order to oppose the 'poisonous ideology of Islamist extremism',[21] and the 'agents of extremism (that) [. . .] spread their ideologies across national borders'.[22] Consequently, fighting extremism had to be developed in the ideological realm, and the main concern of the Council became developing a 'counter-narrative that rejects the language of radicalization'[23] and that could 'inspire young people to make choices based on reality, not ISIL's gangster fantasies'.[24]

The focus on extremist narratives received so much attention that the Council started referring to the need to develop a 'counter-narrative',[25] mirroring the language of 'countering' terrorism. In 2016, the body even entitled its 7,690[th] meeting 'Countering the narratives and ideologies of terrorism'.[26] By 2017, the need to combat ideas had become so institutionalised that the UNSC produced the 'Comprehensive International Framework to Counter Terrorist Narratives'.[27] This dynamic also peaked in 2016, corresponding with the climax of the phenomenon of foreign fighters and the impossibility for states to explain why these individuals, belonging to 'developed' countries, were joining ISIL.

Inheriting a problem-solving vision from the Cold War according to which exists a causal connection between ideology and acts of political violence (Kundnani, 2015), not only behaviours but also ideas, thoughts and views became the locus of intervention and of 'countering extremism'. This construction had two main consequences. On the one hand, the focus on abstract elements such as ideas and thoughts neglected the role of states in co-producing terror and blamed an 'alien ideology' for these acts (Kundnani, 2015). It depoliticised terrorism, neglecting the role of structural and political inequalities and constructing 'narratives' and 'thoughts' as causes of violence.

On the other hand, the merging of extremism with violence brought the criminalisation of the behaviours, ideas and ideologies supposedly behind terrorism. Countering extremism was implemented on the basis that ideas could predict behaviours (Elshimi, 2017). Paraphrasing Orwell (1949), policies started being concerned with 'thought-crimes'. In this case, the focus shifted again. The Council's attention was not only on 'countering' (violent) extremism (CVE) but also on 'preventing' it (PVE). In the name of fighting (violent) extremism, countering extremism became 'preventing' individuals from becoming terrorists but also from assuming specific ideas and ideologies. Preventing extremism could be interpreted as preventing individuals from assuming certain thoughts.

The Council provided a legitimisation for these practices and the implementation of international governmentality of thoughts and ideas. In 2017, the Counter-Terrorism Committee published the Comprehensive International Framework to Counter Terrorist Narratives, where it emphasised 'the role of counter-narrative campaigns as part of a comprehensive approach to the threats of terrorism and violent extremism'.[28] UNSC's CVE measures also included initiatives to control and censor social media and the internet, as stated in the same document. Here, it was also argued that 'in order to effectively counter terrorist narratives, States and others must enter more fully into the "marketplace of ideas"'.[29] Another example may be Resolution 1624 (2005), which called on states to prohibit incitement to terrorism (*apologie*), severely reducing freedom of expression (Kundnani and Hayes, 2018).

Grounded in this construction, states were legitimated to broaden countering extremism to various aspects and to label as 'dissent' also political ideas divergent or critical of the hegemonic mainstream. This had huge repercussions for human and civil rights (Kundnani and Hayes, 2018). Symbolic of this process were, for example, the new measures of societal surveillance and the broadening of the control to 'social media and modern communication technologies'[30], which soon became the object of state interventions and censorship (Grasso and Bessant, 2018).

Moreover, the Council's legitimised securitisation in the name of preventing extremism of domestic, personal and everyday spheres (Auchter, this volume; and Ford, this volume). The Council enforced preventing extremism 'notably through programs at schools and in prisons',[31] and in 'health, social, welfare and education sectors',[32] focusing specifically on 'youth'[33] but also on 'empowering youth, families, women, religious, cultural and education leaders, and all other concerned groups of civil society'.[34] However, as mentioned, the UNSC not only produced a discourse on extremism, but also established new norms and institutions and cemented favourable behaviours and ideas at an international level. It thus produced a global *dispositif* of extremism.

Constructing the Council's international *dispositif* of extremism

The Council was assigned a 'leading and coordinating role'[35] in the international fight against extremism. This allowed the body to standardise and homogenise a new language of counter-terrorism but also new (legal) measures, norms and institutions. The UNSC thus played a central role in what Kundnani and Hayes (2018) named the 'globalisation of Countering Violent Extremism (CVE) policies'. It legitimised this shift, adopting uncritically extremism as a new vocabulary and giving international diffusion and institutionalisation to problematic frameworks (Kundnani and Hayes, 2018). The international counter-terrorism *dispositif* (Ditrych, 2013, 2014) would gradually become the international counter-(violent)-extremism *dispositif.*

The body's discursive merging of terrorism and extremism broadened the discourse to ideas and put forward the assumption that this was a bigger and wider threat to be fought at different levels – but not a new menace. Therefore, the Council considered that 'concrete means and measures need(ed) to be updated and adapted'[36] but not reformulated. This meant that, using Jackson's and Tsui's (2016) Hollywood metaphor, the UNSC lived *Groundhog Day.* Stuck in the same loop, it reproduced analogous approaches and responses to previous counter-terrorism measures. These were supported by a new legitimacy found in this fresh vocabulary and the reformulation of the threat.

The organ reproduced dynamics similar to the ones implemented in the immediate 'post-9/11'. In 2015, acting under Chapter VII, the body condemned extremism and enforced binding measures on members, similar to what it did in 2001 in relation to terrorism. The Counter-Terrorism Committee, the main UNSC body in charge of countering terrorism, was assigned the task of countering and preventing violent extremism. CVE became one of its Focus Areas in 2015.[37]

Symbolic of the merging of the menaces, Resolution 1624 (2005), among the pillars of the UNSC's countering terrorism strategy, was rendered central in its countering extremism policy.[38] Described as a 'natural extension' of Resolution 1624 (2005), the body approved Resolution 2178 (2015), containing binding elements that concerned top-down and state security-led initiatives and that neglected the political roots of extremism (Kundnani and Hayes, 2018). Subsequently, the organ approved Resolution 2242 (2015) – on the role of women in countering extremism – and 2250 (2015) on the role of youth in countering extremism. The Council also focused on specific places of construction of the subject-citizen – that is, schools, places of worship, prisons and so on.

Furthermore, to show how discourses can influence practices, after the adoption of Resolution 2178 (2014), new bodies were created specifically to deal with the issue of extremism. Although not directly dependent on the Security Council, the UN Counter-Terrorism Implementation Task Force established an *ad hoc* Working Group on Preventing Violent Extremism. Moreover, in 2016 the Secretary-General presented a Plan of Action to Prevent Violent Extremism[39] which invited members, regional and subregional organisations to develop national and local plans aimed at preventing violent extremism. It is with these changes that the merging of the two issues was complete.

Linking ideas and aspects of personal life to international terrorism was connecting domestic and international countering extremism. The exceptionality attached to the fight against international terrorism (Benoist, 2013) could be implemented at a local level. Through the discursive development of a 'fight against extremism', actors had given themselves a new vocabulary, a renewed legitimacy and a more extensive scene of action. On this ambiguity was based the deployment of a holistic *dispositif*, which included both spheres in the name of fighting the same threat. In this sense, both personal and domestic matters were linked to the international fight against terrorism.

Considered among the main Council's documents on countering and preventing extremism, Resolution 2178 (2014) is an interesting example of how the incongruent meaning of extremism created the conditions of possibility for this practice to take place at a normative level. The Resolution was centred on the (international) threat posed by foreign fighters, individuals 'recruited by and joining entities such as the Islamic State in Iraq and the Levant (ISIL), the Al-Nusrah Front (ANF) and other cells, affiliates, splinter groups or derivatives of Al-Qaida' (Resolution 2178, 2014, p. 1). The document was thus focused on combating recruitment of individuals by international terrorist organisations.

Nevertheless, the domestic and international spheres were tackled together. Here, many are the references in the Resolution to 'violent extremism', understood as the narrative 'which can be conducive to terrorism' (Resolution 2178, 2014, p. 2). The Resolution also refers to the importance of developing 'non-violent alternatives for conflict prevention' and 'peaceful alternatives to violent narratives espoused by foreign fighters', highlighting the important role of education (Resolution 2178, 2014, p. 7). The construction of the link between private and political realm is also observable in the Council's various calls for the empowerment of youth, women, civil society, teachers and religious leaders, among other figures (Resolution 2178, 2014, p. 6). All of these were non-governmental actors which belonged, mainly, to the domestic and private sphere.

Furthermore, Resolution 2178 (2014) represents an example of how the UNSC was not only reflecting the discourse, but also legitimising and endorsing states' actions and repression. By placing its measures under Chapter VII, the Council imposed on all Members standardised measures. By forcing states to adopt, for example, procedures of extended surveillance, travel restrictions, border control and law enforcement, the Council was standardising and internationalising the *dispositif* of extremism. Deploying what the same organ named a 'comprehensive approach to the challenge of violent extremism [. . .] that directly address the drivers of violent extremism at the local, national, regional and global levels',[40] it constructed an all-encompassing international regime of governmentality.

Fighting violence and combatting ideas became encompassed within the same discourse and allowed the deployment of a comprehensive *dispositif* of countering extremism. By discursively linking phenomena of political violence taking place at an international level with specific behaviour constructed as risky in the domestic and personal realm, the Council was thus providing legitimacy for the deployment of a comprehensive fight in the name of countering extremism.

Hence, the 'war on terror' became a holistic process, not only a military one but a project of international governmentality with different open fronts: internationally fighting against extremism and domestically combating and preventing what were labelled as 'extremist ideas'. The standardisation of these practices provided the legitimacy states needed to implement extensive measures at both a domestic and international level, but also reproduced international standardised governmentality.

Governing domestically and internationally through counter-extremism

The dichotomic discursive construction of extremism as an international and domestic phenomenon and as an ideological and violent threat allowed the broadening of the discourse and linking of the domestic and international, the personal and political, ideas and behaviours, in the name of fighting against a single phenomenon. Countering extremism became countering a kind of violence that stemmed from specific ideas and, at the same time, combating particular ideas that (supposedly) would inevitably lead to violence – that is, international terrorism.

Because of the binary dynamics of language, by criminalising 'extremism', the Council reinforced and promoted as favourable the opposite category 'moderate' (Cuadro, this volume). Individuals were ideologically encouraged to move towards thoughts that were considered 'moderate' and standard, while states were encouraged to promote certain 'moderate' values over others. As Ford argues, 'Such an understanding of extremism cements hegemonic liberal attitudes at the centre of understandings of what constitute legitimate attitudes' (Ford, 2017, p. 128). It thus further delegitimated any – violent or not – opposition and legitimated states' actions in this regard. This produced a process of homologation of thoughts and elimination of dissent, which gave rise to global governmentality of behaviours and ideas.

The homologation of thoughts took place through the criminalisation of radical and extreme thinking. The values at the centre of the 'moderate' were grounded in the Western state identity and were thus mainly liberal ideas, liberalism being the philosophy behind the United Nations and the international order in general (Cuadro, 2013; Peñas Esteban, 2003, 1997). Contrastingly, the ideas and behaviours securitised, illegitimated and, at times, illegalised belonged to specific sub-groups of societies (Eroukhmanoff, 2015). Through this process, even these groups' identity was securitised. When only the 'moderate' is constructed as the normal and the non-threatening, any identity and values that are not presented as the standard are brought into question (Martin, 2014, p. 63).

The Council's focus was on different minorities and sub-groups. However, the inherited in-built assumptions from the discourse on terrorism that securitised Islam (Mavelli, 2013; see also Croft, 2012; Cuadro, 2016), already present in the Council's discourse, constructed Muslims as the primary 'suspect community' (Awan, 2012; Breen-Smyth, 2014). In other words, by promoting 'moderate' ideas, the UNSC's discourse on extremism was criminalising, above all, Islamic dissenting ideas and identities. This reflected the fact that, in Kundnani's words, 'the liberal caveat is that Muslims are acceptable when depoliticized' (Kundnani, 2015): not only should they be silent about politics but – and, above all – they should embrace the liberal norm, an understanding reflected by the Council.

The idea that Muslims must 'subscribe to a form of Islam that is palatable to Western thoughts and beliefs', as Qureshi reminds us, was not new and has its roots in the historical interactions between the so-called 'Western' and the Islamic world (Kundnani, 2007; Qureshi, 2005). Through the discourse on terrorism and then on extremism, this assumption entered the Council, shaped by Western thought and powers, but also by unequal relations of power. These communities became the locus of suspicion, a process based on a 'complex hermeneutic of suspicion, in which cultural, religious, and political signifiers are parsed for signs of allegiance' (Kundnani, 2015).

The Council's new 'hearts-and-minds approach'[41] and the focus on narratives to counter extremism took a different meaning. The shift towards emotions is symbolic of the constructed clash between the Muslim and the liberal world as exclusive and incompatible and of the need to convince individuals of the superiority of the liberal model. Their loyalty to 'Western' liberal values was tested and any shift away from these, even if towards their identity and religion, was interpreted as a betrayal towards the international model (Martini, 2019). The superiority of the liberal societies was also remarked in the debates as it was stated that 'one of the most disturbing aspects is how this conflict (with ISIL) is sucking in our own young people from modern, prosperous societies'.[42]

The discourse securitised the places of construction of the subject which became a locus of concern of preventing extremism. Schools, worship places, prisons and even communities and families became loci of production of the 'liberal citizen', where liberal values could be taught and thoughts could be homologated. The punishment of other conducts and ideas rendered liberal principles non-debatable (Kühle and Lindekilde, 2012) and 'post-political' (Mouffe, 2005, 2013). The Council's criminalisation of different ideas 'prevented democratic participation of the suspected group' in politics (Breen-Smyth, 2014, p. 223). Thus, in various states, the UNSC contributed to the securitisation of the debates on multiculturalism, which started looking more and more like cultural assimilation (Kundnani, 2012). Security policies, focusing on specific subgroups of these societies, rendered these communities 'the domestic fronts of the war on terror' (Kundnani, 2015).

The Council's countering and preventing extremism activity thus resulted in international governmentality. It governed and homologated all spheres of the social and political: from the public political to the domestic and personal realm and from physical violence and behaviours to narratives, ideas and thoughts.

Conclusion

The present chapter has analysed the role the UNSC had within the globalisation and standardisation of countering and preventing extremism policies. It has shown how the body's ambiguous construction of 'extremism' and the consequent formation of an ambiguous *dispositif* has allowed all-encompassing governmentality at a global level. In the name of fighting an ambiguous menace, the *dispositif* of extremism merged the domestic, private and the public, political spheres. Moreover, it securitised behaviours but also ideas, thoughts and narratives.

The Council's international governmentality could thus encompass various social and political spheres. Through its global reach, the organ could standardise behaviours but also ideas and thoughts around the core liberal values behind the Council's constitution and the liberal order in general. Promoting moderate and liberal ideas as desirable, the body illegitimated and securitised different values and identities, specifically linked to the Muslim community.

It is for this reason that it is of extreme importance to reflect on and deconstruct processes that took place at a global level. Through its activity, the Council justified, legitimised and enforced the use of extreme measures under the banner of the exceptionality of the threat. States saw their sovereign powers and (intrusive) policies reinforced and legitimised. Internationally, human and civil rights have suffered severe restrictions in the name of fighting an ambiguous threat, dissent has been criminalised and difference has been securitised. It is only by deconstructing these narratives and highlighting how the consequent *dispositif* works that these processes can be countered and their resulting governmentality resisted.

Acknowledgements

I would like to thank Richard Jackson, Kieran Ford and Griffin Leonard for the valuable comments on previous versions of this chapter. I am forever thankful to Francisco J. Peñas. Moreover, I would like to thank the Sant'Anna School of Advanced Studies for the support provided to conduct this research.

Notes

1 All the documents can be found here: http://research.un.org/en/docs/sc/quick/meetings/2020 (accessed 22 September 2017).

2 Representative of France, S/PV.5104, 17 December 2004, p. 7.

3 Representative of Pakistan, S/PV. 4921, 4 March 2004, p. 17.

4 Representative of China, S/PV.6765, 4 May 2012, p. 13.

5 Representative of Turkey, S/PV.6034, Resumption, 9 December 2008, p. 11.

6 Representative of Russia, S/PV.6765, 04 May 2012, p. 10.

7 Representative of Kyrgyzstan, S/PV.7316, 19 November 2014, p. 55.

8 Secretary of State of the United States of America Hillary Rodham Clinton, S/PV.6390, 27 September 2010, p. 6.

9 Representative of the UK, S/PV.7670, 14 April 2016, p. 10.

10 Representative of Malaysia, S/PV.7690, 11 May 2016, p. 14.

11 Representative of Senegal, S/PV.7690, 11 May 2016, p. 22.

12 President of the Republic of Chad Idriss Deby Itno, S/PV.7272, 24 September 2014, p. 7.

13 Representative of Canada, S/PV.7316, 19 November 2014, p. 18.

14 Representative of Kenya, S/PV.7690, 11 May 2016, p. 60.

15 Representative of Canada, S/PV.7316, 19 November 2014, p. 68. Here, referring to the 2008 Mumbai terrorist attacks.

16 Representative of Saudi Arabia, S/PV.7316, 19 November 2014, p. 30.

17 Representative of Sweden, S/PV.7962, 08 June 2017, p. 7.

18 Representative of Lithuania, S/PV. 7565, 20 November 2015, p. 6.

19 Security Council Presidential Statement 23 (2014), p. 3.

20 Deputy Secretary General, S/PV. 7690, 11 May 2016, p. 3.

21 Representative of the UK, S/PV.7316, 19 November 2014, p.17.

22 Representative of Sri Lanka, S/PV.7316, p. 67.

23 Representative of Spain, S/PV.7453, 29 May 2015, p. 17.

24 Representative of UK, S/PV.7453, 29 May 2015, p. 19.

25 Security Council Presidential Statement 23 (2014), p. 3.

26 Security Council Meeting 7690, 11 May 2016.

27 Security Council Document 375 (2017).

28 UNSC document number S/2017/375, p. 7.

29 UNSC document number S/2017/375, p. 8.

30 Representative of Lithuania, S/PV. 7316, 19 November 2014, p. 16.

31 United Nations Presidential Statement 11 (2015), p. 4.

32 United Nations Security Council Resolution 2396 (2017), p. 10.

33 See, for example, United Nations Security Council Resolution 2250 (2015) on the role of youth in countering and preventing extremism.

34 United Nations Security Council Resolution 2178 (2014) art. 16, p. 6.

35 Representative of China, S/PV.7690, 11 May 2016, p. 18.

36 Representative of Lithuania, S/PV. 7316, 19 November 2014, p. 15.

37 For more information, see www.un.org/sc/ctc/focus-areas/countering-violent-extremism/ (accessed 15 May 2018).

38 See www.un.org/sc/ctc/focus-areas/countering-violent-extremism/ (accessed 10 January 2019).

39 Information available at www.un.org/sites/www.un.org.counterterrorism/files/plan_action.pdf (accessed 15 May 2018).

40 www.un.org/sc/ctc/focus-areas/countering-violent-extremism/ (accessed 11 June 2019).
41 Representative of Malaysia, S/PV.7272, 24 September 2014, p. 41.
42 David Cameron, Prime Minister of the UK, S/PV.7272, 29 September 2014, p. 13.

References

Awan, I., 2012. '"I am a Muslim not an extremist": How the Prevent strategy has constructed a "suspect" community: Extremism and terrorism', *Politics & Policy*, 40(6), 1158–1185.

Baker-Beall, C., Heath-Kelly, C. and Jarvis, L. (eds), 2015. *Counter-Radicalisation: Critical Perspectives*. Routledge, Abingdon and New York.

Benoist, A. de, 2013. *Carl Schmitt Today: Terrorism, 'Just' War, and the State of Emergency*. Arktos Media, London.

Boulden, J., Weiss, T.G. (eds), 2004. *Terrorism and the UN: Before and After September 11*. Indiana University Press, Bloomington, IN.

Breen-Smyth, M., 2014. 'Theorising the "suspect community": Counterterrorism, security practices and the public imagination', *Critical Studies on Terrorism*, 7(2), 223–240.

Brulin, R., 2011. 'Defining "terrorism": The 1972 General Assembly debates on "international terrorism" and their coverage by the New York Times', in Baybars-Hawks, B. and Baruh, L. (eds), *If It Was Not for Terrorism: Crisis, Compromise, and Elite Discourse in the Age of War on Terror*. Cambridge Scholar Press, Cambridge, pp. 12–30.

Comras, V.D., 2010. *Flawed Diplomacy: The United Nations and the War on Terrorism*. Potomac Books, Dulles, VA.

Croft, S., 2012. *Securitizing Islam: Identity and the Search for Security*. Cambridge University Press, Cambridge.

Cuadro, M., 2013. 'La Guerra Global contra el Terror y el universalismo liberal: reflexiones mediante Carl Schmitt', *Relaciones Internacionales*, 22, 109–125.

Cuadro, M., 2016. 'Racismo religioso: el islam en la economía discursiva del terrorismo', *Relaciones Internacionales*, 32, 59–78.

Ditrych, O., 2013. 'From discourse to dispositif: States and terrorism between Marseille and 9/11', *Security Dialogue*, 44(3), 223–240.

Ditrych, O., 2014. *Tracing the Discourses of Terrorism: Identity, Genealogy and State*. Palgrave Macmillan, Basingstoke and New York.

Elshimi, M.S., 2017. *De-Radicalisation in the UK Prevent Strategy: Security, Identity and Religion*. Routledge, Abingdon and New York.

Eroukhmanoff, C., 2015. 'The remote securitisation of Islam in the US post-9/11: Euphemisation, metaphors and the "logic of expected consequences" in counter-radicalisation discourse', *Critical Studies on Terrorism*, 8(2), 246–265.

Fairclough, N., 1992. *Discourse and Social Change*. Polity Press, Cambridge.

Ford, K., 2017. 'The insecurities of weaponised education: A critical discourse analysis of the securitised education discourse in North-West Pakistan', *Conflict, Security & Development*, 17(2), 117–139.

Foucault, M., 1980. *Power/Knowledge: Selected interviews & Other Writings 1972–1977.* Pantheon Books, New York.

Githens-Mazer, J., 2012. 'The rhetoric and reality: Radicalization and political discourse', *International Political Science Review*, 33(5), 556–567.

Grasso, M.T., Bessant, J. (eds), 2018. *Governing Youth Politics in the Age of Surveillance: The Criminalization of Political Dissent.* Routledge, London.

Heath-Kelly, C., 2013. 'Counter-terrorism and the counterfactual: Producing the "radicalisation" discourse and the UK PREVENT strategy', *The British Journal of Politics and International Relations*, 15(3), 394–415.

Hegemann, H., 2014. *International Counterterrorism Bureaucracies in the United Nations and the European Union.* Nomos, Baden-Baden.

Herman, E., O'Sullivan, G., 1989. *The 'Terrorism' Industry: The Experts and Institutions That Shape Our Views of Terror.* Pantheon Books, New York.

Huesmann, L.R., Huesmann, G.R., 2012. 'Poverty and exclusion are not the root causes of terrorism', in Jackson, R. and Sinclair, S.J. (eds), *Contemporary Debates on Terrorism.* Routledge, London and New York, pp. 113–120.

Imber, M., 2006. 'The reform of the UN Security Council', *International Relations*, 20(3), 328–334.

Jackson, R., 2005. *Writing the War on Terrorism: Language, Politics and Counter-terrorism.* Manchester University Press, Manchester.

Jackson, R., 2016. 'Critical Discourse Analysis', in Dixit, P. and Stump, J.L. (eds), *Critical Methods in Terrorism Studies.* Routledge, London and New York, pp. 77–90.

Jackson, R., Tsui, C.-K., 2016. 'War on terror II: Obama and the adaptive evolution of US counterterrorism', in Bentley, M. and Holland, J. (eds), *The Obama Doctrine: A Legacy of Continuity in US Foreign Policy?* Routledge, Abingdon, pp. 70–83.

Kühle, L., Lindekilde, L., 2012. 'Radicalization and the limits of tolerance', *Journal of Ethnic and Migration Studies*, 38(10), 1607–1623.

Kundnani, A., 2007. *The End of Tolerance. Racism in 21st Century Britain.* Pluto Press, London.

Kundnani, A., 2012. *A Decade Lost: Rethinking Radicalization and Extremism.* Claystone Publications, London.

Kundnani, A., 2015. *The Muslims Are Coming! Islamophobia, Extremism and the Domestic War on Terror.* Verso, London.

Kundnani, A., Hayes, B., 2018. *The Globalisation of Countering Violent Extremism Policies: Undermining Human Rights, Instrumentalising Civil Society.* Available at www.tni.org/en/publication/the-globalisation-of-countering-violent-extremism-policies (accessed 13 May 2018).

Martin, T., 2014. 'Governing an unknowable future: The politics of Britain's Prevent policy', *Critical Studies on Terrorism*, 7(1), 62–78 (accessed 15 May 2018).

Martini, A., 2019. *On International Barbarians and Global Civilisations. A Critical Discourse Analysis of the Evolution of the Security Council's Fight against International Terrorism.* (PhD, Doctor of Philosophy) Sant'Anna School of Advanced Studies. Unpublished work.

Mavelli, L., 2013. 'Between normalisation and exception: The securitisation of Islam and the construction of the secular subject', *Millennium – Journal of International Studies*, 41(2), 159–181.

Mouffe, C., 2005. *On the Political. Thinking in Action.* Routledge, New York.

Mouffe, C., 2013. *Agonistics: Thinking the World Politically.* Verso, London.

Nasser-Eddine, M., Graham, B., Agostino, K. and Caluya, G., 2011. *Countering Violent Extremism (CVE) Literature Review.* [online]. Available at www.dtic.mil/get-tr-doc/pdf?AD=ADA543686 (accessed 20 May 2018).

O'Donnell, A., 2016. 'Securitisation, counterterrorism and the silencing of dissent: The educational implications of Prevent', *British Journal of Educational Studies*, 64(1), 53–76.

Onuf, N.G., 2009. 'Making terror/ism', *International Relations*, 23, 53–60.

Orwell, G., 1949. *1984.* Penguin Books Ltd, New York.

Peñas Esteban, F.J., 1997. *Occidentalización, fin de la Guerra Fría y relaciones internacionales.* Alianza Editorial, Madrid.

Peñas Esteban, F.J., 2003. *Hermanos y enemigos: Liberalismo y relaciones internacionales.* La Catarata, Madrid.

Qureshi, A., 2005. 'PREVENT: Creating "radicals" to strengthen anti-Muslim narratives', *Critical Studies on Terrorism*, 8(1), 181–191.

Richards, A., 2015. 'From terrorism to "radicalization" to "extremism": Counterterrorism imperative or loss of focus?' *International Affairs*, 91(2), 371–380.

Saul, B., 2005. 'Definition of "terrorism" in the UN Security Council: 1985–2004', *Chinese Journal of International Law*, 4(1), 141–166.

Schmid, A., 2013. 'Radicalisation, de-radicalisation and counter-radicalisation: A conceptual discussion and literature review', Research Paper. International Centre for Counter-Terrorism, The Hague.

Schmid, A., 2014. *Violent and Non-Violent Extremism: Two Sides of the Same Coin?* ICCT Research Paper, May. Available at www.icct.nl/download/file/ICCT-Schmid-Violent-Non-Violent-Extremism-May-2014.pdf (accessed 15 May 2018).

Stern, M., Öjendal, J., 2010. 'Mapping the security–development nexus: Conflict, complexity, cacophony, convergence?' *Security Dialogue*, 41(1), 5–29.

Stump, J.L., Dixit, P., 2013. *Critical Terrorism Studies. An Introduction to Research Methods.* Routledge, New York.

Townshend, C., 2011. *Terrorism: A Very Short Introduction.* Oxford University Press, Oxford and New York.

United Nations Presidential Statement 11 (2015).

United Nations Security Council Meeting, 6034, Resumption, 9 December 2008.

United Nations Security Council Meeting, 6390, 27 September 2010.

United Nations Security Council Meeting, 6765, 4 May 2012.

United Nations Security Council Meeting, 7272, 24 September 2014.

United Nations Security Council Meeting, 7316, 19 November 2014.

United Nations Security Council Meeting, 7453, 29 May 2015.

United Nations Security Council Meeting, 7565, 20 November 2015.

United Nations Security Council Meeting, 7670, 14 April 2016.

United Nations Security Council Meeting, 7690, 11 May 2016.

United Nations Security Council Meeting, 7962, 8 June 2017.

United Nations Security Council Presidential Statement 23 (2014).

United Nations Security Council Resolution 1373 (2001).

United Nations Security Council Resolution 1624 (2005).
United Nations Security Council Resolution 2170 (2014).
United Nations Security Council Resolution 2178 (2014).
United Nations Security Council Resolution 2195 (2014).
United Nations Security Council Resolution 2178 (2015).
United Nations Security Council Resolution 2242 (2015).
United Nations Security Council Resolution 2250 (2015).
United Nations Security Council Resolution 2396 (2017).

9

International PVE and Tunisia: a local critique of international donors' discourses

Guendalina Simoncini

Introduction

This chapter aims at providing an overview of the vision, the strategy and the language of international donors' funding of preventing violent extremism (hereinafter PVE) programmes in the field of international cooperation in Tunisia. International organisations are increasingly important actors in PVE policies in the country. For this reason, this chapter seeks to provide a reflection about their role in the Tunisian context, problematising their priorities and strategies through a critical analysis of the discourse constructed in the projects' guidelines for civil society applicants and other relevant documents.

Violent extremism is currently at the centre of international organisations' agendas in Tunisia, and numerous PVE programmes in the field of international development cooperation are currently being implemented in the country. Young people are undoubtedly the main targets of such initiatives, together with women, though the ways in which these stakeholders are depicted and the way in which the problem of violent extremism is formulated raises issues related to the securitisation of the young and the instrumentalisation of women in counter-terrorism measures.

Following the revolution, Tunisian youth have been targeted with a high number of international cooperation projects aimed at reinforcing their participation in the transitional process, their freedom of expression and their active citizenship. Starting from 2015, these programmes gradually started integrating a securitarian dimension through the inclusion of PVE. Moreover, according to Somi (2016), the period after 2011 saw a critical transformation at the level of youth policy in the country, which has shifted from a state traditional monopoly to 'a field of competition with international stakeholders'. This is one of the reasons why the study of the priorities and objectives of the international community in Tunisia acquires importance. Starting from a critical analysis of the language employed by international actors in PVE policy papers, this chapter aims at highlighting and discussing the main assumptions on which the donors' discourse is based.

The category of 'youth' will be addressed with the aim of problematising its systematic use in PVE policies. More specifically, securitisation theory offers useful tools with which to understand the link between security and development concerning PVE programmes, as well as revealing the interests in framing extremism as an essentially 'youth problem'. Gender Studies also provides crucial instruments with which to consider the issue of women's participation in PVE policies. Before showing the results of the Critical Discourse Analysis (CDA), this chapter will offer a brief presentation of the Tunisian context and a short introduction to the theoretical framework used to carry out the analysis.

Tracing a brief context of the Tunisian background

The issues of 'terrorism' and 'violent extremism' are currently central themes in the political and public debate of the young Tunisian democracy. The years following the fall of the Ben Ali regime have been severely marked by a climate of growing non-state political violence that has destabilised state institutions and hindered the process of democratic transition that began in February 2011. Starting from 2012, some Salafist jihadist[1] groups have threatened Tunisian institutions, jeopardising the already problematic economic situation by attacking tourist infrastructures and exacerbating the polarisation between Islamists and liberals in the country.

The presence of armed groups operating in the interior and bordering regions has also had negative consequences on the safety of the inhabitants of the affected territories, complicating the already sensitive situation of these historically marginalised areas,[2] as well as creating a stigma between the young inhabitants, considered by public opinion as being young marginalised extremists. The situation of domestic non-state political violence has also been strongly influenced by the instability in neighbouring Libya and by the rise of the so-called Islamic State. It should be recalled that Tunisia is the country of origin of approximately 6,000 'foreign fighters' (Soufan Group, 2015).

The juridical and administrative responses to this situation formulated by the various governments in power since 2011 have been repressive counter-terrorism measures that incidentally questioned the position of Tunisian democracy regarding the respect for civil rights, human rights and its compliance with the rule of law (Bras, 2016; Tamburini, 2018).

Tunisia is often perceived as both a stronghold of, and a key protagonist in, the global war on terror. As reported by Aliaga and O'Farrell (2017), Tunisia is actually at the centre of interest of different international actors who are struggling to impose their control through cooperation in the security sector. Since security assistance offers the opportunity to access valuable information, international donors 'compete to establish privileged relationships with the Tunisian government' (Aliaga and O'Farrell, 2017, p. 5). International donors concentrate on offering security training to Tunisian security forces, disregarding the pressing need to reform the Tunisian security sector, which still has not been done properly after 2011.

Moreover, international donors are also committed to 'softer' preventative initiatives. Even if Tunisian authorities are progressively moving into the PVE field, it can be said that the prevention of 'violent extremism' in Tunisia is currently being mainly explored by international actors and non-governmental organisations. In 2016, the Tunisian National Commission on Counter-Terrorism issued a strategy for fighting extremism and terrorism. This includes the pillar of prevention. Nevertheless, at the moment, the activities carried out by governmental authorities can be considered fragmented and inconsistent. The largest amount of funds in PVE social programmes is actually allocated by international actors as part of multilateral or bilateral cooperation for development. It is important to consider that these PVE policies envisage the application of a wide range of policy instruments and a particular set of assumptions that have been designed in the global North. It is very important to consider the globalisation of PVE policies (Kundnani and Hayes, 2018) when studying the Tunisian context. The emergence of exogenous programmes has brought with it a series of practices and knowledge developed in other social, political and economic environments.

In the coming section, the relationship between violent extremism and development will be addressed using some of the theoretical tools offered by securitisation theory.

Violent extremism, security and development

The discourse of international stakeholders formulates the problem of political violence in the country in terms of 'violent extremism'. In this way, donors legitimise and apply a common set of knowledge, skills and competences that have been geographically conceived far from Tunisia and thus reflect international dynamics and priorities.

Nevertheless, as critical literature indicates, 'violent extremism', like other terms belonging to the same semantic field, such as 'terrorism' or 'radicalisation', is characterised by a strong disagreement about its definition. After all, the notion has been adopted in social policies in the global North before being submitted to the assessment of the scientific community. The literature seems to trace the birth of this concept to 2005, when the international community after the Madrid and London bombings started to move from the framework of the 'war on terrorism' to the 'fight against violent extremism' (Nasser-Eddine, 2011). This paradigm shift was institutionalised ten years later with the adoption of the UN Security Council Resolution 2178 (2014) and the creation of the UN Secretary-General's Plan of Action to Prevent Violent Extremism (United Nations, 2015). Therefore, rapidly, 'the prevention of violent extremism has become a priority for the global community' (Frank and Reva, 2016, p. 2). The United Nations has formulated the need for PVE policies with the justification that security measures alone would not be sufficient to provide an effective response to terrorism (United Nations, 2015). Therefore, PVE has been defined as:

> the use of non-coercive means to dissuade individuals or groups from mobilizing towards violence and to mitigate recruitment, support, facilitation or engagement in ideologically motivated terrorism by non-state actors in furtherance of political objectives. (Khan, 2015, in United Nations Office on Drugs and Crime, 2018)

Although the relationship between 'violent extremism' and 'terrorism' has not clearly been made explicit in policy papers or academic literature, as a matter of fact the link between the two concepts has been constructed as a close one. This is why violent extremism is depicted as a threat to security. Moreover, it is important to stress the fact that PVE policies have been intended to accompany and complement counter-terrorism hard power measures in different policy areas, including the development sector. In fact, in 2016, the Organisation for Economic Co-operation and Development decided that certain PVE activities – previously classified as counter-terrorism – were eligible as Official Development Assistance, opening the way to a further securitisation of development (Aning, 2010).

A large corpus of academic and grey literature has explored the nexus between development and security, a complex relationship that has been described in very diverse terms. As the review of the literature done by Spear and Williams indicates (2012, p. 21), there are different conceptualisations of this relationship, from 'mutually consecutive' to 'hierarchical', passing through 'sequential' or 'interdependent'. The consecutive relation, summed up by the statement 'there is no security without development, and no development without security' (Spear and Williams, 2012, p. 22), can be considered one of the most important positions defended by international donors allocating funds for development.

However, as pointed out by Duffield, this relationship can be insidious: 'through a circular form of reinforcement and mutuality, achieving one is now regarded as essential for securing the other' (2001, p. 27). But for Duffield, the convergence 'is not simply a policy matter. It has profound political and structural implications' (2001, p. 27). The nexus between security and development has proved to be problematic and has been explored by the critical literature. Based on securitisation theory, it has denounced the instrumentalisation of foreign aid to accomplish security and military objectives. Moreover, the context of the 'global war on terror' has significantly affected the convergence of security and development, bringing it closer to security goals, institutions and policies (Howell and Lind, 2009, p. 7).

In the Tunisian context, various observers have already highlighted a trend towards the securitisation of development. As Aliaga and O'Farrell note, 'a consequence of the CVE approach is the securitisation of governance and development work, where non-security programmes are perceived as vectors through which to advance CT and CVE objectives' (2017, p. 22).

The notion of securitisation, originally theorised by Ole Wæver and then popularised by the work of the Copenhagen school, refers to the process through which a given issue 'is presented as an existential threat, requiring emergency measures and justifying actions outside the normal bounds of political procedure' (Buzan et al., 1998, pp. 23–24). Within this process, securitisation theory insists on the importance of discursive practices in the construction of an issue as a 'security threat'. Buzan and Wæver conceptualised securitisation as a 'discursive process' (2003, p. 491), whereby the speech act or the utterance has in itself a performative power to create the reality. Therefore, securitisation theory also provides the tools to explore the social and political implications of constructing something as a security threat. By conducting a Critical Discourse Analysis of international stakeholders' policy documents, and placing texts in their broader context, this study will offer a reflection about what issues or which actors are constructed as 'problematic' for security.

The case explored by this study shows that, besides the securitisation of development, other processes of securitisation take place concerning different issues or social actors, such as young people, that are actually at the centre of the PVE agenda being considered closely linked with the security of the nation. Moreover, the developmental practices show the underpinning of unequal power relations existing between donors and receivers. Part of the literature about development shows how donors base their funding programmes on their own development goals (Reith, 2010; Wallace et al., 2007). An inegalitarian relation between donors and receivers results in an increased dependence of civil society organisations and NGOs on donors, and an increased vulnerability to donor demands (Agg, 2006; Wallace, 1997). In the present case study, donors establish the general theoretical and practical framework in which Tunisian civil society organisations and NGOs necessarily have to develop programmes. By acting in this way, the donors leave the receivers little room for manoeuvre, establishing, reproducing and imposing the hegemonic globalised discourse about violent extremism (Kundnani and Hayes, 2018).

Methodology

With the aim of exploring the vision and the strategy of international donors funding the PVE project in Tunisia, this study is based on the analysis of the discourse constructed in the programme guidelines for applicants contained in the call for proposals of international aid for development and other relevant documents. Applicants' guidelines have been considered crucial documents here. They offer extremely useful information about the perceived background, the project's rationale, the recommended approach, the eligibility criteria and donors' priorities and objectives.

The methodology used to analyse the documents is CDA. CDA is often defined not as a simple method, but rather as a methodology or a technique of analysis of texts and discourses, as well as a way of understanding the connection between discourse and political and social phenomena (Jackson, 2005, p. 24). This method and theory have been considered the best way to conduct a study about the language and the practice of the PVE international actors in Tunisia, due to their capacity to explore the relationship between language, ideology and power.

For the purpose of this study, discourse will be conceived of as a form of social practice both socially conditioned and socially constitutive (Fairclough et al., 2011, p. 258). Exploring the relationship between discourse and power, this chapter inquires into how discursive practices can produce and reproduce unequal power relations (Fairclough et al., 2011, p. 258).

The discourse of international donors about violent extremism

A plethora of PVE activities, conferences, awareness campaigns, debates and so forth have been organised since 2016 all around Tunisia, as its capital is an important centre of activities. Pull and push factors of violent extremist adhesion have been the object of a multitude of reports and surveys, mainly conducted by NGOs and local associations. Nevertheless, some observers censured the superficiality of these initiatives (Aliaga and O'Farrell, 2017) and a general climate of confusion while speaking about 'violent extremism', 'radicalisation' or 'terrorism'. Actually, these three concepts are used sometimes interchangeably (Martini, this volume), and in the majority of cases they are not properly defined even by practitioners. This tendency has been found in the corpus of documents analysed in this study. None of the calls for proposals offers a proper definition of what is meant by 'violent extremism'. This, however, is still described as one of the 'greatest risks that threaten social cohesion' (United Nations Development Programme (UNDP), 2016, p. 1) and as a 'centrifugal tendency' that arises from the feeling of abandonment and exclusion (UNDP, 2016, p. 1). At the level of the vocabulary employed, the violent extremism is set against terms like 'peace', 'dialogue', 'inclusion', 'participation', 'social cohesion', 'non-violence', among others, and linked with words like 'instability', 'radicalisation', 'conflict', 'delinquency', 'smuggling', 'informal working' and 'culture of violence'.

Through this framework, the donors' discourse legitimises and vehiculates a precise knowledge about terrorism and violent extremism, the one produced by international organisations starting in 2005 and that constitutes the basis of most of the PVE initiatives all around the world (Kundnani and Hayes, 2018).

Violent extremism and the 2011 revolution

The totality of the documents analysed start the contextualisation of the 'problem' of violent extremism in Tunisia by mentioning the 2011 uprisings. This systematic reference to 2011 can be seen as naturally recognising the importance of the uprisings in the region. However, the so-called 'Arab Spring' does indeed have a special significance for the international community and donors. Once the authoritarian regime of Ben Ali fell, Tunisia became a new territory of possible intervention for international donors and even, to a certain extent, an experimental territory due to the new context of freedom and democratisation.

However, the general narrative constructed in these documents admits that the 2011 events have improved the life of Tunisians, bringing a new set of democratic institutions and freedom of expression, but at the same time they have failed to provide a socio-economic solution to the demands expressed by citizens. In the donors' view, this situation of unfulfilled expectations leads to frustration, which, in turn, results in 'vulnerability' to violent extremism.

In the European Commission tender, it is argued that the marginalisation and socio-economic disparities – which played a catalytic role in the 2011 revolution – are generating a climate of frustration and disillusionment in which a number of 'young people are turning to smuggling, informal trading and/or being sensitive to the rhetoric of extremist organizations'. (European Commission, 2017). According to UNDP, even if the uprisings of 2011 undoubtedly brought about a series of improvements in terms of citizenship and the relationship with the state, this essentially remains a condition limited to urban intellectual elites. This narrative of a half-failed revolution legitimises the intervention of international donors in the field of democratisation and development of Tunisia.

Moreover, it is necessary to stress the fact that the 2011 events marked a landmark in Tunisian and regional contemporary history. Violent actors that in the past had been repressed by the authoritarian rule certainly took advantage of the post-uprising turmoil. The events of 2011 represent a turning point in the expression of non-state violence that reached its peak in 2013–2015. However, formulating the problem of violent extremism in terms of the 'post-uprising problem' could lead to misunderstanding a problem that existed long before 2011, even if in different forms, importance and characteristics.

Violent extremism as a 'youth problem'

When analysing the texts in question, it became very easy to find out visually who the expected beneficiaries of these projects are. The high occurrence in the text of the words 'young'/'youth' and 'women' prove the priority accorded to these social actors by international donors. This actually reflects an international tendency (Kundnani and Hayes, 2018). The aim of these programmes is globally targeting young people that are described as a category vulnerable to violent extremism, as they are frustrated, weary, disillusioned and in search of identity. Young people are considered at the same time both a category vulnerable to violent extremism, as well as the best potential partnering actors to fight it (European Commission, 2017).

When discussing the issue of violent extremism in Tunisia, the category of 'youth' is often at the centre of the debate in political discourses and news, as well as being the target of specific public policies. However, the category of youth has revealed to be problematic, first, because categories are never neutral, but socially constitutive. Second, because the boundaries between adulthood and youth appear to be very blurry, depending on time and space. The epistemological relevance of the youth category had been questioned by authors like Bourdieu (1993) and Halbwachs (1972), and is still problematised by contemporary scholars studying the nexus between youth and security in the southern Mediterranean region (Murphy, 2018; Paciello and Pioppi, 2018; Pepicelli, 2018).

In recent times, two events increased the interest of researchers and policymakers in the young people of the Arab countries: first, the incidents of 11 September 2001, and second, ten years later, the Arab uprisings of 2010–2011 (Gertel and Hexel, 2018, p. 9). Both events also contributed to establishing even more than before the link between 'youth' and 'security'. As pointed out by Sukarieh and Tannock, the debate on Arab youth has been marked by a systematic reference to the theory of the 'youth bulge' (Sukarieh and Tannock, 2018, p. 576), built on the assumption that a disproportionate[3] and unprecedented percentage of young people can contribute to instability, which can result in conflicts and violence. The other strand of the narrative concerning young people in Arab countries opposes this tale of youth as a menace to stability and instead looks at youth as an 'actor of change' (Paciello and Pioppi, 2018). This kind of discourse places Arab youth at the centre of the interest of neoliberal economy (Sukarieh, 2012) and stabilisation policies.

In the Tunisian context, this juncture is particularly representative. Sukarieh (2012) studied the implications of the shift in attitudes of the global community towards Arab youth, considering their move 'from terrorists to revolutionaries' (p. 424) in the 2010–2011 context. However, Pepicelli argues that the 2011 uprising period saw the rise of the image of Tunisian youth as agents of change and heroes of the nation, but shortly afterwards, this positive and borderline epic narrative was replaced by an opposite image of youth as problematic, as a danger for the stability of the country, downgrading them 'from "hero" to "zero"' (2018).

A large corpus of literature has shown the significance of the process of the securitisation of youth by revealing the implication of linking this unstable social category with security (Murphy, 2018). Sukarieh and Tannock (2018) have problematised PVE policies addressed to youth, starting from the analysis of a number of institutional initiatives taken by various actors on the wave of UN Security Council Resolution 2250 (2015) on Youth Peace and Security (YPS). They argue that the YPS agenda corresponds with the general trends of securitisation of development, linking youth to security and overestimating their role as security subjects and actors. This process of securitisation, according to Murphy, can contribute to overshadowing the context of 'multidimensional hyperprecarity and insecuritisation of young peoples' lives which derive from that same neoliberal economic order and the political structures that sustain it in the SEM [South and East Mediterranean] countries' (2018, p. 21).

It is important to stress the fact that the PVE policies funded by international actors have to combine with the counter-terrorism measures put in place by the state, which often have a major impact on Tunisian youth. At the same time, some of these measures have proved to adversely affect civil rights and disproportionately target young people. For instance, the travel restrictions imposed since 2013, which prevented men and women under 35 from travelling to 'at-risk' countries without their father's authorisation, have been considered by human rights associations as an arbitrary restriction on the right to freedom of movement (Amnesty International, 2018; Human Rights Watch, 2015). The measure, which aimed at containing the departure of Tunisian youngsters to join extremist groups in conflict areas, did not originate from a proper order of the public prosecutor or a national court, but simply followed a Ministry of the Interior's directive (S17), raising issues about arbitrariness.

In the Tunisian context, the disproportionate impact that national and international policies have on youths could turn out to be counter-productive as envisaged by Della Porta and Haupt: 'In a vicious circle, social groups considered vulnerable to radical propaganda because they are excluded and/or discriminated against tend to be treated as potential risks, thereby strengthening those feelings of exclusion and discrimination' (2012, p. 312). The construction of 'violent extremism' as a 'youth problem' paves the way to an infantilisation of the beneficiaries. It would refer to the idea of 'juvenile rebellion', overshadowing the violent actor's political commitment. It proves to be problematic since it entails categorising radical positions and practices as a youth matter, thus depoliticising extremist activism and ideologies, on the basis of a stereotyped young people's naivety.

Moreover, categorising youth as a crucial group both responsible for, and vulnerable to, the problem of violent extremism permits international actors to maintain the control they have been exercising over the sector of youth since 2011 when they replaced the state in the design and implementation of youth policies (Somi, 2016). International donors prioritise young people in PVE policies also in a logic of control of their activism, influencing their way of understanding 'democracy' and 'participation', basically responding to the kind of neoliberal democracies they support (Grasso and Bessant, 2018; Murphy, 2018; Sukarieh and Tannock, 2018).

The essentialised role of women in PVE policies

According to international donors, the other privileged beneficiary and partnering actors in PVE programmes are women, which, coupled with youth, are considered an underrepresented and vulnerable group. One of the most common ideas is that promoting women's role in PVE will reinforce the resilience of communities. In this sense, women are considered 'key actors'. For instance, according to UNDP, the promotion of women's 'capacity of neutralisation' of root causes of violent extremism will strengthen the 'immunity' of rural regions against violent extremism (2016, p. 3).

This kind of representation of women is ultimately problematic because, as pointed out by Ní Aoláin, it tends to 'oversimplify the personal and social contexts in which these women live' and fails to appreciate 'the complexity of the roles they play in their families and communities' (2015, p. 5). At the same time, the praise for women's crucial role in PVE practice remains blurred, since the policy document only superficially specifies the motivation of it. The role of women is exaggerated, as shown by the definition 'pivotal actresses of the community' (UNDP, 2018). Women are seen in essentialised and stereotyped ways and they are reduced to their gender role within the family (Giscard d'Estaing, 2017), viewed as 'beautiful souls', intrinsically peaceful and non-violent (Elshtain, 1987).

Nevertheless, in the CDA analysis, attention should not be placed just on what is said; silences are also significant. The important activism of women in violent Salafi groups in Tunisia is something almost completely neglected in the documents analysed. Although Tunisian women have been part of those people leaving Tunisia to join Islamic State in Iraq and Syria and eventually reached important roles in domestic jihadi Salafist brigades, in the political and mediatic narrative, they are often forgotten or reduced to the figure of 'jihadi brides' (Martini, 2018). Paraphrasing Sjoberg and Gentry (2013), the recognition of women's violence is not sex-neutral, but related with gender roles and stereotypes. Thus, violent women, in contrast with their alleged peaceful nature, have failed as members of society and as women as such (2013, p. 5).

The narrative constructed about young people and extremism discussed earlier has an obvious gender-biased nature. Young men from disadvantaged areas are often seen as potential delinquents, radicalised extremists or illegal migrants (Catusse and Destremau, 2016, p. 16). The perception is indeed very different for extremist women, who have been at the centre of the public debate in another kind of prejudicial mediatic narrative concerning violent extremism, namely, the discourse about *ǧihād al-nikāḥ*, which in Arabic means the jihad of the marriage or the sexual jihad. In fact, this category is not unprecedented, but it reflects the tendency, internationally widespread, that has difficulty in recognising women's agency in violence and terrorism and reduces their activism to 'sexual' or 'romance' *affaires* (Martini, 2018; Sjoberg and Gentry, 2011).

By silencing the violent dimension of Tunisian women's activism and reducing them to the place they occupy in the family and the community, even in terrorist contexts, donors end up negating women's political commitments and depoliticising their actions (Martini, 2018, p. 14). Hence, this representation not only has gender bias, but it also acquires importance in the light of neo-Orientalist discourses and practices, particularly affecting women, described by Akram (2000), consisting in othering and stereotyping Muslims worldwide, both in academia and policies.

Through expressions such as women's 'capacity of neutralisation' of violent extremism (UN, 2015), international donors have so far prioritised a representation of the role of women in PVE as redemptorist, a picture that has in fact been prioritised by policies and campaigns of both international donors and the Tunisian authorities, for example the case of the awareness-raising video issued by the Ministry of the Interior targeting parents, which shows blurred images of a woman sitting in a police car speaking by radio to her son who is involved in a terrorist action. At the end, the video states: 'When we do not pay attention to our children, terrorism can be among us'.[4] The paternalistic phrase and the fact that only the mother but not the father is represented in the video raises several issues concerning gendered narratives in PVE. In fact, this video campaign fits in with the broader tendency to consider mothers disproportionally responsible for the actions of their sons and daughters (Giscard d'Estaing, 2017; Ní Aoláin, 2015).

Rephrasing Giscard d'Estaing (2017), the promotion of the role of women in PVE policies corresponds with an instrumentalisation of their position for security interests. For international donors, they represent 'an entry point to the private sphere of the home, through their role as mothers, wives, and sisters, enabling PVE/CVE programming to reach individuals and groups that are often difficult to access and influence them away from extremism' (2017, p. 106; see also Auchter, this volume).

Territorialising the problem of violent extremism

Marked by a close liaison between youth and extremism, the discourse of international donors contributes more concretely to the construction of a specific sub-category, *the young rural unemployed potential extremist*. As discourses are never compartmentalised but intertextual, this kind of rhetoric can be found in the institutional and mediatic discourse that often contributes to stigmatising a specific portion of 'youth' – that is, the one living in disadvantaged suburban and rural areas. This is the case in two suburbs of Tunis: Douar Hicher and Ettadhamen. The remarkable study by Lamloum and Ben Zina contributes to depicting these young people in their complexity, far from the hegemonic media construction that reduced them to jihadi Salafists (2015, p. 14).

But international donors' programmes are territorialising the problem of violent extremism in border and internal regions that, at the same time, are suffering more from the stigma of their social exclusion and the presence of armed groups active in their territories (as in the region of the Mountain Chaambi in the governorate of Kasserine). The governorates prioritised by donors are Médenine, Tataouine (southern borders with Lybia), Kef, Kasserine (borders with Algeria), Sidi Bouzid, Kairouan (interior), Bizerte (north) and Grand Tunis (Ariana, Ben Arous, Manouba – peri-urban belt of the capital).

The decision to undertake small PVE projects in highly stigmatised and highly impoverished areas can be considered problematic. First, because the superimposition of this kind of project risks adding fuel to the fire of the discriminatory discourse against these populations. Second, this type of initiative alone cannot claim satisfactory results in areas where there is still a historical and structural marginalisation dependent on certain dynamics of the Tunisian state.

Moreover, as space is political (Harvey, 1994), other questions arise from the territorialisation of the threat constructed by donors. For instance, violent extremism is related by international donors with other issues that have in their turn been securitised and closely linked to terrorism, such as smuggling and informal trade. It is not by chance that donors chose to link violent extremism to 'smuggling' and 'informal commerce', placing them in the same sentence as results of the same cause, 'frustration' (European Commission, 2017). As a matter of fact, apart from the development, the bilateral and multilateral international cooperation with Tunisia has an important security component with different dimensions, border control being one of the most important.

Far from denying the existing relationship between smuggling and terrorism, it is important not to forget that establishing discursive links between terrorism and smuggling has had important consequences, in policy terms, on the population of the areas bordering Libya and Algeria. The CVE policies carried out by the Tunisian state with the support of the EU (Délégation de l'Union européenne en Tunisie, 2017), the US (Mullin and Ruabah, 2018) and other partners have led to a heavy securitisation of its borders. This has not only put pressure on the informal economic system which sustained the local population, but has also contributed to worsening the already precarious economic and social conditions because of the lack of the creation of economic alternatives to smuggling for border populations (Gallien, 2018). According to Meddeb, this securitarian approach 'has disrupted the informal and illegal economic networks on which much of the population relies and caused it to lose faith in the government' (2017, p. 1). For Boukhars, it may prove to be counter-productive at the PVE level:

> Tunisia has increasingly relied on the military to bring security to its border region with Libya in response to a growth of jihadism in the region and the rise of new forms of trafficking in the aftermath of the 2011 revolution. But the current approach risks worsening the security situation and playing into the hands of jihadis. In the absence of a concerted program to lift Tunisia's southeast out of poverty, crackdowns on small-time, cross-border traffickers have hurt the traditional economy, creating an even deeper sense of marginalization at a time when a significant number of Tunisian foreign fighters who fought in Iraq, Syria, and Libya are returning to the country. (Boukhars, 2018, p. 1)

Moreover, securitising borders and establishing systematic discursive links between smuggling and terrorism also means reinforcing the construction of 'border violence' that find its roots in the colonial governance of spaces and populations (Mullin and Rouabah, 2018). As highlighted by many authors (Lajili, 2017; Lamloum, 2017; Mullin and Rouabah, 2018), the territorial control of the Tunisian state, and in particular of its frontiers, retains some of the aspects of the colonial-style militarisation and still places this area at the centre of (neo)colonial/imperial interest and violence (Mullin and Rouabah, 2018).

A problematic vision of 'peace'

From a linguistic point of view, the three documents present a very consistent vocabulary; the values of 'peace', 'tolerance' and 'citizenship' are contrasted with 'violent extremism'. 'Participation' and 'social, cultural and political integration' are the alternative to 'conflict', 'isolation' and 'violence'. The civil society is therefore seen as a key actor, reinforcing 'social cohesion', and capable of promoting 'active citizenship' through dialogue and the resolution of conflicts, seen as key elements for the prevention of 'radicalisation'. It is indeed very interesting because the same kind of vocabulary can be found in a number of CVE/PVE policies around the world. As pointed out by Kundnani and Hayes (2018), in recent times we have witnessed the deployment of standardised PVE counter-radicalisation policies around the world.

As in other contexts, the activities envisaged are often awareness activities, capacity-building, construction of spaces for debate, the production of a religious discourse alternative to VE (online and offline) and the promotion of the political participation of the most vulnerable categories. Often, they envisage the identification of key figures to train to deconstruct violent narratives within families (among them mothers), imams and young leaders.

These kind of vocabulary, assumptions and responses are part of the broader context of international policies, guidelines and conferences on youth and security analysed by Sukarieh and Tannock (2018). These two scholars have pointed out that the youth, peace and security agenda fits in with the trends of the broader context of the securitisation of development. Aiming at expanding the involvement of youth as key allies in building resilience against violent extremism, the agenda is open to criticism, since it sponsors moderation and peace in an 'un-problematic way', exaggerating the responsibility of the young as the root of the problem and passing on to them the 'responsibility' of fighting violent extremism (Sukarieh and Tannock, 2018, p. 860). The 'fight' foreseen by these kinds of policies is conducted by a 'moderation' that actually boosts the status quo and maintains ideological support for a neoliberal global order 'that remains massively unequal, and protects and serves the interests of national and global elites in the first instance' (Sukarieh and Tannock, 2018, p. 862).

The entirety of the texts analysed contemplates the need to strengthen trust between the young and the authorities, disregarding the problematic relationship between citizens and the security forces as in the case of the European Commission: 'Strengthening youth participation in decision-making processes related to security and peacebuilding issues including building trust between youth and public authorities (governments / law enforcement / security forces)' (European Commission, 2017, p. 3). However, promoting participation and building trust in public officers without problematising the limits and troubles of these authorities can prove to be problematic. In decentralised regions of Tunisia, historically neglected by the central power, citizens have deep grievances towards public authorities. Historical malpractices that are currently intersecting with terrorism in Tunisia are unlikely to be resolved with PVE programmes. Moreover, none of the texts analysed provides real responses to the need to support the reform of the security sector and the judiciary, envisaged since 2011 as part of the transitional justice process but never achieved. No text addresses the crucial issue of financial conditions imposed by international organisations (such as the IMF) that are throwing the country into a deep economic crisis caused by governmental austerity measures.

Quoting Herrera and Bayat, within some 'grand development narratives, the young are supposed to join, not question, a consolidated global framework for economic and political development' (Herrera and Bayat, 2010, p. 356). It is something that other authors have pointed out even more concretely in the Tunisian context, as did Somi: 'projects targeting young Tunisians tend to confine them in issues and themes that neutralize the possibility for them to be in any way critical of the international order, and, therefore, to aspire to change it' (2016, p. 10)

Conclusion

Through the critical analysis of the discourse of international donors funding PVE programmes in Tunisia, this chapter has highlighted and discussed some of the main assumptions on which the donors' discourse is based, relating them to the broader socio-political context in which they arise. As this chapter has shown in the Tunisian context in a top-down approach, international donors apply knowledge and practices produced by the international community. The framework of development actually provides international stakeholders with the opportunity to determine Western-biased 'rules of play' through which discourses and practices can be framed and controlled.

Different processes of securitisation intersect in the donors' discourse: the securitisation of development actually offers a concrete framework in which youth itself is securitised. As shown throughout this chapter, the measures taken in the field of counter-terrorism and PVE at the national and international levels have been disproportionately addressing Tunisian youth. This fact raises problems because it prevents an understanding of the complexity of Tunisian youths. Far from being a homogeneous category, Tunisian youth experience various forms of insecurity. At the same time, it also prevents a grasp of the often complex dynamics that are at the root of the radicalisation processes driven by the interactions of various political actors within long-lasting processes (Della Porta and Haupt, 2012, p. 317).

The understanding of notions such as peace, inclusion and social cohesion also proved to be problematic as the donors only superficially envisage addressing grievances, and not through a constructive political debate, but rather with the final aim of including marginalised people both in a system that is responsible for their systematic marginalisation and in a neoliberal order that underlies most of the socio-economic insecurity of the beneficiaries of these projects. As pointed out by Attree, 'It is important that actions to stop incitement to violence don't creep into becoming broad clampdowns on dissent' (2018).

Besides, the discourse of international donors concerning women and their role in PVE programmes has essentialised gender relations idealising women's importance in the family and the community. This kind of rhetoric actually indicates the interest that donors have in women's involvement in PVE programmes: having an access point to the private spaces of families and rural communities.

In conclusion, the present chapter proposed a critical analysis of the most problematic assumptions that lie behind PVE practices in Tunisia. Future research should consider the social and political effects of this discourse more practically, for instance conducting surveys among practitioners and beneficiaries with the aim of understanding how these theoretical thoughts and discursive praxis have been translated into practice.

Notes

1   According to the theorisation of Wiktorowicz, the term 'salafist jihadist' is taken to mean those groups that see violence as the main instrument for achieving their goals, which means that they see the minor jihad as the only effective means for establishing the Islamic State (Wiktorowicz, 2004).
2   The Tunisian interior and bordering regions had historically been the object of systemic and intentional marginalisation and exclusion starting from the colonisation period. Nowadays this problem still persists.
3   The Middle Eastern and North African population is marked by 30% of people aged between 15 and 29 (UNDP, 2016, p.22).
4   The original version in Arabic (dialectal register) 'كي نغفلو على أولادنا ..... ينجم يكون الإرهاب بيناتنا'. The video is available at www.facebook.com/ministere.interieur.tunisie/videos/1159190170775024/ (accessed 1 August 2018).

References

Agg, C., 2006. 'Winners or losers? NGOs in the current aid paradigm', *Development*, 49(2), 15–21.

Akram, S., 2000. 'Orientalism revisited in asylum and refugee claims', *International Journal of Refugee Law*, 12(1), 7–40.

Aliaga, L., O'Farrell, K.T., 2017. 'Counter-terror in Tunisia: A road paved with good intentions?', *Saferworld*. Available at https://saferworld-indepth.squarespace.com/counter-terror-in-tunisia-a-road-paved-with-good-intentions/ (accessed 31 May 2019).

Amnesty International, 2018. *They Never Tell Me Why. Arbitrary Restrictions on Movement in Tunisia.* Amnesty International, London. Available at www.amnesty.org/en/documents/mde30/8848/2018/en/ (accessed 4 May 2019).

Aning, K., 2010. 'Security, the war on terror, and official development assistance', *Critical Studies on Terrorism*, 3(1), 7–26.

Attree, L., 2018. 'Shouldn't you be countering violent extremism?', *Saferworld*. Available at https://saferworld-indepth.squarespace.com/shouldnt-you-be-countering-violent-extremism (accessed 4 May 2019).

Boukhars, A., 2018. 'The Potential Jihadi windfall from the militarization of Tunisia's border region with Libya', *Carnegie Endowment for International Peace*. Available at https://carnegieendowment.org/2018/01/26/potential-jihadi-windfall-from-militarization-of-tunisia-s-border-region-with-libya-pub-75365 (accessed 31 May 2019).

Bourdieu, P., 1993. *Sociology in Question (Theory, Culture & Society)*. SAGE, London.

Bras, J.-P., 2016. 'Tunisie: L'élaboration de la loi antiterroriste de 2015 ou les paradoxes de la démocratie sécuritaire', *L'Année du Maghreb*, 15, 309–323.

Buzan, B., Wæver, O., 2003. *Regions and Powers: The Structure of International Security.* Cambridge University Press, Cambridge.

Buzan, B., Wæver, O. and Wilde, J. de, 1998. *Security: A New Framework for Analysis.* Lynne Rienner Publishing, Boulder, CO.

Catusse, M. and Destremau, B., 2016. 'Governing youth, managing society: A comparative overview of six country case studies (Egypt, Lebanon, Morocco, Occupied Palestinian Territories, Tunisia and Turkey)', *Istituto Affari Internazionali Working Paper n°14*. Available at www.iai.it/sites/default/files/p2y_14.pdf (accessed 7 April 2019).

Délégation de l'Union européenne en Tunisie, 2017. *Rapport d'activité. Édition 2017*, Tunis. Available at https://eeas.europa.eu/sites/eeas/files/rapport_activite_due_2017_fr_20062017.pdf (accessed 10 May 2019).

Della Porta, D. and Haupt, H.-G., 2012. 'Patterns of radicalization in political activism', *Social Science History*, 36, 311–320.

Duffield, M.R., 2001. *Global Governance and the New Wars: The Merging of Development and Security.* Palgrave, London.

Elshtain, J.B., 1987. *Women and War.* University of Chicago Press, Chicago.

European Commission, 2017. *Soutien aux acteurs de la société civile du pays pour la prévention des conflits, la consolidation de la paix et la préparation aux crises Lignes directrices à l'intention des demandeurs. Bruxelles.* Available at https://webgate.ec.europa.eu/europeaid/online-services/index.cfm?do=publi.welcome&nbPubliList=15&orderby=upd&orderbyad=Desc&searchtype=RS&aofr=154272 (accessed 15 June 2019).

Fairclough, N., Mulderrig, J. and Wodak, R., 2011. 'Critical Discourse Analysis', in Van Dijk ,T.A. (ed.), *Discourse Studies: A Multidisciplinary Introduction.* SAGE, London, pp. 357–378.

Frank, C. and Reva, D., 2016. 'Preventing violent extremism: South Africa's place in the world', Institute for Security Studies, Africa Portal. Available at www.africaportal. org/publications/preventing-violent-extremism-south-africas-place-in-the-world/ (accessed 12 October 2019).

Gallien, M., 2018. 'An economic malaise lies at the heart of Libya-Tunisia border standoff', *Middle East Eye*. Available at www.middleeasteye.net/columns/economic-malaise-heart-libya-tunisia-border-standoff-883226567 (accessed 15 February 2019).

Gertel, J., Hexel, R., 2018. *Coping with Uncertainty: Youth in the Middle East and North Africa*. Sagi Books, London.

Giscard d'Estaing, S., 2017. 'Engaging women in countering violent extremism: Avoiding instrumentalisation and furthering agency', *Gender & Development*, 25, 103–118.

Grasso, M.T., Bessant, J. (eds), 2018. *Governing Youth Politics in the Age of Surveillance: The Criminalization of Political Dissent*. Routledge, London.

Halbwachs, M., 1972. *Classes sociales et morphologie*. Les Editions de Minuit, Paris.

Harvey, D., 1994. 'The social construction of space and time: A relational theory', *Geographical Review of Japan, Series B*, 67(2), 126–135.

Herrera, L., Bayat, A., 2010. *Being Young and Muslim: New Cultural Politics in the Global South and North*. Oxford University Press, Oxford.

Howell, J., Lind, J., 2009. *Counter-terrorism, Aid and Civil Society: Before and After the War on Terror (Non-governmental public action series)*. Palgrave Macmillan, Basingstoke, New York.

Human Rights Watch, 2015. *Tunisia: Arbitrary Travel Restrictions*. Available at www.hrw.org/news/2015/07/10/tunisia-arbitrary-travel-restrictions (accessed 10 October 2019).

Jackson, R., 2005. *Writing the War on Terrorism: Language, Politics, and Counter-terrorism: New Approaches to Conflict Analysis*. Manchester University Press, Manchester.

Kundnani, A., Hayes, B., 2018. 'The globalisation of countering violent extremism policies', Transnational Institute, New York. Available at www.tni.org/en/publication/the-globalisation-of-countering-violent-extremism-policies (accessed 7 June 2019).

Lajili, M., 2017. 'Franchissement des frontières et contrôle du territoire: le cas du sud tunisien dans les années 1960', in Sghaier, A.A. (ed.), *Terrorisme et Contrebande en Tunisie (1988–2016)*. Mannouba University Press, Tunis, pp. 7–24.

Lamloum, O., 2017. 'Marginalisation, insecurity and uncertainty on the Tunisian–Libyan border. Ben Guerdane and Dhehiba from the perspective of their inhabitants', *International Alert*. Available at www.international-alert.org/publications/marginalisation-insecurity-and-uncertainty-tunisian-libyan-border (accessed 16 May 2019).

Lamloum, O., Ben Zina, M.A., 2015. *Les Jeunes de Douar Hicher et d'Ettadhamen: Une enquête sociologique*. International Alert, Éditions Arabesques, Tunis.

Martini, A., 2018. 'Making women terrorists into "Jihadi brides": An analysis of media narratives on women joining ISIS', *Critical Studies on Terrorism*, 11(3), 458–477.

Meddeb, H., 2017. 'How Europe can help preserve Tunisia's fragile democracy', European Council of Foreign Relations. Available at www.ecfr.eu/publications/summary/peripheral_vision_how_europe_can_preserve_tunisias_democracy_7215 (accessed 12 March 2019).

Mullin, C., Rouabah, B., 2018. 'Decolonizing Tunisia's border violence: Moving beyond imperial structures and imaginaries', *Viewpoint Magazine*, 1 February. Available at www.viewpointmag.com/2018/02/01/decolonizing-tunisias-border-violence-moving-beyond-imperial-structures-imaginaries/ (accessed 14 April 2019).

Murphy, E., 2018. 'The in-securitisation of youth in the South and East Mediterranean', *The International Spectator*, 53, 21–37.

Nasser-Eddine, M., 2011. *Countering Violent Extremism (CVE) Literature Review*. Australian Government Department of Defence, Canberra. Available at https://apo.org.au/sites/default/files/resource-files/2011/03/apo-nid101921–1138111.pdf (accessed 14 February 2019).

Ní Aoláin, F., 2015. 'Jihad, counter-terrorism and mothers', Just Security, 4 March. Available at www.justsecurity.org/20407/jihad-counter-terrorism-mothers/ (accessed 14 February 2020).

Paciello, M.C., Pioppi, D., 2018. 'Youth as actors of change? The cases of Morocco and Tunisia', *The International Spectator*, 53, 38–51.

Pepicelli, R., 2018. 'From "hero" to "zero": Re-thinking youth in post-revolutionary Tunisia. A focus on family, state and public discourse', in El Shabab, W. (ed.), *Images of Transformations between the Two Shores of the Mediterranean*. Genova University Press, Genova, pp. 56–80.

Reith, S., 2010. 'Money, power, and donor–NGO partnerships', *Development in Practice*, 20(3), 446–455.

Sjoberg, L., Gentry, C.E. (eds), 2011. *Women, Gender, and Terrorism, Studies in Security and International Affairs*. University of Georgia Press, Athens.

Sjoberg, L., Gentry, C.E., 2013. *Mothers, Monsters, Whores: Women's Violence in Global Politics*. Zed Books, London.

Somi, O. 2016. 'Youth policies in Tunisia: The internationalisation of youth as public policy issue', *Power2Youth Working Papers*, No. 9 (May). Available at www.iai.it/en/node/6307 (accessed 12 April 2019).

Soufan Group, 2015. *Foreign Fighters: An Updated Assessment of the Flow of Foreign Fighters in Syria and Iraq*. Available at https://wb-iisg.com/wp-content/uploads/bp-attachments/4826/TSG_ForeignFightersUpflow.pdf (accessed 14 February 2019).

Spear, J., Williams, P. (eds), 2012. *Security and Development in Global Politics: A Critical Comparison*. Georgetown University Press, Washington, DC.

Sukarieh, M., 2012. 'From terrorists to revolutionaries: The emergence of "youth" in the Arab world and the discourse of globalization', *Interface: A Journal for and about Social Movements*, 14, 424–437.

Sukarieh, M., Tannock, S., 2018. 'The global securitisation of youth', *Third World Quarterly*, 39, 854–870.

Tamburini, F., 2018. 'Anti-terrorism laws in the Maghreb countries: The mirror of a democratic transition that never was', *Journal of Asian and African Studies*, 53, 1235–1250.

United Nations, 2015. *Plan of Action to Prevent Violent Extremism*. Report of the Secretary-General. Available at www.un.org/en/ga/search/view_doc.asp?symbol=A/70/674 (accessed 14 February 2020).

United Nations Development Programme (UNDP), 2016. *Projet TAMKEEN, pour la promotion de la citoyenneté et le renforcement de la cohésion sociale et de la société civile. Lignes directrices à l'intention des demandeurs. Appel à propositions sur la promotion de la participation citoyenne.* Available at www.onu-tn.org/uploads/appels/1464264417.pdf (accessed 14 February 2020).

United Nations Development Program (UNDP), 2018. *Appel à propositions portant sur la contribution des femmes vivant en milieu rural au renforcement de la résilience communautaire face à l'extrémisme violent.* Available at https://procurement-notices.undp.org/view_file.cfm?doc_id=148283 (accessed 14 February 2020).

United Nations Office on Drugs and Crime, 2018. *Counter-Terrorism Module 2 Key Issues: Preventing & Countering Violent Extremism.* Available at www.unodc.org Available at www.unodc.org/e4j/en/terrorism/module-2/key-issues/index.html (accessed 14 February 2020).

Wallace, T., 1997. 'New development agendas: Changes in UK NGO policies and procedures', *Review of African Political Economy*, 24, 35–55.

Wallace, T., Bornstein, L. and Chapman, J., 2007. *The Aid Chain: Coercion and Commitment in Development NGOs.* Practical Action Publishing, Rugby.

Wiktorowicz, Q., 2004. *Islamic Activism: A Social Movement Theory Approach.* Indiana University Press, Bloomington, IN.

10

Communication as legitimation in Spanish CVE: bringing lessons from the past

Laura Fernández de Mosteyrín

Introduction

In recent decades, Western states have overdeveloped counter-terrorist structures. Policy debates on counter-terrorism (CT hereafter) are based on problem solving, anticipation and orthodox epistemologies. As programmes for countering violent extremism (CVE) globalise (Kundnani, 2015), much of what is being done across countries reproduces a policy paradigm – a set of ideas and worldviews that become hegemonic to underpin political interventions (Hall, 1993). While this paradigm offers a clear-cut diagnosis of problems and solutions, it also adapts to the socio-political specificities of national contexts. The primary objectives of this chapter are to show how this transposition is happening in Spain, how a Western CVE policy paradigm is being implemented and how, in this process, authorities draw on global discourses and institutions, while also tapping lessons from past experiences. To this end, the chapter examines the recent past to shed light on the present, and it develops an account of the process of terrorism's delegitimation as a source for CT and, eventually, for CVE.

The Spanish CVE strategy (PEN-LCRV)[1] was approved in 2015. It is currently in early implementation stages with most activity falling within the field of rhetoric and communication. Exploring the reasons behind the delay in implementation of this programme in comparison to neighbouring countries, and the strategy's focus on 'communicating' as a priority, sheds light on specificities present in Spain and on global diffusion of CVE. Therein lie the reasons for policy paradigm transfer (Rose, 2004) combined with policy learning, too (Hall, 1993). In fact, changes in Spanish CT dating from 1998 were essential to counter ETA's[2] terrorism. But it was only upon building social consensus around the need to reform criminal codes and expand behaviours considered terrorism that innovations became acceptable. Therefore, in addition to the argument of 'context-specific' transposition, it is a secondary goal of this chapter to argue that in the expansion of state powers, accumulation of coercion is heavily dependent on social legitimisation.

By examining the legitimation of CT since 1998, the Spanish case becomes relevant to our understanding of CVE policies for various reasons. This chapter explores how global paradigms and hegemonic policy programming are subject to contextual forces that shape each case, and also illuminates how legitimisation is central to state coercion. The goal is to shed light on a rarely explored dimension of CVE: the way state authorities mobilise discourses to build consent for the expansion of power, and how this is a socio-political process that turns from one that is top-down to an interaction between state and society.

Bringing historical and cultural sociology into the analysis

Critical scholarship provides findings on the epistemological flaws underpinning CVE strategies (Kundnani, 2015). There is evidence in many countries of societal impacts like institutional Islamophobia (Massoumi et al., 2017), control of dissent (Grasso and Bessant, 2018) and use of welfare apparatuses for surveillance (Heath-Kelly, 2013). At the same time, the state's expansion into a security state with the power to designate, surveil and punish is being assessed across the social sciences (Boukalas, 2014; Neocleous, 2012). An authoritarian turn is stimulating the expansion of states' powers to reshape state/citizen interactions. We can identify how this has happened across the globe in the ideological and institutional context of the neoliberal *war on terror*.

To understand policy changes, we need to consider the bellicosity of the context. Not every nation-state contains the same amount of coercion or the same capacity for consent. States need to 'write' the war on terror if they are to deploy their troops in a sovereign nation-state (Jackson, 2005); and they need to create the narrative regarding threats and enemies to implement political programmes that use bureaucratic apparatuses to monitor populations. In the making of Western nation-states through progressive accumulation of coercion, nationalism provided the framework for legitimisation. This happened historically through centrifugal ideologisation, a mass phenomenon, spread by political and cultural elites through the state, religious organisations, military institutions and social movements geared towards mass population:

> while the social organizations help disseminate and institutionalise the ideological message (through mass media, education institutions, public sphere, governmental agencies, police and military), groups in civil society and family networks buttress the normative scaffolding which ties the ideological macro level narrative with the micro level solidarity of face to face interactions. (Malesevic, 2010, p. 11)

The legitimisation of state coercion is, therefore, a relational process produced at different levels of interaction between state and society; it emerges at the centre and expands throughout multiple settings. It encompasses institutions, worldviews, discourses and practices of authority, of belonging, of rights and of duties. CT programmes, which are central to state coercive power, operate in the same way and are dependent on consent. By examining how Spanish CT found societal support in the past and how contemporary CVE is 'communicated' to the public, this chapter anchors in the macro–meso level terrain of 'centrifugal ideologicalisation' and draws on the recent past to trace how this happened. I explore recent efforts to legitimise CVE to better understand this as a priority by first examining the path from terrorism to extremism in Spain.

As a cultural process, legitimation entails understanding culture as context, as discourse and as embedded practice (Bonnell et al., 1999); ideology is the set of discourses, symbols, practices, narratives and schemas to confer political meaning to social life. In the legitimisation of CT there are narratives – plotted storylines about the origin, nature and prospects of terrorism (Polleta, 2008) – and also 'ideological dilemmas' (Billig et al., 1988) that span liberty–security, inclusion–exclusion, we–them etc. The process does not happen only top down, so we need a relational approach to explore how it is co-produced in the interaction between state and society. Goffman's (1974) dramaturgical analysis becomes especially helpful in accounting for the interactive process by which collective actors exchange meaningful interactions through specific narratives and practices.

My argument explores how the measures that expanded coercion relied on the mobilisation of narratives to support that exercise of power against ETA and also transposes this effort across time. The chapter unfolds in a three-part account. First, I situate the Spanish CVE programme within the context of Spanish CT policy. I then outline how new regulations and institutions developed since the 2000s to combat ETA resulted in the mobilisation of narratives regarding the conflict and its solution. Finally, I describe how new developments in national security, CT and CVE are being legitimised.

My case builds upon various sources. The first part of this text draws on my original research on CT in the Basque conflict after 9/11, which comprises an in-depth examination of historical and secondary sources, together with twenty-seven expert interviews with key stakeholders (Fernández de Mosteyrín, 2013a). To explore the contemporary legitimisation of CT and CVE, I examine textual materials, primary documents and online content (blogs, websites, twitter accounts, promotional and streaming video) of political and social organisations, dating from 2015 onward. Descriptions come from participant and non-participant observation in public security awareness events.[3]

The case and the context

The Spanish CVE strategy was born ten years after the Madrid bombing on 11 March 2004 that killed 193 people, and long after the EU's CVE policy was unveiled. The strategy, one of the first outcomes of the Spanish National Security Strategy (2013), is oriented towards anticipating radicalisation defined as 'the development of extremist, dogmatic or hate behaviour for xenophobic or ideo-logical reasons' (Government of Spain, 2015b, p. 5). The programme aims to be 'an effective tool for the early detection of violent extremism, by working with vulnerable communities and groups at risk' (Government of Spain, 2015b, p. 5). The focus is set on ideas and worldviews (2015b, p. 3), and the targets are mainly Muslim communities and youth. Actors called into the programme are intelli-gence institutions, security agencies, social services, care providers, civil society and private citizens. The three core aspects of the programme are locality, antic-ipation and cooperation across sectors. Even though no additional resources have been supplied for setting this in motion at the local level, about twelve major local Spanish governments have, in 2018, set up the mechanisms for implementation. With aims of fostering community cohesion and resilience in countering extremism, Malaga, a member of the UN's Strong Cities Network, and the city of Fuenlabrada were designated as pilot cities for the CVE pro-gramme, with regional strategies also being put in place in the Basque Country and Catalonia.

Despite a lack of public debate around it, this policy stands to face potential challenges in the Spanish socio-political context for at least two reasons. First, the Spanish state is highly decentralised and most policies are articulated through regional governments and municipalities. There are two major national law enforcement agencies (*Policía Nacional* and *Guardia Civil*), three regional police agencies (*Policía Foral*, *Ertzaintza* and *Mossos d'Esquadra*) and almost 8,000 local government police agencies. Second, Spain has undergone signifi-cant political change since 2011 when anti-austerity movements shifted socio-logical bipartidism, eventually impacting the composition of parliament and mainstream agendas (Revilla and Molina, 2016).

Nevertheless, though CVE programmes are new in Spain, 'extremism' has been successfully prosecuted since the early 2000s, when the crime of terrorism expanded in the context of the Basque conflict to include acts of speech indicted as glorification. Spain has extensive experience fighting ETA with a solid set of measures for tackling terrorism (Reinares, 2009). Since the 11 March bombing, Spanish CT has become more sophisticated, especially as far as intelligence and police cooperation are concerned. Police operations are efficient in countering jihadist violence and the criminal justice system has an array of tools for indictment and prosecution. According to the Spanish Ministry of Interior, between 2008 and 2015 there were 405 detentions and indictments of ETA members. Since 2004, 148 police operations have taken place, resulting in 761 detainees being charged with international terrorism.

Fighting ETA through delegitimation

Since its very birth in 1978, Spanish democracy had to deal with the problem of violence within the Basque nationalist conflict,[4] a key source of instability during the transition to democracy. For three decades, terrorism was a principal concern for Spanish society, a priority for every government and a frequent source of polarisation among parties. According to the Spanish Centre for Sociological Research (Centro de Investigaciones Sociológicas (CIS), 2018), terrorism was one of the top three concerns for public opinion until 2008, and from the year 2000, CT reforms were widely supported, including penal regulations and police powers.

By the mid-1990s, ETA increased its targeting of civil society representatives (e.g., journalists, businesspeople, local politicians). This spurred a large coalition to emerge from civil society against terrorism. A 'constitutional movement' made up of victim groups (*Asociación de Víctimas del Terrorismo, AVT*; *Colectivo de Víctimas del Terrorismo, COVITE*; *Fundación Víctimas del Terrorismo, FVT*) allied with civic organisations (*Movimiento Manos Blancas, Iniciativa Ciudadana Basta Ya, Fundación Foro de Ermua*) to campaign from 1998 to 2008. Calls for tougher CT were politicised and a new narrative was disseminated through mass demonstrations, court-trial accusation and public engagement activities (lectures, seminars, workshops, periodical publications) in Spain and abroad (Fernández de Mosteyrín, 2013b).

According to the Spanish Interior Ministry, there were 4,000 demonstrations against terrorism between 1998 and 2006, with 2,697 of those demonstrations taking place from 2000 to 2001. Excluding the 2003 anti-war mobilisation, terrorism was, for many years, the only issue to stimulate mass demonstrations across the country. Terrorism was presented as a non-political irrational evil for which no dialogue could be developed: 'the first thing you have to do to deter terrorism is to delegitimize it'.[5] The 'politics of delegitimation' was the process by which victims and civic organisations, in coalition with political parties and governments, mobilised CT narratives that eventually embedded themselves in Spanish institutions. Several years later, the 11 March bombing took place during this time of active debate surrounding terrorism. Though CT served as a bipartisan priority, under Aznar and Zapatero the conservative government in power during the bombing aligned itself with the Bush administration's war on terror.

During the 1990s, Basque civic movements (*Gesto por la Paz* and *Elkarri*) had deployed a pacifist narrative in which terrorism was envisaged as the by-product of a political conflict (Funes, 1998). In opposition to this view, the new diagnosis that emerged in later years declared terrorism non-political in nature and was predicated as the biggest challenge to the Spanish constitutional regime; the cultural basis of that irrational violence was what needed to be confronted. While nationalism was envisioned as the source of violence, the discursive space of the Basque problem narrowed to a dichotomy of 'we (democrats) / them (criminals)'. According to a leading politician in the coalition:

> There is no politics in terrorism (. . .) there is a will to put down and destroy the morale of men and women and their convictions (. . .) it is a statement with which only those who participate in terror, or those who are set to obtain political assets from the exercise of terror by others, can disagree.[6]

At that point, those in disagreement were nationalist political parties and organisations. This confrontation culminated during the 2002 regional elections, after which acts of rejection became ritualised in Spanish politics. This unofficial requirement turned into social practice in response to acts of violence; the practice of *condemnation* crystallised as proof of democracy, as ritual of access to public debate. The request for condemnation ended up limiting discourse and criminalising dissent by eventually expanding from car bombing to photos, events and, more recently, to music lyrics and humour expressing 'glorification' (Bessant, 2017).

Simultaneously, the language of *the rule of law* became prominent. ETA was described as a criminal organisation challenging state power; terrorism was a key threat to democracy. While terrorism took aim at the rule of law, it was the very rule of law that offered a cure (Al Sumait et al., 2009). During the 1990s, controversies about past 'dirty wars' had polarised public debate with the accepted 'lesson learned' that it was within the rule of law that terrorism would be defeated. The idea of 'the full force of law' was associated with the defence of law enforcement, criminal justice and the support of all legal changes required for stopping ETA's community of legitimation:

> Terrorism has a common enemy; liberal democracy and rule of law. Its main enemies are political systems that protect free individuals and rule of law; systems in which legitimate violence is only exercised by the State. (Foro de Ermua, 2004, p. 1)

Since the 1990s, the 'Spanish way' of channelling terrorism through the criminal justice system created concern among scholars (Llobert-Anglí and Masferrer, 2015) that most legal provisions exceed the limits of 'standard' criminal law, though *special powers* are not invoked.

This new diagnosis disregarded pacifism as politically naïve. In the binary of 'we' (democrats) versus 'them' (evildoers), 'buenismo'[7] was the rhetorical tool used to label political views considered utopian and/or idealistic:

> The problem in this society is not a peace problem . . . I am not a pacifist (. . .)
> I believe in the legitimate coercion of the State . . . I believe in the State's monop-
> oly of force. Police, judges and so forth: I think that the pedagogy of the rule of
> law is essential.[8]

The pedagogy worked, thereby crystallising the narrative against ETA and radical nationalism. It was inscribed in the policy known as *Agreement for Liberties and against Terrorism* (Anti-terrorist Agreement) that was signed by the two major parties in 2000: PSOE (Socialist) and PP (Conservative). The policy toughened criminal codes, brought increased sophistication to the police, improved international cooperation and gave a voice and support to victims. 'Glorification' was codified as a crime and criminal regulations were expanded throughout the decade to criminalise further behaviours as terrorism.

The most controversial regulation resulting from this consensus was the Political Parties Act (2002), which about 64% of Spaniards supported (CIS, 2002). As a result, radical nationalist parties were proscribed, initiating the decline of ETA's community of support (Fernández de Mosteyrín, 2013b; Whitfield, 2014). 'Glorification' was central to this regulation. To be considered legal, political parties were required to declare their rejection of violence. This is how the practice of *condemnation* was eventually codified. As the discursive space narrowed after the Anti-terrorist Agreement (Guittet, 2008), rejection became an obsession in Spanish politics, with almost every public intervention, and even scholarly works on terrorism, starting with a sort of disclaimer stating 'I reject'.[9] Many legal changes took place further under this consensus and they spread to anti-austerity (Fernández de Mosteyrín and Limon, 2018). By 2010, all political parties and most civil society organisations (except Basque civil rights and radical nationalist organisations) interviewed found this law unproblematic and no further public debate has taken place around it.[10]

When ETA was coming to an end in 2011, the Spanish socio-political landscape was changing. The *Indignado* movement developed a cycle of mobilisation that peaked around 2014 (Romanos, 2016). The state further developed its security apparatus. In addition to 2015's *Gag Law*, some legal provisions designed to deter ETA's community of legitimation were used to control dissent. The notion of 'radical' became essential to punish and surveil. Amnesty International (2018) reported that most of those indicted for 'glorification' were linked to anti-austerity demands and had no relation to Islamic terrorism; the report was titled 'Tweet if you dare'. This expansion of control made civil society aware and led to an emerging civil rights movement campaigning against these regulations.

Nevertheless, when in 2014 ISIS propelled many young Europeans to join the Caliphate, Spanish authorities brought the problem of Islamic terrorism back to the forefront and laid out, together with the Socialist Party, a new agreement. The *Counter-jihadist Agreement* (2015) invigorated the 2000s in promoting measures for expanding CT capacities and was clearly oriented towards Muslim communities, encompassing the codification of individual terrorism, foreign fighters, recruitment, training (including passive), the use of social media for propaganda, the improvement of intelligence capacities (including online under-cover policing) and the implementation of active CVE policies.

However, the mentioned 'eventful transition' (2011–2015) had eroded 'major' political parties, leading to their being challenged from the margins. Catalan and Basque nationalist parties, and leftist parties Podemos and Izquierda Unida, refused this consensus. Terrorism was no longer a major focus of public opinion, whereas unemployment, the economy and corruption were coming to the fore-front (CIS, 2018). Given the contention over the recent *gag law*, criminal laws and the resonance of justice's miscarriage in relation to 'glorification' and free speech, the road to a public debate around CVE did not seem expedited.

Delegitimation for CVE

In 2015, two years after the Spanish government approved its first National Security Strategy, I attended a three-day seminar at a Spanish public univer-sity intended for students and the general public. The audience of about 200 consisted of people in uniforms, press professionals and the wider public. The panel included CT scholars, practitioners and policymakers and members of the intelligence community and national security staff. Opening remarks by local authorities and university chancellors emphasised something relatively new for the author: the importance of building a 'culture of security'[11] and raising awareness in society to tackle 'multidimensional' and 'volatile' new threats.

Throughout the event certain expressions seemed normalised. Some were familiar, such as the 'delegitimation of terrorism', while others were less so, such as 'counter-narrative', 'hearts and minds', 'resilience' and 'co-responsibility'. Most of the speakers, operators and politicians referred to Spain's extensive experience with CT and Spanish society's resilience in the face of suffering. Some expres-sions seemed *taboo*; 'conflict', when mentioned, came with air quotes. 'Western foreign policy' was one of the 'many' variables in this complex threat, but ruled out as a meaningful one. DAESH (not ISIS) was authoritatively highlighted as the 'right expression' to avoid the legitimisation of an organisation claiming to be a state. To sum up, language seemed paramount to the panellists. There were many mentions of 'powerful ideas' that 'we all' (the public) should keep in mind. What was going on?

In keeping with symbolic interaction, I have attended and followed many events of this sort in an effort to understand the socio-political situation involved. For, just like in the early 2000s, during the effervescence of the 'politics of delegitimation', I argue that much of what happens in these events is the construction and mobilisation of narratives to support CVE. The rest of this account stems from this ongoing research.

Performing security awareness

In recent years, security agencies have been working on strategic communication and developing programmes to raise awareness. According to the Spanish Open Information Agency, about €600,000 has been allocated to universities, think tanks and private organisations since 2013 to develop events promoting 'security culture'.[12] Although not all events referred to are funded under this scheme, most are inspired by it. Other organisers include private sector organisations, research institutes and stakeholders such as victims' organisations. Panels are inter-sectoral combining public/private entities, internal/external security agencies, intelligence communities, scholars and civil society organisations. Some of the specific segments of society that participate include students in higher education, scholars, and professionals in the sector or adjacent fields such as education, social care and youth instructors.

These events are well disseminated online through email newsletters and social media. Titles and programmes are attractive enough and usually include expressions such as 'challenges', 'future', 'threats/risks', 'security' and 'global'. These programmes circulate online generating much twitter conversation among participants and prospective audiences. What happens onsite is preceded by online preparation, synchronic streaming and tweeting, and post-event resonances. As collective situations, both online and onsite, these events are settings that offer exceptional opportunities to observe how what starts from the centre moves to the periphery – in encounters where the state meets society.

Following a dramaturgical approach (Goffman, 1974), we can explore these social interactions through a theatrical metaphor in which characters play narratives in interaction with active audiences. Throughout the play, beliefs are set in motion, and idealisations are emotionally communicated in order to raise awareness of security issues. By doing so, a story is told (Polleta, 2008) and worldviews are politicised. The story is about 'our enemies', 'our response', 'the sacrifices' and the societal 'effort'; but it is also a story about distribution of power. I will break down how this happens by focusing on characters and narratives.

Characters

Using Weberian 'ideal types', we can set up a preliminary typology of the social characters and their role in this performance:

a) *Institutions and security institutions* are local/regional/national authorities, invited diplomats, representatives of international organisations and foreign governments, and high-level bureaucrats in the field. Institutions are also observable through *males*, mostly, in uniform. This presence of military and police officials, while normalised in recent times, is totally new in Spanish socio-political life. After the Francoist regime ended, the Spanish armed forces and Spanish society turned their backs on each other; the institutional presence of law enforcement agencies at social events was unusual. Approaches to terrorism vary among the military, the semi-military law enforcement agency *Guardia Civil* and the national civil police. While military elites develop erudite geopolitical explanations,[13] law enforcement is prone to sharing (partial) operative knowledge on how CT works.

b) *Scientific community and 'experts'* are ever-present. One of the most remarkable features is the increasing collaboration between public and private universities in the diffusion of security culture. This collaboration comes in the form of sponsorship and scientific participation. There are at least nine public universities collaborating with the National Intelligence Agency on programmes, either oriented towards formal education or for diffusion. Although these events are difficult to quantify, a look at the universities' extension programmes for the summer of 2018 reveals that ten major Spanish universities hosted at least one event related to security, CT or radicalisation. Far from being specific to the case, Price (2015) shows how this is a trend across many countries that results in the normalisation of the military and an intelligence ethos. The *scientific expert* is devoted to presenting empirical accounts of the global order, and the theological basis of Islamic terrorism, jihadist profiles and the processes of radicalisation. Their knowledge is venerated as much as science is venerated in our epoch. Even though there are controversial approaches, accounts frequently reproduce the epistemological pitfalls of mainstream research, as Stampnitzky (2013) found in her seminal work on the links between experts and the creation of terrorism. And still, the same few experts make their role evident as nodes in the policy network of CT (Miller and Mills, 2009).

c) *Public and private operators* are diverse. There is a wide spectrum of intelligence, policing and criminal justice sectors. Much of what they address is wrapped in secrecy and alarm; it is very difficult to follow, to trace by other means and even to counter argue. The most unintelligible terrain for this type of expression is cyberspace, particularly the deep *dark web*, as a metaphor of unknown evil and the darkest future; it is, however, a sphere in which the co-participation of lay citizens is predicated as essential.

d) *Engaged civil society* varies depending on whether the promoters are victims, media, financial institutions, universities, private sector companies or civil liberties organisations. They embody the societal effort against terrorism. It is part of 'what we learned' fighting ETA, but is also the new CT *ethos* of enlisting society. Among them, victims are especially powerful characters that are mobilising for CVE. In fact, they represent the continuation of CT efforts after ETA laid down their arms. The Group of Victims of Terrorism, founded in 1989 (COVITE), has a leading role in contemporary CVE. In conjunction with scholars and other stakeholders, the group promoted the International Terrorism Observatory (OIET) 'for the prevention of radicalization and the diffusion of democratic principles'.[14] Even when not present at an event, victims represent *resilience* and are considered authoritative voices for confronting extremism.

e) *Muslim communities*, even though not often present, are a central character as well. They become essential to the narrative as the first line of detection. It is 'their' problem so they should stand against terrorism. In clear continuity with the *practice of condemnation*, the Muslim community is required to take a stance against terrorism and watch for their communities.

f) *Terrorists and radicals* are core to the narrative, but not a character of their own. They are deemed to have no status as 'actors' and are depicted as evildoers, irrational and morally 'stupid' in early versions of the narrative (after the bombing of 11 March 2004), or as hyper-ideological (not so much religious) individuals. Potential extremists are envisaged as being vulnerable to 'ideological abusers', and women are given special gendered roles as caregivers and are especially 'vulnerable' (Martini, 2018; Tellez, 2018).

g) *The audience* is difficult to decipher but includes university students in search of ideas and professional prospects, uniformed attendees looking for training, motivated retired people (including from the military), press professionals and community managers, and 'unknowns' that are very well-connected with the panellists. It is among this nameless public that one final character emerges:

h) *The do-gooder.* As explained previously, pacifism turned politically naïve in CT discourse in the 2000s. In the narrative of the 'political ingenuousness' that is becoming dominant in many areas of Spanish political debate, sometimes this character emerges from the panels. Sometimes it is a lay citizen who challenges the narrative. *El buenista* turns out to be the touchstone for delegitimising those who do not stand in one clear 'bloc'. The *do-gooder* is the participant unpleasantly addressed with condescendence and lectured to about the centrality of language, the 'battle' of ideas in which there are 'powerful words' to be used while others should be avoided. Engaging in a public debate is difficult and doing so in a public session while being recorded and streamed can result in self-censorship. And yet this character always shows up in the public with the role of initiating controversy, thereby becoming essential to understanding these encounters as co-construction.

As a whole, these characters participate in CVE awareness. In doing so, discourses 'from above' meet discourses 'from below' and an *encounter* takes place between the state and society for the co-production of such legitimisation.

The narrative of the 'counter narrative'

Across events, a chorale of collective voices that speak, write and act via many outlets, symbols and practices compose a narrative, a discursive sequence of event-based explanations, about the origins and core drivers of terrorism, along with a 'solution' that 'we' (society as a whole) should work on. I will break down some components of this narrative that resemble previously tested scripts against ETA, while adding in new global CVE normativity.

The problem
An initial layer of threats to security is the opening of an event. It later becomes a main discursive cluster – a bloc around which specific discussions happen to create a diagnosis. The National Security Strategy is mentioned by authorities and operators, and is regarded as the official layout of threat and responses.[15] There are numerous threats as the world has changed since 9/11. Most of them are 'volatile', 'multidimensional' and 'diffuse' to the extent that security agencies alone are not enough without society's participation. This is what justifies the event and why, according to the National Security Strategy, it is a task that belongs to 'us all'. Terrorism is the priority; radicalisation and extremism are regarded as drivers of violence. Although in 2015 terrorism was still predicated as an 'existential threat', it is quite a contested issue among panellists and publics.

When it comes to causes, there are geopolitical factors that explain terrorism, but the essence of the problem is cultural and ideological. 'Political' accounts draw on an erudite Clausewitzian vision of terrorism as asymmetric warfare, and in fact this is the source of numerous events in recent years. In this military gaze, the objective of terrorism is to 'defeat the will' of democracies so that the public will implore politics to come in. It is a 'battle of intentions'. Terrorists attack our values and Western way of living. Strategies to counter this threat are varied and may include military action, but resilience and civil society's cooperation is predicated as paramount. As stated by a navy officer explaining the National Security Strategy, 'there are casualties in all wars; we should resist the impacts. Our way of life, values and legal norms should resist' (Fieldnotes, Event 6, 2018).

However, *war* is a contested term: while military personnel frame the issue in their own *ethos*, this term is avoided or disputed. In 2012, while addressing the Spanish victims' organisations, a high-level military representative used Basque terrorism as an example to explain jihadist in terms of intentions:

> What can be done? What you people do . . .Resist. We should resist. We should strengthen our society . . . even if there are attacks . . . we need to fight (. . ..) the first and foremost strategy is negation. It is to convey the message that you will never gain political ends. It is impossible! . . . This is why we need to stimulate resilience as the capacity of all society around its victims.[16]

Negation remits to the past. Spanish CT discourse constantly relies on *lessons learned* from the past. Most importantly, how we speak of the problem and how we disseminate the proper narrative is essential for defeating terrorism. Conveying learning is a way to express moral superiority and political effectiveness:

> Spain has extensive experience in CT. Throughout many decades, we have combated the terrorist gang ETA that caused intense suffering to Spanish society, yet was defeated. So, Spain is among the countries in the international community that shows that it is possible to defeat terrorism with determination, courage and the rule of law.[17]

There are at least four core 'lessons' that are constantly raised by politicians and experts: *the negation of conflict is effective*. ETA was 'a gang', not an organisation. Here is why language is important and why there is so much effort to avoid certain frames and why there are certain 'powerful ideas' to convey:

> DAESH and not Islamic State (. . .) among my colleagues and security agencies personnel we refuse to speak of Islamic State because to some extent it is legitimizing. It is DAESH, an international terrorist organization. And this is something we should start making publicly aware and remark on, we need to say each thing in its own terms.[18]

By dealing with terrorism as with any other form of delinquency, the problem can be channelled through criminal justice without invoking special powers. This is also why *the rule of law works*. In fact, the mobilisation of society in the 2000s was essential for CT innovations, so *pedagogy works* too and there should be a societal effort to communicate the right narrative. Finally, *victims are essential* for pedagogy because they are exemplars of collective resilience; they represent 'determination and courage', so making them bearers of the counter narrative makes stronger societies.

The solution and the calling

Geopolitics might be the context but what really matters is how to prevent people being drawn into 'extremism'. Explanations turn psycho-social, focusing on vulnerable communities and individuals at risk (i.e., Muslims and youth). To further a solution, the participation of key actors is essential: 1) frontline bureaucrats; 2) Muslim communities; 3) society; and 4) victims. This must happen at the local level, in everyday interactions with people showing 'signs' of radicalisation. It should happen at the level of 'street bureaucrats' (Lipski, 1980) like paediatricians, social workers, elementary-school teachers and librarians. Paraphrasing James Scott (Scott, 1999), the state needs to 'see' via its administrative standardised measures, communication systems and online applications to monitor what it would otherwise not prevent. And this is why the wider state and society is incarnated in some panels. Frontline care providers and ordinary citizens are in advantageous positions to anticipate:

> If we act before radicalization settles in a family, within the mind of a youngster or woman . . . if we are able to make society aware, if we are able to train people to read those indicators and signs that an individual or a group are at risk or vulnerable of being drawn into extremism before radicalizing, it is much better than reacting once the process is finished.[19]

Awareness of threats is used to get societal cooperation. *Stop radicalismos* is an online platform for reporting to police agencies 'any sign of radicalisation or extremism'. Since its launch in 2015, at least 5,485 anonymous reports have been submitted (Government of Spain, 2017a, p. 27). Even if not every citizen is in a position to detect and report terrorism, 'we all' should be resilient because it is our way of life, our Western values that are at stake:

> At the end. . . [it] is not only the work of security, intelligence and law enforcement agencies. It is a task of the society as a whole . . . the most important thing in this fight against terrorism is our own certainty in our values and in the principles we believe in. Because, terrorism is not only a threat to security . . ., but to our liberty, our democratic system and our way of life; to the model of society we want to live in. This is why the strength of society is so important in the fight against terrorism.[20]

At this point, ideological diagnoses converge with solutions. An ideological problem requires a *counter-narrative* as the answer; a story in which the non-political nature of terrorism, the misappropriation of Islam by radicals and the superiority of Western values are put forward. According to a private-sector professional with extensive experience engaging *foreign fighters* online: 'we need to use the religious fact to abort recruitment' (Fieldnotes, Event 6, 2018). In this task, Muslim communities are regarded as essential to engage radicals and to 'moderate' their positions with public and unambiguous rejection. Still, the societal group with moral superiority in representing society's efforts are the victim's organisations, and this is where the transposition of a narrative against ETA is most prominent:

> Terrorists' victims should be at the forefront of counterterrorism, not only for adequate recognition, but as an instrument for countering radicalization and violent extremism. The dissemination of counterterrorist culture, through pedagogic exercises over past events and hate dissolution, is paramount. (National Security Strategy, 2017, p. 26)[21]

Diffusion becomes construction?

This exploration of how narratives are transposed for legitimisation sheds light on the sort of effort that lies in awareness programmes. Controversial issues and debates that surround this otherwise monolithic narrative are symptoms that point at the constructive nature of building consent. They also support the argument that these events are interactive encounters between the state and society. The result is not an inert composition, but a symphony played at specific sites. Regardless of what authorities may wish to convey, publics are diverse. Within the symbolic universe of threats and risks, challenging this narrative might prove difficult.

But we can catch a glimpse in the contentious issues that emerge in panel discussions and are predicated on other sites of 'counter-hegemonic' discourse (from civil rights organisations, social movements, international cooperation organisations, political parties, etc.): the financing of terrorism brings organisations and capabilities to the debate, helping to challenge ideological explanations. Also, foreign policy comes up to point at structural factors like inequality, imperialism or the welfare–warfare nexus (Mills, 1958). Whenever these topics emerge, they play into the discourse of 'well intended but unrealistic pacifism', even with accompanying exhortations and/or spontaneous acts of *condemnation*. But they add to the making of the CT narrative. The switch from terrorism as an 'existential threat' (in 2004) to terrorism as a 'priority threat' (in 2016), *vis-à-vis* climate change or nuclear war, may be regarded as part of this discursive resistance.

Other contentious topics in awareness events, although still marginal, are surveillance or Islamophobia. They remit to the diversity of society and make evident how consent for CT is under construction. As the mainstream narrative keeps flowing in Spain, debates over CVE programmes are only emerging. The chorale of characters and narratives faces contestation as CVE comes to the forefront of the 'conversation'. In the end, a hegemonic narrative is predicating ways of being a citizen (who is in and who is out, who we are, what the essence of our identity is and what the duties of the willing citizens are) and specific modes of interaction between the state and citizens.

Conclusions: delegitimation and legitimation

The chapter examined how CVE paradigms are being transposed in Spain and how they are adapted to socio-political specificities and legacies of the past. It further examined how CVE encompasses the need for consent building and how this is happening through the raising of awareness about threats. As argued in the first part, the Spanish case shows how CT policies found consent through the mobilisation of narratives of delegitimation. A genealogy of these narratives and its institutional inscription sheds light on how the global implementation of CVE policy paradigms combines hegemonic visions of counter-extremism with the specific features of each context. It explains how, along with the assimilation of dominant paradigms, policy learning from the past is drawn on as well.

Nevertheless, the legitimating of CVE is an open process. It is an elite initiative, but *centrifugal ideologisation* happens through interactions between the state and society. The examination of characters and narratives in contemporary Spain point at a story-building and storytelling taking place; one that resembles the recent past.

Still, further research is needed on a number of issues. We need deeper understanding of the co-constructive nature of legitimisation. To this end, the examination of the role of the state and elite movements (Massoumi et al., 2017) is especially promising, together with the institutionalisation of Islamophobia. We also need in-depth knowledge of how legitimisation happens in micro-social everyday interactions. As CVE narratives portray ideals of the 'good citizen', research that connects this political normativity with the micro-level experience of lay citizens is needed as well.

The delegitimisation of terrorism, the depoliticisation of violence and the surveillance of political worldviews has an opposite movement of rationalisation of the state's power to control. As such, it is an overall process of power distribution and one that happens interactively between certain spheres of the state and specific parts of society. It is the task of critical scholars to further the analysis of how and on behalf of whom this power is distributed.

Acknowledgements

Part of this research was supported by the SecurityCulture Project: CSO2017–86985-R. 2018–2020, Spanish Research Agency: Challenges to Society Programme #8 Security, Protection and Defence. An early version of this chapter was first discussed at the ISA Annual Conference (2018, San Francisco). I appreciate the many comments and feedback received in the panel 'Governing through

Suspicion: Countering-Terrorism, Countering-Extremism, and the Evolving Regime of Governing through Fear'. I would also like to thank the editors of this volume, Alice Martini, Kieran Ford and Richard Jackson, for the many insightful comments to the piece and for their supportive editorial style.

Notes

1 It is part of the Spanish Counter-terrorism Strategy (EICTIR).
2 The Basque armed organisation Euskadi Ta Askatasuna (ETA).
3 I draw on: two online events and five on-site observations (1–3 days each) 2015–2018. The seven events include public/private cooperation, universities, security agencies and/or terrorism victim organisations: (1) Guardia Civil University, July 2015 (on terrorism, radicalisation); (2) National Security University (on cyber threats and terrorism financing), September 2016; (3) Military/Defence University (on asymmetrical warfare), November 2016; (4) Private University Spanish Senate (hybrid warfare), May 2017; (5) Victim organisation University (on CVE), November 2017; (6) Private University (on CVE), March 2018; and (7) Think tank (on women and CVE), March 2018. All events were promoted as diffusion of the 'culture of security'. I use extensive field notes, informal talks with participants and online follow up to explore beliefs, meaning-making, characters and narratives.
4 In the process ETA killed around 800 people. State-sponsored violence happened during the 1970s and 1980s, with around thirty people being killed by paramilitary groups- (Grupos Antiterroristas de Liberación (GAL)) and 4,113 complaints of torture and police abuse (Etxeberría et al., 2017).
5 Author's interview with Foro de Ermua, a civic association, Madrid, 2010.
6 Rosa Díez, *BastaYa* supporter. Interview published in Garzón (2006).
7 This expression is the Spanish expression for 'do-gooder' – a well-meaning, but unrealistic, politically naive person.
8 Author's interview with civic supporter, Bilbao, 2010.
9 See, for instance, the first footnote of a scientific article recently published. Immediately after a funding disclosure it states: 'the author of this piece does not intend to defend, support or justify violence related to "jihadist terrorism" or any other hate crime. The objective is to reflect on the ways the threat of this sort of terrorism is instrumentalised for the exercise of other forms of violence (structural and political) based on fear and suspicion' (Tellez, 2018, p. 1).
10 Very recently, this piece has been part of the public debate again in the context of the Catalonian conflict.
11 The diffusion of the 'culture of security' is a priority for the National Security System. Organic Law 5/2005 for National Defence; Guidelines for National Defence 1/2012; and National Security Law 36/2015 are legal provisions stressing the need for strategic communication to raise security awareness (Congreso de los Diputados, 2005).

12 Source: Office of Transparency, Access to Information and Corporate Government. Available at www.infosubvenciones.es/bdnstrans/GE/es/concesiones (accessed 15 January 2020).
13 For extensive accounts on terrorism from a military view, see publications by the Spanish Institute for Strategic Studies. Available at www.ieee.es (accessed 15 January 2020).
14 See https://observatorioterrorismo.com/ (accessed 15 January 2020).
15 The first *Spanish National Security Strategy* was developed in 2013 and reformulated in 2015 and 2017. It is the blueprint for political and operators' risk assessment. It was followed by the *National Security Law* (2015), which was subjected to modest public discussion.
16 Address by Miguel Angel Ballesteros, General, Spanish armed forces and Chief Director of the Instituto Español de Estudios Estratégicos (Institute for Strategic Studies) to the Asociación Víctimas Terrorismo (Spanish Victims' Association) (Ballesteros, 2012).
17 Interview with Ignacio Cosidó, former director of the Spanish National Policy Agency (Instituto de Seguridad y Cultura, 2017a).
18 María Luz González Martín, Chief Analyst of the Spanish Intelligence Agency for Terrorism and Organised Crime, Spanish Ministry of Interior (Real Instituto Elcano de Estudios Estratégicos, 2017).
19 María Luz González Martín, Chief Analyst of the Spanish Intelligence Agency for Terrorism and Organized Crime, Spanish Ministry of Interior (Real Instituto Elcano de Estudios Estratégicos, 2017).
20 Interview with Ignacio Cosidó, former director of the Spanish National Policy Agency (Instituto de Seguridad y Cultura, 2017b).
21 (SNSS, 2017, p. 26).

References

Al-Sumait, F., Lingle, C. and Domke, D., 2009. 'Terrorism's cause and cure: The rhetorical regime of democracy in the US and UK', *Critical Studies on Terrorism*, 2(1), 7–25.
Amnesty International, 2018. *'Tweet If You Dare': How Counterterrorist Laws Restrict Freedom of Expression in Spain*. Report EUR 41/7924/2018. AI, Madrid.
Ballesteros, M.A., 2012. 'El terrorismo en el mundo de hoy: retos y desafíos', XXXth Conference of Spanish Victims Association: 'Las víctimas en primera persona. Logros y retos en la lucha frente al terrorismo'. Section: 'Desafíos del terrorismo actual'. 19 January 2012. Madrid: Palacio de Exposiciones y Congresos. Available at www.youtube.com/watch?v=3_GwQ1RVqqQ (accessed 15 January 2020).
Bessant, J., 2017. 'Digital humour, gag laws and the liberal security state', in Luppicini, R. and Baard, R. (eds), *Digital Media Integration for Participatory Democracy*. IGI Global, Hershey, PA, pp. 204–221.

Billig, M., Condor, S. and Edwards, D., 1988. *Ideological Dilemmas: A Social Psychology of Everyday Thinking*. SAGE, New York.

Bonnell, V.E., Hunt, L. and Biernacki, R., 1999. *Beyond the Cultural Turn: New Direction in the Study of Society and Culture*. University of California Press, Berkeley, CA.

Boukalas, C., 2014. *Homeland Security, Its Law and Its State: A Design of Power for the 21st Century*. Routledge, London.

Centro de Investigaciones Sociológicas (CIS), 2002. *Estudio 2466, Septiembre*. CIS, Madrid.

Centro de Investigaciones Sociológicas (CIS), 2018. *Barómetro 3223, Septiembre*. CIS, Madrid.

Congreso de los Diputados, 2005. *Ley Orgánica 5/2005 de 17 de noviembre, la Defensa Nacional*. BOE, Madrid.

Congreso de los Diputados, 2015. *Ley 36/2015 de 28 de Septiembre, de Seguridad Nacional*. BOE, Madrid.

Etxeberría, F., Martín Bertistain, C. and Pego, L., 2017. *Informe Final Proyecto de investigación de la tortura y los malos tratos en el País Vasco entre 1964–2014*. Secretaría General de Derechos Humanos, Convivencia y Cooperación, Gobierno Vasco.

Fernández de Mosteyrín, L., 2013a. 'La Guerra contra el Terror y la transformación de umbrales de violencia tolerada: un estudio de la violencia en el País Vasco (1998–2010)', PhD thesis, Universidad Complutense de Madrid, 2013. Available at http://eprints.ucm.es/20050/ (accessed 18 May 2020).

Fernández de Mosteyrín, L., 2013b. 'Las demandas de seguridad y las políticas antiterroristas tras el 11-S', in Morán, M.L. (ed.), *Actores y Demandas en España: Análisis de un inicio de siglo convulso*. La Catarata, Madrid, pp. 157–184.

Fernández de Mosteyrín, L. and Limón, P., 2018. 'Controlling dissent through security in contemporary Spain', in Grasso, M. and Bessant, J. (eds), *Governing Youth Politics in the Age of Surveillance*. Routledge, London, pp. 48–61.

Fore de Ermua, 2004. Hoja de Ermua, May.

Funes, M.J., 1998. 'Social responses to political violence in the Basque Country: Peace movements and their audiences', *Journal of Conflict Resolution*, 42(4), 493–510.

Garzón, B., 2006. *La lucha contra el terrorismo y sus límites*. Adhara, Madrid.

Goffman, E., 1974. *Frame Analysis: An Essay on the Organizational Experience*. Harvard University Press, Cambridge, MA.

Government of Spain, 2011. *Estrategia Española de Seguridad*. DSN, Madrid.

Government of Spain, 2012. *Directiva de la Defensa Nacional, 1/2012 'Por una defensa necesaria, por una defensa responsable'*. Ministerio de Defensa, Madrid.

Government of Spain, 2013. *Estrategia de Seguridad Nacional: Un Proyecto Compartido* DSN, Madrid.

Government of Spain, 2015a. *Informe Anual de Seguridad Nacional*. DSN, Madrid.

Government of Spain, 2015b. *Plan Estratégico Nacional de Lucha contra la radicalización violenta PEN LCRV*. Ministerio del Interior, Madrid.

Government of Spain, 2016. *Informe Anual de Seguridad Nacional*. DSN, Madrid.

Government of Spain, 2017a. *Estrategia de Seguridad Nacional: un proyecto compartido de todos y para todos*. DSN, Madrid.

Government of Spain, 2017b. *Informe Anual de Seguridad Nacional*. DSN, Madrid.

Grasso, T., Bessant, J., 2018. *Governing Youth Politics in the Age of Surveillance*. Routledge, London.

Guittet, E.P., 2008. 'Is consensus a genuine democratic value? The case of Spanish political pact against terrorism', *Alternatives*, 33(3), 267–291.

Hall, P.A., 1993. 'Policy paradigms, social learning, and the state: The case of economic policymaking in Britain', *Comparative Politics*, 25(3), 275–296.

Heath-Kelly, C., 2013. 'Counter-terrorism and the counterfactual: Producing the "radicalisation" discourse and the UK PREVENT strategy', *The British Journal of Politics and International Relations*, 15(3), 394–415.

Instituto de Seguridad y Cultura, 2017a. *Interview with Ingacio Cosidó, former director of the Spanish National Police Agency*, 12 June 2017. Available at www.youtube.com/watch?v=gb5a_VSZLzI (accessed 15 January 2020).

Instituto de Seguridad y Cultura, 2017b. *Conference on hybrid war organised in collaboration with US Embassy and NATO*, 18 May 2017. Madrid: Palacio del Senado. Available at seguridadycultura.org/guerra-hibrida-nuevas-amenazas/ (accessed 15 January 2020).

Jackson, R., 2005. *Writing the War on Terrorism: Language, Politics and Counter Terrorism*. Manchester University Press, Manchester.

Kundnani, A., 2015. *The Muslims Are Coming! Islamophobia, Extremism and the Domestic War on Terror*. Verso Books, London.

Lipski, M., 1980. *Street Level Bureaucracy: Dilemmas of the Individuals in Public Service*. SAGE, New York.

Llobert-Anglí, M., Masferrer, A., 2015. 'Counterterrorism, emergency and national laws', in Lennon, G. and Walker, C. (eds), *Routledge Handbook of Law and Terrorism*. Routledge, London, pp. 38–51.

Malesevic, S., 2010. *The Sociology of War and Peace*. Cambridge University Press, Cambridge.

Martini, M., 2018. 'Making women terrorists into "Jihadi brides": An analysis of media narratives on women joining ISIS', *Critical Studies on Terrorism*, 11(3), 458–477.

Massoumi, N., Mills, T. and Miller, D., 2017. *What is Islamophobia? Racism, Social Movements and the State*. Pluto Press, London.

Miller, D., Mills, T., 2009. 'The terror experts and the mainstream media', *Critical Studies in Terrorism*, 2(3), 414–437.

Mills, C.W., 1958. *The Causes of the Third World War*. Ballantine, New York.

Neocleous, M., 2012. 'Don't be scared, be prepared': Trauma-anxiety-resilience', *Alternatives: Global, Local, Political*, 37(3), 188–198.

Polleta, F., 2008. 'Storytelling in politics', *Context*, 7(4), 26–31.

Price, D.H., 2015. *Weaponizing Anthropology: Social Science in the Service of the Militarized State*. Counterpunch, Oakland, CA.

Real Instituto Elcano de Estudios Estratégicos, 2017. *La mujer en la prevención de la radicalización violenta y desradicalización*, in collaboration with UK Embassy, US Embassy, Canada Embassy. 30 March 2017. Available at www.youtube.com/watch?v=SvClQpQvLRE (accessed 15 January 2020).

Reinares, F., 2009. 'After the Madrid bombings: Internal security reforms and prevention of global terrorism in Spain', *Studies in Conflict & Terrorism*, 32(5), 367–388.

Revilla, M., Molina, C., 2016. 'Explaining electoral reorganization in Spain (2010–2015): 15-M, mareas and the uprising of new parties'. Paper presented at the General Conference ECPR, Prague, 8–10 September. Panel S56PO14.

Romanos, E., 2016. 'Late neoliberalism and its indignados: Contention in austerity Spain', in Della Porta, D., Andretta, M., Fernandes, T., O'Connor, F., Romanos, E. and Vogiatzoglou, M. (eds), *Late Neoliberalism and Its Discontents in the Economic Crisis: Comparing Social Movements in the European Periphery*. Palgrave Macmillan, Basingstoke, pp. 131–167.

Rose, R., 2004. *Learning from Comparative Public Policy: A Practical Guide*. Routledge, London.

Scott, J.C. 1999. *Seeing like a state. How certain schemas to improve human condition have failed*. Yale University Press, New Haven, CT.

Stampnitzky, L., 2013. *Disciplining Terror: How Experts Invented 'Terrorism'*. Cambridge University Press, Cambridge.

Tellez, V., 2018. 'El "Pacto Antiyihadista" y las estrategias de lucha contra la "radicalización violenta": Implicaciones jurídicas, políticas y sociales', *Revista de Estudios Internacionales Mediterráneos*, 24, 9–30.

Whitfield, T., 2014. *Endgame for ETA: The Elusive Peace in the Basque Country*. Oxford University Press, Oxford.

11

Extremists or patriots? Racialisation of countering violent extremism programming in the US

Priya Dixit

Introduction

Throughout 2017, there were reports of increasing hate crimes and murders committed by right-wing extremists in the US.[1] The Anti-Defamation League (ADL) reported there were thirty-four extremist-related killings in 2017, with white supremacist-inspired killers responsible for seventeen deaths. This was more than double the number of the previous year (ADL, 2018a, 2018b; Gstalter, 2018). The New America Foundation reported 104 Americans were killed by 'jihadi' extremists and eighty-six by 'far right-wing' extremists from 11 September 2001 to November 2018 (New America Foundation, 2018). A 2014 study conducted by academics Charles Kurzman and David Schanzer with the Police Executive Research Forum showed that 74% of 382 US law enforcement agencies surveyed reported anti-government extremism as one of the top three terrorist threats in their jurisdiction (Kurzman and Schanzer, 2015).

Overall, far-right extremist violence has proliferated in recent years in the US. Many around the world are aware of the 2017 events of Charlottesville, Virginia where white supremacists and their allies clashed with counter-protesters, killing one person. In October 2018, a man sent sixteen pipe bombs to critics of President Trump and another shot three and killed two Black supermarket shoppers in Kentucky. The deadliest anti-semitic attack in US history also occurred in October 2018 as a far-right extremist killed eleven worshippers and injured six at a Pittsburgh synagogue. All these were connected to the far right. Various organisations that track far-right violence all agree it is becoming increasingly more common (Lee et al., 2015; Lowery et al., 2018). Despite this, however, government policies on extremism in the US remain focused mainly (and, often, only) on jihadist extremism and ignore the rising violence from right-wing extremists.[2]

This chapter addresses this gap with regard to violent extremism in the US, wherein right-wing violent extremists are often ignored in government policies and programmes on preventing and countering extremism in general. It argues that this erasure of right-wing extremism, both violent and non-violent, from discussions and policies regarding extremism in the US creates a context wherein violence by white perpetrators is excused and normalised as part of everyday life. Countering violent extremism (CVE) programmes are established to counter potential and actual violence by persons of colour, often Muslims and Arab-Americans. Examining US CVE through the lenses of Islamophobia and 'suspect communities' opens up discussions of how extremism is racialised, constituting people who appear to be Muslim as dangerous 'others' and as 'suspect communities'.[3] CVE programmes marginalise and stereotype Muslim and Arab-Americans, while making invisible the ongoing violence by white nationalists and white supremacists.[4] Such an absence means extremist violence committed by militia and far-right groups is not defined or prosecuted as 'extremism'. Other related outcomes of this silencing of white/far-right violence is a suppression of dissent by minorities and positing of persons of colour as un-American.

This chapter is organised as follows. The next section outlines some recent examples to direct attention to broader questions regarding how 'violent extremism' is conceptualised and managed in the US. The section following offers an outline of racialisation and 'suspect communities' scholarship in relation to CVE. This is followed by a genealogy of official CVE in the US, evaluating Department of Homeland Security-supported programmes. The section after draws together key points regarding racialisation of extremism in the US. This includes discussions of race and how the US state manages predominantly white 'patriot' violence, as compared with violence committed by minorities, especially Muslims and Arab-Americans, in the post-9/11 period. Overall, this chapter illustrates how an inconsistent definition of 'extremism', erasure of white violence from CVE and targeting of Muslim and Arab-Americans in CVE programmes constitutes Muslim and Arab-Americans both as vulnerable to and responsible for extremism. This shapes popular perception of 'extremists' as brown persons/persons of colour while similar violence by white Americans is made invisible in CVE programmes.

Patriots and extremists: suspect communities and countering violent extremism

A deeper look at three recent events will illustrate differences in how the US state represents and manages extremist violence (Table 11.1).

As can be noted in Table 11.1, penalties imposed on those arrested were racialised, with militia (white) violence taken less seriously than actions by

Table 11.1 Overview of three illustrative events regarding racialisation of extremist violence in the US

Event	What happened?	Reasons given	Outcome	Extremism?
2014 Bundy Ranch (April–May)	Armed militants – majority white – led by Bundys confronted government officials after refusing to pay grazing fees on public land	Anti-government, for freedom and God	Government backed down to end standoff; nineteen charged. By early 2018, majority had charges dropped (Levin, 2018)	Not charged with extremism or terrorism
2016 Malheur Refuge	Armed occupation of refuge by predominantly white militia	Anti-government, claimed US state had no constitutional authority to own and manage public lands	Twenty-seven militants indicted and twelve pled guilty. Of these, eight convicted of felonies and misdemeanours with sentences ranging from probation to thirty-seven months in jail (Bernstein, 2018, Wilson, 2018)	Not charged with terrorism or extremism.
2014 Minneapolis	Nine Somali-American young men (late teens to early twenties) arrested for attempting to travel to join so-called Islamic State. None of them were armed.	Travel to Syria to fight for so-called Islamic State	In 2016, sentenced for five to thirty-five years in jail (two for thirty years; one for thirty-five years; one suspended sentence for cooperating with government) (Montemayor, 2016; Yuen and Xaykaothao, 2016). Extensive media attention and framing of Minneapolis as centre of jihadist extremism (Varvelli, 2016)	Yes, terrorism. Charged with providing material support to terrorism (alongside other charges)

persons of colour. The Minneapolis case was considered supporting 'terrorism', while neither terrorism nor extremism charges applied for the Bundy ranch and Malheur refuge armed standoffs. When examined in terms of targets, actions and perpetrators, we could argue that armed attacks against the state fit in well with definitions of violent extremism, perhaps even more so than thinking about or even planning to go fight overseas. The Federal Bureau of Investigation (FBI) defines 'violent extremism' as 'encouraging, condoning, justifying, or supporting the commission of a violent act to achieve political, ideological, religious, social, or economic goals' (FBI, n.d.). In other words, at the Bundy ranch and the Malheur refuge, the perpetrators took up arms against the government for a political cause; in Minneapolis, there was no violent act committed and nor were the men armed. And yet the sentences for the armed anti-government militia were far more lenient than those for the young men in Minneapolis. This indicates differences in how 'extremism' and 'terrorism' are defined in the US, with different penalties imposed.

These examples illustrate how US extremism is racialised, with brown bodies seen as dangerous and potential extremists, while the majority white far-right extremists are not depicted as such. Examining these discrepancies in penalties through an Islamophobia framework illustrates mechanisms of CVE policymaking that structure these differences in how extremism is managed and the consequences of such differences. We might ask why were the Malheur refuge and Bundy Ranch confrontations *not* designated as 'terrorism' or even 'domestic extremism', both designations which carry substantial penalties?[5] Compare this with the Minneapolis youth who were charged with providing material support to terrorism (among other charges). This is partly connected to the conceptual and legal confusion over terrorism in the US, where federal charges for 'domestic terrorism' are hard to enforce (Myre, 2017a, 2017b). Yet we can also ask ourselves: if events fit into definitions of extremism and terrorism, should they not be labelled as such and the perpetrators prosecuted? Why is the state not engaged in CVE programmes against militia and 'patriot' movements, while Minneapolis is one of the sites for the Department of Homeland Security's 'pilot' programmes for CVE? The absence of white perpetrators from CVE discussions limits conversations and policy debates on CVE to only jihadist extremists.

While not everyone at the Bundy and Malheur standoffs had far-right views (Gallaher, 2016), mainly anti-immigrant and anti-Muslim 'patriot' groups were present at both events. Yet their actions have not been categorised as extremism. The absence of groups like the patriot movement from discussions and policymaking regarding extremism creates a context where extremist ideas by the mostly white 'patriots' and others are not scrutinised or managed (Childress, 2017; Sullivan, 2016). 'Patriot' beliefs are a combination of anti-immigrant, pro-gun rights (second amendment) and anti-government. The Southern Poverty

Law Center, which tracks extremist and hate groups, reported that the number of 'patriot' groups rose from 149 in 2008 to 1,360 in 2012 and then declined to 998 in 2015 and to 623 by 2016 (Welsh, 2017). Patriot group members and white nationalists are standing for office and even winning seats in some cases (Wilson, 2018). The patriot movement recruits through family and peer networks, has extensive online presence and also conducts military-style training (PBS, 2017b).

Returning to the examples in Table 11.1, it is worthwhile considering how a Muslim or Arab-American group which established training camps and gathered individuals for armed resistance against the US government would be received by the majority of the US public, media and authorities. In a 2016 report titled, 'Why the law turns a blind eye to militias', a reporter for *Mother Jones* wrote about armed training camps run by militia groups:

> These military-style trainings have no connection to the US military or a government-sponsored militia. Yet they are legal so long as they don't cross the line into inciting violence or civil unrest. Under California law, it is illegal for a 'paramilitary organization' to train with weapons if it engages in 'instruction or training in guerrilla warfare or sabotage.' Violators are subject to one year of imprisonment and/or a fine of up to $1,000. When I asked the California attorney general's office if there was any reason to believe that [California state militia's] activities might violate state law, a spokeswoman said the office was unable to provide any legal analysis and declined to comment further. (Rathod, 2016)

This glimpse into how authorities respond to militia activities directs our attention to two key issues relevant to understanding extremism in the US: one, unlike many other democracies, the US has legislation that permits large-scale militarised 'training' activities as long as the participants are not 'inciting violence'. The understanding of what and when groups are inciting violence can be interpreted differently. Second, the 'no comment' here also indicates disinterest on the part of authorities to grapple with questions of whether and how militarised training could become dangerous to society or the state. Understandings of extremism and extremists in the US are racialised, as militia and patriot actions including militarisation and training are usually seen as part of US culture (PBS, 2017a, 2017b, 2018). This means programmes to counter extremism almost exclusively focus on persons of colour. This affects US CVE policies and programmes as discussions of far-right violence including militia violence become erased from discussions of ways to counter extremism.

An analysis that centres race and identifies processes of racialisation is useful to explain these differences in how extremism is conceptualised and managed in the US. Differences in definitions of extremism are not just about how the term is inconsistently applied, but about how such inconsistencies produce different racialised groups – white 'patriots' and brown/Black 'extremists' and racialised meanings of violence. Racialisation is best understood here as a process in which members of a certain group, for example 'Muslim-Americans', are ascribed specific features (e.g., vulnerability to extremism, potential for being recruited by terrorists, etc.) that are then linked to race (Gans, 2017). At the same time, militia and 'patriot' movements are also racialised in that their white-ness links them to cultural practices (e.g., carrying guns, establishing military training camps around the country) that are authorised under the US constitution.

Centralising race in analysis of terrorism and extremism makes visible counter-extremism practices that are inconsistently applied and which target communities of colour. A race-based analysis also directs attention to the multireligious and multihistorical connections between various parts of the world, interrogating and overturning mainstream counter-terrorism discourses wherein minorities, especially Muslim and Arab minorities in the West, are seen as new and potentially threatening an imagined 'Western' identity. These framings are connected with a forgetting of the intertwined global histories of the so-called global North and global South. This forgetting contributes to the formation of 'suspect communities', wherein minorities become conceptualised as 'suspect' due to their perceived potential for violence and their connection to 'terrorism' (Breen-Smyth, 2014; Cherney and Murphy, 2016). Related to this is the relative absence of race, class and gender-based analyses in much of CVE scholarship, especially those that get cited in US government policymaking. This absence hides differential impacts of counter-terrorism policies on communities of colour.

The absence of discussions of race can also be noted in the concealment of structural effects of counter-terrorism practices, including how communities have become racialised as dangerous (Considine, 2017). Conceptually, Islamophobia is useful to analyse the development of US CVE policies, especially to explain how and why white perpetrators are excluded from definitions and policies regarding extremism. Structural processes connected to counter-terrorism which racialise the terrorist subject in the West are often ignored in discussions and policymaking (Beydoun, 2018a). Beydoun's definition of Islamophobia as having multiple dimensions of private, structural and dialectical (2018a, p. 29) is critical to thinking about how racialisation of counter-terrorism policies impacts minority communities. Beydoun notes that Islamophobia is presented as a private problem, a few bad apples as it were, when it actually has structural dimensions (2018a, pp. 29–30). This means concerns regarding raced and gendered practices like the surveillance of Muslim-Americans (Pilkington, 2018) or the psychological and security impacts of CVE on those targeted are often ignored in US CVE policymaking.

Recent concerns about US CVE include increased unease among the US Muslim and Arab communities that CVE programmes unfairly target Muslim- and

Arab-Americans by constituting them as having the responsibility to conform to mainstream – however understood – society, while not acknowledging the unintended consequences of targeting mainly Muslims and Arab-Americans with CVE interventions (Ibrahim, 2016). These consequences include increasing Islamophobic attitudes and violence. The FBI's Hate Crimes Report for 2017 showed a 17% rise in hate crimes (Li, 2018).[6] Additional concerns include that CVE programmes could further stigmatise and marginalise the Muslim-American community by holding an entire community responsible for the actions of some individuals. This can have the effect of suppressing dissent and categorising persons of colour as suspect if they do not align with the state's CVE and counter-radicalisation policies or if they disagree with the majority.

Expressions of dissent by minority groups can automatically be deemed suspicious to the nation-state. This is problematic within a democracy (Neumann, 2013; Price, 2016). The current lack of definitions of extremism and radicalisation in the US actually allows the state to claim it *is* including all forms of extremism in its discussions and policies. However, in practice (Appendix 11.A), it is mainly Muslim/Arab-Americans and Islam itself that are linked with extremism in CVE programmes. This is problematic as it constructs Muslims and Arabs as a suspect community while also ignoring similar or even more violent actions committed by right-wing perpetrators. In other words, by pre-emptively producing Muslim- and Arab-Americans as potential threats but also as vulnerable to extremism, the state is able to authorise practices of surveillance and detention against them. Such practices are unable to be authorised in relation to far-right extremists, who are almost always white. In this case, whiteness of militia and far-right extremists inoculates against being considered 'extremist' and being produced as a 'suspect community'. The next section provides a brief genealogy of US policies and programmes on CVE.

CVE in the US: a brief genealogy

Despite being relatively new as compared with CVE and counter-radicalisation programmes in other Western countries, US CVE programmes have similar outcomes of governing lives of minorities. They do so by producing 'the Muslim population' as a homogenous group to be scrutinised, managed and penalised while, at the same time, excluding far-right/white violent extremism from similar interventions (Appendix 11.A). When CVE programming was first established in the US under the Obama administration, it was controversial. After some Americans travelled overseas to fight for extremist groups in the 2000s, the US government began focusing on CVE, both financially and in terms of pilot programmes and strategies. The US involvement in CVE was formalised in 2011 with the government's publication of its CVE strategy, called *Empowering Local Partners to Prevent Violent Extremism in the United States* (White House, 2011). Important aspects of this strategy included an emphasis on al Qaida/jihadist extremism to the exclusion of other forms of extremism, an emphasis which has continued in subsequent US CVE policies and programmes. The strategy also proposed a 'community-based approach' to CVE without, however, including many details of which communities would be selected and the criteria for selection (White House, 2011). Many minority activists perceived CVE as discriminatory (Mauleon, 2018), while conservatives saw it as empowering 'Islamic supremacists' (Schachtel, 2017).

The government's CVE policy grew quickly but lacked coordination. Many government and non-governmental organisations established different departments and programmes to counter extremism, leading to a lack of cohesion and communication. The 2011 Strategy was followed by the establishment of CVE units in the FBI, the Department of Homeland Security (DHS), the Department of Justice (DOJ) and related government departments.[7] In April 2015, the White House held a global summit to discuss causes of violent extremism and consider ways and means to counter it (White House, 2015). Domestic CVE initiatives included a pilot programme that started in 2015 and focuses on three cities: Boston, Los Angeles and Minneapolis-St Paul. The DHS, DOJ, FBI and United States Agency for International Development (USAID) all began CVE and anti-radicalisation programmes (DHS, n.d.b). Of the nearly $1 billion available in the Homeland Security Grant Program for 2017, DHS outlined CVE as a 'program priority'. The DHS was supposed to be the lead in an 'interagency CVE task force' that was prioritised for 2016 (DHS, 2016). CVE efforts also took off internationally with the *Department of State and USAID Joint Strategy on Countering Violent Extremism* released in May 2016. This connected domestic CVE in the US with USAID's international efforts (US Department of State, 2016). As such, it linked Muslim and Arab communities inside and outside of the US as susceptible to violent extremism.

While 'community-owned' aspects of CVE were given importance during the early years of US CVE, this changed as funding priorities shifted towards law enforcement after the 2016 election (Appendix 11.A). There was significant increase in funding to law enforcement agencies, with agencies in Colorado, Minnesota, California, Washington and others receiving around half a million dollars each. A CVE task force established under the Obama administration was de-funded and its head resigned in July 2017. The only organisation focused on the far right – Life After Hate – had its DHS funding revoked (Hannsler, 2017). This emphasis on law enforcement had the effect of militarising CVE and further removing local ownership of programmes. Additionally, the Office for Community Partnership at the DHS was disbanded and the 'Countering Violent

Extremism' page at DHS had its name changed to 'Terrorism Prevention Partnerships', thus automatically securitising their actions as 'preventing terrorism'. For the 2018 budget, more than $300 million was to be cut from various CVE-related programmes throughout the government (Kopan, 2017). There were reports that the State Department had left unused millions of dollars that were meant to develop programmes to counter online extremism (Toosi, 2017), indicating a lack of government interest in CVE.

Two key issues emerge here regarding CVE and the formation of 'suspect communities': the state's overwhelming focus on Muslim- and Arab-Americans as target of CVE interventions, and a lack of cohesion regarding design and implementation of CVE programmes. In a 2018 report for the Brennan Center, Patel et al. (2018) write:

- At least 85% of CVE grants, and over half of CVE programs, now explicitly target minority groups, including Muslims, LGBTQ Americans, Black Lives Matter Activists, immigrants, and refugees.
- The amount of CVE funding going to law enforcement has tripled, from $764,000 to $2,340,000.

As Appendix 11.A illustrates, numerous agencies which were selected to receive CVE funding during the Obama administration had their funding reduced or cut altogether by the Trump administration. Some organisations, including the Claremont School of Theology, rejected grants after the 2016 election as anti-Muslim rhetoric grew (Ali, 2017).

This change in funding priorities is not linked with a consistent definition, as definitions of extremism and radicalisation remain unspecified and vague. A review of policies and programmes on radicalisation and CVE in the US indicate that concepts such as 'radical', 'radicalisation' and 'extremism' have multiple meanings. For example, the DHS CVE programme describes *where* violent extremist threats arise from ('a range of groups and individuals') and *how* (small groups of people may be radicalised or travel overseas; use of social media), but does not actually define *what* is extremism in the first place (DHS, n.d.a). Does extremism, then, mean someone who holds different ideas than those of mainstream society? It is difficult to have a clear and consistent notion of which ideas and acts can be categorised as 'extremist' and 'radical', as definitions of these often are not provided. The lack of definitions also means it would be possible for a government agency to inconsistently define some violence as 'extremism' and others not, which is what has been happening.

Even when definitions are provided, they are often vague and can be made to fit numerous widely different acts and actors. The US government's August 2011 policy document on CVE defines 'violent extremists' as 'individuals who support or commit ideologically-motivated violence to further political goals' (White House, 2011). It states that violent extremist threats within the US can come from a range of extremist groups and individuals, including 'Domestic Terrorists and Homegrown Violent Extremists (HVEs)' (White House, 2011). But further clarification or examples are not provided. The DHS defines CVE as follows:

> The term 'Countering Violent Extremism' refers to efforts focused on preventing all forms of ideologically based extremist violence, to include prevention of successful recruitment into terrorist groups. (DHS, n.d.a)

As can be noted here, while the phrase 'ideologically based extremist violence' is provided, the line following it limits it to 'recruitment into terrorist groups'; not right-wing groups, not other forms of 'ideologically based groups', but specifically 'terrorist groups'. The sections following this mention that the Muslim community is vulnerable, again linking Muslim-Americans with (potential and actual) extremism. There is no mention, for example, that young white males may also be vulnerable to extremism, considering the recent rise in far-right violence.

Therefore, the US CVE programme is inconsistent in its definition of 'extremism' and shifted funding from community-based organisations to law enforcement. This removes agency of minority community-focused groups and shapes them as 'suspect communities'. This partly explains the discrepancy in referring to events such as the Malheur refuge as an 'occupation' and not as 'extremism' or 'terrorism'. The absence of militia and related far-right groups from consideration of CVE intervention constitutes actions by the Bundys and their supporters as separate to extremism, even though such actions fit within the US government's definitions of extremism. On this note, it is worth recalling the discussions surrounding the DHS 2009 report on right-wing extremism titled *Rightwing Extremism: Current Economic and Political Climate Fueling Resurgence in Radicalization and Recruitment* (DHS, 2009). Immediately after its publication, conservative commentators attacked both the report and the DHS. Conservative Michelle Malkin called it 'one of the most embarrassingly shoddy pieces of propaganda I'd ever read out of DHS' (Montopoli, 2009). A Republican politician said the report was 'political profiling' (Fox News, 2009). DHS eventually withdrew the report and its lead author claimed this was due to political pressure (Ackerman, 2012; Johnson, 2012, 2017; Levin, 2011). In the years that followed, DHS would reduce its domestic terrorism unit while expanding focus on 'jihadist' extremism.

The lack of definitions is combined with a focus on minorities as having the responsibility to build and maintain 'social cohesion'. Social cohesion and resilience are offered as goals for many CVE programmes, but there is a lack of clarity about what they entail. The 2011 US government strategy, along with the CVE pilot programmes in Boston, Los Angeles and Minneapolis, all emphasise the need to build community resilience to counter violent extremism. However, the process of how to achieve resilience is left unspecified. Often, the responsibility for community cohesion is placed on the minority group that is being targeted. In other words, the way US CVE policies are framed, it is the minority group – brown bodies in this case – which has the responsibility for creating and maintaining cohesion. This leads to programming which targets communities of colour almost exclusively, framing them both as vulnerable to radicalisation with the potential for becoming extremists and also as the ones responsible for creating and maintaining community cohesion. Of the programmes reviewed in Appendix 11.A, almost all are concentrated on Muslim and Arab-American populations, thus targeting them as causes of a potential lack of social cohesion. This selective targeting has increased concern among the US Muslim/Arab communities that CVE programmes unfairly target them by constituting them as having the responsibility to conform, while not acknowledging the consequences of CVE interventions (Ibrahim, 2016).

US CVE thus constitutes minorities – Muslims and Arab-Americans in this case – as having the responsibility to deal with extremism. Of the three cities involved in the pilot CVE programmes, Minneapolis-St Paul has received the most attention. The programme statement for the Minneapolis-St Paul CVE programme mentions that it was developed in conjunction with the Somali Minnesotan community. The programme itself is called 'Building Community Resilience' and its goal is to identify what the community considers 'roots' of radicalisation (DOJ, 2015). However, the emphasis has been on Muslim communities and not on other forms of extremism which are also present in the area. For example, in June 2016, two Muslim men in Minneapolis were shot. The *Star Tribune* reported, 'an assailant allegedly made disparaging remarks about Muslims before opening fire on five young men clad in Muslim prayer robes called qamis' (Sawyer, 2016). These killings and many other anti-Muslim incidents across the US have received relatively little attention in the media and especially in DHS CVE programmes. In Minneapolis and elsewhere, men like the Bundys and the 'patriot' movement have not been targeted for intervention or tasked with building community resilience and maintaining social cohesion.

Racialisation of extremism in the US

The targeting of Muslim and Arab-American communities for CVE interventions, as indicated in Appendix 11.A, constitutes them as a suspect community prone to radicalisation. Their loyalty and presence in the US state's space is questioned and their everyday behaviour is deemed 'suspect', while similar behaviour is considered 'acceptable and unremarkable for ordinary white Christians' (Alimahomed-Wilson, 2018). Research with Muslim-Americans has revealed their perception that the US state views them as suspicious due to their Muslim-ness (Selod, 2015). The actions of a few, such as the Minneapolis young men discussed earlier, are taken as indicators for how all Muslim- and Arab-Americans will act. They are taken as how a geographical area can be stereotyped. This stereotyping was seen in President Trump's remarks about Minnesota as a state where Somali refugees arrived in large numbers and then proceeded 'spreading extremism all over our country and all over the world' (Trump, 2016). These claims of un-Americanness and disloyalty to the state are not something that white Americans are charged with, even when they engage in violence (Alimahomed-Wilson, 2018). As Appendix 11.A and the examples earlier in this chapter indicate, there has not been a parallel move towards racialisation – in the sense of constituting a 'white American suspect community' – of anti-government extremists or of 'patriot' movements. Instead, the rights to bear arms and of freedom of speech are often invoked in militia and far-right-led anti-government armed actions.

Constituting Muslim- and Arab-Americans as 'suspect communities' ties in with various facets of Islamophobia. Beydoun's understanding of Islamophobia as multifaceted is relevant here (Beydoun, 2018a). It is not just individual personal animosity and anti-Muslim hate crimes that are indicators of Islamophobia; it is also the overrepresentation of violent acts by Muslims in the media (Kearns et al., 2017) and the inconsistencies in government policies in defining and implementing policies on extremism as noted here. Islamophobia is not limited to individual acts of hate against those perceived to be Muslim but has been institutionalised and is prevalent in US society (Considine, 2017; Marusek, 2018). Considine writes, 'in the context of the "war on terror", the racialisation of American Muslims generates local and palpable experiences of exclusion and abuse for both Muslims and non-Muslims [who are perceived to be Muslim]' (2017, p. 1). Statistics indicate assaults against Muslims in America rose between 2015 and 2016 to levels higher than in 2001 (Kishi, 2017). Kearns et al.'s (2017) study concluded that terrorist attacks committed by Muslims received five times more attention than those committed by white perpetrators (Kearns et al., 2017).

Far-right extremists and the communities they are from do not face similar abuse or exclusion. Indeed, CVE policies' overemphasis on Muslims as targeted communities can facilitate the normalisation of far-right and militia violence as, legally, they receive lower penalties for acts of violence (Table 11.1), and their violence is not labelled as 'extremism' or 'terrorism'. Furthermore, the notion of a 'lone-wolf' attacker is often used to describe white perpetrators of mass violence, suggesting such attackers are disconnected from communities they are from. The 'lone-wolf' designation also serves as presumptive exemption from terrorism for white persons, an exemption that Muslims are not given (Beydoun, 2018b). Thus, the ignoring of far-right/white violence in CVE programmes is shaped by and itself shapes Islamophobia, especially at the structural level.

Right-wing ideologies are often de-linked from violence even when the perpetrator has been part of white supremacist or neo-Nazi movements (Simi, 2013, pp. 145–146). Factors including the election of Barack Obama, a steep economic downturn and increasing anti-immigration sentiments contributed to the rise of right-wing extremism in the 2000s (Simi, 2013). Yet there was no corresponding political or government-level intervention of the kind paralleling CVE programmes. Simi gives the example of Timothy McVeigh who was inspired by *The Turner Diaries* and was connected to white supremacist communities, and yet an FBI profile of him initially called him a 'lone-wolf' attacker (Simi, 2013, p. 145). Indeed, Simi (2013, p. 146) argues that one of the implications of seeing right-wing violence as individualised and not connected to a larger strategy of right-wing extremism is that this constitutes right-wing extremism as of no great concern.

The absence of right-wing extremists from government discussions and legislation and from CVE programmes is noteworthy, as it ignores not just rising far-right threats, but also plentiful existing scholarship on US militia, white supremacists and anti-government extremists (e.g., Gallaher, 2002; Mulloy, 2005; Potok, 2010). This was especially the case prior to 9/11. Other scholars have investigated goals and motivations of various types of right-wing extremists both in the US and abroad (Gallaher, 2002; Johnson, 2012; Mulloy, 2005; Von Mering and McCarty, 2013). By ignoring this scholarship, US CVE was limited in its outlook. In CVE policies and programmes, a range of actions can be justified in the name of preventing 'extremism'. By rewording the DHS 'community partnership program' as 'terrorism prevention', the Trump administration can classify a range of actions (e.g., building interethnic linkages, community policing, interfaith efforts, etc.) as somehow connected with 'terrorism prevention'. Furthermore, the programme itself has moved away from non-military CVE efforts to more militarised responses. As minorities are deemed to be potentially suspect, even non-violent behaviour is often criminalised, with entire communities considered vulnerable to extremism and in need of intervention.

As existing official CVE practices became increasingly militarised and continue to target minority Muslim and Arab communities while excluding far-right and militia perpetrators, they were hardly exemplary. There is a twofold effect that bears consideration. First, the defunding of DHS's CVE by the Trump administration does not necessarily mean that practices of surveillance and ste-reotyping of minorities has ended. Indeed, by 'invisibilising' CVE through making it part of law enforcement work or implemented as part of broader pro-grammes, it makes it more difficult to scrutinise and evaluate CVE actions by various government agencies. Second, taking right-wing extremism seriously could mean adding right-wing extremists to programmes on CVE and sub-jecting additional areas and communities to similar levels of scrutiny as those faced by Muslim- and Arab-Americans. However, merely adding right-wing extremism to the already problematic CVE programmes would not deal with the racialisation of extremism and the normalisation of militia-type activities. Instead, a shift in official thinking regarding the role of CVE programming would be useful – what would a de-militarised CVE that takes all forms of extremism seriously look like? Does the US even need CVE programmes at all?

Overall, this chapter fits in within critical scholarship that centres race – about Islamophobia and the formation of 'suspect communities' – in analysis of extremism. The US CVE programmes borrowed from other de-radicalisation and CVE models, rather than developing local versions best suited for the US context (Coolsaet, 2016, p. 35). The US is different to many other industrialised countries especially in its easy access to guns, increasing police militarisation and an active militia movement. Black and brown bodies and the spaces they are present in have been conceptualised as bodies and spaces of danger (Beydoun, 2018a; Browne, 2015; Jones, 2016; Kundnani, 2014) while far-right users of vio-lence have not. In a 2016 testimony to the US Congress, Richard Cohen, Presi-dent of the Southern Poverty Law Center, quoted a report that claimed 'between 1990 and 2014, far-right domestic extremists were responsible for four times as many ideologically based homicidal incidents as extremists associated with al Qaeda and related movements' (Cohen, 2016). He further added that this threat does not receive much attention in the US. As indicated above, many of the pol-icies put in place for CVE and to build social cohesion target Muslim-Americans and minority communities while leaving the majority alone. In this way, extrem-ism and CVE policies are racialised – portraying minority communities and minority 'extremists' as dangers to society and the state. This, instead of building cohesion, can exacerbate social divisions and further research needs to con-sider such impacts.

Acknowledgements

I am grateful to the editors and to the anonymous reviewers for their enormous help with this chapter.

Notes

1   This chapter addresses events and policies until January 2019.
2   Right-wing and far-right extremism are used interchangeably in this chapter. There
    is no one agreed-upon definition for 'far-right' and 'right-wing' extremism. Norris
    argues far-right and right-wing political parties are a cluster. Mudde suggests the
    different ideological commitments of far-right extremists means clear conceptual
    criteria are difficult to produce. Both Norris and Mudde cited in Gaston (2017).
    There is an overview of right-wing extremism in Carter (2018), with a description
    of groups in the US context in Ford (2017). Mudde found at least twenty-six
    definitions in recent scholarship about right-wing extremism in Caiani et al. (2012).
    Ford (2017) has a taxonomy of the US far right.
3   Bleich (2012) offers an overview of defining and researching Islamophobia.
4   Perlman (2017) defines white supremacists as believing the white race is superior to
    others, while white nationalists want a nation of white people.
5   Wiles (2018) includes a list of charges.
6   As the FBI report is based on self-reporting by law agencies, it can undercount hate
    crimes as not all agencies report (Green, 2018).
7   Bjelopera (2014) has a summary of US CVE efforts. McCants and Watts (2012)
    provide a short assessment.

References

Ackerman, S., 2012. 'DHS crushed this analyst for warning about far-right terror',
    Wired.com, 7 August. Available at www.wired.com/2012/08/dhs/ (accessed
    10 September 2018).
Ali, S.S., 2017. 'Islamic school walked away from nearly $1m in federal funding because
    of Trump', *NBC News*, 6 March. Available at www.nbcnews.com/news/us-news/
    islamic-school-walked-away-nearly-1m-federal-funding-because-trump-n727746
    (accessed 10 November 2018).
Alimahomed-Wilson, S., 2019. 'When the FBI knocks: Racialized state surveillance of
    Muslims', *Critical Sociology*, 45(6), 871–887.
ADL (Anti-Defamation League), 2018a. *A Dark and Constant Rage: 25 Years of
    Right-wing Terrorism in the United States*. Available at www.adl.org/sites/default/
    files/documents/CR_5154_25YRS%20RightWing%20Terrorism_V5.pdf (accessed
    10 September 2018).
ADL (Anti-Defamation League), 2018b. *Murder and Extremism in the United States in
    2017*. Available at www.adl.org/resources/reports/murder-and-extremism-in-the-
    united-states-in-2017 (accessed 10 September 2018).
Bernstein, M., 2018. 'Judge sentences Oregon refuge occupier Ryan Payne to over
    3 years in prison', *The Oregonian*, 28 February. Available at www.oregonlive.com/
    oregon-standoff/2018/02/federal_judge_sentences_oregon.html (accessed
    10 September 2018).

Beydoun, K.A., 2018a. *American Islamophobia: Understanding the Roots and Rise of Fear*. Chicago University Press, Chicago.

Beydoun, K.A., 2018b. 'Lone wolf terrorism: Types, stripes, and double standards', *Northwestern University Law Review Online*, 112(5), 1213–1244.

Bjelopera, J.P., 2014. *Countering Violent Extremism in the United States*, Congressional Research Service, 19 February. Available at https://fas.org/sgp/crs/homesec/R42553.pdf (accessed 10 September 2018).

Bleich, E., 2012. 'Defining and researching Islamophobia', *Review of Middle East Studies*, 46(2), 180–189.

Breen-Smyth, M., 2014. 'Theorising the "suspect community"? Counterterrorism, security practices and the public imagination', *Critical Studies on Terrorism*, 7(4), 223–240.

Browne, S., 2015. *Dark Matters: On the Surveillance of Blackness*. Duke University Press, Durham, NC.

Caiani, M., Della Porta, D. and Wagemann, C., 2012. *Mobilizing on the Extreme Right: Germany, Italy, and the United States*. Oxford University Press, Oxford.

Carter, E., 2018. 'Right-wing extremism/radicalism: Reconstructing the concept', *Journal of Political Ideologies*, 23(2), 157–182.

Cherney, A., Murphy, K., 2016. 'Being a "suspect community" in a post 9/11 world – the impact of the war on terror on Muslim communities in Australia', *Australian & New Zealand Journal of Criminology*, 49(4), 480–496.

Childress, S., 2017, 'A guide to the new militia movement', *PBS Frontline*, 17 May. Available at http://apps.frontline.org/militia-movement/ (accessed 10 September 2018).

Cohen, R., 2016. 'Testimony of J. Richard Cohen President, Southern Poverty Law Center before the subcommittees on national security and government operations committee on oversight and government reform U.S. House of Representatives: Radicalization in the US and the rise of terrorism', 14 September. Available at www.splcenter.org/sites/default/files/rc-writtentestimony-9–14–16_house.pdf (accessed 10 September 2018).

Considine, C., 2017. 'The racialization of Islam in the United States: Islamophobia, hate crimes, and "flying while brown"', *Religions*, 8(9), 165–185.

Coolsaet, R., 2016. '"All radicalization is local": The genesis and drawbacks of an elusive concept', Egmont Royal Institute of International Relations Paper No. 84, May. Available at www.egmontinstitute.be/all-radicalisation-is-local/ (accessed 10 September 2018).

Department of Homeland Security (DHS), 2009. *Rightwing Extremism: Current Economic and Political Climate Fueling Resurgence in Radicalization and Recruitment*. Available at https://fas.org/irp/eprint/rightwing.pdf (accessed 10 September 2018).

Department of Homeland Security (DHS), 2016. *Fact Sheet: DY 2017 Budget*, 9 February. Available at www.dhs.gov/news/2016/02/09/fact-sheet-dhs-fy-2017-budget (accessed 10 September 2018).

Department of Homeland Security (DHS), n.d.a *Terrorism Prevention Partnerships*. Available at www.dhs.gov/terrorism-prevention-partnerships (accessed 14 September 2018).

Department of Homeland Security (DHS), n.d.b *Fact Sheet: A Comprehensive US Government Approach to Countering Violent Extremism*. Available at www.dhs.gov/sites/default/files/publications/US%20Government%20Approach%20to%20 CVE-Fact%20Sheet_0.pdf (accessed 10 September 2018).

Department of Justice (DOJ), 2015. *Building Community Resilience: Minneapolis-St Paul Pilot Program: A Community Led Local Framework*, February. Available at www.justice.gov/usao-mn/file/642121/download (accessed 10 September 2018).

Federal Bureau of Investigation (FBI), n.d. *What is violent extremism?* Available at www.fbi.gov/cve508/teen-website/what-is-violent-extremism (accessed 10 September 2018).

Ford, M., 2017. 'The "far right" in America: A brief taxonomy', *The Atlantic*, 22 January. Available at www.theatlantic.com/politics/archive/2017/01/far-right-taxonomy/509282/ (accessed 10 September 2018).

Fox News, 2009. 'Chorus of protest grows over report warning of right wing radicalization', 15 April (updated 24 December 2015). Available at www.foxnews.com/politics/chorus-of-protest-grows-over-report-warning-of-right-wing-radicalization (accessed 20 February, 2020).

Gallaher, C., 2002. *On the Fault Line: Race, Class, and the American Patriot Movement*. Rowman and Littlefield, Lanham, MD.

Gallaher, C., 2016. 'Placing the militia occupation of the Malheur national wildlife refuge in Harney County, Oregon', *ACME: An International Journal for Critical Geographies*, 15(2), 293–308.

Gans, H.J., 2017. 'Racialization and racialization research', *Ethnic and Racial Studies*, 43(3), 341–352.

Gaston, S., 2017. *Far-right extremism in the populist age*, Demos briefing paper. Available at www.demos.co.uk/wp-content/uploads/2017/06/Demos-Briefing-Paper-Far-Right-Extremism-2017.pdf (accessed 10 September 2018).

Green, F.T., 2018. 'Is federal data misstating the state of hate?', *Pacific Standard*, 21 February. Available at https://psmag.com/social-justice/is-federal-hate-crime-data-misstating-the-state-of-hate (accessed 10 September 2018).

Gstalter, M., 2018. 'ADL warns of rise in white supremacist violence', *The Hill*, 18 January. Available at http://thehill.com/homenews/news/369552-study-murders-by-white-supremacists-doubled-in-2017 (accessed 10 September 2018).

Hannsler, J., 2017. 'DHS shifts focus of funding to counter violent extremism', *CNN Politics*, 4 July. Available at https://edition.cnn.com/2017/07/01/politics/cve-funding-changes/index.html (accessed 10 September 2018).

Ibrahim, M., 2016. 'Community response to feds' MN anti-terror recruiting efforts', *MPR News*, 23 February. Available at www.mprnews.org/story/2016/02/23/somali-community-response-anti-terror-recruiting (accessed 10 September 2018).

Johnson, D., 2012. *Right-wing Resurgence: How a Domestic Terrorist Threat Is Being Ignored*. Rowman and Littlefield, Lanham, MD.

Johnson, D., 2017. 'I warned of right-wing violence in 2009. Republicans objected. I was right', *Washington Post*, 21 August. Available at www.washingtonpost.com/news/posteverything/wp/2017/08/21/i-warned-of-right-wing-violence-in-2009-it-caused-an-uproar-i-was-right/?utm_term=.61aeea9975a1 (accessed 10 September 2018).

Jones, D.M., 2016. *Dangerous Spaces: Beyond the Racial Profile*. Praeger International, Denver and Santa Barbara.

Kearns, E., Betus, A. and Lemieux, A., 2017. 'Why do some terrorist attacks receive more media attention than others?', *SSRN*, 7 March. Available at https://papers.ssrn.com/sol3/papers.cfm?abstract_id=2928138 (accessed 10 September 2018).

Kishi, K., 2017. 'Assault against Muslims in US surpass 2001 level', *Pew Research Center*, 15 November. Available at www.pewresearch.org/fact-tank/2017/11/15/assaults-against-muslims-in-u-s-surpass-2001-level/ (accessed 10 September 2018).

Kopan, T., 2017. 'Domestic terrorism programs would be cut under Trump', *CNN Politics*, 1 November. Available at https://edition.cnn.com/2017/10/02/politics/trump-administration-cuts-domestic-terrorism/index.html (accessed 10 September 2018).

Kundnani, A., 2014. *The Muslims Are Coming! Islamophobia, Extremism, and the Domestic War on Terror*. Verso Books, London.

Kurzman, C., Schanzer, D., 2015. *Law enforcement assessment of the violent extremism threat*. Triangle Center on Terrorism and Homeland Security, 25 June. Available at https://sites.duke.edu/tcths/files/2013/06/Kurzman_Schanzer_Law_Enforcement_Assessment_of_the_Violent_Extremist_Threat_final.pdf (accessed 10 September 2018).

Lee, J., Canon, G. and Patterson, B., 2015. 'The rise of violent right-wing extremism, explained', *Mother Jones*, 30 June. Available at www.motherjones.com/politics/2015/06/right-wing-extremism-explainer-charleston-mass-shooting-terrorism/ (accessed 10 September 2018).

Levin, B., 2011. 'Controversial '09 DHS rightwing report author responds to critics', *Huffington Post*, 26 July. Available at www.huffingtonpost.com/brian-levin-jd/daryl-johnson-dhs-interview_b_909786.html (accessed 10 September 2018).

Levin, S., 2018. 'Stunning victory for Bundy family as all charges dismissed in 2014 standoff case', *Guardian*, 8 January. Available at www.theguardian.com/us-news/2018/jan/08/bundy-family-charges-dropped-nevada-armed-standoff (accessed 21 February, 2020).

Li, D.K., 2018. 'Hate crimes in America spiked 17 percent last year, FBI says', *NBC News*, 13 November. Available at www.nbcnews.com/news/us-news/hate-crimes-america-spiked-17-percent-last-year-fbi-says-n935711 (accessed 19 November 2018).

Lowery, W., Kindy, K. and Tran, A.B., 2018. 'In the United States, right-wing violence is on the rise', *The Washington Post*, 25 November. Available at www.washingtonpost.com/national/in-the-united-states-right-wing-violence-is-on-the-rise/2018/11/25/61f7f24a-deb4–11e8–85df-7a6b4d25cfbb_story.html?utm_term=.a6876eaf1f55 (accessed 27 November 2018).

Marusek, S., 2018. 'Inventing terrorists: The nexus of intelligence and Islamophobia', *Critical Studies on Terrorism*, 11(1), 65–87.

Mauleon, E., 2018. 'Worst suspicions confirmed: Government reports show domestic anti-terrorism efforts target minorities', *Just Security*, 3 October. Available at www.justsecurity.org/60940/worst-suspicions-confirmed-government-reports-show-domestic-anti-terrorism-efforts-target-minorities/ (accessed 19 November 2018).

McCants, W., Watts, C., 2012. 'US strategy for countering violent extremism: An assessment', Foreign Policy Research Institute e-notes, December. Available at www.files.ethz.ch/isn/162046/McCants_Watts_-_Countering_Violent_Extremism.pdf (accessed 10 September 2018).

Montemayor, S., 2016. 'Minneapolis ISIL trial opens with tense scene between attorney and defendant', *Minneapolis Star Tribune*, 9 May. Available at www.duluthnewstribune.com/news/4028505-minneapolis-isil-trial-opens-tense-scene-between-attorney-and (accessed 21 February, 2020).

Montopoli, B., 2009. 'DHS report warns of right wing extremists', *CBS News*, 14 April. Available at www.cbsnews.com/news/dhs-report-warns-of-right-wing-extremists/ (accessed 10 September 2018).

Mulloy, D.J., 2005. *American Extremism: History, Politics, and the Militia Movement*. Routledge, London and New York.

Myre, G., 2017a. 'What is, and isn't, considered domestic terrorism?', *NPR*, 2 October. Available at www.npr.org/2017/10/02/555170250/what-is-and-isnt-considered-domestic-terrorism (accessed 10 September 2018).

Myre, G., 2017b. 'Why the government can't bring terrorism charges in Charlottesville', *NPR*, 14 August. Available at www.npr.org/2017/08/14/543462676/why-the-govt-cant-bring-terrorism-charges-in-charlottesville (accessed 10 September 2018).

Neumann, P.R., 2013. 'The trouble with radicalization', *International Affairs*, 89(4), 873–893.

New America Foundation, 2018. *What is the Threat to the United States Today?* Available at www.newamerica.org/in-depth/terrorism-in-america/what-threat-united-states-today/#americas-layered-defenses (accessed 10 November 2018).

Patel, F., Lindsay, L. and DenUyl, S., 2018. 'Countering violent extremism in the Trump era', Brennan Center, 15 June. Available at www.brennancenter.org/analysis/countering-violent-extremism-trump-era (accessed 12 September 2018).

PBS, 2017a. 'Why armed militia groups are surging across the nation', 19 April. Available at www.pbs.org/newshour/show/armed-militia-groups-surging-across-nation (accessed 10 September 2018).

PBS, 2017b. 'American patriot: Inside the armed uprising against the federal government', *PBS Frontline*, 16 May. Available at www.pbs.org/wgbh/frontline/film/american-patriot-inside-the-armed-uprising-against-the-federal-government/ (accessed 10 September 2018).

PBS, 2018. 'Documenting hate: New American Nazis', *PBS Frontline*, 20 November. Available at www.pbs.org/wgbh/frontline/film/documenting-hate-new-american-nazis/ (accessed 27 November 2018).

Perlman, M., 2017. 'The key difference between "nationalists" and "supremacists"', *Columbia Journalism Review*, 14 August. Available at www.cjr.org/language_corner/nationalist-supremacist.php (accessed 10 November 2018).

Pilkington, E., 2018. 'NYPD settles lawsuit after illegally spying on Muslims', *Guardian*, 5 April. Available at www.theguardian.com/world/2018/apr/05/nypd-muslim-surveillance-settlement (accessed 10 September 2018).

Potok, M., 2010. 'Rage on the right', *Southern Poverty Law Center Intelligence Report*, March. Available at www.splcenter.org/fighting-hate/intelligence-report/2010/rage-right (accessed 10 September 2018).

Price, M., 2016. 'FBI guidelines weaken separation of community outreach and intelligence gathering efforts', *Just Security*, 8 June. Available at www.justsecurity. org/31440/fbi-guidelines-weaken-separation-community-outreach-intelligence-gathering-efforts/ (accessed 10 September 2018).

Rathod, S., 2016. 'Why the law turns a blind eye to militias', *Mother Jones*, 25 October. Available at www.motherjones.com/politics/2016/10/paramilitary-militia-laws-training/ (accessed 10 September 2018).

Sawyer, L., 2016. 'Shooting of Muslim men will be investigated as possible hate crime', *Minneapolis Star Tribune*, 30 June. Available at www.startribune.com/cair-to-hold-news-conference-on-alleged-hate-crime-in-minneapolis/385086311/ (accessed 20 February, 2020).

Schachtel, J., 2017. 'White House keeps failed "countering violent extremism" program', 28 July. Available at www.conservativereview.com/news/white-house-keeps-failed-countering-violent-extremism-program/ (accessed 14 November 2018).

Selod, S., 2015. 'Citizenship denied: The racialization of Muslim American men and women post-9/11', *Critical Sociology*, 41(1), 77–95.

Simi, P., 2013. 'Cycles of right-wing terror in the US', in Von Mering, S. and McCarty, T.W. (eds), *Right-wing Radicalism Today: Perspectives from Europe and the US*. Routledge, New York and London, pp. 144–161.

Sullivan, K., 2016. 'Primed to fight the government', *Washington Post*, 16 May. Available at www.washingtonpost.com/sf/national/2016/05/21/armed-with-guns-and-constitutions-the-patriot-movement-sees-america-under-threat/?noredirect=on&utm_term=.233f7580a27c (accessed 10 September 2018).

Toosi, N., 2017. 'Tillerson spurns $80 million to counter ISIS, Russian propaganda', *Politico.com*, 2 August. Available at www.politico.com/story/2017/08/02/tillerson-isis-russia-propaganda-241218 (accessed 10 September 2018).

Trump, D., 2016. 'Trump says Minnesota "has suffered enough" from immigration', *The Washington Post*, 6 November. Available at www.washingtonpost.com/video/politics/trump-says-minnesota-has-suffered-enough-from-immigration/2016/11/06/2ef1dfa2-a499–11e6-ba46–53db57f0e351_video.html?utm_term=.cdbf0d1ddaf3 (accessed 10 November 2018).

US Department of State, 2016. *Department of State and USAID Joint Strategy on Countering Violent Extremism*, May. Available at https://pdf.usaid.gov/pdf_docs/PBAAE503.pdf (accessed 10 September 2018).

Varvelli, A. (ed.), 2016. *Jihadist Hotbeds: Understanding Local Radicalisation Processes*. Edizioni Epoke – IPSI, Milan.

Von Mering, S., McCarty, T.W. (eds), 2013. *Right-wing Radicalism Today: Perspectives from Europe and the US*. Routledge, New York and London.

Welsh, T., 2017. 'Domestic militia groups plummet 40 percent amid Trump rise', *Miami Herald*, 15 February. Available at www.miamiherald.com/news/nation-world/national/article132948254.html (accessed 10 September 2018).

White House, 2011. *Empowering Local Partners to Prevent Violent Extremism in the United States*, 3 August. Available at https://obamawhitehouse.archives.gov/the-press-office/2011/08/03/empowering-local-partners-prevent-violent-extremism-united-states (accessed 10 September 2018).

White House, 2015. *Fact Sheet: The White House Summit on Countering Violent Extremism*, 18 February. Available at https://obamawhitehouse.archives.gov/the-press-office/2015/02/18/fact-sheet-white-house-summit-countering-violent-extremism (accessed 10 September 2018).

Wiles, T., 2018. 'Acquitted, convicted, fined or free: After the Oregon standoff', *High Country News*, 12 April. Available at www.hcn.org/articles/malheur-national-wildlife-refuge-acquitted-convicted-fined-or-free-malheur-sentences (accessed 10 November 2018).

Wilson, C., 2018. 'Occupation leader Ryan Payne sentenced to 37 months in prison', *Oregon Public Broadcasting*, 27 February. Available at www.opb.org/news/series/burns-oregon-standoff-bundy-militia-news-updates/ryan-payne-sentence/ (accessed 10 September 2018).

Yuen, L., Xaykaothao, D., 2016. 'Judge sentences three men to decades in prison in ISIS trial', *MPR News*, 16 November. Available at www.mprnews.org/story/2016/11/16/third-day-of-isis-trial (accessed 10 September 2018).

Appendix 11.A   Countering violent extremism grants funded by the Department of Homeland Security (data from Patel et al., 2018)

Grant recipient (state)	Programme name	Change in funding in US$ (Obama to Trump)	Targeted group(s)	Policy document	Type of programme	Evaluation
Alameda, CA County Sheriff's office (CA)	Operation E Pluribus Unum	0 to 499,125	Current or recent prisoners, mostly Muslim. Approx. 120 individuals	https://www.dhs.gov/sites/default/files/publications/EMW-2016-CA-APP-00087%20Full%20Application.pdf	Deradicalisation, social service, intervention	Yes: internal and external
Denver, CO Police Department (CO)	Countering Violent Extremism Collaborative Grant Program	240,000 to 481,313	"Faith communities, diverse communities, refugee communities, LGBTQ communities and Black Lives Matter in Denver" (Patel et al., 2018)	https://www.dhs.gov/sites/default/files/publications/EMW-2016-CA-APP-00381%20Full%20Application.pdf	Intervention, community outreach	Yes: participants and police both
Hennepin County Sheriff's Office (MN)	Community Engagement: A Frontline Strategy for Countering Violent Extremism	0 to 347,600	Somali, Liberian, Oromo, East African, Native American and Latino communities in Hennepin County and the Minneapolis area	https://www.dhs.gov/sites/default/files/publications/EMW-2016-CA-APP-00081%20Full%20Application.pdf	Intervention; community outreach; CVE online	Yes, including data on online reporting
Las Vegas, NV Metropolitan Police Department (NV)	Southern Nevada Community Resiliency and Intervention Coalition	425,000 to 500,000	14–24-year-olds in Southern Nevada, with a focus on Muslim and refugee youth	https://www.dhs.gov/sites/default/files/publications/EMW-2016-CA-APP-00102%20Full%20Application.pdf	Intervention, social service	Unclear, though says tools to be developed

Grant recipient (state)	Programme name	Change in funding in US$ (Obama to Trump)	Targeted group(s)	Policy document	Type of programme	Evaluation
Seattle, WA Police Department (WA)	Countering Violent Extremism Program	0 to 409,390	'Immigrants and refugees', 'disengaged youth' aged 5–18 and 'disenfranchised Seattleites' (this includes African American, Native American, Latino, Asian/Pacific Islander and homeless populations) (Patel et al., 2018)	https://www.dhs.gov/sites/default/files/publications/EMW-2016-CA-APP-00236%20Full%20Application.pdf	Community outreach, social service	Yes: surveys
Masjid Mohammad Inc (DC)	Developing Credible, Authentic and Constructive Muslim Voices to Prevent Extremism	450,000 to 531,195	Muslims in DC and nationwide	https://www.dhs.gov/sites/default/files/publications/EMW-2016-CA-APP-00253%20Full%20Application.pdf	CVE online	Yes: participation rates and data assessment
Crisis Intervention of Houston Inc (TX)	Countering Violent Extremism Training and Engagement Initiative	400,000 to 500,000	810,000 youth of the Greater Houston region and nearly 1.5 million family households, with a focus on Muslim communities	https://www.dhs.gov/sites/default/files/publications/EMW-2016-CA-APP-00158%20Full%20Application.pdf	Intervention, social service	Yes: activities, workshops, surveys
Global Peace Foundation (NJ)	CVE Train-the-Trainer and Cross Community Engagement	150,000 to 453,497	Muslims; 'immigrants and other marginalized populations' and at-risk young 'Latinos, African-American, Asian Indians, Caucasian and Arabs' in Camden, Jersey City and Peterson	https://www.dhs.gov/sites/default/files/publications/EMW-2016-CA-APP-00104%20Full%20Application.pdf	Intervention; CVE online; community outreach	Yes: semi-annual survey, focus groups

(Continued)

Appendix 11.A   Continued

Grant recipient (state)	Programme name	Change in funding in US$ (Obama to Trump)	Targeted group(s)	Policy document	Type of programme	Evaluation
Heartland Democracy Centre (MN)	Empowering U	165,435 to 423,340	Minnesota's Somali population	https://www.dhs.gov/sites/default/files/publications/EMW-2016-CA-APP-00401%20Full%20Application.pdf	Intervention	Surveys to evaluate mental health issues
Nashville, TN International Centre for Empowerment (TN)	Proactive Engagement to Achieve Community Empowerment (PEACE)	0 to 445,110	500+ 'New Americans' (i.e., refugees, immigrants and children of immigrants) in the middle Tennessee area	https://www.dhs.gov/sites/default/files/publications/EMW-2016-CA-APP-00066%20Full%20Application.pdf	Intervention, social service	Yes: DHS CVE framework; youth assessment
Tuesday's Children (NY)	Project COMMON BOND: Building Resilience and Long-Term Healing in Youth, Families & Communities	147,154 to 386,670	Individuals, especially young people aged 15–20, families and communities, who have been impacted by terrorism, violent extremism or war	https://www.dhs.gov/sites/default/files/publications/EMW-2016-CA-APP-00264%20Full%20Application.pdf	Social service, CVE online	Yes: Surveys, programme evaluation, expert consultations
National Governors' Association for Best Practices (DC)	State Approaches to Violent Extremism (S.A.V.E.) Policy Academy	0 to 500,000	Governors who will implement the programme's 'CVE roadmap'	https://www.dhs.gov/sites/default/files/publications/EMW-2016-CA-APP-00276%20Full%20Application.pdf	Intervention	Yes: regular communication
Police Foundation (MA)	Youth and Police Initiative Plus (YPIP)	463,185 to 484,835	120 Somali immigrant youth and their families in Boston's Roxbury neighbourhood	https://www.dhs.gov/sites/default/files/publications/EMW-2016-CA-APP-00112%20Full%20Application.pdf	Community outreach; social service; potentially intervention	Yes: conducted by Police Foundation

Appendix 11.A Continued

Grant recipient (state)	Programme name	Change in funding in US$ (Obama to Trump)	Targeted group(s)	Policy document	Type of programme	Evaluation
University of San Diego (CA)	Connected Youth-Resilient Communities Initiative	0 to 634,769	Somali, Iraqi and refugee youth in San Diego and El Cajon, CA	https://www.dhs.gov/sites/default/files/publications/EMW-2016-CA-APP-00212%20Full%20Application.pdf	Community outreach, social service	Institute for Peace and Justice at UCSD will evaluate goals and objectives
Houston, TX Mayor's Office of Public Safety and Homeland Security (TX)	Countering Violent Extremism Training and Engagement Initiative	400,000 to 500,000	'810,000 youth of the Greater Houston region and nearly 1.5 million family households, with a focus on Muslim communities'		Intervention, social service	Some, including surveys, but unclear what will be measured
Massachusetts Executive Office of Public Safety and Security (MA)	New Freedoms Intervention	0 to 500,000	139 men being released from maximum security prison in Massachusetts	https://www.dhs.gov/sites/default/files/publications/EMW-2016-CA-APP-00336%20Full%20Application.pdf	Deradicalisation, social service	Somewhat: various evaluation objectives mentioned

(Continued)

Appendix 11.A   Continued

Total funding = $10 million each year in 2016 and 2017 (all data from Patel et al., 2018)

Organisations that rejected grants or withdrew their applications after the Trump administration's shift in priorities (2017):

- Ka Joog Nonprofit Organization ($499,998 to 0)
- Muslim American Leadership Alliance ($40,000 to 0)
- Unity Productions Foundation ($396,585 to 0)
- Leaders Advancing and Helping Communities ($500,000 to 0)
- Claremont School of Theology ($800,000 to 0)

Organisations that had funding withdrawn by the Trump administration after review of CVE (2017):

- University of North Carolina, Chapel Hill ($866,687 to 0)
- Project Help, Nevada, Inc. ($150,000 to 0)
- Music in Common ($159,000 to 0)
- Life After Hate Inc. ($400,000 to 0)
- Coptic Orthodox Charities ($150,000 to 0)
- Muslim Public Affairs Council Foundation ($393,800 to 0)
- Los Angeles, CA Mayor's Office of Public Safety ($825,000 to $425,000)

12

The CVE paradox: inapplicability and necessity in Bosnia and Herzegovina

Tanja Dramac Jiries

Introduction

Bosnia and Herzegovina's (BiH) war was the first 'never again in Europe' public discourse to be broken after World War II had devastated the continent (Andjelic, 2003; Bieber, 2010; Djokić and Ker-Lindsay, 2010; Dzihic and Hamilton, 2012; Glenny, 1996, 2001; Malcolm, 1994). The small, heart-shaped country in the Western Balkans was the epicentre of a nearly four-year conflict, one of the bloodiest of the 1990s, which only ended following American intervention. The Dayton Peace Accords (DPA) proved to be an effective truce. Soon after the war's end, Bosnia held its first democratic elections, internally displaced persons and refugees began returning back to their pre-war homes, and the International Criminal Tribunal for the former Yugoslavia issued the first indictments for crimes against humanity.

A number of foreign fighters from North Africa, the Middle East and the Gulf States who had fought for BiH in the 1990s war received honorary citizenship for their services. After the US government launched a global 'war on terror' after 9/11, Bosnia again became a country of interest. After the 9/11 attacks, in an effort to demonstrate that it was a US ally, the BiH government stripped the majority of these individuals of that privilege and forced them to leave the country (Mustapha, 2013). Since then, a number of Bosniaks have joined conservative Salafi communities led primarily by foreign fighter veterans who had been allowed to stay in the country because of marriage or who had studied in Saudi Arabia or Malaysia.[1] At the same time, when ISIS arose and flourished, more than 250 individuals left Bosnia to join the ranks of its armies without any prior connection to Syria or Iraq.[2] Although the Salafi movement in BiH has several thousand estimated members, it is important to note that not all are considered violent, and they are far from being a monolithic group.[3] It is, however, a reasonable assertion that all 250 of those who left for Syria and Iraq adhered to the most conservative Islam practised in Bosnia.[4]

Today, many years after the war, the socio-political situation in BiH is far from stable and flourishing. With the highest unemployment rate in Europe, rampant corruption, political party and state capture, and inefficient and dead-locked state institutions, BiH is the leading underperformer in the region and on the continent. In terms of politics, the lack of a cohesive vision of a common future and resentment of the past create an atmosphere in which elections held every two years serve only as megaphones for ethno-nationalist leaders to remind their constituencies who threatens them and who will stand up for them in the event of another war.

In such circumstances, any policy agenda or security strategy that aims to deter violence is important. In short, the goal should be at least to prevent armed conflict and at best to build a long-lasting peace. The essential problem with BiH's only State Strategy against Terrorism for 2015–2020 is that it is very nar-rowly defined towards violent Islamist extremism and ignores various other rad-ical groups that permeate the country, including those with political connections. The Strategy also fails to address inflammatory hate speech, violent nationalistic groups and divisive education agendas plagued with historical revisionism (Government of Bosnia and Herzegovina, 2015). Since the current Strategy will soon end and the government will consider a new one in 2019, this chapter argues for abandoning the current approach in favour of strengthening existing peace education and violence-reduction programmes that are national responses to domestic constituencies and not the result of external pressure from Europe and the US. Drawing from the literature that deals with 'Counter-productive CVE/CT' as well as identifying the deficiencies of externally driven democracies and troubles for peacebuilding in such contexts, the following discussion argues for recalibrated holistic peacebuilding strategies rooted in indigenous needs and drive from within the country.

The BiH countering violent extremism (CVE)/ counter-terrorism (CT) strategy

The study of CVE and CT has spawned many critical responses that look at the deficiencies of suggested approaches and find the reductionist and often misled efforts to be 'counterproductive CVE' (Aziz, 2017). In an effort to address it, one early response by scholars was to approach it as a multi-layered and multifaceted process that could be carried out through the capacity building of both govern-ment and non-governmental actors, emphasising the latter to 'soften the approach' (Crelinsten, 2007; Mroz, 2009). In addition, many scholars highlighted the significant erosion of civil liberties and deterioration of human rights that resulted from dense CVE strategies, which actually generated further grievances and backlash (Hanlon, 2007; Hocking, 2007). A more straightforward approach has come from scholars who viewed mainstream CVE as an extension of failed democratisation efforts overseas (de Graaf, 2010). As an externally driven democracy and a semi protectorate, Bosnia had to address the challenge of its citizens travelling to take part in the wars in Syria and Iraq while it was receiving assistance from the Organization for Security and Co-operation in Europe (OSCE) and European Union (EU). When the foreign fighters from the region departed to Syria and Iraq *en masse*, the governments in the region, including BiH, amended their existing legislation to criminalise the participation of their citizens in foreign wars. In addition, most countries eventually opted for the urgent adaptation of national strategies to counter terrorism and violent extremism. These strategies relied heavily on international and EU-facilitated approaches that nominally necessitate multilevel and multisector involvement, including security structures, local communities, media, academia, civil society and other actors, in a joint effort to counter radicalisation that leads to violence (Government of Bosnia and Herzegovina, 2015). In addition to adopting new national strategies, each country appointed a special coordinator to oversee these responses as well as coordinating groups consisting of local experts to advise and inform the work of the coordinator and other working groups (Government of Bosnia and Herzegovina, 2015). Furthermore, Bosnia established two inter-agency bodies tasked with coordinating efforts to prevent and combat terrorism and violent extremism. The first was the Supervisory Body for Monitoring the Implementation of the Strategy and Action Plans; the second, working at the operational level, was the Task Force for Combatting Terrorism, which consisted of representatives from all levels of the government. The Action Plan includes measures aimed at rehabilitating and reintegrating former foreign fighters, but these have yet to be operationalised.

As defined by the country's Council of Ministers' Strategy for countering terrorism for the 2015–2020 period, 'the greatest present threat to safety and security interests of Bosnia and Herzegovina, comes from the following terrorist organizations, or individuals and groups inspired by their ideologies: Al Qaeda, ISIL and Al-Nusra Front' (Government of Bosnia and Herzegovina, 2015). The only state strategy promulgated during the five-year period that deals with violent extremism challenges is significant, so the nature and repercussions of its terminology are crucial in keeping the peace in the country. The document was drafted in consultation with civil society and with the support of the OSCE. Bibi van Ginkel and Steven Westervelt (2009) argue that regional organisations (such as the OSCE) are uniquely suited to ensure that states adopt legitimate counter-terrorism measures, thus avoiding ethical bottlenecks. As the legislation was adopted, the OSCE stressed that 'through its activities in the area of countering violent extremism (CVE), the Mission directly supports the prevention pillar of the Strategy and provides targeted assistance in other areas. The Mission will continue with these activities in the upcoming period whilst streamlining CVE within its human rights, rule of law, governance and education programs' (OSCE, 2017).

While the Strategy does not address CVE per se, the OSCE Mission, under whose guidance and support the document was drafted and promoted, makes no distinction between countering terrorism and countering and preventing violent extremism; in fact, it promoted the document as such – a blended approach that equalises terrorism and violent extremism. The Strategy addresses violent extremism and radicalisation that can lead to terrorism but, at the same time, it also declares that, as an aspirant state with the Stabilization and Associ-ation Agreement with the EU coming into force, 'Bosnia and Herzegovina also has a legal obligation to harmonize its legislation with the EU legislation' (Government of Bosnia and Herzegovina, 2015). While it might hold true that the Strategy serves an additional goal, namely, to bring BiH closer to candidate status for EU membership and closer to Euro-Atlantic integration as a whole, one must consider the impact of EU conditionality on already fragile democracies.

Simply put, there is no concrete evidence that the EU's current approach to CVE is working when it comes to addressing the challenge of violent extremism. To that end, there is a wealth of scholarship that suggests precisely the opposite – that the EU approach has failed and needs to be rethought. Lasse Lindekilde's study (2015) on measures implemented to prevent violent extremism in Den-mark, for example, is but one of many empirical studies that questions the cur-rent approach by an EU member state that is considered to be the most proactive and far-reaching; it has even worked on the individual level, through mentoring programmes. It comes as no surprise that Bosnia's Strategy relies heavily on har-monising its approach with one of its mentors, but the problem does not rest there. The EU has had its fair share of examples of tolerating or turning a blind eye to autocratic governments in the region and their deficiencies as long as they deliver on EU harmonised legislation and tick boxes that are, in a nutshell, inconsistent with the complexities of the problems it is trying to solve.

Furthermore, the goal of the Strategy is to 'counter all forms of extremist and terrorist activity respecting the values of democracy, rule of law and human rights and freedoms – to make Bosnia and Herzegovina a place safe for the life and work of all its citizens and others within its territories' (Government of Bosnia and Herzegovina, 2015). It further states that 'Bosnia and Herzegovina is essentially facing and is to counter the very same global terrorist threats as all other member states in the Anti-Terrorist and Anti-ISIL Coalition' (Government of Bosnia and Herzegovina, 2015). A major deficiency of the Bosnian approach is that, due to a sense of urgency, the government not only adopted laws criminalising the departure of foreign fighters but also manufactured a strategy without first ensuring proper public debate and contextualising the issue prior to putting it forward for adoption by Parliament. The authors of the document did not consider the specific Bosnian factors that could pose other threats to the security of the country, particularly that recruits to radical Islamist forces are, by and large, fuelled precisely by other types of extremism in the country that are propelled by the country's complex and difficult past. It is now understood that 'reciprocal extremism' permeates the Bosnian public discourse.[5] The country is dominated by extreme voices and groups that are violent and, more often than not, politicised.[6] Embarrassed by the US embassy in Sarajevo being attacked a few years ago by local extremists and the stigma of the 1990s from 'importing foreign fighters' into its army, Bosnia's officials have made every effort to make it clear to the international community and its US and European allies that the state has opted to counter rather than endorse terrorists. Bosnian politicians were keen to prove where their global loyalty lies, given some initial glitches with extraditing war veterans in the early 2000s and the reluctance to actually strip them of the citizenship they received for their service.

The main shortcoming of Bosnia's CVE/CT strategy is that it does not account for all types of groups that encourage and galvanise violent extremism – particularly right-wing extremist organisations and paramilitary groups (Zuvela, 2018). The Strategy does not take a hardline approach as was the case with the UK and US programmes that surveilled and pressured their Muslim communities (Kundnani, 2015). These top-down repressive measures were employed in places where Muslim communities are a minority, whereas in Bosnia, according to the latest (2013) poll, Muslims make up the majority of the population. As a result, any attempt to blatantly subject the majority to such an approach would be outright dismissed and fiercely opposed. However, as Arun Kundnani and others (Hassain, 2008; Kundnani, 2015) have observed, the possibility of identifying 'suspect Muslim communities' in the form of the many Salafi communities that reside in BiH to represent a 'potential threat', despite the fact that not all advocate for violence, does label one community over another and further securitise the issue.

Given the long-standing strong influence of civil society organisations on understanding public perspectives, Bosnia's policymakers and academics ought to be more precise and deliberate when assessing possible threats within the country. For example, it is well documented that during the 1990s conflict Serbian and Croatian paramilitaries closely tied to secret police units utilised sports connections to recruit and radicalise young men who committed some of the worst atrocities in Bosnia (Newman, 2012). Today, the Minister of Security is warning of the presence of similar paramilitary groups who recently marched in full combat gear into the administrative capital of Banja Luka. The highly contentious military parade marked a disputed national holiday in one of the country's two autonomous regions (Zuvela, 2018). In fact, a number of far-right groups registered in Serbia and Croatia are also operating in Bosnia through their ethnic counterparts, exploiting freedom of the internet and online outreach capabilities to engage in illegal military training offline.[7] The growth of extreme nationalism and the emergence and tolerance of illiberal and far-right civil society groups are challenges that are not being tackled strategically. These threats do not appear even once in Bosnia's State Security Strategy, which showcases an absolute lack of understanding by policymakers about how Bosnian history, culture, social relations and political systems generate certain societal outcomes. Without debating which extremism is more dangerous or how it lacks a plethora of empirical evidence, it is quite apparent that the state's current CVE Strategy is deficient in its framework of analysis and is in immediate need of revision. In addition, a deliberate ethno-nationalist paradigm started the Bosnian war, so the imminent danger lays precisely in that issue. Finally, there is little evidence to demonstrate how in fact the government is implementing the Strategy. Two annual reports do not reveal much more than regular meetings and conferences, and there has been no update on the implementation of the Action Plan.

The paradox

As demonstrated in the paragraphs above, the main paradox of the BiH CVE Strategy, aside from the necessity to protect its citizens while doing quite the opposite, is that it does not shelter its constituency from its most imminent danger – an extreme, divisive and nationalistic public discourse. Mentioned a couple of times, the document recognises hate speech as a threat but does not prescribe any penalty for it. Policymakers took *one* illustrative example of a hard security threat and portrayed it as the *only* security threat, which in turn nourished an encompassing nationalistic paradigm. The document evokes the need to produce a comprehensive state strategy that would foresee and include all soft and hard security threats. Such a document should not reinforce impunity for ethnic leaders but, on the contrary, properly sanction them, thus preventing the segregation paradigm from becoming normalised. Singling out one issue in a complex country like Bosnia is short-sighted and dangerous.

Once the 'conscience' and epicentre of the international community, Bosnia is no longer the focus of international attention, making it more prone to the influences of ethnic leaders who masquerade their political ineffectiveness by provoking ethnic bigotry. Perhaps the single most worrying sign of Bosnia's deterioration is the level to which historical revisionism about the 1990s conflict and other wars in the country's history permeates public discourse. It is the narratives of past wars that are being used to rekindle and spread anger and fear among ethnic groups through classic 'divide and conquer' rhetoric, thus inspiring violent extremists. A principal reason why the country is unable to move forward is a lack of progress in facing the past and its legacies. Why is it paramount to remember and underline the role of the UN International Criminal Tribunal for the former Yugoslavia (ICTY) in a discussion about CVE? Why do we need to dig into the past and instruments for dealing with the past to understand violent extremism today?

With the ICTY's 2017 closure came additional challenges that the country has not been able to overcome. Bringing perpetrators to trial to face their war-related charges is understood as a *precondition* for effective peacebuilding efforts. The ad-hoc tribunal was established in 1993; it was the first court of its kind since the WWII Nuremberg trials of a former Nazi official for some of the most egregious crimes against humanity. The court had convicted approximately ninety people, including former presidents, generals and other military and secret service leaders, most of whom were given lengthy prison sentences in an effort to put an end to the culture of impunity in the region. The ICTY has often been criticised by many for a variety of reasons; however, nothing can lessen its importance and the incredible body of evidence that it accumulated and archived. Even after some controversial verdicts, such as in the cases of Croatian General Ante Gotovina, who was initially sentenced to twenty-four years in prison but was later released on appeal days prior to Croatia joining the EU, and Serbian General Momcilo Perisic, who was first sentenced to twenty-seven years and later released, the ICTY laid a foundation for evidence-based truth-seeking that would influence the rebuilding process of societies across the Balkans. Even the court's staunchest critics can agree that, had it been left to national tribunals to prosecute war criminals, the results would have been much more modest and the quest for justice would have been trivialised.

Paralleling these obstacles was the fearful outcry against the ICTY's involvement and convictions by local political leaders, who made sure to undermine, sabotage and discredit its work. Despite the ICTY's verdicts and lengthy processes, there has not been progress in normalising public discourse on dealing with the past or reforming the education system to institutionalise the tribunal's legacy and set a course that would heal society rather than reversing its work and the work of other peacebuilding programmes initiated at the war's end (Kunovich and Hodson, 2016; Russo, 2000; Torsti, 2007).

Once the ICTY's initial verdicts were handed down, politicians railed unsanctioned and unchecked about victimhood and the politics of spite. Instead of facing the past in a constructive and productive manner, the country witnessed the propagation of policies like 'two schools under one roof', the practice of seg-regating education in one of Bosnia's entities. This practice was largely ignored by the international community, even though it must have understood its far-reaching consequences. Public figures and the media also fostered the glorifica-tion and normalisation of war criminals and far-fetched historical revisionism. Just how far the reinterpretation and other processes have advanced is demon-strated by the fact that Bosnian students study three different versions of the so-called 'national group of subjects', including language, geography and history (Soldo et al., 2017). 'The Others' – members of the country's other ethnic or religious groups – are typically presented through the prism of the enemy, thwarting any possibility for the reconciliation and reconstruction of a multicul-tural society (Torsti, 2007). In cooperation with compliant educators, public officials continue to name public places, student dormitories and schools after convicted war criminals and proven Nazi collaborators.

Current reports on CVE initiatives and activities in the country call for pre-ventative and counteractive measures against extremism to be directed through the school system, noting that informal education, camps, youth exchanges and other youth-oriented activities can have an impact on at-risk youth (Perry, 2016). The problem with this recommendation is that, in a segregated education system, CVE-related initiatives are likely to be segregated as well; as such, if these recommendations are included in the state's strategy, they will be doomed to produce only more marginalisation and stigmatisation.

Bosnia's ethnic leaders continue to engage in public denial, justification and trivialisation of major atrocities committed during the war. The aim is the nor-malisation and desensitisation of this political practice, which promotes societal polarisation and further segregation. Due to the institutional make-up of the country as set forth by the rigid DPA, which stridently divided territories and competences along ethnic lines, the post-war political climate has been particu-larly conducive to the use of hate speech. In addition, politicians continue to frequently employ the ridiculing of other communities' war traumas and expe-riences as a political strategy. Within this context, contentious positions on war-time events and war-time figures are frequently instrumentalised in order to exacerbate ethnic antipathies. The ultimate goal of these political practices is, of course, to win votes, given that these ethnic leaders deliberately set themselves up as protectors of their own ethnic groups. But over the long term, their goals are not so short-sighted – they are breeding and institutionalising separation and inspiring secessionism.

In addition, regional political leaders often exaggerate the number of sus-pected terrorists or extreme Islamists that have left Bosnia, doing irreparable damage not only to the country's reputation internationally, but thwarting any progress made towards reconciliation thus far. The presidents of Croatia and the Czech Republic have both made public claims about 'thousands of foreign fighters who are coming back to Bosnia and will cause war', which was obviously not true.[8] By making up numbers and highlighting the issue of Islamic extremism, they are further dividing and provoking fear among ethnic groups.

Rethinking CVE as a part of rethinking peacebuilding in Bosnia

In addition to traditional peacekeeping operations and preventive diplomacy and mediated negotiations around the world, the functions of the UN forces during the post-Cold War era expanded considerably to include peacemaking and peacebuilding as effective approaches to ensure self-sustainable and peaceful post-conflict transitions. Former UN Secretary-General Boutros Boutros-Ghali described these additional functions in detail in his reports *An Agenda for Peace* (1992) and *Supplement to an Agenda for Peace* (1995) (UN Secretary-General, 1992, 1995). Peacebuilding, as defined by these strategies, is an active process of design and implementation that considers activities aimed at sustaining peace over the long-term with a clear focus on reducing chances for the deterioration into further conflict. Peacebuilding is seen as a broader policy framework that is context-dependent and strengthens the connection between related efforts of conflict prevention, peacemaking, peacekeeping, recovery and development.

Peacebuilding also serves as an educational mechanism that is a part of a collective and sustained effort to build permanent peace and to prevent communities from ever relapsing into armed conflict. Many scholars claim that it is understood that there is no preference of one activity over another, since the one that will most likely reap success is the one that creates an environment supportive of integrating civil society, repairing damaged societal fabric and reconciling and facing past opponents. A successful strategy is also one that addresses the underlying dynamic which enabled conflict to become possible in the first place, and which successfully instituted the rule of law to enforce civil liberties and encourage peace activism and education to thrive and flourish. Researchers and practitioners have found that the precondition for any successful peacebuilding process is local ownership of the process and a deep native understanding of the variables and contexts that lead to conflict and peace (De Coning, 2013). In this context, if long-lasting peace is understood as merely the absence of war, then twenty-three years after the DPA was signed, Bosnia is experiencing peace. However, just a cursory glance at the current state of Bosnia, including the political party capture, endemic corruption, number of ethnic-related incidents, hate speech and other worrying signs, clearly demonstrates that the country is not on the path to permanent peace (Chandler, 2000).

Although the term 'frozen conflict' had its roots in the breakaway crises across the former Soviet Union in the 1990s, the definition is applicable in the case of Bosnia as well. The DPA that ended the violence in 1995 in Bosnia allowed for the continuation of war by other means, given the agreement's deficiencies (Aggestam and Björkdahl, 2011). In other words, a major element of the term is the inactivity or ineffectiveness of processes to be resolved (Grant, 2017). Critics of the DPA agree that the treaty was necessary at the time and efficient at securing a ceasefire, but shortsighted vision prevented it from being more flexible and inclusive of all the changes that require a sustainable peace (Chandler, 2000). Two decades after, DPA's favourable treatment of the 'three constituent people', group rights and rigid power-sharing arrangements favours ethnic lines only. In addition, as notable experts have observed, the situation in post-Dayton Bosnia can be described as a frozen conflict due to an international presence that tolerates an imperfect peace as long as it sees incremental reforms (Perry, 2009).

As per Roland Paris (2004, p. 6) who examined fourteen peacebuilding missions following 1990s conflicts, including the one in Bosnia, 'peacebuilding was nothing less than an enormous experiment in social engineering, aimed at creating the domestic conditions for durable peace within countries just emerged from civil wars'. He further ascertains that peacebuilding missions in the 1990s sought to transform war-shattered states into 'liberal market democracies' as quickly as possible' (Paris, 2004, p. 6). Johan Galtung's definition of peacebuilding (1969) is very broad and, beyond armed conflict, includes the observance of human security as well as socio-economic development, combined with other elements. Galtung also argues for a distinction between 'negative peace' and 'positive peace', which is quite relevant for Bosnia. Negative peace refers to the absence of violence; when a truce is enacted and operationalised, a negative peace will supervene. This effectively happened in Bosnia following the signature of the Dayton Accords. In contrast, 'positive peace' denotes constructive aspects such as restoration of relationships, creation of a system that serves the constituency and repair of social bonds and the social fabric as a whole – which effectively did not take place in Bosnia.

However, given the problem of externally governed democracies like Bosnia, the most fitting definition and approach to peacebuilding is offered by Catherine Goetze (2016), who sees it mostly in the context of Western domination and global inequalities. Goetze believes that 'The people, organizations, institutions, and agencies that claim to build peace in foreign lands exist and act on the grounds of specific patterns of power and domination in the world' (Goetze, p. 2). This is not to reject outright peacebuilding as a concept, but merely to recognise it as it is: externally driven with little local ownership in Bosnia and largely a failure, given the current state. With Galtung's lack of 'positive peace' and Goetze's concern about the social reproduction of power structures in globalisation processes, how can peacebuilding efforts be expanded to absorb CVE efforts in Bosnia?

Although CVE in its various definitional applications is not necessarily associated with Islamic radicals, it is now impossible to claim that it has not been indelibly linked with the 30,000 foreign fighters who left nearly ninety countries to aid various rebel groups in the Syrian civil war. CVE has *de facto* become a Western application of the new 'war on terror' paradigm. Indeed, as commentators have pointed out, 'if you blinked, you might have missed it – the Obama administration has unofficially rebranded the "war on terror" phrase that dominated public discourse throughout the Bush administration. The replacement phrase, carefully chosen, is "CVE" – Countering Violent Extremism' (Ambinder, 2010).

During this time, the proliferation of CT discourses emerged again. According to some scholars, extremism is defined as a convergence of activities, attitudes, beliefs and characters which are not normal, ordinary or mainstream (Coleman and Bartoli, 2015, p. 2). By the time an alarmed academia once again warned that CVE and its sister acronyms were fuelling Islamophobia in an increasingly xenophobic environment of the Western democracies, it was already too late.[9] A number of initiatives and grantmaking policies to support civil society's CVE efforts were put in place without taking into account the limitations of the concept and the context in which it was employed.[10] Donors were openly requesting that the theme of violent extremism become a part of project submissions. Indeed, without the catchphrase 'CVE', a grant might not be guaranteed.[11] Externally driven democracies have an issue with the legitimacy and accountability of its institutions. Externally driven programmes implemented by local civil society groups will also create issues with their legitimacy and accountability. The symbolic capital created around the term 'CVE' has plagued Bosnia's civil society with unfair elbow-style competition over funds that are effectively already drying up.[12]

The notion that the external is superior to the local is not a novel one – it stems from the Bosnian history of an external ruler as well as from the country's current institutional setup. Bosnia, in the not so distant past, was an Ottoman and Austro-Hungarian colony, followed by being a part of a Yugoslavia broken up by war. Following the conflict, which ended indeed only after the external intervention, the DPA foresaw an external Office of the High Representative (OHR) as the most powerful and final authority to oversee the full implementation of the agreement, including the prevention of hindrance assured by the Bonn Powers and the country's further democratisation and subsequent EU accession.[13] In a seminal work produced from a postcolonial perspective (1997), Maria Todorova argued that there is a discourse termed 'Balkanism', a subset of Edward Said's 'Orientalism', which creates a stereotype of the Balkans as something inherently inferior to Europe. Todorova holds that the Balkans have often served as a depository for adverse features upon which a positive and self-pleasing image of the 'European' has been constructed. The argument suggests, in simplified form, that the Balkans hold exclusivity over 'barbarianism', as opposed to the advanced and peaceful Europeans, and for that they have been subjected to condemnation from outsiders, mostly other Europeans (Todorova, 1997). This external, paternalistic and biased view fed into myths of 'ancient hatreds as the cause of the war' in Western media reporting, further damaging the interpretation, and led to the oversimplification of the events of the 1990s. Furthermore, in arguing for the expansion of the postcolonial critique to include the Balkans, some authors (Rexhepi, 2018) saw the Europeanisation process as equal to the EU accession process, in terms of a move from colonial Europe to a (post)colonial EU. In such an environment, favouring externally driven programmes and external experts, while at the same time undermining local efforts and conditions, is viewed as detrimental to the peace progress.

Based on Georgia Holmer's observation, peacebuilders operate with a broader and more neutral understanding of violence and its causes, and can engage with a larger range of actors. This more expansive approach also affords greater explanations and more nuanced analysis of causes, which in turn helps to map more contextually relevant interventions.[14] In similar fashion, peacebuilding is generally understood as a 'do not harm' process at its core, whereas many other practices borrowed from the counter-terrorism methodology under the CVE umbrella, such as active surveillance, policing and raids, and the further marginalisation of specific communities, do not adhere to this no-harm practice.[15] Although measuring the impact of both peacebuilding and CVE outcomes is difficult due to multiple external variables that can aid or hinder the process, the peacebuilding strategy seems to notably enable wide-ranging societal progress. Because peacebuilding organisations and efforts focus on preventing conflict, highlighting success becomes a long-term effort, and work with both state and civil society actors, including the media and academia, is then uniquely positioned to contribute to the objectives of CVE programmes if paired and carefully complemented.[16] Another important highlight to be understood is the importance of local ownership of the national progress raised by scholars. Despite the growing emphasis on local ownership, a close look at interventions shows that states remain underdeveloped or suspended in a large web of international agencies, donors, third-party governments and other social forces (Schlichte, 2005).

Whereas peacebuilding rests upon the premise of the importance of the local contribution, CVE seems rather like an imposed practice that drives a local agenda while maintaining that it engages the local community. This is exemplified by the donor preference for projects that mention 'CVE' over those that do not. 'Western interventions in countries plagued by violent extremism are often characterized by an external versus internal dichotomy that privileges the external "expert" theory and praxis' (Schwoebel, 2017, pp. 3–8). As many authors have observed, this approach, in turn, creates a status of 'perpetual transition and state of exception' (Majstorovic and Vučkovac, 2016). Effectively, it has turned Bosnia into the international community's surrogate child, who – more than two decades after the Dayton Accords were signed – is just barely learning to crawl. As is the case in other places around the world, external actors attempting to de-privilege their 'expertise' in order to create scientific distance often romanticise or 'Orientalise' the local, but do not engage him or her as much (Schumicky-Logan, 2017).

Concluding remarks

The 1995 DPA and international troops stationed in the country were extremely effective in fashioning a truce after nearly four years of bloodshed, after which peacemaking efforts took a turn for the better. The process that came shortly after, peacekeeping, also seems to have started well, notwithstanding problems that commonly accompany an immediate ceasefire. At the time, the devastated nation and international community gave a ubiquitous sigh of relief that the violence had finally ended. The immediate question on everybody's mind was what happens next and how the process of peacebuilding would commence. In other words, when would the 'positive peace' commence and who would guarantee its sustainability?

Two decades after, it is apparent from the state of current affairs that Bosnia has failed to face its past in a coherent, ethical and systematic manner. The ICTY judgments that were supposed to provide a clean slate were not accompanied by a reformed education system nor responsible politicians. The Constitution never saw the amendments necessary to move the country forward. Most Bosnian politicians' electoral campaigns still rely on fostering further societal divisions along ethnic lines and openly flirting with extremist groups by endorsing and normalising their views while normatively aligning and harmonising legislation with the EU.

Bosnia is far from a 'positive peace'. Given that the country remains in a continuous election cycle every two years, it is nearly impossible to measure the effects and implications of two decades of such societal damages. But it is certain that Bosnian society has remained in a catatonic state of affairs. Political leaders do not shy away from bringing family members of convicted war criminals to their political rallies to garner popular support and further whip up fear of the 'others', and they frequently engage in historical revisionism. With the highest unemployment rates in Europe, constant reminiscence of past wrongdoings and

divisive politics and education, stagnancy and resignation permeate the foundations of Bosnian life. Add to that the groups that thrive on war traumas and
grievances and you most certainly have a recipe for an outburst when circumstances are ripe. Or, in another words, '[A] precarious peace agreement [. . .] is
administered by an international elite that pursues a strict liberalization program and legitimizes weak and corrupt governments, which, in turn, suffer from
porous governance and are unable to provide any perspective to their citizens in
the face of rising levels of unemployment and poverty' (Goetze, 2016, p. 217).

In addition, the global attention given to al Qaida and then to ISIS, exacerbated by inadequate reporting about the state of affairs in Bosnia, has further
propelled the country into the global spotlight again. It is also true that approximately 260 Bosnian individuals have either left to take up arms in countries
they had never visited before, alongside recruits they had never met, against
enemies they had never encountered, or to aid the Islamic state in other ways
(Dramac, 2016). However, the main argument is that, without further contextualisation of the problem, the country has no means by which it can prevent and
counter the problem of violent extremism. To be able to assess violent and
extreme groups in Bosnia, we would first and foremost need to examine cap-
tured civil society, biased media and compromised academic professionals, and
nationalist political and other groups in Bosnia, Croatia and Serbia, given the
diverse ethnic composition of Bosnia, and find out how these groups operate
across borders. Relegated only as an issue of extreme Islamists, the assessment of
violent extremism in Bosnia will remain incomplete and, at worst, will drive the
implementation of inadequate policies that will only exacerbate problems.

Indeed, this holistic perspective does not seek to minimise the issue of foreign
fighters, violent extremism or the extremist religious activists who put extremist
views to practical use. There is a profound need to add more pieces to the bigger
picture and to understand the larger problem at stake: if the Bosnian state does
not deal with its past, if it does not amend its education system and its constitution, if it does not sanction divisive rhetoric and hate speech, if it does not account
for all extremist groups and decisively deal with them using an overarching CVE
paradigm with a larger peacebuilding agenda – the prospect of the country experiencing another civil war in the near future is real. While peacebuilding is a long
process, and one that has most certainly lagged behind and stalled in post-war
Bosnia, a CVE strategy that does not deem all forms of violent extremism relevant
is only bound to undo any peacebuilding progress made in Bosnia, no matter how
small it has been over the years. Additionally, given that it deals with security
issues, in particular those that cannot be neglected in a post-war setting, an effective CVE strategy must be designed to recognise and dispel all forms of potential
threats, including right-wing extremism and threats to stability.

To counteract such dire prospects, what is needed is greater support for peacebuilding goals by applying a reformatted and better thought out security strategy that reflects Bosnia's unique experience. While flawed in its current form, Bosnia still needs an effective and comprehensive programme to counter violent extremism as an integral part of its peacebuilding mechanisms. Peace-building efforts must act as a holistic framework that includes education, dealing with the past programmes, and other processes conducive to peace rather than conflict. Depending on whether internal actors align with this framework and implement strategies that reflect knowledge of the complex web of variables that constitute Bosnian society, the future of the region will hang on the whim of self-serving political interests that manipulate the vulnerabilities, fears and expectations of a wounded nation.

An alternative model of CVE rooted in peacebuilding and peace educa-tion is an option that has not yet been explored thoroughly, but it is one that has a chance to yield results. By engaging in policy debates and initiatives related to violent extremism, peacebuilders may find opportunities to shift the debate towards a broader, earlier and more preventive approach to peacebuild-ing that addresses the drivers of conflict. The potential for an alternative approach to CVE based on anti-violence and peacebuilding is enormous but, alas, the long-term approach will not tick any of the EU's conditionality boxes, nor will it satisfy international donors' eager fascination to demonstrate 'suc-cess stories'.

There are a number of examples, led by indigenous voices, which demon-strate how small, organic initiatives can bridge communities. The co-option of these initiatives by external regulators and experts has failed before, and it will fail again. External authorities should utilise their leverage to systematically aid the country in overcoming its perpetual political and systematic crisis, while in parallel assisting organic, local initiatives to drive the healing of soci-ety. In the words of Kemal Pervanic, a former concentration camp survivor and a prominent peace activist, 'It is evident by now that what this country needs is a complete reset, a system-wide reset on the way peacebuilding is conducted, CVE included. We need peace education that includes as many young people as possible'.[17] To conclude, does multi-ethnic Bosnia, whose sov-ereignty is continually contested, need a strategy that aspires to sideline extreme voices that stop just short of violence? Absolutely. Does the current CVE strategy respond to the needs and realities of post-Dayton Bosnia? Abso-lutely not. This analysis shows that inadequate, detrimental state strategies need to be abolished all together in favour of expanded parallel peace pro-cesses that would aid overall peacebuilding and, more importantly, sustainable reconciliation in Bosnia.

Notes

1　In regard to the ethnic composition in Bosnia, according to the 2013 census, Bosniaks make up 50.11%, Serbs 30.78% and Croats 15.43% of the population. The institutional setup stemming from the 1995 DPA rests on the principle of the balance and equality of the three 'constitutive peoples' – Bosniaks, Serbs and Croats.

2　None of the Bosnian individuals was known to have had any connection with Syria or Iraq prior to his or her departure, as opposed to some other recruits from Western Europe. The Islamic State of Iraq and the Levant (ISIL), Islamic State of Iraq and Syria (ISIS), Islamic State (IS) or Da'esh all refer to the same movement in the same region. In this article, the name used to refer to the group is ISIS because this term dominated the discourse.

3　For more on the need to differentiate between the diverse trends of Salafi groups in Bosnia, see Becirevic (2016). The four-type typology was developed by the leading Bosnian theologian Muhamed Jusić (2017).

4　The author acknowledges that a term such as 'Salafi' contributes to the labelling and generalising practice. However, I opted to use it because the members of the communities refer to themselves as such, as confirmed in interviews with them.

5　Conversation with Vlado Azinović, June 2018.

6　As demonstrated by the violence at the football match, which resulted in one person being killed. See www.balkaninsight.com/en/article/thousands-mourn-killed-sarajevo-football-fan (accessed June 2017).

7　For a detailed analysis of the groups operating in the Balkans and their specific modus operandi, see http://javno.rs/analiza/balkanske-ultra-desnicarske-grupe-preplavile-internet- ; for paramilitary training, see www.theguardian.com/world/2018/jan/12/russian-trained-mercenaries-back-bosnias-serb-separatists (accessed June 2018).

8　One of the most illustrative examples was the ill-informed claim made by the Croatian President that caused a regional stir: www.vecernji.hr/vijesti/grabar-kitarovic-iz-islamske-drzave-u-bih-se-vraca-tisuce-boraca-1133717 (accessed June 2018).

9　For the proliferation of related terms and norms that terminology can reinforce, see: www.peacedirect.org/wp-content/uploads/2017/09/Peacebuilding-low-res.pdf (accessed 13 June 2018).

10　As an illustration, the Bosnian Office of the International Organization for Migration received $16 million for CVE programmes in the country. In addition, USAID Bosnia is also 'piloting new approaches to engaging youth to mitigate external pressures that lead to violent extremism'. See http://pdf.usaid.gov/pdf_docs/PBAAE884.pdf (accessed June 2018).

11　Paraphrased from a March 2018 interview with Velma Saric, the founder of the award-winning Post-Conflict Research Center.

12　Also paraphrased from the March 2018 interview with Velma Saric.

13　The 'Bonn Powers' were added in 1997 as substantial powers for the OHR that help to avoid the implementation of the Dayton Agreement being delayed or obstructed by local nationalist politicians.

14 Paraphrased from: Georgia Holmer, United States Peace Institute, 'Countering Violent Extremism: A Peacebuilding Perspective', www.icnl.org/research/library/files/files/Transnational/CVEUSIP.pdf (accessed June 2018).
15 In an interview with the State Investigative and Protective Unit's Head of Counterterrorism, he confirmed that there are a number of Salafi villages that they tour at least once a week.
16 Paraphrased from: Georgia Holmer, United States Peace Institute, 'Countering Violent Extremism: A Peacebuilding Perspective', www.icnl.org/research/library/files/files/Transnational/CVEUSIP.pdf (accessed June 2018).
17 Interview with Kemal Pervanic, March 2018.

References

Aggestam, K., Björkdahl, A., 2011. *Just Peace Postponed: Unending Peace Processes and Frozen Conflicts. JADBPbP Working Paper No.10.* Nordic University Press, Lund.

Ambinder, M., 2010. 'The new term for war on terror', *The Atlantic (2010).* Available at www.theatlantic.com/politics/archive/2010/05/the-new-term-for-the-war-on-terror/56969 (accessed 12 March 2018).

Andjelic, N., 2003. *Bosnia-Herzegovina: The End of a Legacy. Southeast European Politics.* Frank Cass Publishers, London.

Aziz, S.F., 2017. 'Losing the "war of ideas": A critique of countering violent extremism programs', *Texas International Law Journal,* 52(255); Texas A&M University School of Law Legal Studies Research Paper No. 17–22. Available at https://ssrn.com/abstract=2913571.

Becirevic, E., 2016. *Salafism vs. Moderate Islam: A Rhetorical Fight for the Hearts and Minds of Bosnian Muslims.* Atlantic Initiative, Sarajevo.

Bieber, F., 2010. 'Popular mobilization in the 1990s: Nationalism, democracy and the slow decline of the Milošević regime', in Djokic, D. and Ker-Lindsay, J. (eds), *New Perspectives on Yugoslavia.* Routledge, London, pp. 161–175.

Chandler, D., 2000. *Bosnia: Faking Democracy after Dayton.* Pluto Press, London.

Coleman, P., Bartoli, A., 2015. *Addressing Extremism.* The International Center for Cooperation and Conflict Resolution, New York. Available at www.libertyunderattack.com/wp-content/uploads/2015/06/Addressing-Extremism-ICCCR-ICAR.pdf (accessed 7 February 2018).

Crelinsten, R., 2007. 'Counterterrorism as global governance: A research inventory', in Ranstorp, M. (ed.), *Mapping Terrorism Research: State of the Art, Gaps and Future Direction.* Routledge, Abingdon, pp. 210–235.

De Coning, C., 2013. 'Understanding peacebuilding as essentially local', *Stability: International Journal of Security and Development,* 2(1), 1–6.

de Graaf, B., 2010. 'Redefining "us" and "them"', *Countering Violent Extremist Narratives.* National Coordinator for Counterterrorism, The Hague, pp. 36–45. Available at www.ris.uu.nl/ws/files/20779441/Countering_Violent_Extremist_Narratives_2_tcm126_444038_2_.pdf (accessed 21 March 2018).

Djokić, D., Ker-Lindsay, J. (eds), 2010. *New Perspectives on Yugoslavia: Key Issues and Controversies.* Routledge, London.

Doyle, M., 2002. 'Strategy and Transitional Authority'. in Stedman Stephen, J., Rothchild, D. and, Cousens, E. (eds.), *Ending Civil Wars: The Implementation of Peace Agreements.* Boulder, Lynne Rienner Publishing, Boulder, CO, December 1, 2002.

Dramac, T., 2016. 'Radicalization as a prop in Bosnia's elections', *The Cipher Brief,* 24 June. Available at www.thecipherbrief.com/radicalization-as-a-prop-in-bosnias-elections (accessed 18 March 2018).

Dzihic, V., Hamilton, D. (eds), 2012. *Managing Hatred and Distrust: The Prognosis for Post-Conflict Settlement in Multiethnic Communities in the Former Yugoslavia,* 4 April. SAIS Center for Transatlantic Relations, Washington, DC.

Galtung, J., 1969. 'Violence, peace, and peace research', *Journal of Peace Research,* 6(3), 167–191.

Ginkel, B., Westervelt, S., 2009. 'The ethical challenges of implementing counterterrorism measures and the role of the OSCE', *Security and Human Rights,* 2, 123–142.

Glenny, M., 1996. *The Fall of Yugoslavia: The Third Balkan War,* 3rd edition. Penguin Books, London.

Glenny, M., 2001. *The Balkans: Nationalism, War & the Great Powers (1804–1999).* Penguin Books, London.

Goetze, C., 2016. *The Distinction of Peace: A Social Analysis of Peacebuilding.* University of Michigan Press, Ann Arbor, MI.

Government of Bosnia and Herzegovina, 2015. *Strategy of Bosnia and Herzegovina for Preventing and Combating Terrorism, 2015–2020.* Available at http://msb.gov.ba/PDF/STRATEGIJA_ZA_BORBU_PROTIV_TERORIZMA_ENG.pdf (accessed 18 March 2018).

Grant, T., 2017. 'Frozen conflicts and international law', *Cornell International Law Journal,* 50(3), 361–413.

Hanlon, L., 2007. 'UK anti-terrorism legislation: Still disproportionate?', *The International Journal of Human Rights,* 11(4), 481–515.

Hassain, M., 2008. 'Defending the faithful: Speaking the language of group harm in free exercise challenges to counterterrorism profiling', *The Yale Law Journal,* 117, 920–969.

Hocking, J., 2007. 'Counter-terrorism and the politics of social cohesion', in Jupp, J., Nieuwenhuysen, J.P. and Dawson, E. (eds), *Social Cohesion in Australia.* Cambridge University Press, Melbourne, pp. 182–190.

Jusić, M., 2017. 'The complex narratives and movements in Bosnia and Herzegovina', in Azinović, V. (ed.), *Between Salvation and Terror: Radicalization and the Foreign Fighter Phenomenon in the Western Balkans.* Atlantic Initiative, Sarajevo, pp. 43–57.

Kundnani, A., 2015. *The Muslims Are Coming! Islamophobia, Extremism and the Domestic War on Terror.* Verso, London.

Kunovich, R., Hodson, R., 2016. 'Ethnic diversity, segregation, and inequality: A structural model of ethnic prejudice in Bosnia and Croatia', *The Sociological Quarterly,* 43(2), 185–212.

Lindekilde, L., 2015. 'Refocusing Danish counter-radicalization efforts: An analysis of the (problematic) logic and practice of individual de-radicalization interventions', in Baker-Beall, C., Heath Kelly, L. and Jarvis, L. (eds), *Counter-radicalization, Critical Perspective*. Routledge, New York, pp. 223–241.

Majstorovic, D., Vučkovac, Z., 2016. 'Rethinking Bosnia and Herzegovina's post-colonialism: Challenges of Europeanization discourse', *Journal of Language and Politics*, 15(2), 147–172.

Malcolm, N., 1994. *Bosnia: A Short History*. New York University Press, New York.

Mroz, J., 2009. 'Countering violent extremism: Lessons learned', *EastWest*. Available at www.files.ethz.ch/isn/104324/2009-07-22-Counterning_Lessons-Learned.pdf (accessed 8 June 2015).

Mustapha, J., 2013. 'The mujahedeen in Bosnia: The foreign fighter as cosmopolitan citizen and/or terrorist', *Citizenship Studies*, 17(6–7), 742–755.

Newman, J., 2012. 'The origins, attributes, and legacies of paramilitary violence in the Balkans', in Gerwarth, R. and Horne, J. (eds), *War in Peace: Paramilitary Violence in Europe after the Great War*. Oxford University Press, Oxford, 145–163.

Organization for Security and Co-operation in Europe, 2017. 'BiH Council of Ministers adopts an action plan for the implementation of the Strategy for Preventing and Combatting Terrorism 2015–2020', *OSCE Mission to Bosnia and Herzegovina*. Available at https://polis.osce.org/node/1371 (accessed June 2017).

Paris, R., 2004. *At War's End: Building Peace after Civil Conflict*. Cambridge University Press, Cambridge.

Perry, V., 2009. 'At cross purposes? Democratization and peace implementation strategies in Bosnia and Herzegovina's frozen conflict', 10(1), 35–54.

Perry, V., 2016. *Initiatives to prevent/counter violent extremism in South East Europe: A survey of regional issues, initiatives and opportunities*, July. Regional Cooperation Council, Sarajevo.

Rexhepi, P., 2018. 'The politics of postcolonial erasure in Sarajevo', *Interventions*. Available at 10.1080/1369801X.2018.1487320 (accessed 10 April 2018).

Russo, C., 2000. 'Religion and education in Bosnia: Integration not segregation?', *European Journal for Education Law and Policy*, 4(2), 121.

Schlichte, K., 2005. *The Dynamics of States: The Formation and Crises of State Domination*. Ashgate, Aldershot.

Schumicky-Logan, L., 2017. 'Addressing violent extremism with a different approach: The empirical case of at-risk and vulnerable youth in Somalia', *Journal of Peacebuilding & Development*, 12(2), 66–79.

Schwoebel, M., 2017. 'Peacebuilding approaches to preventing and transforming violent extremism', *Journal of Peacebuilding & Development*, 12(2), 3–8.

Soldo, A., Trbić, D., Husremović, D., Veličković, N., Čelebičić, I. and Ibrahimović, N., 2017. 'Education in Bosnia and Herzegovina: What do we (not) teach children? Content analysis of textbooks of the national group of subjects in primary schools'. Available at http://promente.org/index.php/en/news/486-research-report-education-in-bih-what-do-we-not-teach-our-children (accessed 18 March 2018).

Todorova, M., 1997. *Imagining the Balkans*. Oxford University Press, Oxford.

Torsti, P., 2007. 'How to deal with a difficult past? History textbooks supporting enemy images in Post-war Bosnia and Herzegovina', *Journal of Curriculum Studies*, 39(1), 77–96.

UN Secretary-General, 1992. *Agenda for Peace*. Available at www.un.org/ruleoflaw/files/A_47_277.pdf (accessed 10 April 2018).

UN Secretary-General, 1995. *Supplement for Peace*. Available at www.securitycouncilreport.org/atf/cf/%7B65BFCF9B-6D27-4E9C-8CD3-CF6E4FF96FF9%7D/UNRO%20S1995%201.pdf (accessed 10 April 2018).

Zuvela, M., 2018. 'Bosnia to investigate suspected Serb paramilitary group', *Reuters*, 16 January. Available at www.reuters.com/article/us-bosnia-security-paramilitary/bosnia-to-investigate-suspected-serb-paramilitary-group-idUSKBN1F51ZW (accessed 18 June 2018).

13

Drivers or decoys? Women and the narrative of extremist violence in Pakistan

Afiya Shehrbano Zia

Introduction

It would be inaccurate to suggest that any overarching countering violent extremism (CVE) policy has caught the imagination of the people or even Pakistani state officials. This makes any critique of some stable CVE a futile exercise. Such acronyms mean little and often have no local, linguistic or cultural resonance. Rather, certain events and incidents are intuitively categorised or labelled as acts of terrorism (*daishad gardi*) or inspired by extremism (*inteha pasandi*) by the media and communities. Usually, these refer to armed attacks on state institutions, religious minorities, unarmed communities or individuals, secular sites, practices or politics, or on defiant women and individuals who refuse to adhere to the prescribed bounds of male-defined customs, religious codes or traditions.

The CVE project – if it is understood as a loosely defined approach to end extremism and curtail, arrest and/or de-radicalise 'mainstream' religious militants – is not just challenged by insurgent groups and right-wing Islamists as an American ruse to end Islam. In fact, over the past fifteen years, several scholars and conservative Pakistani commentators have also produced defensive and sanitised analyses of Islamists' politics. It is disconcerting too, that despite the efforts of the United Nations to institutionalise the Women, Peace and Security (WPS) agenda beyond conflict contexts and to include terrorism and counter-terrorism (Ní Aoláin, 2016, p. 277), the terms of such expansion remain male-dominated and the emphasis stresses the use of force and argues for an expansion of security regimes, which only increases insecurity for women.

Many member countries developed National Action Plans to implement United Nations Security Council Resolution (UNSCR) 1325, which urges nations and stakeholders to address the impact of violent conflict and war on women and girls. The Resolution also calls for attention to the crucial role that women should and already do play in conflict prevention, conflict resolution, peace-making and peacebuilding (United Nations, n.d.). According to the International League for Peace and Women (PeaceWomen), by 2016, sixty-three member nations had developed a National Action Plan. A civil society effort in Pakistan attempted to do so after the tenth anniversary of the Resolution in 2010 but the project stalled. Those who support Resolution 1325 in Pakistan argue that women's participation in peacebuilding is linked to the larger gender inequality issue. They urge for the recognition of women's agency in peacebuilding, strengthening their voice in peace and security matters, building their resilience and reducing their vulnerability.

However, there are two important obstacles to achieving such aims in Pakistan. The first is the limited influence of civil society in such efforts, given that the driver of the National Action Plan is the military establishment and the inclusion of women is non-existent or negligible. Second, the refusal to recognise, and in fact the active discrediting of, any secular resistance, alternatives or voices has meant that the counter-narrative to extremism remains limited to one defined in and by religious identities, references, agency and goals. Such asphyxiated and narrow frames for countering violent extremism exclude women and religious minorities and simply become majoritarian masculine sites and determinants.

For the purpose of this chapter, I apply Furlow and Goodall's (2011) framing of extremist narrative and rhetoric techniques in relation to acts of violence. I reference Laird Wilcox's (2005) explanation of the manner in which extremists who are 'at war' with an opposing group or idea engage their battles with specific uses of language. These include character assassination and name calling and assuming moral and even divine authority to legitimise their cause and intimidate their opponents. I argue that CVE efforts, however defined, need to push back the extremist discourse by an understanding of the power of narrative and by developing social networks and communicative forms that demystify the abstraction and symbolic falsity that drives hate-inspired narratives.

Second, this chapter recognises how women serve as mediating tools across which community-based rules, conduct and laws are contested, and disputes are settled. Femininity is part of the construction of extremist-defined oppositional politics that ultimately inspires violence (Haq, 2007; Saigol, 2013). A more meaningful CVE policy would examine the role of women within the context of extremist acts and the associated narratives that endorse, encourage and independently support, sustain and justify extremism, rather than limiting analysis to just Muslim women's 'docile' agency, as defined in Saba Mahmood's influential work on the subject (2005).

The chapter discusses the role of Islamist women as contributors to a masculinist religio-nationalist narrative of extremism. It recalls cases of those who have paid the price of consequent violence in Pakistan. I refer to Islamist women not as a binary distinction from Muslim women but, rather, in recognition of the former's political persuasion, consciousness or activism. I also note that among Islamist women (and men), some recognise the Pakistani state and constitution, while others contest the legitimacy of both and aspire to a more global cross-border Muslim imaginary/community. I do, however, use the term as inclusive of those women who lead and associate with pietist or mosque movements in recognition of their self-defined subjectivity or agency, which I consider political. All through the chapter, I point to the counter-intuitive and counter-productive role of Pakistani scholars (cited below) who have attempted to defend Islamist politics and offer Islamic alternatives by critiquing liberal and/or secular resistance to extremist narratives and strategies.

Since my research and scholarship speaks to the discipline of women's studies, the chapter focuses mainly on the gendered nature of these events and the narratives represented and claimed by women associated with religious politics – mainstream or extremist – as well as those who have been victims and survivors of extremism. This chapter discusses some of the multi-layered debates on terrorism, extremism and militancy following Pakistan's induction as the front-line ally of the US-led war on terror. It offers some thoughts on the ineffectuality of the project to develop an alternative definition and imaginary of/for Pakistan's religious and political identity for the purposes of CVE. It then points out how these contradictions and confusions divided national opinion during the climactic events of the Lal Masjid siege of 2007, and how they are indicative of the difficulties in maintaining a stable counter-violence narrative in Pakistan. It cites some of the major encounters where women were the drivers of the Islamists' narratives, but only serve as decoys to be appeased by religious or heavenly rewards rather than beneficiaries of equal, secular, political and material rights. The legacy of the signifying event of the Jamia Hafsa or women's madrasa associated with the Lal Masjid confirms the importance, and also the tenuous ground, on which the counter-extremism narrative is resting and the marginal role of women within it.

Incomplete and competing narratives

It is a difficult task to sift through the mountainous heaps of research studies, analyses and theories on terrorism and extremism in Pakistan generated over the past fifteen years (Abbas, 2004, 2014; Cohen et al., 2011; Haqqani, 2005; Haroon, 2007; Lodhi, 2011; Rashid, 2008; Shah, 2014). After the attacks of 9/11 in America in 2001 and Pakistan's induction as the front-line ally of the US war on terror, the bulk of early literature produced was an attempt to identify the actors and causes of religious militancy. Much of this later body of work tends to be non-academic, journalistic and contradictory (Gul, 2010; Latif and Munir, 2014; Lieven, 2011; Shahzad, 2011; Mir, 2010). As Pakistan received millions of dollars for military assistance under General Musharraf's regime (1999–2008), some of these studies and analyses became heavily funded projects.

Even with the incorporation of partnerships with academia in the UK, US and Pakistan, much of the findings of this 'research' have been counter-intuitive and dependent on a new form of war anthropology and research methods that have relied on fixers, handlers, translators, NGO research and No Objection Certificates awarded by the military authorities at their discretion. In terms of political and academic research interest on Pakistan, the war on terror has been not just overly deterministic with regard to analyses, scholarship and projects, but also a pretty lucrative business and path to academic renown (Siddiqa, 2007). Many academics working on Muslim identities, newly minted 'experts' on Islam, terrorism, jihad, security and conflict studies found careers in think-tanks associated with British and American governments, while others moved to a Western academia that was keen to learn about 'Muslims', especially Muslim women (Bano, 2007; Cheema and Mustafa, 2009; Iqtidar, 2011; Tahir, 2013b; Zakaria, 2017). Ex-military personnel and freelance journalists found jobs as security advisors and informants for international media and researchers.

Several civil and military regimes since 2001 have scrambled to introduce legal changes and devise strategies to counter extremism, but these policies have remained limited to an accumulation of unpronounceable acronyms and ineffectual results. Despite all this, Pakistan seems to have entered a post-conflict détente, even if it cannot be said that extremist violence has been countered or its threat diminished. Rather than being holistic, CVE responses have been anaemic, *ad hoc* and abstract experiments. Since 2004, Pakistan has carried out several military operations with the purported aim to eradicate extremist sanctuaries and hideouts and to target the supporters of terrorist activities. In terms of humanitarian and economic costs, according to Pakistan's Economic Survey for 2015–2016, the war on terror has cost $118 billion thus far.[1] In terms of loss of human lives, Physicians for Social Responsibility published a report in 2015 stating that Pakistan has lost 81,860 civilians, journalists and military personnel over the last fifteen years (Physicians for Social Responsibility, 2015).

Pakistan also introduced a number of non-military measures, such as madrasa (seminary) reforms, the Anti-Terrorism Amendment 2001, which banned sectarian and militant organisations, and several Anti-Terrorism Ordinances. The bulk of Pakistan's CVE strategy has focused on military measures and multimillion-dollar international financial assistance for development and peacebuilding measures. More recent legal and policy measures include: the Pakistan Protection Ordinance 2013, which amended the legal frameworks to give more power to law enforcement officials; the Political Parties Act (2010); the Reforms Agenda for Federally Administered Tribal Areas (FATA) (2011); banning hate speech and the illegal FM 96 (a radio station in the Swat/Malakand region to counter terrorist propaganda launched by Pakistani Taliban leader Mullah Fazulluah, popularly known as Mullah Radio); and several embedded media campaigns to counter militant rhetoric and curtail their savvy use of mainstream media. After 2014, the Prevention of Electronic Crimes Act 2016 was passed to curtail terrorism, hate speech and harassment.

The scope and role of visual and electronic material used to promote the extremists' narrative is too broad to be included in this chapter. However, it is important to note that the range of extremist rhetoric in Pakistan has often conflated with the master narrative of al Qaida about the US–Zionist–Crusades theme of the war on terror, but also departed via a metanarrative that focused far more on historical struggles against British colonial rule and over issues of sectarianism, blasphemy and inter-faith issues. Al Qaida's narrative (and that of its franchise, the Tehreeq e Taliban Pakistan – TTP) cast Pakistan as un-Islamic and as a US protégé, and equated its democratic status as anathema to Sharia, while the Pakistan army was seen as the enemy that persecuted tribal Muslims and its media as the false messiah that misled the masses.

While 'narrative' itself is a rhetorical device used by story tellers, novelists, entertainers, historians, preachers and polemics, its use by political groups enables its weaponisation. Some common traits that define Islamist extremist narratives include the opposition to a philosophy, government or religions connected to a geographical entity known as 'the West'; a linking of current enemies to historical villains of the past (dating to the time of the Crusades); justification of violence through use of texts such as the Quran and ancillary texts or oral tradition, and *fatwas* (religious edicts) – all of which are often contextualised with folklore for cultural resonance; appeals to the theme of martyrdom and sacrifice, jihad, or holy struggle for survival; and references to sexual corruption as a key signifier of difference between Muslims and the West (Furlow and Goodall, 2011).

Furlow and Goodall (2011, p. 222) make a comparative case for extremist narratives in the US and Arab world but recognise the difference in intentions between extremist groups who advocate violence and politicians who invoke fear narratives. They summarise: 'The narrative provides a reason and divine justification for extremist action and as such serves as an inspiration and motivation for "true believers" [. . .] What is unique about extremist groups is religion is used to justify their actions while simultaneously using political avenues to enforce religious ideas'. The core narrative of extremists is that the world is in chaos and must be saved and set right by political action inspired and ordained by 'the divine' (Furlow and Goodall, 2011, p. 222). The authors note that just as

Waterloo has a meaning that exists beyond its specific historical reference, so does the Battle of Badr for the Muslim imaginary. Certain rhetorical techniques must be deployed to move the 'trajectory' of these narratives 'by a hero from the story line to the streets' (Furlow and Goodall, 2011, p. 221). Hate-filled narratives require supportive environments in order to manifest themselves as physical violence; that is, words can lead to violence if enabling conditions are provided. All of these drivers, props and appeals are found to be applicable to Pakistan's experiences with extremist narratives and remain a challenge, especially when the role of women, feminine vulnerability and sacrificial iconography is invoked to feminise the stakes.

Some of the early and key media debates[2] that framed the public narrative on religious extremism in Pakistan following 9/11 included: whether the war on terror was Pakistan's war or a US war on Muslims; whether the religious militants were motivated by religious extremist ideologies and teachings or by Islamophobia, drones and the stereotypical 'vengeance philosophy' of the tribals; whether the same Pakistani military that created the Taliban could be trusted to void their strategic asset jihadists; whether moderate Islam was the antidote to extremist and jihadist versions; whether religious politics and seminary or madrasa education were drivers or a viable alternative to extremist politics; and if democracy and Islam were compatible or anathema. There were micro debates that were offshoots of these, such as whether suicide bombings and/or intra-Muslim killing was permissible under jihad conditions, and the legitimacy of fatwas and their issuers in the absence of a state church or religious authority in Islam.

In the period 2003–2007, another important division was the series of failed peace talks with the militants in the tribal areas and the subsequent use of US drones against all militant targets in FATA. Deeply contentious and much debated, the complication was the realisation that, despite feigning disagreement, the Pakistani military was collaborating with US drone warfare. All through the war on terror years, many violent protests were held on the issue of blasphemous material in the West but no meaningful, sustained anti-drone protest was observed in Pakistan. The political correctness of condemning drone warfare as a violation of sovereignty by governments was simply a masquerade (Zia, 2012). Some scholar-activists who initiated campaigns via PhD theses and documentaries rendered the drone attacks as imperialist savagery with no mention of the militants and their decimation of tribal communities and brutal recruitment drives (see Akbar Zaidi, 2013; Bennett Jones, 2013; Sabri, 2013; Tahir, 2013a on debates around this). When women members of the US group Codepink joined the single, half-baked and quickly aborted protest march on drones in 2012 led by aspiring politician Imran Khan, they were the only women participating and lent a kind of reverse exotica to the war on terror politics (Zia, 2012).

The role of women remained fairly marginal in the initial framings of these debates, but after 2007 the growing feminisation of extremist politics in Pakistan peaked in significant manner. The Lal Masjid siege in 2007 was not only a trigger for the subsequent surge of extremist violence and a backlash that took Pakistan to the brink of civil war, it was also a critical signifier of how militant narratives converge with mainstream Islamist ones and depend on, drive and overlap with nationalist anxieties across the ideological spectrum. In particular, the role of the women of the Jamia Hafsa madrasa (connected to the Lal Masjid) raised attention to the challenges of women piety/mosque and madrasa movements on the one hand, and secular resistance to Islamic politics on the other.

Women crusaders: drivers or decoys?

The role of women as part of religio-nationalist iconography that has informed the founding of Pakistan as an Islamic Republic and in the project of subsequent nation-building has been explored closely by some feminist scholars (Khattak, 2006; Saigol, 2016). During the rule of General Zia ul Haq (1977–1988), the project became hinged exclusively on an orthodox Islamisation strategy. But in 1999, General-President Pervez Musharraf positioned himself as a liberal dictator invested in steering the nation towards a path of religious moderation in the days following 9/11.

Musharraf championed women's rights as part of a convenient theme for his self-proclaimed vision for 'Enlightened Moderation' and as a *raison d'être* for his overthrow of a democratic government in 1999. The paradox of a liberal governance led by Musharraf's regime that depended on an alliance with conservative and Islamist parties, the Muttahida Majlis-e-Amal (MMA), which had campaigned for the 2002 elections on a platform of bitter opposition to Pakistan's alliance with the US, was lost.

On forming a government in the North-West Frontier Province (now Khyber Pakhtunkhwa), the political culture under the pro-militant sympathies harboured by the MMA government created an enabling environment for the spillover of the insurgency into Pakistan's tribal belt adjoining Afghanistan (Brohi, 2006). When the MMA formed government in the province (2002–2008), it worked towards actively subverting all constitutional women's rights, including the right to vote, legislating for a vice and virtue police to restrain women's mobility in public spaces (Hisba Bill), campaigning against theatre, films, music, Indian TV/films and family planning messages. Women's shelters were shut down and participants in sporting activities were harassed and attacked (Brohi, 2006). These are all instances of where mainstream Islamists' agendas intersect closely with those of the militants'. It is this nexus that allowed the militants to devastate the social fabric of the province during the Islamists' rule. All the while, they were able to represent an 'authentic' politics – one which was *for* (restricting) women *by* women.

While some defensive scholars tease out the differences between Islamists and militants in Pakistan, they avoid a discussion of the similarities, overlaps and consequences of their shared schemas. During this period, such scholarship justified Islamist women's politics by suggesting they were agentive and independently following an alternative empowerment discourse to that of Western feminist goals. This was done by whitewashing the consequences and convergence of such politics that was based on patriarchal means and exclusionary goals (Aziz, 2005; Bano, 2012; Iqtidar, 2011; Jamal, 2005).

Over the entire course of the war on terror operations in Pakistan, Anatol Lieven notes,

> the Pakistan Army's campaigns were not accompanied by the looting, random brutalization and most especially extensive rape carried out by US and South Vietnamese forces, and by the Pakistani Army in East Pakistan in 1971. Rape has never been credibly alleged in the recent Pakistani campaigns... because of the intense Pashtun concern with female 'honour'... [and]... the effects of war crimes are to some extent culturally specific. A counter-insurgency force may be able to get away with a considerable number of reasonably targeted extra-judicial executions, where even a very small number of rapes would ruin its whole position. (Lieven, 2017, pp. 177–178)

After the passage of UNSCR 1325, further Security Council resolutions followed, all demonstrating a particular preoccupation with sexual violence. However, such violations (on either the part of the militants or the army) were not an overwhelming concern for Pakistani activists. Ní Aoláin argues that

> the pattern of selective entreaty in multiple Security Council resolutions, as well as the language of 2242 essentializing women as either wicked purveyors of extremist violence or virtuous saviours of sons, husbands and communities, underscores the inconsistency in using women and the WPS agenda to advance the sustained protection of women and their rights in situations of armed conflict and collective violence. (Ní Aoláin, 2016, p. 282)

However, the rescue narrative assigned for Muslim women as justification for the occupation of Afghanistan in particular has often been extended falsely as a 'liberal-secular' feminist project applicable to all Muslim-majority contexts (Abu Lughod, 2002; Hirschkind and Mahmood, 2002). Despite the embrace of a gender-responsive governance as a means to gain approval of the international community and demonstrate Musharraf's purported commitment to counter-terrorism policies, Pakistan has not been at the receiving end of the kind of 'colonial feminist' counter-insurgent efforts that have been repeatedly criticised with reference to post-9/11 conflict zones. Neither has there been any sustained or consistent campaign of fear-mongering or demonising of Islamist women.

In fact, the situation in Pakistan has been quite the reverse, such that it has been the Islamists in Pakistan who have been invested in rescuing brown Muslim women from white infidel men and Western libidinal cultures. Simultaneously, a narrative has been built up against 'liberal-seculars' as anti-Islam and pro-drone and as imperialist collaborators and Zionist agents. This anxiety runs in continuation with prior nationalist concerns over cultural corruption as represented by a 'Hindu' India from which Pakistan separated as a Muslim homeland in 1947. Political Islamists historically milked the rescue narrative for political advantages long before the war on terror. However, this motif became a more opportune peg in the years after 2001 as it now included post-secular scholars and conservative commentators as defenders of Islamists.

This narrative technique was most manifest in the case of Afia Siddiqui, the US-based Pakistani female scientist who was put on the FBI wanted list in 2005 and extradited from Pakistan by General Musharraf to the US, where she was tried, incarcerated and sentenced for suspected terrorism in 2010. The right-wing Islamists, especially the *Jamaat e Islami*, used her as an icon of global Islamophobia, US injustices and Muslim victimhood in national campaigns in Pakistan (Zia, 2018).

The influential study by Saba Mahmood of Muslim women's piety in Egypt (2005) and her critique of secular feminism has encouraged a body of defensive academic works by Muslim scholars, including Pakistanis, who agree and apply the theory of Muslim women's docile agency as an alternative to liberal autonomy (Zia, 2018). These works do not focus on Muslim women's economic status, unequal access to legal rights, violence perpetrated against them by Muslim men and, certainly, not on their sexual agency. Many of these propose the fusion and hybridisation of Islam with modernity, or for Islamic rights as postcolonial alternatives.

The piety movement by the Al-Huda in Pakistan is one such model that has received considerable academic attention (Ahmad, 2009). However, the more radical turn for Islamist women's roles came with the rise of the *Jamia Hafsa* women's force in 2007, but analysis within Pakistan has remained circumspect about the motivations or agentive potential of Islamist women and their role in religious extremism.

'Sharia or martyrdom'

The Lal Masjid (Red Mosque) siege followed in the wake of a series of radical activist campaigns initiated by Islamist women of the associated madrasa of the

Jamia Hafsa, and effectively ruptured the façade of the extremist discourse as a purely masculine purview. The government-appointed head cleric (*khateeb*) of the Lal Masjid, Abdul Rashid Ghazi, was a vocal opponent of joint Pak/US military operations and used the space of the Red Mosque to wage a campaign against them. Two generations of clerics claimed to have enjoyed historical support from members of Pakistan's intelligence community (Rashid, 2008; Sarwar, 2007).

In 2004, the mosque had issued a fatwa declaring that Pakistani soldiers killed in tribal Waziristan should be denied an Islamic burial, whereas only militants who died in confrontation qualified as 'martyrs' for the Islamic cause (Ali, 2014; Munir, 2011; The News, 2013). The effect of such an edict was said to have resulted in refusals by soldiers to enter the battlefield and was later echoed by the amir of the mainstream Islamist party, *Jamaat e Islami*. In April 2007, the Red Mosque set up its own Sharia courts and warned of thousands of suicide attacks if the government tried to shut these courts down.

The uprising of the Jamia Hafsa women students in Islamabad in 2007 was the only serious political confrontation to General Musharraf's dictatorial regime of nine years by any group of women activists. These girl students belonged to a religious school or madrasa, attached to the Lal Masjid in an upscale location in the capital, Islamabad. The women clerics who ran the girls' madrasa were related to the male imams (clerics) of the main mosque, who in turn were suspected for their affiliation with radical religious militants in the north of the country, in the wake of the war on terror.

In 2007, the young women of the Hafsa madrasa led by Umme Hassan, after a series of vigilante activities in the city, illegally occupied the premises adjoining the mosque land. This was in protest against the government's threat to demolish and reclaim this property (and other illegally constructed mosques in the city) because it was suspected to have become a hotbed for terrorist indoctrination. The Jamia Hafsa women wore complete black veils, carried banners in English and Urdu and wore headbands declaring *Sharia ya Shahadat* (Sharia or martyrdom). They carried bamboo sticks and kidnapped a woman from the neighbourhood whom they accused of running a prostitution enterprise. They only let her free once she 'repented'. The imagery soon caught the attention of global media and challenged the notion of Muslim women as veiled and victimised by oppressive religious practices of their male counterparts and, at times, in need of liberation through military or non-military interventions (Abu-Lughod, 2002; Razack, 2007). This was in diametric opposition to the image of feminine victimhood that the Islamist men were invested in soon after the all-out military operation that followed.

Once negotiations between Musharraf's government and the Lal Masjid leaders broke down, the state seemed bent on a show of force that resulted in the

evacuation of 1,200 occupants, the death of Abdul Rashid Ghazi and an estimated 100–200 fatalities (Bokhari and Johnson, 2007). The spectacle of Maulana
Aziz escaping the smoke-filled complex of the Lal Masjid under the disguise of a
burqa earned him the mocking and emasculating title of 'Mulla Burqa' by critics.
After the siege was over, breaking the vow that it was un-Islamic to be photo-
graphed, Aziz went on to invoke the victim card and castigate the government in
the media and in sermons (Dawn, 2014). He remains a cleric at the reconstructed
Lal Masjid at a new site in Islamabad and continues to call for a caliphate to be
established in Pakistan.

Umme Hassan too, appeared in the media and justified the kidnapping of
Shamim Akhtar by saying 'She was a factory of Aids and if we got her brothel
closed, what is wrong about it?' (Ansari, 2007). Hassan referred to the government as a 'lazy mother' who is neglectful of her duties and claimed that the girls
of Jamia Hafsa were only carrying out the government's job in cleaning up the
brothels since the police were unable to crack down on prostitution without
retaliation from influential government officials who themselves patronised
these brothels (Perlez, 2007). The Jamia Hafsa women claim several of their
female students were killed, although the state denies this and there has been
no evidence or legal testimony confirming this assertion. The army's willingness to bomb a site of worship became proof of the state's brutality and its
anti-Islam orientation. For years following, Umme Hassan and her students
continued to narrate graphic stories about the atmosphere of death and destruction inside the mosque during Operation Silence. Many have appeared on television to mobilise sympathy and support through their stories of grief. This
strategy of 'truth-telling' and invocation of gendered tropes to counter the official state narrative surrounding the operation has been immensely successful
(Yusuf, 2011).

The state used the uprising to justify the need for more operations against
deep-seated terrorist infiltration, and the Islamists marketed it as confirmation
that Musharraf's regime was acting as proxy for anti-Islamic, US governmental
interests. The narrative of the survivors reminisced the sufferings of Kashmiri
women in a land occupied by non-Muslim infidels and mimicked the Shia tradition of enacting public lamentations during the Islamic month of Muharram to
commemorate the historic cruelties suffered by the martyrs of Karbala.

In a booklet entitled *Saniha Lal Masjid: Hum Par Kya Guzri* that was later
published by the mosque administration, Umme Hassan narrates the horrors of
the siege and cites last wills posted by the residents on the inside walls and pillars
of the mosque as the young women allegedly prepared themselves for the possibility of 'martyrdom'. The two strongest emotions invoked in such narrations are
of grief and forfeiture of feminine desires for the larger political cause. A strategic difference between this and the other women's religious movements lies in

how they appropriate and deploy constructs of 'woman-as-nation' in their political activism (Yuval Davis, 1997).

The most pious movement of the *Al-Huda* in Pakistan emphasises religious
education so that women can raise pious children and families and build more
Islamically aligned nations (Ahmad, 2009). For mothers of the militant group
Lashkar-e-Tayyaba, their cause is the willingness to sacrifice their sons to become
martyrs for the movement and Islamic nation (Haq, 2007). However, the state's
perceived willingness to compromise sovereignty to infidels' interests motivates
the women of Jamia Hafsa to break out of the private, domestic and protective
sphere, discard their invisibility and engage in an aggressive moral-cleansing
campaign in order to re-build an Islamic nation-state themselves.

Liberal commentators disparagingly viewed these 'ninjas', 'burqa brigades'
and 'chicks with sticks' (Shamsie, 2007) as mere pawns in the hands of the Red
Mosque's male leadership, citing their impoverished class backgrounds as the
reason behind their susceptibility to manipulation by a powerful leadership
seeking a popular base. On the other hand, sympathetic scholars (Bano, 2012)
sanitised the politics of the Lal Masjid by denying its historical role with
state-sponsored jihadist strategies (Ahmed, 2016; Hussain, 2013) and glorifying
the social significance that the women disciples of the Jamia Hafsa derive in their
roles as mothers, sisters, wives and daughters, as they spread their Islamic learn-
ings. Bano (2012, p. 146) argues madrasa education and learned piety 'empower[s]
the girls to deal with material scarcity' and cope with peer pressure against
observing Valentine's Day and fashion trends. Such scholars advocate support
for Islamic female leadership as a viable alternative to Western feminism. Some
even described the Jamia Hafsa vigilantism as a civil society movement (Devji,
2008, p. 21).

The important point here is that agentive embodied performances are not
always docile. This form of 'agency' relies on self-construction as authentic
moral actors who oppose a supposedly secular state beholden to foreign interests. The cultural purity claimed by the Jamia Hafsa women is invested in rigidly
patriarchal constructions of gender and sexuality. Their narrative supports the
discipline and purpose of gendered bodies and prescribes their roles and representations in public spaces. The common charge against Islamic militants is that
they simply deny women's agency. This was progressively challenged as militants
recognised the potential in offering women temporal roles in the insurgency and
immortality as martyrs.

The *Sharia ya Shahadat* (Sharia or Martyrdom) slogan adopted by the Jamia
Hafsa women is a radical promise, but who does their activism serve? Haq (2007,
p. 1043) holds reservations about the agency of the *Lashkar-e-Tayabba* (LeT)
mothers of martyrs, arguing that the agency of the mothers is tapped by the LeT
leadership who simply 'becomes the agent that mines the mothers' private grief

to enact a public jihadi community'. As such, the agentive potential of Islamist women can only have limited bearing and, ultimately, offers them mainly sacrificial roles for the larger cause of saving the threatened community of the Muslim ummah. A culture of recognition, even when it unveils women's agency, can also serve as a sealant of otherwise transformative possibilities for women as individuals or as feminine collectives. To serve as the bearer of culture can turn out to be a 'fundamentalist defence of internal power structures – patriarchy, caste, class – rather than a systemic critique of these' (Sarkar, 2001, p. 234). The conditions and challenges under which Islamist women's agency is currently being articulated in Pakistan is in compliance with the larger male-dominant ideologies of Islamist politics. Unless women's religious agency is unpacked with this understanding and challenged for serving Islamist male causes, gender-blind CVE policies will not prevent the price that women are paying for their sacrifices.

A simmering stalemate

In 2017, a decade after the Lal Masjid siege, I interviewed Umme Hassan in the relocated premises of the Jamia Hafsa in Islamabad. She maintained that the cause of her disciples was to realign the anti-Islamic society of Pakistan (citing the prevalence of alcohol, zina/extra-marital sex, obscenity, corruption, fraud and a *wadera* (feudal culture as evidence of paganism) with that of its originary promise of an Islamic Republic. In pursuit of that goal, Hassan insisted that the Jamia Hafsa and Lal Masjid movements 'are a positive force but to bring change, conflict is imperative'. While believing in the compatibility of the parliamentary system with the goals of Islamic welfare she categorically rejected the current political governance of the country. Recalling the state siege of 2007, Hassan insists the women of Jamia Hafsa had not been conducting vice and virtue moral drives to shut down markets selling music or films, but since Sharia demands action they simply pamphleteered and encouraged shopkeepers and men in the communities to act on their own Muslim conscience.

Hassan's rhetoric is considerably tempered after the siege and the curtailment on the Lal Masjid activities under the National Action Plan. She cited disagreement with the methods of the TTP, saying she doesn't believe in bloodshed and categorically rejected alleged support for Daesh, even when I cited earlier video interviews of her announcing allegiance with the Islamic State. She did, however, register disagreement with the beliefs of the Shia sect and emphatically declared the Ahmedi sects as *kaafirs* or apostates. On the constitutional rights of Pakistanis, she agreed that all citizens were equal but insisted that Muslims should not enter Christian households or communities.

Hassan opined that Al-Huda was not different in ideological bent from the dis-ciples of the *Jamia Hafsa* but 'bahadar nahi humare jaise' (they are not as coura-geous as us). She claimed the Lal Masjid disciples felt the closest ideological resonance with the mainstream Islamist party of the *Jamaat e Islami* while the others simply tow the government line. She recounted the confessionary role of Jamia Hafsa and as arbiter in community issues, with followers seeking advice and justice on cases of incest and sex crimes. She maintained that women cannot be heads of state and can work, provided they observe the veil. Reflecting on the siege of her madrasa, she invoked the sacrifice metaphor in recalling that 'our sacrifice stands testament to the very notion of how this state inflicts injustice to Islamic forces and exposes its own anti-Islamic bent. Women have been inspired by us and so we have a duty to carry the mission on. If the state remains unrepentant then we will be forced to take radical measures. . . felling mosques is an unIslamic act'.

She spoke at some length on the moral decline of Pakistani society, citing Islamic verses and history and then ended the interview by explaining that the most demonic influence was that of the 'free media'. I cited the media's devotion to religious programming and reminded her of her own TV appearance and publicity campaigns, as well as those of Abdul Aziz, but she dismissed this by repeating 'Media Islam dushman hai, dushman hai, dushman hai' (the media is the enemy of Islam). Nearly all her contentions, except support of democratic governance for Pakistan, fall within the narrative framing of the TTP.

Hassan claims she is deeply respected in the same markets that she was accused of shutting down. She challenged my citing her reputation as an extrem-ist by retorting, 'If I was an "extremist" I would not be sitting here in the heart of the capital city'. She went on to assure me that, 'However, I can destroy peace in Islamabad in one stroke'. On reminding her of her pledge and commitment to peaceful means she responded with confidence and said, 'I'm not saying I will. . . I'm simply saying I can be the matchstick that starts fires'.[3]

Legacy of war on terror narratives

In the fallout of the decade of the war on terror, a series of murderous attacks on women officials and human rights activists have taken place. After the assassina-tion of Benazir Bhutto in 2007, apparently the indemnity that women are sup-posedly extended as non-combatants in holy war was stripped. Between 2006 and 2009, the Taliban's invasion of Swat in the Himalayan region of Pakistan was followed by their systematic and violent pogrom to enforce their version of Sharia on the already-Islamic Republic of Pakistan (Perlez, 2009). The Taliban destroyed Swat's famed tourist industry through a series of public beheadings and hangings (of prostitutes, barbers and entertainers) in town squares. Once they controlled Swat, over their three-year siege the Taliban prohibited polio vaccination campaigns, destroyed 165 girls' schools and twenty-two barber shops and banned all music, cinema and most NGOs in the area (Din et al., 2012). Reportedly, health workers were also killed by the Taliban as they attempted to save people wounded in suicide blasts (Din et al., 2012). Women have been recruited as TTP suicide bombers while women state officials (polio/health workers, officials in women's shelters, those serving in the Levies (paramilitary law-enforcement organisations – *gendarmerie* – in Pakistan)) have been targeted for reprisal attacks by religious militants.

The minister Zill e Huma, political candidate Zahra Shahid (Dawn, 2013) and prominent activists, such as Parveen Rahman (BBC News, 2013), Farida Afridi (Haddadi, 2012) and Sabeen Mahmud (Dawn, 2015) have all been murdered for their political views by those associated with religious organisations or with faith-based motivations. Women lawyers and human rights activists have been under constant threat for defending the rights of women and minorities and require around-the-clock security. Women singers, teachers, health workers, artists and those simply residing in tribal areas have been direct victims of religious militancy and 'collateral victims' by drone attacks and military operations conducted by the state.

Yet, in 2012, despite the assassination attempt on the 14-year-old Malala Yousufzai, who defied the Taliban's edict prohibiting girls from attending school in Swat, critics of human rights activists continued to accuse them of deploying 'authenticity as a weapon to legitimize racist violence against Muslims, while undermining the work of scholars and activists engaged in genuine anti-imperialist and anti-racist work in the West' (Toor, 2012, p. 154). Reluctant to 'rescue Muslim women' (Abu-Lughod, 2002), they argued for contextualising such violence in 'the web of social, economic and political power relations within which acts such as these are embedded' (Manchanda, 2012). Such academic endeavours did not assist in countering extremist violence in any manner.

It was only after February 2014, when the Pakistani Taliban murdered twenty-three prisoners from the Frontier Corps whom they had been holding hostage that equivocation over the terrorist threat began to wane. The military also exerted pressure on the media to take an unequivocal stance against the militants (Lieven, 2017). This determination came full circle after the brutal massacre of 141 children and teachers at an Army Public School in Peshawar on 16 December 2014. After this attack on children as the most vulnerable victims, and following the adoption of a joint National Action Plan by the government and military, even the Pakistani Islamist parties ceased to advocate peace.

Operation Zarb e Azb (2014) had a decisive impact on suppressing the insurgency in the tribal areas. However, the fragmentations of extremism have resulted in regroupings by way of an emboldening of domestic Islamist politics, which has dug its heels in on the blasphemy law, anti-Ahmadiyya activism (Ahmadi Muslims believe in the Messiah, Mirza Ghulam Ahmad of Qadian) and on the basis of sectarian differences. At the same time, the military establishment's resolve seems not to have translated into the sociology of counter-extremism narratives. In 2017, the army spokesperson justified the release of self-confessed recruit of the Islamic State, Noreen Leghari, who had been planning an attack on a church on Easter day, by suggesting she could be rehabilitated and it would serve no purpose to treat her as a terrorist. In light of the bombings of churches in Pakistan, including one on Easter 2016, the Christian community released a statement expressing their insecurity at this decision to release an intended terrorist.

Despite the launch of a new National Internal Security Policy in June 2018, the rise of two new religious parties, Milli Muslim League (MML) and the Tehreeq e Labaik Pakistan (TLP), representing radicalised derivations of otherwise pietist Islamic schools, signal the constant reinvention and radicalisation of mainstream Islamist politics in Pakistan. In the run up to the national elections of July 2018, no political party has outlined preventive or counter-extremist policy frameworks revealing a concession to the military establishment on this issue. On the contrary, extremist groups that were banned organisations and listed on the 'fourth schedule' have now been allowed to contest elections on the pretext of 'mainstreaming' them. As Basit notes, 'by participating in the electoral process, [banned religious outfits] gain public legitimacy and create space for their extremist narratives and agendas' (Basit, 2018).

The CVE narrative is unlikely to stabilise as long as the state's approach to jihadist outfits, sectarian groups and Islamist parties is dealt with through selective operations – that is, force against those who threaten the state on the one hand, but appeasement and accommodation for those considered guardians of Islamic morality, defenders against India and of the sovereignty of the Islamic Republic, on the other hand. This whack-a-mole approach simply weakens the narrative for resistance against extremism.

Meanwhile, the defence of Islamist women's 'agency' seems to be making them more attractive as decoys for whom the circumscribed rewards of martyrdom, pride, nationalism, spiritual duty, iconography, paradise and piety will be offered as substitutive to any individual or tangible rights. This is beneficial for a male-dominant religio-nationalist status quo. Pietist agency does not challenge nor contravene radical Islamist aims or activism – in fact, it prepares the societal grounding and pious agents serve as foot soldiers and rationalisers of the larger cause of Islamising the nation.

The marginality or absence of women from CVE strategies internationally is the result of the gender-blindness of its architects. In Pakistan, women religious activists are not the drivers of Islamist politics but can serve as decoys, lured into the rhetoric of sacrifice and heavenly rewards as promised in the scripts of extremists. Layered on such limited roles has been a defensive criticism and dismissal of human rights, feminism or NGO activism as 'Western', 'secular' or 'liberal' and inapplicable for Muslim contexts. It is imperative to understand how women have been deployed in the narrative of extremism through specific cases rather than abstract academic, religious or international frames of terrorism or counter-extremism that may not even apply to Pakistan.

Pakistan's National Action Plan claims 'successes' in stemming terrorism and crime across the country, but in its text and spirit, as well as in the policy guidelines for 2018 as provided in the National Counter Terrorism Authority formed in 2009, gendered considerations or women's voice and participation are non-existent. Unless there is a convincing counter-narrative that exposes the limitations of women's religious agency and offers tangible alternative benefits from women's democratic political empowerment, and their voice is meaningfully included in the CVE discourse and its outcomes, women will remain decoys for extremist ends rather than as drivers for countering extremist violence in Pakistan.

Notes

1 www.finance.gov.pk/survey/chapters_16/Annexure_IV_War_on_terror.pdf (accessed 23 February 2020).
2 See multiple publications by Pakistan Institute for Peace Studies, www.pakpips. com/publications (accessed 23 February 2020).
3 As this went to publication in 2020, the women of the Jamia Hafsa resurfaced briefly to deface a feminist mural bearing images of sisterhood painted by young women in preparation for the Aurat March (Women's March) for International Women's Day in Islamabad (Ali, 2020).

References

Abbas, H., 2004. *Pakistan's Drift into Extremism: Allah, the Army, and America's War on Terror.* M.E. Sharpe, Armonk, NY.
Abbas, H., 2014. *The Taliban Revival: Violence and Extremism on the Pakistan-Afghanistan Border.* Yale University Press, Yale.
Abu-Lughod, L., 2002. 'Do Muslim women really need saving? Anthropological reflections on cultural relativism and its others', *American Anthropologist New Series,* 104(3), 783–790.
Ahmad, S., 2009. *Transforming Faith; The Story of Al-Huda and Islamic Revivalism Among Urban Pakistani Women.* Syracuse University Press, New York.
Ahmed, K., 2016. *Sleepwalking to Surrender: Dealing with Terrorism in Pakistan.* Penguin/Viking, New York.
Akbar Zaidi, S. 2013. 'Pakistan: Misrepresentation and imperialism', *The News,* 8 November. Available at www.thenews.com.pk/archive/print/465659-misrepresentation-and-imperialism (accessed 23 February 2020).
Ali, K., 2014. 'Legally, Abdul Aziz is not the khateeb', *Dawn,* 27 December. Available at www.dawn.com/news/1153401 (accessed 23 February 2020).

Ali, K., 2020. 'Jamia Hafsa students claim responsibility for defacing feminist mural in Islamabad', *Dawn*, 5 March. Available at www.dawn.com/news/1538478 (accessed 21 April 2020).

Ansari, M., 2007. 'Female Madrassa students battle Musharraf', *Telegraph*, 15 April. Available at www.telegraph.co.uk/news/worldnews/1548680/Female-madrassa-students-battle-Musharraf.html (accessed 23 February 2020).

Aziz, S., 2005. 'Beyond petition and redress: Mixed legality and consent in marriage in Pakistan', *Bayan*, IV, 55–70. Simorgh Publication, Lahore.

Bano, M., 2007. 'Contesting ideologies and struggle for authority: State-madrasa engagement in Pakistan', Working Paper 55. University of Birmingham and DFID: Religions and Development Research Programme, UK. Available at http://epapers.bham.ac.uk/1566/1/Bano_Pakistan.pdf (accessed 23 February 2020).

Bano, M., 2012. *The Rational Believer: Choices and Decisions in the Madrasas of Pakistan.* Cornell University Press, Ithaca.

Basit, A., 2018. 'Pre-poll violence', *The News*, 22 July. Available at www.thenews.com.pk/print/344683-pre-poll-violence (accessed 23 February 2020).

BBC News, 2013. 'Pakistan mourns murdered aid worker Parveen Rehman', 14 March. Available at www.bbc.com/news/world-asia-21783304 (accessed 23 February 2020).

Bennett Jones, O., 2013. 'A dangerous debate', *The News*, 24 December. Available at www.thenews.com.pk/archive/print/474749-a-dangerous-debate (accessed 23 February 2020).

Bokhari, F., Johnson, J., 2007. 'Rage in the madrassa belt', *Financial Times*, 10 July. Available at www.ft.com/content/2f7aa178–2f0c–11dc-b9b7–0000779fd2ac?segmentId=9b41d47b-8acb-fadb-7c70–37ee589b60ab (accessed 23 February 2020).

Brohi, N., 2006. 'The MMA offensive; Three years in power 2003–2005', Monograph. Action Aid, Islamabad.

Cheema, M.H., Mustafa, A.-R., 2009. 'From the Hudood Ordinances to the Protection of Women Act: Islamic critiques of the Hudood Laws of Pakistan', *UCLA Journal of Islamic and Near Eastern Law (2008–2009)*, 8, 1–48.

Cohen, S.P. et al., 2011. *The Future of Pakistan.* Brookings Institution Press, Washington DC.

Dawn, 2007. 'Garhi Khuda Bux awaits another Bhutto: Benazir felled by assassin's bullets; 21 others killed in suicide bombing; Asif Zardari, children taking remains to Larkana', 28 December. Available at www.dawn.com/news/282027 (accessed 23 February 2020).

Dawn, 2013. 'PTI senior leader Zahra Shahid killed on eve of Karachi re-polls', 19 May. Available at www.dawn.com/news/1012155 (accessed 23 February 2020).

Dawn, 2014. 'TTP negotiator rejects peace talks under Constitution', 7 February. Available at www.dawn.com/news/1085510 (accessed 23 February 2020).

Dawn, 2015. 'Director T2F Sabeen Mahmud shot dead in Karachi', 24 April. Available at www.dawn.com/news/1177956 (accessed 23 February 2020).

Devji, F. 2008. 'Red mosque', *Public Culture*, 20(1), 19–26.

Din, I.U., Mumtaz, Z. and Ataullahjan, A., 2012. 'How the Taliban undermined community healthcare in Swat, Pakistan', *The BMJ*. Available at www.bmj.com/content/344/bmj.e2093 (accessed 23 February 2020).

Furlow, R.B., Goodall, H.L., 2011. 'The war of ideas and the battle of narratives: A comparison of extremist storytelling structures', *Cultural Studies ↔ Critical Methodologies*, 11(3), 215–223.

Gul, I., 2010. *The Most Dangerous Place: Pakistan's Lawless Frontier*. Viking Penguin, New York.

Haddadi, A., 2012. 'Pakistani women's rights activist Fareeda "Kokikhel" Afridi shot dead in Peshawar', *International Business Times*, 5 July. Available at www.ibtimes.co.uk/woman-activist-fareeda-kokikhel-shot-dead-peshawar-359823 (accessed 23 February 2020).

Haq, F., 2007. 'Militarism and motherhood: The women of the Lashkar-i- Tayyabia in Pakistan', *Signs: Journal of Women in Culture and Society*, 32(4), 1023–1046.

Haqqani, H., 2005. *Pakistan: Between Mosque and Military*. Carnegie Endowment for International Peace, Washington, DC.

Haroon, S., 2007. *Frontier of Faith: Islam, in the Indo-Afghan Borderland*. C. Hurst and Co, London.

Hirschkind, C., Mahmood, S., 2002. 'Feminism, the Taliban, and politics of counter-insurgency', *Anthropological Quarterly*, 75(2), 339–354.

Hussain, Z., 2013. *The Scorpion's Tail: The Relentless Rise of Islamic Militants in Pakistan –and How It Threatens America*. Free Press, New York.

Iqtidar, H., 2011. *Secularizing Islamists? Jamaat-i-Islami and Jama`at-ud-Da`wa in Urban Pakistan*. Chicago University Press, Chicago and London.

Jamal, A., 2005. 'Feminist "selves" and feminism's "others": Feminist representations of Jamaat-e-Islami women in Pakistan', *Feminist Review*, 81(1), 52–73.

Khattak, S.G., 2006. 'Inconvenient facts: Women's political representation and military regimes in Pakistan', in *Transforming Institutions of Power: Towards Gender-responsive Governance*.Monograph. Rozan, Islamabad.

Latif, A., Munir, H.S., 2014. 'Terrorism and jihad, an Islamic perspective', *Journal of Islamic Studies and Culture*, 2(1), 69–80.

Lieven, A., 2011. *Pakistan: A Hard Country*. Allen Lane, London.

Lieven, A., 2017. 'Counter-insurgency in Pakistan: The role of legitimacy', *Small Wars & Insurgencies*, 28(1), 166–190.

Lodhi, M. (ed.), 2011. *Pakistan: Beyond the 'Crisis State'*. Oxford University Press, Karachi.

Mahmood, S., 2005. *Politics of Piety; The Islamic Revival and the Feminist Subject*. Princeton University Press, Princeton, NJ.

Manchanda, N. 2012. 'Out of nowhere? The Taliban and Malala', open Democracy, 7 November. Available at www.opendemocracy.net/opensecurity/nivi-manchanda/out-of-nowhere-taliban-and-malala (accessed 23 February 2020).

Mir, A., 2010. *Talibanisation of Pakistan: From 9/11 to 26/11 and beyond*. Pentagon Press, New Delhi.

Munir, A., 2011. 'Lal Masjid siege – four years on', *Express Tribune, 2 July*. Available at https://tribune.com.pk/story/201068/lal-masjid-siege--four-years-on/ (accessed 23 February 2020).

Ní Aoláin, F., 2016. 'The "war on terror" and extremism: Assessing the relevance of the Women, Peace and Security agenda', *International Affairs*, 92(2), 275–291.

Perlez, J., 2007. 'Pakistani students capture masseuses to make a point', *The New York Times*, 25 June. Available at www.nytimes.com/2007/06/25/world/asia/25islamabad.html?_r=1&pagewanted=2 (accessed 23 February 2020).

Perlez, J., 2009. 'Taliban seize vital Pakistan area closer to the capital', *The New York Times*, 22 April. Available at www.nytimes.com/2009/04/23/world/asia/23buner.html?pagewanted=all&_r=0 (accessed 23 February 2020).

Physicians for Social Responsibility, 2015. *Body Count: Casualty Figures After 10 Years of the "War on Terror"*, March. Available at www.ippnw.de/commonFiles/pdfs/Frieden/Body_Count_first_international_edition_2015_final.pdf (accessed 23 February 2020).

Rashid, A., 2008. *Descent into Chaos: The US and the Disaster in Pakistan, Afghanistan, and Central Asia*. Penguin Press, New York.

Razack, S., 2007. 'Stealing the pain of others: Reflections on Canadian humanitarian responses', *Review of Education Pedagogy and Cultural Studies*, 29(4), 375–394.

Sabri, Z., 2013. 'Timid treatment', *The News*, 24 December. Available at http://tns.thenews.com.pk/timid-treatment/#.W1TmhiOB0Y0 (accessed 23 February 2020).

Saigol, R., 2013. *The Pakistan Project: A Feminist Perspective on Nation and Identity*. Women Unlimited, New Delhi.

Saigol, R., 2016. 'Feminism and the women's movement in Pakistan: Actors, debates and strategies', A Country Study (Pakistan). Friedrick Ebert Stiftung, Islamabad.

Sarkar, T., 2001. *Hindu Wife, Hindu Nation: Community, Religion and Cultural Nationalism*, Indiana University Press, Bloomington, IN.

Sarwar, B., 2007. "Boots, beards, burqas and bombs', *Himalmag*, August. Available at https://countervortex.org/node/4496 (accessed 23 February 2020).

Shah, A., 2014. *The Army and Democracy: Military Politics in Pakistan*. Harvard University Press, Cambridge, MA.

Shahzad, S., 2011. *Inside Al Qaeda and the Taliban: Beyond Bin Laden and 9/11*. Pluto Press, London.

Shamsie, K., 2007. 'Hostage to a story line', *Index on Censorship*, 36(12), 12–17.

Siddiqa, A., 2007. *Military Inc: Inside Pakistan's Military Economy*. Pluto Press, London.

Tahir, M., 2013a. 'Drones, wounds and privilege', *The News*, 14 November. Available at www.thenews.com.pk/archive/print/466862-drones-wounds-and-privilege (accessed 23 February 2020).

Tahir, M., 2013b. *Wounds of Waziristan*. Journeyman Pictures, 25 November. Available at www.youtube.com/watch?v=sk7fD5umakg (accessed 23 February 2020).

The News, 2013. 'Lal Masjid reissues 2004 fatwa to support JI chief', 13 November. Available at www.thenews.com.pk/archive/print/466701-lal-masjid-reissues-2004-fatwa-to-support-ji-chief (accessed 23 February 2020).

Toor, S., 2012. 'Imperialist feminism redux', *Dialectical Anthropology*, 36 (3–4), 147–160.

United Nations, n.d. Available at www.un.org/womenwatch/osagi/wps/ (accessed 23 February 2020).

Wilcox, L., 2005. 'What is political extremism?', *Scribd*. Available at www.scribd.com/document/20270033/What-is-Political-Extremism-Defamation (accessed 23 February 2020).

Yusuf, H., 2011. 'The future of Pakistan', *US Institute for Peace*, 31 January. Available at www.c-spanvideo.org/program/297769–1 (accessed 23 February 2020).

Yuval-Davis, N., 1997. *Gender and Nation*. SAGE, Thousand Oaks, CA, London.

Zakaria, R., 2017. 'Terror and the family: How jihadi groups are redefining the role of women', *World Policy Journal*, 34(3), 41–44.

Zia, A.S., 2012. 'The political correctness of drone activism', *openDemocracy*, 5 November. Available at www.opendemocracy.net/5050/afiya-shehrbano-zia/political-correctness-of-drone-activism (accessed 23 February 2020).

Zia, A.S., 2018. *Faith and Feminism in Pakistan*. Sussex Academic Press, Brighton.

14

The Mayor of Abuja and the 'Pied Piper' of Maiduguri: extremism and the 'politics of mutual envy' in Nigeria?

Akinyemi Oyawale

Introduction

Countering extremism, as a 'softer' approach to countering terrorism, has received heightened attention in Nigeria following the failure of erstwhile 'hard' approaches to combating Boko Haram. Much of the initial effort to counter Boko Haram was based on a strict coercive counter-terrorism strategy, where the Nigerian military primarily focused on forcefully vanquishing militants. In response to the various criticisms which the state received for alleged human rights violations and abuse, there has been a shift towards a more comprehensive approach not only transcends violence but incorporates non-violent means to tackle underlying 'causes' or 'ideologies', such as Salafi and Wahhabi doctrines, that purportedly 'enable' or 'cause' terrorism. This chapter critically examines the politics behind these interventions through postcolonial and poststructuralist lenses.

To vividly capture the politics of extremism in Nigeria and the transformation of Boko Haram from the non-violent religious study group that it used to be, the chapter adapts insights from The Pied Piper of Hamelin to capture how the Nigerian government (Mayor), has been locked in a mimetic relationship with Boko Haram (Piper) which captures what will be described as the 'Politics of Mutual Envy'. As an early prebuttal, Abuja has no 'Mayor' (it has a minister) and Maiduguri has no 'Pied Piper' (Abubakar, 2014b). The 'Mayor of Abuja' serves as a metaphor for the Nigerian government (and state), while the Pied Piper serves as a metaphor for non-state challenges to state authority that emerge from within society and may enjoy some legitimacy from sections of the population (Loimeier, 2011, 2012).

The chapter contends that terrorism is not a product of independent or isolated causal factors that instigate particular actors to engage in violence, but rather is an interaction between disparate actors (Jackson et al., 2011; Kundnani, 2015). In this sense, rather than viewing Boko Haram as a product of root causes, extremist ideology and in particular Salafism or Wahhabism, it can best be understood as an interaction between the group and the Nigerian state which has been driven by an intractable politics of mutual envy (PME). It becomes important to ask how the Nigerian way of defining and combating threat has been expanded (at least nominally) from countering terrorism to countering ideology, i.e., violent extremism, and what purpose this transformation serves. This chapter argues that countering violent extremism (CVE) in Nigeria is a form of mimicry of Western – especially Anglo-American – ways of constructing and dealing with threat, and that this introduction of a 'softer' approach to countering terrorism ignores the cultural, political and historical realities of Nigeria.

First, the chapter engages with contemporary literature on extremism and radicalisation more broadly, and in Nigeria more specifically. Current literature concerns itself with explaining how particular extremist ideologies may cause terrorism and how these could be reversed through the deradicalisation of victims, mostly convicted militants or those awaiting trial; hence, it is more remedial than proactive. Second, the chapter conceptually situates its central arguments in poststructuralist and postcolonial thoughts through addressing the origin and journey of extremism and radicalisation as interrelated concepts within the UK and how it has been adopted in Nigeria as a 'soft' makeover on its previously 'hard' approach to countering Boko Haram.

Third, the chapter addresses extremism through an entangled reading of British and Nigerian countering-violence and violent-extremism projects, thus showing how governments attempt to delegitimise the *Other* to further the goals of the self. Fourth, the chapter addresses the reciprocal envy by non-state actors in their bid to challenge the authority and legitimacy of states through examining local discourses on Boko Haram. Ultimately, extremism and radicalisation should be viewed as a process where both state and non-state actors are locked in a continuous PME about an imagined *Other*.

Literature review

Radicalisation and extremism form a duo of concepts that drive the new 'soft' measures – deradicalisation and preventing violent extremism (PVE) – that have been incorporated into the previously 'hard' counter-terrorism approach to Boko Haram in Nigeria (Eji, 2016). While this so-called 'soft' approach to counter-terrorism has received increasing attention and commendation both locally and internationally, a review of current literature on the origin and evolution of the concept more broadly or its journey into the Nigerian security policy and scholarship reveals how problematic radicalisation and extremism and the policy prescriptions that they underpin are, both internationally and within the Nigerian context (Eji, 2016; Kundnani, 2012, 2015). To properly critique radicalisation within the Nigerian context, it is important to engage with local literature on the concept and critically examine their assumptions and taken-for-granted 'Truths' from postcolonial and poststructuralist perspectives, which will serve as a point of departure for the main arguments made in this chapter.

The most prominent debate on radicalisation and extremism in Nigeria research is situated within broader religious terrorism research on Boko Haram, where the concern with radicalisation follows from the initial acknowledgement that Boko Haram is driven by an extremist ideology. These studies seek to examine macro factors that make people susceptible to extremism. Onuoha (2014), Agbiboa (2013, 2014), Sodipo (2013) and Ojochemnemi et al. (2015), among others, all advance – to varying degrees – the 'root cause' argument, highlighting how structural factors such as poverty and political marginalisation could predispose citizens to the appeal of radical Islamist views. Sodipo (2013) makes a causal connection between some form of deprivation, i.e., economic or political, and predisposition to radicalisation. In other words, since Northern Nigeria is economically deprived and politically marginalised, this can explain why Boko Haram emerged and has succeeded there (Sodipo, 2013). Alao (2013) views radicalisation as 'reactionary' against five main factors that cause radicalisation in Nigeria, namely, traditionalism, desecration (of the Prophet), Christianisation – or Pentecostalism more specifically – since the 1980s, socio-economic deprivation and purported attack on the Ummah.

Another prominent concern for scholars in Nigeria is about the effectiveness of CVE. Besides the earlier macro-explanations for why people could be predisposed to radicalisation and eventually engaging in terrorism, authors such as Barkindo and Bryans (2016) and Clubb and Tapley (2018) have specifically engaged in primary work to assess deradicalisation success. Barkindo and Bryans (2016) investigated the disengagement and deradicalisation scheme at Kuje Prison in Abuja, which examined the effectiveness of counter-narratives in changing the views of convicted militants or those awaiting trial for suspected involvement in terrorism. This version of Nigeria's CVE is remedial in that it seeks to reverse much of what is considered primarily causal in why those militants joined Boko Haram (Barkindo and Bryans, 2016, p. 1). Their approach is similar to prisoner rehabilitation assessments where success is measured based on lack of, or low percentage of, recidivism among beneficiaries. In a similar evaluative work, Clubb and Tapley (2018) introduce a more community-based evaluative approach which does not merely stop at lack of recidivism but, rather, the successful social reintegration of 'disengaged' and 'deradicalised' individuals back into their communities. These studies all provide a solid attempt to evaluate the success of a state policy to fulfil its objectives, which is evident in their problem-solving nature that treats the status quo as a given (Cox, 1981).

For the initial arguments about radicalisation in Nigeria, 'root cause' arguments advance structural, 'macro-explanations' for terrorism, i.e., structural woes such as poverty, illiteracy, socio-economic factors and political marginalisation may predispose people to being receptive to violent extremism (Jackson et al., 2011). This is partly a combination of the 'frustration-aggression hypothesis', which was proposed by Berkowitz (1989), and rationalist arguments (Crenshaw, 1981; Jackson et al., 2011). Monocausality has been challenged by various scholars, for example, Malečková (2005), Krueger and Malečková (2002) and Berrebi (2003), who have all refuted these 'poverty' and 'illiteracy' causes by questioning their empirical validity, while experts within the critical security tradition usually shy away from making direct causal arguments which have positivist undertones (Jackson et al., 2011). In this sense, it is difficult to differentiate between correlation and causation, and almost impossible to prove why these same factors do not lead to radicalisation and terrorism elsewhere in the absence of a control group (Jackson et al., 2011; Kundnani, 2015).

For studies that have evaluated the success of reversing or countering the process of radicalisation, i.e., disengagement and deradicalisation, the paucity of evaluative work on the radicalisation project in Nigeria may be because of the project's recency (Office of the National Security Advisor (ONSA), 2016). Nigerian CVE policy was officially adopted by the government in a move towards a 'softer' approach to counter-terrorism which was established in the National Counter-Terrorism Strategy (NACTEST) in 2014 (Eji, 2016). This makes it difficult for these studies to definitely know if deradicalisation or disengagement actually work, without benefit of long-term data, results or even enough time for these courses to be completed by inmates. In much of these works, radicalisation as a concept is treated as unproblematic and the status quo is taken for granted, which can be viewed as their 'problem-solving' nature.

From a critical perspective, three main issues are discernible as weaknesses within extant studies on radicalisation and extremism within the Nigerian context. They ignore the historical, social and cultural context within which Nigeria and its political and cultural conflicts have evolved, which is largely responsible for their treatment of radicalisation as an unproblematic and objective phenomenon. This chapter argues that this represents a *mimicry* of European, and particularly Anglo-American, ways of defining and countering threat (Bhabha, 1984; Heath-Kelly, 2016). In the UK, where these concepts evolved in the aftermath of the 9/11 and 7/7 attacks, effectiveness studies on policies developed to counter them, i.e., deradicalisation, are largely inconclusive and fraught with practical and theoretical difficulties (Kundnani, 2015), which further complicates why such untested methods have been adopted by Nigeria without caution.

These are neither neutral nor value-free, but are rather value-laden commitments that are often largely unacknowledged.

To be sure, this chapter argues that it is important and indeed beneficial to examine the politics of (de-)radicalisation through construing extremism, rather than as an objective phenomenon which can be transplanted to a variety of contexts, towards viewing it as a socially constructed ontology which serves an ideological purpose (Heath-Kelly, 2016; Kundnani, 2015). First, it serves the purpose of elites and political entrepreneurs both locally, i.e., to appeal to citizens that the state is doing something and also as a weapon of governmentality, and internationally, to appeal to a global Western-oriented and dominated disciplinary regime that has made particular universal security frameworks and ideals best practices that must be adopted by non-Western states to prove that postcolonial states are doing enough. This can be viewed as a 'rite of passage' for acceptance into the 'international society' of states.

From a poststructuralist perspective, it becomes possible to expose the workings of power, i.e., the relationship between knowledge and power (Foucault et al., 1997; Heath-Kelly, 2014). So-called foundational concepts such as sovereignty, legitimacy and political authority cannot be treated as *givens*, which in turn may be understood as the increasing *marketisation* of Nigerian security research to serve both local and global interests (Barnard-Wills and Moore, 2010; Chowdhry, 2007). Locally, it serves the demands of the state in terms of the problem-solving nature where policy relevance drives research and there is a competition among scholars to advance the best possible ways to solve the problem of violent extremism, even when defining such a concept is not straightforward and when the state itself may be implicated in fostering conditions which permit such problems (Jackson et al., 2011). On a global level, liberal funding and publications in high-impact international (more precisely Anglo-American) journals serve as a self-interested *disciplinary regime* for Nigerian academics who need to make headway, both financially and career-wise. Thus, there are tendencies that their arguments do not challenge the so-called liberal world order through calling out its premises and how it is implicated in creating a global *Western Utopia* which continuously upholds a *mythical* West vs. anti-West binary.

What is usually not discussed is that for radicalisation to be convincing, the premise of extremism must be accepted alongside the typological and categorical presumptions of Islamist or religious terrorism with its inherent essentialist, universalist and causative arguments (Gunning and Jackson, 2011; Jackson et al., 2011). From an essentialist standpoint, Boko Haram is an Islamist group because other attributes such as ethnic, cultural and political factors (for example, state repression) are less important; from a universalist perspective, Boko Haram is Islamist, meaning that it must *behave* like other so-called jihadi groups or, for more ambitious positivists, must belong to a global jihad network that wants to topple the West; causatively, the group's 'barbaric' violence, unprecedented bravado and wanton destructiveness, and incorrigibility are all *caused* by its transcendental objectives steeped in irrational religious beliefs and fundamentalist (mis-)interpretation of the Quran (Gunning and Jackson, 2011; Jackson et al., 2011; Weber, 2013). These myths all flounder on closer scrutiny (Kundnani, 2014, 2015).

To prevent an overextension, the *Pied Piper* metaphor is not an analytical framework but rather a metaphor which helps to capture the PME that has plagued Nigerian counter-terrorism more broadly, deradicalisation more specifically and, to an extent, extremism and radicalisation as concepts that emerged and blossomed in the UK and other Western countries, post 9/11 and 7/7 (Heath-Kelly, 2016; Kundnani, 2012, 2015). My contention is that construing the politics of extremism as involving PME serves to capture the various layers of dynamics at play in understanding Boko Haram violence itself (Kundnani, 2015). Causation – especially *monocausality* – within radicalisation scholarship and policy in Nigeria is treated as unproblematic, which raises similar questions about how the complex interplay of factors such as those highlighted by earlier pre-9/11 scholars such as 'political context and organisational decision-making [as well] as individual motivation and ideology' (Kundnani, 2015, p. 24; Crenshaw, 1981).

This multidimensional approach captures macro, meso and micro factors that may influence – not necessarily *cause* – gravitation towards terrorism and other forms of political violence (Jackson et al., 2011; Pisoiu and Hain, 2017). Like most arguments on radicalisation, while much effort is put into discussing the process through which certain influential radical clerics (associated with particular radical groups) identify and indoctrinate susceptible youths (individually motivated) into engaging in terrorism (Hearne and Laiq, 2010), the process is reified so much that the origin of this 'conveyor belt' receives almost no attention.

Finally, as already discussed, current research ignores African identity and its historical representation as the Other (to the West) in their engagement with *Western* concepts and ideas (Said, 1978). This is not only reckless but complicit in perpetuating unequal power relations that have characterised European–African relations for almost half a millennium. The concept of *traveling theory* by Said (1983) reminds us of the context-dependency of theory, while Cox's (1981, p. 128) popular maxim that 'theory is always for someone and for some purpose' reminds us of the interest-driven tendencies of theoretical postulations. Postcolonial curiosities are totally absent in these endeavours, or how do they not find Chinua Achebe's (1977) epigrammatic expressions in *Image of Africa* – which took issue with Joseph Conrad's (1996) representation of Africa and Africans in his seminal work *Heart of Darkness* – particularly discerning? To Achebe (1977, p. 783), Africa was represented as 'the other world [. . .] the antithesis of Europe and therefore of civilization. What this implies is that Africa and Africans are much more historically and culturally maligned than the 'Islamic' 'Other' that Europe has created as an antithesis of the Western Self in a 'clash of civilisations' thesis (Huntington, 1993), or in earlier more graphic narratives concerning Africa and Africans (Hegel and Sibree, 2004).

A contrapuntal reading and understanding of African and European history, or more specifically, Nigerian and British history, reveals how these histories are intertwined rather than being independent, with British history and identity valorised – in contrast to the Other – as the conqueror, coloniser, superior, and Nigerian history considered antithetical, i.e., everything which British history and identity is or was not, colonised, inferior and uncivilised, among others (Chowdhry, 2007; Darwish, 2007; Said, 1983).

This chapter pays attention to these dynamics and unequal power relationships to address how radicalisation, extremism and other cognate concepts have been adopted and replicated within the Nigerian context and how this mimicry of Western ways of constructing and dealing with threat can be unpacked through the Pied Piper metaphor and postcolonial and poststructuralist commitments which will serve to show how both the UK and Nigeria, as state actors, engage in politics of envy to demonise and suppress dissent and challenges to their authority and legitimacy. Non-state actors, mainly al Qaida, ISIS and Boko Haram, have reciprocated this practice in what can best be understood as politics of mutual envy.

The Piper and the Mayor, politics of mutual 'envy'

The envious gaze which the state casts on Boko Haram is astounding, i.e., as an entity that can be reckless without repercussions, be ruthless without sanctions, be 'legitimate' without responsibility, even if it is at the cost of being labelled enemy combatants without full legal status. In a way, is this not what the greatest despots aspire to? Even so-called self-acclaimed 'advanced' climes have had a Cromwell, a Napoleon, a Hitler and a Mussolini, among others (Barducci, 2008; Hertzler, 1940). This is the objective of the 'performance of political authority' that knows no bounds (Heath-Kelly, 2014, p. 41); the biggest 'organised criminal' in town without sanctions (Tilly, 1985); the promotion of a 'secular ministry' by the biggest organised criminal (Heath-Kelly, 2014, p. 78), so to speak. Under military regimes in Nigeria, blatant force has served despotic purposes, but this is now difficult to achieve or sustain, especially when Boko Haram itself has metamorphosed – like most contemporary non-state actors – to exploit the weaknesses of monstrous state actors through becoming masters of subterfuge and trickery or, even more rewarding, *publicity* (Schmid, 1989).

This *gaze* is present in the Pied Piper's story when the Mayor watches the itinerant Piper accomplish what s/he struggled in vain to achieve, i.e., getting rid of the rats which had plagued Hamelin in the story, but within the Nigerian context, generated a fervour that colonialism more or less stripped through amalgamation and the bifurcation of society and the state – the former serving the purpose of belonging and a source of ontological security and the latter serving political and economic ends (Ekeh, 1975; Giddens, 1991). Reciprocally, the Piper watches the population and resources of Hamelin with envy; with all his magical tunes and power to serenade, he is just an itinerant spirit with neither a stable abode nor friends (Browning, 1888). The Mayor's position with its accompanying status, wealth, power, prestige and authority must be desirous (Browning, 1888). Taking the children away to an underground country must be a way of fulfilling this fantasy of secession and establishing its own political community.

The 'collective memory' of the state's wrongdoing and exploitation has to be mythologised and then embedded in a specific 'projective narrative' to depict what wrongs have been done and construct what past or future space can best right these wrongs. In other words, it involves the constructive manipulation of temporality such that past wrongs and wrongdoers are considered still present and productive of future challenges. The wrongdoing is not an invention but the discursive construction of it by actors to serve their purpose. This may be associated with the argument that there are many cases of poverty, deprivation, political exclusion, grievances and ideologies that may glorify or promote violence, but there are few cases of terrorism (Jackson et al., 2011). The predictive value of the transformation of Boko Haram becomes much weakened from this perspective, just as the earlier experience of the Nigerian state with *Maitatsine* – a heterodox militant 'Islamist' group in the 1970s and 1980s – offered almost no roadmap for the Nigerian government and stakeholders about the best ways to manage the Boko Haram situation where a crackdown resulted in an escalation and helped to make the group more extremist and violent (Loimeier, 2011).

Kanem-Bornu or Sokoto Caliphate narratives are not out there and much of the support base of Boko Haram are youths and middle-aged people who never experienced those epochs first hand or have access to verify claims or counterclaims about their rise and demise. It is often taken for granted that particular ethnic and religious identities are associated with specific groups, but then very little is said about how these constructions are established and sustained. For example, how does Boko Haram manage to string together a chain of biographical narratives that interweave incompatible or even mutually exclusive epochs to forge a seemingly 'homogenous' past that seeks to re-establish itself? Kanem-Bornu Empire and the Sokoto Caliphate were never coterminous, either geographically or culturally. Both entities were usually in conflict after the rise of the Sokoto Caliphate and differed ideologically and ethnically (Loimeier, 2017).

The rise of the Caliphate strongly weakened Kanem-Bornu before they were both conquered by European colonial powers: France conquered the latter in 1900 (Hiribarren, 2016), while British forces conquered the former in 1903 (Oliver, 1985). In fact, both kingdoms were at war and it took the bravery of Al-Kanemi, a warrior-leader, to help rally support within Kanem-Bornu to resist the forays of the Sokoto Caliphate, which meant that it remained independent of the larger and increasingly more formidable empire until the European conquests (Brenner, 1973). While this recreation narrative may be inconsistent in itself, it can also be argued that the recreation discourses do not explain the various trajectories that Boko Haram could have taken, since it ignores the interaction of the group with the various state and non-state actors over the years (Kundnani, 2015). What it only achieves is to reduce Boko Haram to an Islamist ideology which derives its legitimacy and inspiration from the Sokoto Jihad which brought the Sokoto Caliphate into existence (Last, 1967; Lovejoy and Hogendorn, 1990).

From the perspective of states, this so called fanatical adherence to an Islamist ideology serves to undermine the state's own position through acknowledging the possibility of an authority above the state. Citizens who occupy one end of this continuum may be constructed as unpatriotic, while being on the other end may represent treason. For totalitarian regimes, allegiance is usually top down and enforced through coercion, which means that the discontinuation of this coercion or threat of violence may spell the end of such deference, for example, through its renouncement for a better life (Makarychev and Yatsyk, 2017). This is why 'home-grown' terrorism did not make much sense when the Madrid, London and Amsterdam attacks were carried out not by citizens from so-called 'backward' countries with constant repression and various characteristics that Western societies view as conducive to terrorism – such as the 9/11 perpetrators being mostly from the Middle East – but, rather, citizens of 'advanced', liberal democratic Western societies (Heath-Kelly, 2016; Kundnani, 2015). These citizens had a choice, to live in a so-called free and multicultural society or to die for the cause of an ideology that sought to destroy 'freedom' or so-called Western values; they chose the latter (Kundnani, 2014).

Within the Nigerian context, Boko Haram's *ideology* and ongoing project only acquires its meaning from its interaction with various alternative communities (Adesoji, 2011; Campbell, 2014). As discussed earlier, the ideologies that underpinned the empires that emerged in Kanem-Bornu and Sokoto Caliphate had distinctly advanced views on their idea of community and also emerged within specific historical, cultural and political contexts (Brenner, 1973; Hiribarren, 2016; Last, 1967). The colonial administration would have been the extremist challenger to Islamic community at various times, including at the turn of the 20th century when both Islamic political communities eventually fell to superior

European firepower (Kanya-Forstner and Lovejoy, 1994; Lovejoy and Hogendorn, 1990). In this sense, viewing Boko Haram as anti-Western in terms of sharing a similar ideology with other groups such as al Qaida and Islamic State advances a dangerous essentialisation, universalisation and decontextualisation of violence in Nigeria that offers very little analytical value (Jackson et al., 2011). The same argument applies to extremism and radicalisation as concepts, which seek to divert attention from local context-specific dynamics that influence terrorism and distinguish one form of violence from another, making generalisation quite difficult (Jackson et al., 2011), especially from a very Westerncentric perspective. An entangled reading of the evolution of the concept within both contexts may help to shed light on how postcolonial mimicry has plagued African states in their security practice, and how a more critical engagement with Western concepts can serve to advance knowledge (Barnard-Wills and Moore, 2010).

Mayors' attempts to Prevent (UK), Forestall (Nigeria) and possibly 'reverse' radicalisation

Two main policies exemplify attempts by the British and Nigerian governments to combat terrorism through improvised untraditional ways of countering or reversing ideologies that transform ordinary people into monsters: Prevent and Forestall (Kundnani, 2012, 2014; Home Office, 2011; ONSA, 2016). The mayors in this context purportedly serve the interest of the citizenry through being the custodian of popular legitimacy and are recognised by the international community as representatives of the state. The question is not whether these mayors are legitimate or not; the argument here is that the practice of security, both locally and internationally since 9/11, has represented the conjuring up of an imaginary Other who constitutes a death knell to the state's very existence. Radicalisation and extremism serve this Other's purpose and Prevent and Forestall are not only remedial but can be understood as a version of the state's own *extremist* ideology; deliberately digressing from what used to be the norm, expressed through enhanced powers, intrusion into private lives and all-round interventions that undermine the fundamental concepts that those societies were built upon.

In the West, there is a continuous worry that Western liberalism does not offer enough tools to adequately combat extremism in terms of the freedoms that it provides, especially through having individual liberty as its core principle. David Cameron took a more pragmatic stance in 2011 through his rejigged concept of 'muscular liberalism', where liberal countries could effectively combat dangerous Islamic doctrines through a more 'extremist' version of liberalism, in what can be viewed as profoundly oxymoronic (Kundnani, 2015; Latour, 2012).

The envy here is that liberalism promotes multiculturalism, which serves to allow rights and liberties that enemies of the state exploit to promote their own version of political community. This argument is an extension of causal relationships that experts have attempted to propose between liberal democracies and terrorism, such that terrorism only thrives in societies where rights and liberties are protected (Wilkinson, 1986, 2011); liberty condones insecurity. It could be argued that David Cameron's speech was not merely a one-off or a divergence from broader conceptions of the performance of the preponderant Western ideology (liberalism), against Islamism or, more specifically, Islamic fundamentalism, but rather a continuous politics of mutual envy which requires continuous antagonism with the *Other* (Piper). Fukuyama (1989) pulled no punches in his argument about competitors to Western liberal democracy.

A quick examination of the definition of extremism advanced by the UK's pre-eminent counter-radicalisation policy captures this juxtaposition of values and the 'either or' logic that has bedevilled anti-terrorism, counter-terrorism and counter-radicalisation rhetoric since the 9/11 attack on the US. Within Prevent, the politics of mutual envy is expressed through the definition of extremism as characterised by the absence of 'fundamental British values' (Kundnani, 2015):

> Extremism is vocal or active opposition to fundamental British values, including democracy, the rule of law, individual liberty and mutual respect and tolerance of different faiths and beliefs. We also include in our definition of extremism calls for the death of members of our armed forces, whether in this country or overseas. (Home Office, 2011, p. 107)

In the equivalent policy document within the Nigerian context, NACTEST, its PVE/CVE stream (Forestall) fails to explicitly define extremism but constructs it as being antithetical to 'Nigerianness'. While so-called British values are vague, especially when the politics of mutual envy has required the extirpation of some of those vaunted ideals, for example, freedom of expression, tolerance and multiculturalism among others, it does not make much sense to establish so-called radical Islam as antithetical to a particular idealised notion of Nigerian 'values'. The UK can at the very least point to a Judeo-Christian historical tradition. But in Nigeria, several communities in the North – for example, the Kanem-Bornu Empire – can trace Islam to the 12th century, which makes Western liberal democracy the alien tradition (Loimeier, 2011, 2017).

Nigeria has so much internal diversity that multiculturalism is not a desire, but a necessity; visions of a non-multicultural or culturally homogenous Nigeria are a nightmare for most communities invested in the Nigerian political community. In this sense, a homogenous 'Us' vs. 'Them' which constitutes an 'either or', 'Manichean' dichotomy rhetoric, is not only problematic within the Nigerian context but potentially dangerous (Merskin, 2004). Without much value in the politics of extremism within the Nigerian context, it can be argued that Forestall is an adaptation of Prevent, which continues a long tradition of (post-)colonial mimicry where the colony adopts policies and measures from the metropole, even when such ideas or concepts may be irrelevant to the (post-)colony (Bhabha, 1984).

As discussed, at the heart of the politics of mutual envy is legitimacy. These bunch of 'extremists' believe in the legitimacy of a different authority and will fight to accomplish its objectives over those of the British, American, French and German authorities, which very often are constructed along the lines of the Ummah (Kundnani, 2014). This is at the heart of the 'Suspect Community' argument where a community becomes suspected *en masse* as problematic and dangerous and is consequently disproportionately targeted with extraordinary measures (Breen-Smyth, 2014; Hillyard, 1993; Nickels et al., 2012; Pantazis and Pemberton, 2009). Far-right groups and individuals are treated with less disdain because the world which they envision and the community which they 'imagine' are not significantly different from the current status quo; it is a matter of degree and they may be considered to uphold 'British values' more than liberals and conservatives (Anderson, 2006; Goodwin and Milazzo, 2015). Perhaps this explains why right-wing political parties such as the UK Independence Party (UKIP) or the right-wing populist party in France, the National Rally (known as the National Front until June 2018), usually become popular when there is a strong anti-immigration sentiment and when xenophobia gains political salience (Wodak et al., 2013). Thomas Mair, the murderer of Jo Cox, was everything but a terrorist, and despite a history of far-right terrorism, National Action, a neo-Nazi group, was the first far-right group to be banned in December 2016 (Noor et al., 2018).

It is patriotic for British soldiers to sing 'God Save the Queen' and happily fight for and die for the Crown – the embodiment of British values – in faraway wars, and a refusal to follow orders to do so is mutiny and a serious offence of '*unpatriotism*' (Bradley, 2012). Basically, the mutual envy is centred on the preponderant custodian over the political 'power to make live or let die' (Foucault and Ewald, 2003, p. 241) and on whose terms these are defined and executed. As Makarychev and Yatsyk (2017, p. 1) argue, 'biopolitical instruments of power are indispensable components of discourses and practices of making and shaping national identities', although they may be manipulated to further an 'us' which is mutually exclusive to the 'them'.

Within the Nigerian setting, several soldiers and officers have been court-martialled, with some sentenced to death for not being as devout to the Nigerian cause as Boko Haram militants and abandoning their positions when overwhelmed by daredevil Boko Haram militants, who consider the imagined Islamic community as worthy of their ultimate sacrifice (Anderson, 2006; BBC Africa, 2014; Foucault, 1990). It is not extremists' dedication to a 'fanatical' creed that is the problem, it is the icon at the heart of their allegiance. It is through viewing radicalisation and extremism not as objective or ontologically stable phenomena or signifiers that refer to a nonarbitrary 'signified' that opens up possibilities for addressing their underlying politics, the identities of actors that construct and assign these labels to agents and the goals which they serve.

The Piper's reciprocal 'politics of envy'

The ongoing argument has centred on addressing how states are envious of the support and fervency that certain non-state actors command, despite lacking the resources, population and political influence that the state possesses. This section takes the argument further by addressing how the concept of 'radicalisation' – which describes a process of being exposed to extremist ideology, embracing such views and transitioning from non-violence, across an imaginary 'conveyor belt' into violent extremism and ultimately terrorism – is reversed by Boko Haram (Kundnani, 2015). From the Pied Piper of Hamelin, the Piper is envious of the territory, power, authority and resources that the Mayor of Hamelin enjoys in contrast to its own existence as a wayfarer; the envy is mutual and becoming one means not being the other and the desire to be the other and not quite the other involves a continuous and never-ending iteration (Browning, 1888). Boko Haram is envious of the attention, resources, power and recognition that the Nigerian state enjoys, which means that it is on the weaker end of the asymmetric power struggle.

The desires and aspirations of the group are directed towards emulating the Nigerian state through showing that it can imagine, establish and administer an alternative political community built around its version of Islam (Loimeier, 2011). However, this obsession is mutual as the Nigerian government is enraged by the attention that Boko Haram gets as well as the dedication and piety, which it commands from its members in the absence of the authority that the state commands. Even if this is not acknowledged, the group understands that for it to succeed, its version of political community must be recognised both by the people it seeks to rule and by the international society (Kelsen, 1941). It can be argued that the double narratives of re-establishing the Sokoto Caliphate and Kanem-Bornu Empire adopted interchangeably by Boko Haram may at best serve to build legitimacy and cohesion among sections of the population to achieve the former, but to be recognised as the new

Mayor requires a different type of justification (Loimeier, 2011). This can be viewed as the zenith of the envy where, despite the legitimacy the group may command at the expense of the state, it dawns on it that it may never attain such level of authority and recognition, which may be evident in the irony of the Islamic State being unrecognised despite labelling itself as such (Al-Turabi et al., 1983).

There is nothing inherently Islamist about Boko Haram's violence or the discourse of reinventing itself in the image of past dynasties just as with other similar references within Nigeria to pre-colonial ethnic heritage – *Egbe Omo O'dua*, for example – or non-religious violence which is built on challenging the sanctity of Nigerian sovereignty – Biafra, for example (Lowman, 2014). Saying that Boko Haram is one thing and that such ideological underpinning is mechanically causal denies a very rich understanding of how the group has morphed into what it is today through a constant interaction and relation with its main arch enemy, the Nigerian state. Kundnani (2015) makes a similar argument by finding parallels in the gravitation towards violence in groups that can be considered non-religious. He finds various trigger factors: 'the violent suppression of the Paris Commune in 1871, in which tens of thousands were killed, that triggered the turn to dynamite and assassination across Europe', the crackdown on 'the nationalist civil rights movement in Northern Ireland' for the Provisional Irish Republic Army's (PIRA's) violence, and the broadcast of images of the impact of the global war on terror in the Middle East – especially the widespread torture at Abu Ghraib Prison in Iraq – that galvanised the July 7 attackers, rather than any change in ideology per se (Eisenman, 2007; Hersh, 2004; Kundnani, 2015, p. 25; Rehman, 2007).

If ideology is foregrounded as causal, and terrorism the effect, *Salafism* (Wahhabism for some), which is often highlighted as the culprit, does not fully explain why Boko Haram gravitated towards widespread violence after 2009 and has engaged in more widespread civilian violence since 2013. How do so-called radicalisation towards extremism arguments account for change and transformation? Boko Haram's ideology has not changed since the 'non-violent' days even if its rhetoric has increasingly become anti-state, which cannot be detached from the group's interaction with the Nigerian state, where the latter's hostile actions towards the former culminated in the heavy-handed crackdown which led to the deaths of hundreds of suspected militants, including the founding leader, Muhammed Yusuf, his father-in-law Baba Fugu and his financier, Buji Foi (Abubakar, 2014a; Blanquart, 2012; Comolli, 2015; Loimeier, 2012). Ignoring these realities and the role played by Nigerian forces in the evolution of the group, while paying attention to it, foregrounds the politics of mutual envy that has characterised the evolution of both the Nigerian state and Boko Haram, which has resulted in mimetic terrorist and counter-terrorist interactions and the escalation of violence.

It can be argued that Boko Haram and the Nigerian state both became *extremist* when the *Other* became increasingly threatening to the legitimacy and continued existence of the *Self*. Despite being co-opted by politicians and traditional elites to achieve legitimacy and win political elections, the fallout between the group and local elites based on the mutual accusation of debauchery in terms of reneging on earlier promises meant that the group's leaders and political elites found co-optation no longer viable. The crisis that ensued involved attacks on public facilities, infrastructure and the death of security operatives (Anyadike, 2013). The response by the state was heavy-handed and resulted in the extrajudicial killing of hundreds of suspected militants (Adibe, 2014).

What this shows is that, for Boko Haram, this was the moment that the Self had to reformulate its objectives in a situation where the Nigerian Other had not only become an existential threat but had attempted and failed to annihilate the group, mostly unlawfully (Comolli, 2015; Loimeier, 2012). The extrajudicial killings, for example, were unlawful within the Nigerian constitution and international conventions and protocols that the country is a signatory to but it became necessary for the state to become more extremist in dealing with a challenger to its throne; in a way, it was a securitisation of ideologies which were considered causal to future acts of terrorism (Kundnani, 2015). Experts have often paid attention to the radicalisation of Boko Haram but not to that of the state; Boko Haram and the state deviated significantly from the norm, thus becoming mutually *extremist* and intolerant of the dangerous *Other*.

It is important to add that the arguments made here so far should not be misinterpreted as a recommendation for state apathy or a veiled suggestion that the Nigerian state or other states lack legitimacy. Of course, the Nigerian state has become the internationally recognised political authority just as the UK within these jurisdictions, which brings with it enormous responsibilities. Re-evoking the Pied Piper metaphor, the Mayor has more authority and responsibilities than the Piper, but the fact that such authority must be continuously practised and performed to stave off competitors shows that states must continuously justify their existence; it is not given (Weber, 1998).

Despite aiding this cause, the politics of mutual envy deflects attention from what states should be doing and also undermines the fundamental principles of democratic governance that states promise to uphold, which are not necessarily universal but inflected by various cultural and historical factors in different parts of the world. Within the Nigerian context, the widespread abuse by state forces in an attempt to 'outdo' Boko Haram has only escalated the crisis and served as fodder for the fire of militancy, which has consumed over 30,000 Nigerians

(BBC Africa, 2015; Buchanan, 2015; Campbell and Harwood, 2018; CNN Library, 2017; Ojo, 2010).

Conclusion

This chapter has examined the politics of extremism and radicalisation in Nigeria through engaging with various projects which the state had deployed to identify, counter and reverse it. The adoption of a 'soft' approach to fighting Boko Haram through countering ideologies that are considered causal to terrorism is a form of postcolonial mimicry where the Nigerian government has adopted European ways of defining and fighting threat which have significant implications within a Nigerian context where Islam is an integral part of the culture and history of the northern parts of the country. For various reasons, the state and academics find it expedient to adopt Western concepts uncritically, as it serves various material and non-material purposes.

Retaining the Western ways of othering, the Nigerian state has to battle with Boko Haram for legitimacy, which has led to the politics of mutual envy, as was evident with the Pied Piper of Hamelin metaphor. It may not be a problem for states to be *envious* of other competitive actors, but when such gazes become an obsession and *means* become justified by their *ends*, states compromise the very foundation of their existence. In the case of Boko Haram, it has been shown how the politics of mutual envy has driven both actors towards becoming more intolerant of the other, which has resulted in the foreclosure of other approaches that could have produced better results. By construing Boko Haram as an effect of extremist ideology, the state has managed to deflect its own role in the development of the group through direct and indirect influences. Directly, the draconian approach of security forces made it impossible to have a dialogue or address the differences that the group had with the state in the north-east, which could have produced different outcomes.

The attempted extermination of the group only managed to further push it underground and view the state as an existential threat, thus leading to a full-blown insurgency. Indirectly, the longstanding socio-economic realities in the north-east become excluded or relegated to mere secondary factors in terrorism, when it can be argued that terrorists are primarily driven by an extremist ideology. What this means is that the state is able to exonerate itself from various leadership failures that do not necessarily cause terrorism but could contribute to various forms of political violence in one way or the other. This chapter makes a strong case for capturing these dynamics and stepping away from problem-solving approaches that only seek to find solutions to groups and ideologies that threaten the state's existence, thus taking the status quo for granted.

References

Abubakar, A., 2014a. 'Boko Haram mount dynamite raid, rob bank, in looting spree', *Business Insider*, 5 November. Available at www.businessinsider.com/afp-boko-haram-mount-dynamite-raid-rob-bank-in-looting-spree-2014-11?IR=T (accessed 21 October 2015).

Abubakar, I.R., 2014b. 'Abuja city profile', *Cities*, 41, 81–91.

Achebe, C., 1977. 'An image of Africa', *The Massachusetts Review*, 18, 782–794.

Adesoji, A.O., 2011. 'Between Maitatsine and Boko Haram: Islamic fundamentalism and the response of the Nigerian state', *Africa Today*, 57, 98–119.

Adibe, J., 2014. 'Explaining the emergence of Boko Haram', *AFRICA in Focus*. Available at www.brookings.edu/blog/africa-in-focus/2014/05/06/explaining-the-emergence-of-boko-haram/ (accessed 20 July 2015).

Agbiboa, D.E., 2013. 'Why Boko Haram exists: The relative deprivation perspective', *African Conflict & Peacebuilding Review*, 3(1), 144–157.

Agbiboa, D.E., 2014. 'Boko-Haram and the global jihad: Do not think jihad is over. Rather jihad has just begun'. *Australian Journal of International Affairs*, 68(4), 400–417.

Al-Turabi, H., 1983. 'The Islamic State', in Esposito, J.L. (ed.), *Voices of Resurgent Islam*, Oxford University Press, Oxford and New York, pp. 241–251.

Alao, A., 2013. 'Islamic radicalisation and violent extremism in Nigeria', *Conflict, Security & Development*, 13(2), 127–147.

Anderson, B., 2006. *Imagined Communities: Reflections on the Origin and Spread of Nationalism*. Verso Books, London.

Anyadike, N.O., 2013. 'Boko Haram and national security challenges in Nigeria; causes and solutions', *Journal of Economics and Sustainable Development*, 4(5), 12–23.

Barducci, M., 2008. 'Oliver Cromwell, European historical myth? The case of the Italian states in seventeenth-century representations of Cromwell', *The Seventeenth Century*, 23, 54–71.

Barkindo, A., Bryans, S., 2016. 'De-radicalising prisoners in Nigeria: Developing a basic prison based de-radicalisation programme', *Journal for Deradicalization*, 1(7), 1–25.

Barnard-Wills, D., Moore, C., 2010. 'The terrorism of the other: Towards a contrapuntal reading of terrorism in India', *Critical Studies on Terrorism*, 3(3), 383–402.

BBC Africa, 2014. 'Boko Haram crisis: Nigerian soldiers "mutiny over weapons"'. Available at www.bbc.co.uk/news/world-africa-28855292 (accessed 9 November 2015).

BBC Africa, 2015. 'Boko Haram crisis: Nigerian army accused of 7,000 deaths'.

Berkowitz L., 1989. 'Frustration-aggression hypothesis: Examination and reformulation', *Psychological Bulletin*, 106(1), 59–73.

Berrebi, C., 2003. 'Evidence about the link between education, poverty and terrorism among Palestinians'. *Princeton University Industrial Relations Section Working Paper No. 477*. Available at https://papers.ssrn.com/sol3/papers.cfm?abstract_id=487467 (accessed 23 February 2020).

Bhabha, H., 1984. 'Of mimicry and man: The ambivalence of colonial discourse', *October*, 28, 125–133.

Blanquart, G., 2012. 'Boko Haram: Terrorist organization, freedom fighters or religious fanatics? An analysis of Boko Haram within Nigeria, an Australian perspective and the need for counter terrorism responses that involves prescribing them as a terrorist organization'. 3rd Australian Counter Terrorism Conference. Perth, Australia: SRI Security Research Institute.

Bradley, I., 2012. *God Save the Queen: The Spiritual Heart of the Monarchy*. Bloomsbury Publishing, London.

Breen-Smyth, M., 2014. 'Theorising the "suspect community": Counterterrorism, security practices and the public imagination', *Critical Studies on Terrorism*, 7(2), 223–240.

Brenner, L., 1973. *The Shehus of Kukawa: A History of the Al-Kanemi Dynasty of Bornu*. Oxford University Press, New York.

Browning, R., 1888. *The Pied Piper of Hamelin*. George Routledge and Sons, London and New York.

Buchanan, R.T., 2015. 'Isis overtaken by Boko Haram as world's deadliest terror organisation', *Independent*, 17 November. Available at www.independent.co.uk/news/world/africa/boko-haram-overtakes-isis-as-worlds-deadliest-terror-organisation-a6737761.html (accessed 7 December 2015).

Campbell, J., 2014. 'Boko Haram: Origins, challenges and responses', *Norwegian Peacebuilding Resource Centre*, Oslo.

Campbell, J., Harwood, A., 2018. 'Boko Haram's deadly impact', 20 August. Council on Foreign Relations. Available at www.cfr.org/article/boko-harams-deadly-impact (accessed 23 February 2020).

Chowdhry, G., 2007. 'Edward Said and contrapuntal reading: Implications for critical interventions in international relations', *Millennium*, 36(1), 101–116.

Clubb, G., Tapley, M., 2018. 'Conceptualising de-radicalisation and former combatant re-integration in Nigeria', *Third World Quarterly*, 39(11), 2053–2068.

CNN Library, 2017. Boko Haram Fast Facts. Available at http://edition.cnn.com/2014/06/09/world/boko-haram-fast-facts/index.html (accessed 17 October 2017).

Comolli, V., 2015. *Boko Haram: Nigeria's Islamist Insurgency*. Oxford University Press, London.

Conrad, J., 1996. *Heart of Darkness*. Springer, London.

Cox, R.W., 1981. 'Social forces, states and world order: beyond international relations theory', *Millennium: Journal of International Studies*, 10(2), 126–155.

Crenshaw, M., 1981. 'The causes of terrorism', *Comparative Politics*, 13(4), 379–399.

Darwish, M., 2007. 'Edward Said: A contrapuntal reading: Translated by Mona Anis', *Cultural Critique*, 67(2),175–182.

Eisenman, S., 2007. *The Abu Ghraib Effect*. Reaktion Books, London.

Eji, E., 2016. 'Rethinking Nigeria's counter-terrorism strategy', *The International Journal of Intelligence, Security, and Public Affairs*, 18(3), 198–220.

Ekeh, P.P., 1975. 'Colonialism and the two publics in Africa: A theoretical statement', *Comparative Studies in Society and History*, 17(1), 91–112.

Foucault, M., 1990. *The history of sexuality: An introduction*. Vintage, New York.

Foucault, M., Ewald, F., 2003. *'Society Must Be Defended': Lectures at the Collège de France, 1975–1976*. Macmillan, Basingstoke.

Foucault, M., Rabinow, P. and Hurley, R., 1997. *The Essential Works of Michel Foucault, 1954–1984*. Penguin Books, London.

Fukuyama, F., 1989. 'The end of history?', *The National Interest*, 16, 3–18.

Giddens, A., 1991. *Modernity and Self-identity: Self and Society in the Late Modern Age.* Stanford University Press, Stanford, CA.

Goodwin, M., Milazzo, C., 2015. *UKIP: Inside the Campaign to Redraw the Map of British Politics.* Oxford University Press, London.

Gunning, J., Jackson, R., 2011. 'What's so "religious" about "religious terrorism"?', *Critical Studies on Terrorism*, 4(3), 369–388.

Hearne, E., Laiq, N., 2010. 'A new approach? Deradicalization programs and counterterrorism', *International Peace Institute. Conference on Countering Violent Extremism: Learning from Deradicalization Programs in Some Muslim-Majority States*, Meeting Notes. International Peace Institute, New York.

Heath-Kelly, C., 2014. 'Counter-terrorism: The ends of a secular ministry', in Jarvis, L. and Lister, M. (eds), *Critical Perspectives on Counter-terrorism*. Routledge, Abingdon, pp. 41–55.

Heath-Kelly, C., 2016. 'Post-structuralism and constructivism', in Jackson, R. (ed.), *Routledge Handbook of Critical Terrorism Studies*. Routledge, Abingdon, pp. 76–85.

Hegel, G.W.F., Forbes, D., 2004. *Lectures on the Philosophy of History.* Cambridge University Press, Cambridge.

Hersh, S.M., 2004. 'Torture at Abu Ghraib', *The New Yorker*, 30 April. Available at www.newyorker.com/magazine/2004/05/10/torture-at-abu-ghraib (accessed 23 February 2020).

Hertzler, J., 1940. 'Crises and dictatorships', *American Sociological Review*, 5(2), 157–169.

Hillyard, P., 1993. *Suspect Community: People's Experience of the Prevention of Terrorism Acts in Britain.* Pluto Press, London.

Hiribarren, V., 2016. 'Kanem-Bornu Empire', in Dalziel N and MacKenzie JM (eds), *The Encyclopedia of Empire*. Wiley Online Library. Available at https://onlinelibrary.wiley.com/doi/abs/10.1002/9781118455074.wbeoe014 (accessed 23 February 2020).

Home Office, 2011. *Prevent Strategy*. HM Government, London.

Huntington, S.P., 1993. 'The clash of civilizations?', *Foreign Affairs*, 72(3), 22–49.

Jackson, R., Breen-Smyth, M., Gunning, J. and Jarvis, L., 2011. *Terrorism: A Critical Introduction.* Palgrave Macmillan, London.

Kanya-Forstner, A., Lovejoy, P.E., 1994. 'The Sokoto Caliphate and the European Powers, 1890–1907', *Paideuma*, 40, 7–14.

Kelsen, H., 1941. 'Recognition in international law', *American Journal of International Law*, 35(4), 605–617.

Krueger, A.B., Malečková, J., 2002. 'Education, poverty, political violence and terrorism: Is there a causal connection?', *National Bureau of Economic Research Working Paper No. 9074*. NBER, Cambridge, MA.

Kundnani, A., 2012. 'Radicalisation: The journey of a concept', *Race & Class*, 54(2), 3–25.

Kundnani, A., 2014. *The Muslims Are Coming!: Islamophobia, Extremism, and the Domestic War on Terror.* Verso Books, London.

Kundnani, A., 2015. *A Decade Lost: Rethinking Radicalisation and Extremism.* Claystone, London.

Last, M., 1967. *The Sokoto Caliphate.* Longman, London.

Latour, V., 2012. '"Muscular liberalism": Surviving multiculturalism? A historical and political contextualisation of David Cameron's Munich speech', *Observatoire de la Société Britannique*, 13(2), 199–216.

Loimeier, R., 2011. *Islamic Reform and Political Change in Northern Nigeria*. Northwestern University Press, Evanston, IL.

Loimeier, R., 2012. 'Boko Haram: The development of a militant religious movement in Nigeria', *Africa Spectrum*, 47(2–3), 137–155.

Loimeier, R., 2017. *Islamic Reform in Twentieth-Century Africa*. Edinburgh University Press, Edinburgh.

Lovejoy, P.E., Hogendorn, J.S., 1990. 'Revolutionary Mahdism and resistance to colonial rule in the Sokoto Caliphate, 1905–6', *The Journal of African History*, 31(2), 217–244.

Lowman, T., 2014. 'Biafra and Boko Haram: Different conflicts, common themes', *African Arguments*. Available at http://africanarguments.org/2014/07/18/biafra-and-boko-haram-different-conflicts-common-themes-by-tom-lowman/ (accessed 13 March 2018).

Makarychev, A., Yatsyk, A., 2017. 'Biopolitics and national identities: Between liberalism and totalization', *Nationalities Papers*, 45(1), 1–7.

Malečková, J., 2005. *Impoverished Terrorists: Stereotype or Reality*, in Bjørgo, T (ed.), *Root Causes of Terrorism Myths, Reality and Ways Forward*. Routledge, London, pp. 33–43.

Merskin, D., 2004. 'The construction of Arabs as enemies: Post-September 11 discourse of George W. Bush', *Mass Communication & Society*, 7(2), 157–175.

Nickels, H.C., Thomas, L., Hickman, M.J. and Silvestri, S., 2012. 'Constructing "suspect" communities and Britishness: Mapping British press coverage of Irish and Muslim communities, 1974–2007', *European Journal of Communication*, 27(2), 135–151.

Noor, M., Kteily, N., Siem, B. and Mazziotta, A., 2018. '"Terrorist" or "mentally ill": Motivated biases rooted in partisanship shape attributions about violent actors', *Social Psychological and Personality Science*, 10(4), 485–493.

Office of the National Security Advisor (ONSA), 2016. *National Counterterrorism Strategy (NACTEST)*, 57. Abuja.

Ojo, E., 2010. 'Boko Haram: Nigeria's extra-judicial state', *Journal of Sustainable Development in Africa*, 12(2), 45–62.

Ojochemnemi, D., Asuelime, L. and Onapajo, H., 2015. *Boko Haram: The Socio-Economic Drivers*. Springer, New York.

Oliver, R.A., 1985. *The Cambridge History of Africa. 6. From 1870 to 1905*. Cambridge University Press, Cambridge.

Onuoha, F.C., 2014. *Why Do Youth Join Boko Haram?*. US Institute of Peace, Washington, DC.

Pantazis, C., Pemberton, S., 2009. 'From the "old" to the "new" suspect community: Examining the impacts of recent UK counter-terrorist legislation', *British Journal of Criminology*, 49(5), 646–666.

Pisoiu, D., Hain, S., 2017. *Theories of Terrorism: An Introduction*. Routledge, London.

Rehman, J., 2007. 'Islam, "war on terror" and the future of Muslim minorities in the United Kingdom: Dilemmas of multiculturalism in the aftermath of the London bombings', *Human Rights Quarterly*, 29(4), 831–878.

Said, E., 1978. *Orientalism: Western Representations of the Orient*. Pantheon, New York.

Said, E.W., 1983. *The World, the Text, and the Critic*. Harvard University Press, Cambridge, MA.

Schmid, A.P., 1989. 'Terrorism and the media: The ethics of publicity', *Terrorism and Political Violence*, 1(4), 539–565.

Sodipo, M.O., 2013. 'Mitigating radicalism in northern Nigeria', Africa Security Brief no. 26, August. Africa Center for Strategic Studies, Washington DC.

Tilly, C., 1985. 'War making and state making as organized crime', in Evans, P.B., Rueschemeyer, D. and Skocpol, T. (eds), *Bringing the State Back In*. Cambridge University Press, Cambridge, pp. 169–191.

Weber, C., 1998. 'Performative states', *Millennium*, 27(1), 77–95.

Weber, C., 2013. *International Relations Theory: A Critical Introduction*. Routledge, Abingdon.

Wilkinson, P., 1986. *Terrorism and the Liberal State*. Macmillan, London.

Wilkinson, P., 2011. *Terrorism versus Democracy: The Liberal State Response*. Routledge, Abingdon.

Wodak, R., Khosravinik, M. and Mral, B., 2013. *Right-wing Populism in Europe: Politics and Discourse*. A&C Black, London.

Index

EU authorised representative for GPSR:
Easy Access System Europe, Mustamäe tee 50,
10621 Tallinn, Estonia
gpsr.requests@easproject.com

www.ingramcontent.com/pod-product-compliance
Lightning Source LLC
Chambersburg PA
CBHW051952270326
41929CB00015B/2623